Introduction to
PASCAL and
Structured
Design

Introduction to PASCAL and Structured Design

Nell Dale

The University of Texas at Austin

David Orshalick

The University of Texas at Austin

D. C. Heath and Company

Lexington, Massachusetts / Toronto

This book is dedicated to our students,
for whom it was begun and
without whom it would never have been completed.

Preface

In the past there have been two distinct approaches used in introductory computer science texts. One approach focused on problem solving and algorithm design in the abstract, leaving the learning of a particular language to a supplemental manual or to a subsequent course. The second approach focused on the syntax of a particular programming language, and assumed that the problem-solving skills would be learned later through practice.

We believe that neither approach is adequate. Problem solving is a skill that can and should be taught—but not in the abstract. Students must be exposed to the precision and detail required in actually implementing their algorithms in a real programming language. Because of its structured nature, Pascal provides an effective vehicle for combining these two approaches. This book teaches problem-solving heuristics, algorithm development using top-down design, and good programming style concurrently with the syntax and semantics of the Pascal language.

ORGANIZATION AND PEDAGOGY

The organization of the subject matter as well as the organization of the book itself reflects our pedagogical beliefs. Chapter 1 effectively dispels machine anxiety. By Chapter 2, students are ready to start programming the computer.

Each chapter contains the amount of material that a student can absorb in approximately one week. Some topics may require two chapters, or one chapter may group several short topics together.

Examples in the book have been drawn from everyday experience. We believe that a student with a strong math background can relate to examples from other disciplines, but a student with a weak math background has difficulty with math examples. All problems and examples have been carefully chosen to require only high school algebra.

It has been our experience that there are three concepts that give beginning students considerable trouble:

1. Separation of program from data. (Why doesn't the card or line with the data values immediately follow the READ statement?)
2. Subprograms and argument transmission.
3. Arrays. (Using a variable to access another variable?)

Special attention has therefore been paid to these concepts. What happens during the compilation phase and the execution phase is stressed in both Chapter 2 and Chapter 3 and then reinforced again in later chapters. Top-down design methodology is introduced in these chapters and constantly reinforced.

Boolean expressions and the selection control structure are introduced in Chapter 4. The looping control structure is introduced in Chapter 5. Different types of loops are examined and implemented with the WHILE statement. The REPEAT and FOR statements are not covered until later. We have found that students learn the concept of a loop more easily if they are not confused by having to decide which syntactic construct to use.

Procedures are introduced early in the book (Chapter 6) to reinforce the use of modular programming and top-down design. Two chapters are devoted to this topic since it is one with which students often have trouble. The use of parameters is introduced immediately so that students are encouraged to communicate with procedures through parameter lists rather than develop the bad habit of referencing global variables directly from inside the procedure. Scope rules and techniques for preventing side effects are discussed.

Chapter 8 is a collection of topics that make up a week's worth of material. Functions are introduced at the beginning of the chapter to reinforce the concepts of structured programs and argument transmission. The REPEAT and CASE control structures, along with more on real numbers and real arithmetic, are also covered here.

Chapter 9 introduces user-defined types, one-dimensional arrays, and the FOR statement. Chapter 10 presents five case studies to demonstrate the use of one-dimensional arrays and to provide students with experience in reading programs. Chapter 11 covers multi-dimensional arrays. Devoting three chapters to arrays provides students with a solid grounding in this difficult concept.

Records are covered in great depth in Chapter 12. All of the additional Pascal data structures—packed arrays, files, and sets—are covered in Chapter 13.

Our beginning course is taught using Chapters 1 through 13. Chapter 14, which covers pointer variables and dynamic data structures, has been added to make the book complete. Pointers and linked lists are covered in detail, but dynamic data structures such as stacks, queues, and binary trees are only briefly discussed.

Although a linear approach to using the book is strongly recommended, the sections on REPEAT, CASE, and FOR could be covered whenever desired. The order of presentation of the built-in Pascal data structures, Chapters 9 through 13, could also be modified.

ADDITIONAL FEATURES

Class Tested: We have used the book for seven semesters in a beginning computer science course; it has benefited tremendously from student feedback as well as from reviewers' comments. Students tell us that the material is easy to understand and absorb. We have also used the book in other courses, especially an accelerated course for students who already program in another high-level language. These students also like the level of presentation and appreciate the detailed explanations and numerous examples.

Testing and Debugging: Beginning with Chapter 4, each chapter contains a section on testing and debugging, in which typical errors associated with each new construct are pointed out. Internal data checking and choice of external test data are emphasized.

Top-Down Design: Top-down design is used throughout. The notation used to express the top-down designs is a combination of Pascal control structures and English. We make no attempt to standardize this notation into a formal pseudo-code, since this would only add an additional level of complexity. Students should feel comfortable expressing their designs and not worry about whether they have used correct notation.

Exercises and Pre-Tests: With the exception of Chapter 1, each chapter has paper and pencil exercises and a pre-test. The exercise answers are in the back of the book; the pre-test answers are in the Instructor's Guide. Actual programming assignments for each chapter are included in the Instructor's Guide along with sample input data and output.

Goals: Beginning with Chapter 2, the goals for each chapter are listed at the beginning of the chapter. These goals are then tested in the exercises and pre-tests.

Illustrations: The book is rich in figures and illustrations, and color is used effectively to highlight both the figures and the text. Definitions of important terms are highlighted in color throughout and collected, along with other terms, in a glossary at the back of the book.

Instructor's Guide: Answers to the pre-tests, two versions of tests for each of Chapters 2 through 13, cumulative review tests, test keys, and programming assignments for each chapter are all included in the Instructor's Guide. In addition, there are case studies for each chapter suitable for class lecture.

The book can be used by those doing batch or interactive programming on either mainframes, minicomputers, or microcomputers. We present standard Pascal as defined in the *Pascal User Manual and Report*, Second Edition (Kathleen Jensen and Nicklaus Wirth, Springer-Verlag, 1975). All of the program examples and fragments have been run on a dual CDC Cyber 170/750, a DEC-2060, or a microcomputer using Pascal/M (very similar to UCSD Pascal).

ACKNOWLEDGMENTS

We would like to thank the many individuals who have helped us. We are indebted to the members of the faculty of the Computer Sciences Department at the University of Texas at Austin, especially A. G. Dale, James Bitner, Joyce Brennan, Alan Cline, and James L. Peterson. Thanks also to Marilla Svinicki from the Center for Teaching Effectiveness, Douglas McCallum, George Edwards, and Kathy Pardue. For their many helpful suggestions, we would like to thank the teaching assistants and student proctors who run the course for which this book was written and the students themselves.

We would also like to thank the following people who reviewed the manuscript: J. W. Atwood, Concordia University; Richard E. Bolz, Air Force Academy; Lori A. Clark, University of Massachusetts; Carl Crosswhite, Miami University; James W. Lea, Jr., Middle Tennessee State University; Barry Levine, San Francisco State University; Gregory F. Wetzel, University of Kansas; and Michael R. Ziegler, Marquette University. Chip Weems, University of Massachusetts, deserves special thanks for doing detailed reviews at two different stages of the manuscript.

Special thanks go to K. F. Carbone for her careful typing and proofreading of the manuscript as well as for machine-testing the example programs and program fragments. Last, but certainly not least, we thank our families for their support and encouragement.

Nell Dale
David Orshalick

Contents

Sample Problems

Overview of Programming

1

COM·PUT·ER

one that computes; specif: a programmable electronic device that can store, retrieve, and process data.

What a short definition for something that has in 30 short years changed the way of life in industrialized societies! We come in contact with computers in all areas of our daily life: when we pay our bills, when we drive our car, when we use the telephone, when we go shopping. In fact, it would be easier to list those areas of our lives not affected by computers.

It is sad that a device that does so much good is so often feared and maligned. How many times have you heard (or said) "I'm sorry, our computer is broken," or "I just don't understand computers, but I never was good at math anyway"?

The very fact that you are reading this book, however, means that you are ready to set aside prejudices and learn about computers. Be forewarned, this book is not just about computers in the abstract. This is a text to teach you how to use them.

WHY PROGRAMMING?

Human behavior and human thought are characterized by logical sequences. Since infancy, we have been learning how to act, how to do things. We learn to "expect" certain behavior from other people as well as what is "expected" of us. Our lives have a certain order to them; this is what we feel most comfortable with.

A lot of what we do every day is done automatically, on an unconscious level. Fortunately, it is not necessary for us to consciously think of every step involved in something as simple as turning this page by hand. If we had to consciously think:

lift hand,
move hand to right side of book,
grasp corner of top page,
move hand from right to left until page is positioned so that you can read what is on the other side,
let go of page,

we would all be illiterate. Think how many muscles must respond to how many neurons that must fire, all in a certain order or sequence, to achieve a smooth motion of arm and hand. Yet we do it unconsciously.

Much of what we do unconsciously we once had to learn. Watch the intense concentration of a baby putting one foot before the other while learning to walk. Then watch a group of three-year-olds playing tag. Another example of a learned logical sequence of steps is brushing our teeth. We were carefully taught to put the toothpaste on the brush, put it in our mouth and clean our teeth in a certain way. Now the action is completely automatic.

On a broader scale, mathematics could never have been developed without logical sequences of steps for solving problems or proving theorems. Music requires definite sequences of notes in order to be recognizable. Anything produced requires a logical sequence of steps. Mass production of the products we use requires certain operations to take place in a prescribed order. Our whole civilization is based upon the order of things and actions.

Ordering, both conscious and unconscious, is an important part of our lives. This ordering is achieved through a process we could call programming.

PROGRAMMING

The planning, scheduling or performing of a task or an event.

This book is concerned with the programming of one of our tools, the computer.

COMPUTER PROGRAMMING

The process of planning a sequence of instructions for a computer to follow.

Just as a program for a concert or play is a printed outline with annotations of the action to be performed, a computer program is a listing of the set of instructions outlining the steps to be performed.

COMPUTER PROGRAM

A sequence of instructions outlining the steps to be performed.

From now on when we say "program" and "programming," we mean computer program and computer programming.

The computer allows us to do tasks more efficiently, quickly and accurately than we could do them by hand—if we could do them by hand. In order to use this powerful tool, we must specify exactly what we want done and the order in which to do it. This is done through programming; this is why we learn programming.

WHAT IS PROGRAMMING?

Our definition of programming leaves a lot unsaid. In order to write a sequence of instructions for a computer to follow, we must go through a certain process. This process is composed of a problem-solving phase and an implementation phase. (See Figure 1-1.)

PROBLEM-SOLVING PHASE

Analyze—Understand (define) problem.

General Solution (Algorithm)—Develop a logical sequence of steps to be used to solve the problem.

Test—Follow the exact steps as outlined to see if the solution truly solves the problem.

IMPLEMENTATION PHASE

Specific Solution (Program)—Translate the algorithm into a programming language (code).

Test—Have the computer follow the instructions. Check the results and make corrections until the answers are correct.

Use—Use the program.

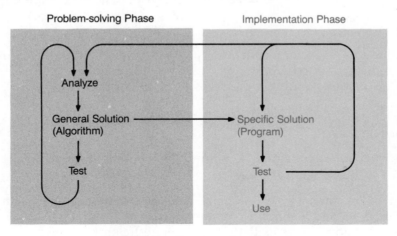

Figure 1-1. Programming Process

The computer, alas, is not intelligent. It cannot analyze a problem and come up with a solution. The programmer must arrive at the solution and communicate it to the computer. The problem solving is done by the programmer—not the computer.

The programmer analyzes the problem and develops a general solution called an algorithm. Understanding and analysis of a problem take up much more time than the illustration would imply. They are the heart of the programming process; more will be said about them in Chapter 2.

ALGORITHM

A step-by-step procedure for solving a problem in a finite amount of time.

We use algorithms every day. They are simply a verbal or written description of logical sequences of actions. Cooking recipes, laundry detergent instructions and refrigerator defrosting instructions are examples of written algorithms.

When we start our car we go through a step-by-step procedure. The algorithm might look something like this:

1. Insert key.
2. Make sure transmission is in Park (or Neutral).
3. Depress the gas pedal.
4. Turn the key to the "start" position.
5. If the engine starts within 6 seconds, release the key to the "ignition" position.
6. If the engine doesn't start in 6 seconds, wait 10 seconds and repeat steps 3 through 6 (but not more than 5 times).
7. If the car doesn't start, call the garage.

Without the phrase "but not more than 5 times" in step 6 it would be possible to be stuck trying to start our car forever. Why? Because, if something is wrong with the car, repeating steps 3 through 6 over and over again may not start it. That never-ending situation is known as an infinite loop. So if the phrase "but not more than 5 times" is left out of step 6, then our algorithm does not fit our definition. An algorithm must terminate in a finite amount of time for any possible conditions.

The programmer might need an algorithm to determine an employee's wages for the week. The algorithm would reflect what would be done by hand.

1. Look up employee's pay rate.
2. Determine the # of hours worked during the week.
3. If the # of hours worked is less than or equal to 40.0, multiply the # of hours by the payrate to get regular wages.
4. If the # of hours is greater than 40.0, multiply the pay rate by 40.0 to get regular wages and multiply one and a half times the payrate by the

difference between the # of hours worked and 40.0 to get overtime wages.

5. Add regular wages to overtime wages (if any) to get total wages for the week.

The final solution to be used by the computer is very often the same as the solution done by hand.

After developing a general solution the programmer then "walks through" the algorithm by performing each step mentally or manually. If this testing of the algorithm doesn't produce the correct answers, the process is repeated by analyzing the problem again and coming up with another algorithm. When the programmer is satisfied with the algorithm, it is then translated into a programming language. We use the Pascal programming language in this book.

PROGRAMMING LANGUAGE

A set of rules, symbols and special words used to construct a program.

Translating the algorithm into a programming language is called coding the algorithm. The resulting program is tested by running it (executing each statement) on the computer. If the program fails to produce the desired results, the programmer must analyze and modify the program as needed.

If the definition of a computer program and an algorithm look suspiciously alike, it is because all programs are algorithms. An algorithm can be in English, but when it is specified in a programming language it is also called a program.

Some students try to take a shortcut in the programming process by going directly from the problem definition to the coding of the program. (See Figure 1-2.) This shortcut is very tempting and it might seem at first to save a lot of time. However, for many reasons which will become obvious to you as you read this book, this approach actually takes *more* time and effort. By not taking the time initially to think out and polish your algorithm, you will spend a lot of extra time correcting errors (debugging) and revising an ill-conceived program. So think first and code later! The sooner you start coding, the longer it will take to get a correct program.

Program documentation and maintenance are also part of programming and will be covered in detail later. Briefly, documentation is written text and comments that make a program readable, understandable and more easily modified. Maintenance is the modification of a program to take care of changing requirements or any errors (bugs) that might show up after the program is put into use.

Programming involves more than simply writing a program. A programmer must understand and analyze the problem in order to develop a correct solution, because the program must solve the specific problem and do so

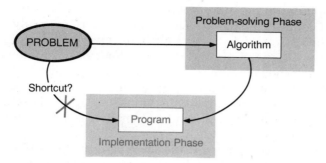

Figure 1-2. Programming Shortcut?

correctly. Developing a general solution before actually writing the program helps the programmer manage the problem, keep thoughts straight and avoid unnecessary errors. In addition, most programs will be used over and over again. Program modification often becomes necessary. Problem requirements may change and/or errors may show up. Careful design and good program documentation prove invaluable during this maintenance phase.

WHAT IS A COMPUTER?

We don't need to know much about a computer in order to use it as an effective tool. We can learn a programming language such as Pascal, write programs and learn the procedure for running (executing) these programs. However, if we know something about the parts of a computer, we can better understand the effect of each instruction in the programming language.

COMPUTER

A programmable electronic device that can store, retrieve and process data.

The verbs store, retrieve, and process imply the five basic components of most computers: memory unit, arithmetic/logic unit, control unit, and input and output devices.

Memory is an ordered sequence of storage cells, each containing a piece of information. It is similar to an old-fashioned post office with a bunch of pigeon holes for mail. These memory storage cells are known variously as memory cells, memory locations, or a place in memory. Each memory cell has a distinct address by which it is referred to in order to store or retrieve information.

In a computer, information is represented, stored and processed in binary form (a coding scheme of 1's and 0's). Memory is simply a set of cells containing this information (data) encoded (represented) in binary bits (a series of binary digits of 1's and 0's). We don't have to know this binary coding scheme. The computer converts the numbers and letters we use to represent information automatically. (We will use the word "data" throughout this book. Information in symbolic form, such as numbers and letters, is known as data. We have to represent information as data before it is usable by the computer.)

Because of our coding scheme, the same pattern of binary bits in a memory cell can be interpreted as a number, as an alphanumeric character or even as an instruction in a program. We tell the computer how to interpret that pattern through the programs we write. Memory does not know or care what kind of information is contained in a cell. It is simply a storage place.

MEMORY UNIT

The internal data storage of a computer.

The memory holds data (input data or the results of computation) and instructions (your program). (See Figure 1-3.)

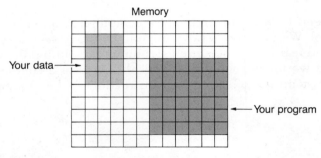

Figure 1-3. Memory

The combination of the arithmetic/logic unit and the control unit is called the central processing unit (CPU).

ARITHMETIC/LOGIC UNIT

The computer component that performs arithmetic operations (addition, subtraction, multiplication, division) and logical operations (comparison of two values).

CONTROL UNIT

The computer component that controls the actions of the other components in order to execute instructions (your program) in sequence.

CENTRAL PROCESSING UNIT

The "brain" of a computer which interprets and executes instructions.

In order for us to use computers, we must have some way of getting data into and out of them. The input and output devices perform this function.

INPUT/OUTPUT (I/O)

Media and devices used to achieve man/machine communication.

This is a stylized diagram of the basic components of a computer.

INPUT DEVICE	CENTRAL PROCESSING UNIT	OUTPUT DEVICE
	ARITHMETIC/LOGIC UNIT	
	CONTROL UNIT	
	MEMORY UNIT	

Computers simply move and combine data in memory. The differences among various computers involve the size and speed of memory, the efficiency with which data can be moved or combined, and limitations on I/O devices.

When a program is executing (the instructions are being followed), the computer proceeds step by step through the instruction execution cycle:

1. The control unit fetches the next coded instruction from memory.
2. The instruction is decoded into control signals.
3. The control signals tell the appropriate unit (arithmetic/logic, memory, or I/O device) to perform the instruction.
4. The sequence is repeated from step 1.

Computers can have a wide variety of peripheral devices attached to them. (See Figure 1-4.)

PERIPHERAL DEVICE:

An input, output or auxiliary storage device of a computer.

Typical auxiliary storage devices are magnetic tape drives (similar to a tape recorder) and disk drives. Disk drives might be thought of as a cross between a record player and a tape recorder because they use a thin platter made out of a magnetic material. A read/write head travels across the spinning disk and retrieves or records data.

A typical input device is the card reader which reads the data from punched cards prepared by a keypunch machine. A typical output device is the line printer which prints out data on computer fan-fold paper. Some devices are used for both input and output such as the teletypewriter and video display terminal. Teletypewriters (TTY) are similar to typewriters; communication with the computer is printed on continuous-feed paper. Video display terminals consist of a keyboard for typing in characters and a cathode-ray-tube (CRT) screen for displaying the data (the same principle as a television set). The CRT terminal is a very common way of communicating with the computer.

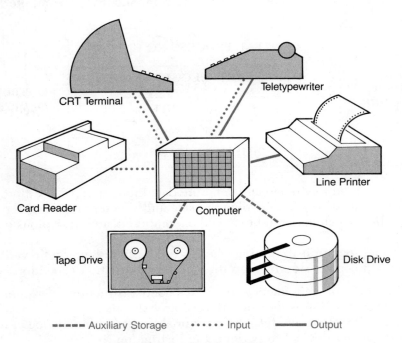

Figure 1-4. Peripheral Devices

When you use the computer there is an interface between you and the computer.

INTERFACE

A shared boundary where independent systems meet and act on or communicate with each other.

The physical interface involves the particular I/O device (such as a terminal) you are using.

When you are communicating directly with the computer through a terminal you are using an interactive system.

INTERACTIVE SYSTEM

Direct communication between the user and the computer; a terminal/computer connection allowing direct entry of programs and data and providing immediate feedback to the user.

Submitting your program and data on cards through the card reader is a form of batch processing.

BATCH PROCESSING

A technique for executing programs and data without intermediate user interaction with the computer.

Typically, batch processing involves input of programs and data on cards, and output in printed form from the line printer.

A computer *system* is composed of hardware and software.

HARDWARE

The physical components of a computer.

SOFTWARE

Computer programs; the set of all programs available to a computer.

Hardware is usually fixed in design, but the software can be easily changed. The ease of manipulating software is what makes the computer such a versatile and powerful tool. There are programs in the computer, besides yours, designed to simplify the user/computer interface, that make it easier for you to use the machine.

As we have seen, a computer is composed of different functional parts. It can store data in memory and on tape or disk, manipulate this data (arithmetic/logic and control units) and communicate with the user (input and output devices).

WHAT IS A PROGRAMMING LANGUAGE?

We use programs to get the computer to work for us. These programs are written in one of the many programming languages in use today. However, when computers were first developed, the abundance of programming languages we have today did not exist. All that was available at first was the primitive instruction set of each machine known as machine language (or machine code).

MACHINE LANGUAGE

The language used directly by the computer and composed of binary coded instructions.

Even though most computers perform the same kinds of operations, the designers may have chosen a different set of binary codes of 1's and 0's to stand for each instruction. So the machine code for one computer is not the same as for another. (We mention "binary codes of 1's and 0's." Remember that this is how data is stored and used in the digital computer, whether it is alphabetic or numeric data or instructions.)

Early computers were programmed in machine language. Programmers had to remember the codes for the various operations of the computer. This was a tedious and error-prone process. The resulting programs were difficult to read and modify, so assembly languages were developed to make the programmer's job easier. An instruction in assembly language is in an easy-to-remember form called a mnemonic (pronounced "ni-mon´ik"). Typical instructions for addition and subtraction might look like this:

Assembly Language	Machine Language
ADD	100101
SUB	010011

The only problem was that the computer could not execute directly the assembly language instructions. So a program was written to translate the assembly language instructions into machine language instructions.

ASSEMBLER

Program that translates an assembly language program into machine code.

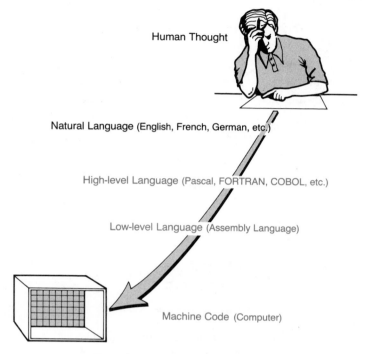

Human Thought

Natural Language (English, French, German, etc.)

High-level Language (Pascal, FORTRAN, COBOL, etc.)

Low-level Language (Assembly Language)

Machine Code (Computer)

Figure 1-5. Levels of Abstraction

This was a step in the right direction, but the programmer was still forced to think in terms of individual machine instructions. Because humans solve problems and communicate in natural languages such as English, higher level programming languages were then developed to be closer to human thought than the limiting level of machine code. (See Figure 1-5.) In these higher level languages (such as Pascal, COBOL and FORTRAN) programs require translation into machine language instructions. This translator program is called a compiler. Higher level languages are now called high-level languages.

COMPILER

Program that translates a high-level language program into machine code.

By writing a program in a high-level language, you can run it on any computer that has the appropriate compiler. (See Figure 1-6.)

Your program in a high-level language is called a source program. After you compile the source program by running (executing) the compiler with

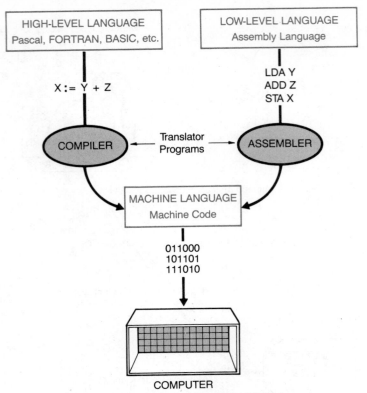

Figure 1-6. Use of Programming Languages

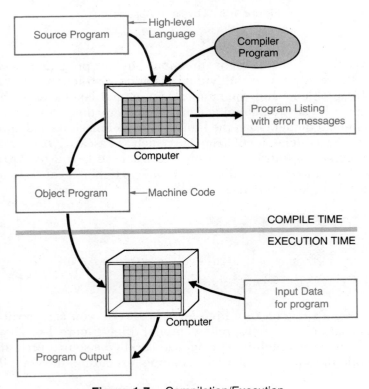

Figure 1-7. Compilation/Execution

your program as data, you have a machine language program called the object program. Your object program can be run directly on the computer. (See Figure 1-7.)

We saw that a computer system is composed of both hardware and software. System software is the set of programs that improve the efficiency and convenience of using the computer:

- the operating system is a set of programs that manage all computer resources (it can input your program, call the compiler, execute the resulting object program and carry out any of the other system commands you enter);
- the compiler translates your high-level programs into machine code (object program);
- the editor helps you create and modify your program text. (See Figure 1-8.)

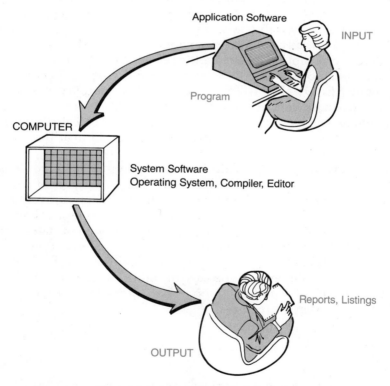

Figure 1-8. Man/Machine Interface

We said that a programming language is a set of rules, symbols and special words used to construct a program. There are rules for both syntax (grammar) and semantics (meaning).

SYNTAX

The formal rules governing the construction of valid constructs in a language.

SEMANTICS

The set of rules which give the meaning of a language construct.

Pascal has such rules and we begin discussing them in Chapter 2.

When designing an algorithm, a programmer should keep in mind the things a computer can do. By being aware of the allowable instructions, a programmer won't make the mistake of including an impossible step such as "perform a somersault" in an algorithm meant for the computer.

The instructions available in a programming language reflect the things a computer can actually do. The computer can transfer data from one place to another. It can input data from an input device such as a terminal and output data to an output device such as a printer. Most programming languages have READ and WRITE statements for these purposes. The computer can also store data in and retrieve data from its memory and its secondary storage (such as tape or disk). The computer can also compare two data values for equality or inequality, and it can perform arithmetic operations such as addition and subtraction very quickly.

Programming languages require certain structures for us to be able to express algorithms as a program. There are four basic ways of structuring statements (instructions): sequentially, conditionally, repetitively and procedurally. These structures are known by different names as shown in the illustration. (See Figure 1-9.) The *sequence* is composed of statements executed one after another. The conditional structure (*selection*) executes different statements depending upon certain conditional values. The *loop* structure repeats statements while certain conditions are met. And the *procedure* enables us to replace a group of statements by a single statement. Pascal has all of these structures.

WHAT IS PASCAL?

The programming language Pascal was designed by Niklaus Wirth in 1968. He named it after the French mathematician Blaise Pascal (1623–1662).

Originally intended to be a teaching tool for programming concepts, Pascal has now achieved acceptance and use in industry. Pascal compilers have been implemented on various large and small computers.

Pascal was created to avoid many of the problems and pitfalls of the programming languages in widespread use at the time of its development.

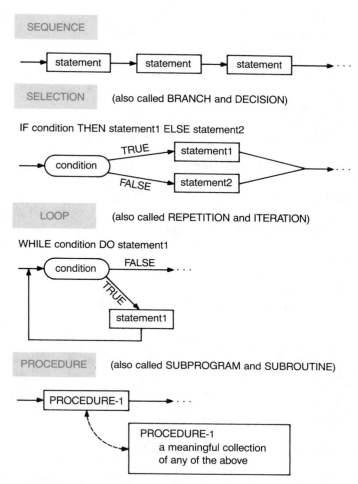

Figure 1-9. Basic Structures of Programming Languages

Because it is a highly structured language, it lends itself well to modern programming techniques. Its simplicity and readability make it one of the best languages for teaching the concepts of programming and instilling good habits. After learning Pascal, you will find it easy to learn other programming languages such as FORTRAN, COBOL and BASIC. The added bonus is that the methods, techniques and habits you learn with Pascal are applicable to other languages as well, thus increasing your skill and value as a programmer.

The following program, Program PAYROLL, is an example of what a Pascal program looks like. But before we look at the program, let's look at the algorithm it was coded from.

This algorithm parallels what is done by hand to compute the wages for each employee in a company and the total wages for the company. However, it was kept in mind that the program would be interactive—the person using the program would interact with the program via a terminal. Here is the algorithm:

1. Prepare to write a list of the employee wages (open file PAYFILE).
2. Prompt the user for the employee # (put message on the screen).
3. Read the employee #.
4. If the employee # is zero then continue with step 13.
5. Prompt the user for the employee's pay rate.
6. Read the pay rate.
7. Prompt the user for the hours worked.
8. Read the hours worked.
9. If the hours worked is greater than 40.0, then
   wages = (40.0 × pay rate) + (hours worked − 40.0) × 1.5 × pay rate
   otherwise, wages = hours worked × pay rate.
10. Add the employee's wages to the total payroll.
11. Write the employee #, pay rate, hours worked and wages on the list (file PAYFILE).
12. Continue with step 2.
13. Write the total company payroll on the screen.
14. Stop.

Here is the Pascal program for the algorithm we just discussed. This example program is just to give you an idea of what you'll be learning. If you have had no previous exposure to programming, you will probably not understand most of the program. Don't worry about it, you will soon. In fact, as each new construct is introduced, we will refer you back to its occurrence in Program PAYROLL.

```
PROGRAM PAYROLL (INPUT,OUTPUT,PAYFILE);     (*This program computes
                        the wages for each employee and the total payroll for the company*)
VAR PAYRATE,                                          (*employee's pay rate*)
    HRS,                                                 (*hours worked*)
    WAGES,                                              (*wages earned*)
    TOTAL   : REAL;                                     (*total payroll*)
    EMPNUM : INTEGER;                              (*employee ID number*)
    PAYFILE : TEXT;                                 (*company payroll file*)
BEGIN
  REWRITE(PAYFILE);                                  (*open file PAYFILE*)
  TOTAL := 0;
  WRITE('ENTER EMPLOYEE #: ');            (*prompting message on screen*)
  READLN(EMPNUM);                            (*read employee ID number*)
  WHILE EMPNUM <> 0 DO            (*repeat until a zero emp.# is entered*)
    BEGIN
      WRITE('ENTER PAYRATE: ');                    (*prompt on screen*)
      READLN(PAYRATE);                  (*read hourly pay rate for emp.*)
      WRITE('ENTER HOURS WORKED: ');              (*prompt on screen*)
      READLN(HRS);                       (*read hours worked by employee*)
      IF HRS > 40.00                              (*check for overtime*)
```

```
      THEN WAGES := (40.0 * PAYRATE) +
                    (HRS - 40.00) * PAYRATE * 1.5
      ELSE WAGES := HRS * PAYRATE;
   TOTAL := TOTAL + WAGES;                    (*add wages to payroll*)
   WRITELN(PAYFILE, EMPNUM, PAYRATE, HRS, WAGES);
                            (*put employee wage data in file PAYFILE*)
   WRITE('ENTER EMPLOYEE #: ');               (*prompt on screen*)
   READLN(EMPNUM)
 END;
WRITELN('TOTAL PAYROLL IS ',TOTAL:10:2)   (*print total payroll on
                                                          screen*)
END.
```

NOTE: Comments are enclosed in the "(* *)" symbol pair and are ignored
by the compiler.

PROGRAM ENTRY, CORRECTION, AND EXECUTION

Up to this point we have talked about programming in the abstract. We
have described the programming process as having two phases: problem
solving and implementation. In fact it isn't until the testing section of the
implementation phase that the word "computer" is used.

Aren't we talking about computer programming? Yes, but remember, the
computer is only a tool. We analyze and solve our problem intellectually for
the general case. We code our solution in a programming language in order
to test our solution.

Now that you have your program written on paper, how do you get it into
the machine? There are two common ways: punched cards in a batch system or a terminal in an interactive system.

Card Interface

Let's talk about the card system first because it is conceptually simpler. A
keypunch machine is like a typewriter. Cards are placed in the hopper at
the upper right and you hit the "feed" button twice to get a card in the
proper place to begin. You then type in your program, one card per line. If
you make a mistake you simply remake the card. (Don't forget to remove
the bad one!)

When you have finished transferring your program to cards, you are
ready to compile and run your program. Remember, before you can run
(execute) your program you must translate it into machine code. The following diagram shows the process.

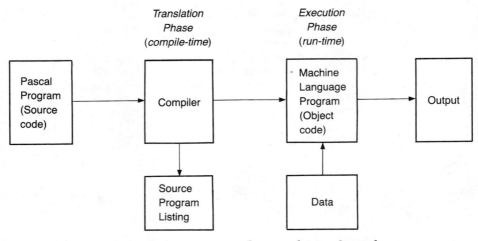

In order for the operating system to know what to do with your program, you must give it some instructions. These instructions to the operating system are called control statements and vary widely across machines. The following is an example from the job control language of the UT2D operating system at The University of Texas at Austin.

Cards	Description
CSXY432	User identification
ABC	User password
PASCAL.	Call to the Pascal compiler
LGO.	Command to execute the compiled program
7/8/9	System separator
⋮	Your Pascal program goes here
7/8/9	System separator
⋮	Your data cards go here (if needed)
6/7/8/9	System separator

Remember, this is only an example. Your system manual will give you the proper control cards for your computer system. They will, however, follow the same basic pattern:

User identification
Compilation information (specific language the program is in)
Execution information

When your job deck is complete, you submit the deck of cards to the machine operator. The cards are put in the card reader and you sit back and wait for the output. Depending on your system you might wait 30 seconds or 30 minutes. What you will get back is your card deck and a listing of your program. (The compiler generates this listing.)

If your program contains syntax errors—mistakes in grammar—an appropriate error message will be written on the listing. You go back to the keypunch and remake the cards which contain errors. When you have corrected all the errors, you resubmit your card deck for running.

When your program is free of syntax errors, the compiler is able to complete the translation of your program. Then the code that the compiler generates can actually be executed. It is possible, but highly unlikely, that your program will be syntactically correct the first time. However, the more careful you are in planning, the more likely this is to happen.

Now that your program can be executed three things can happen: two bad and one good. The good thing is that your program runs to completion and gives you the right answers. The bad things are that your program runs to completion but gives you the wrong answer or that your program halts with an error message (run-time errors).

How do you know if the answers are correct? Because at the end of the problem-solving phase you take some actual values—data—and go by hand through the algorithm. You use these same values to test your program. The results should be the same for both hand testing and machine testing.

If your program halts prematurely or gives the wrong answers, you either have an error in the encoding of the algorithm or an error in the algorithm itself.

Once the errors are found and the appropriate cards have been corrected, the deck is resubmitted and the cycle continues until you get the correct answer. (See Figure 1-10 on page 22.) We will have much more to say throughout this book about how to locate errors.

Terminal Interface

On most of today's computer systems you will be using a terminal as an interface. Cards, once the main means of communicating with the computer, are rapidly being replaced by CRT terminals. A CRT terminal has a screen similar to a television and a typewriter-like keyboard.

You input a line of code and see it on the screen. You indicate the end of the line by pressing what is called the RETURN key. Your lines of text are saved for you by the computer itself. This is both good and bad. You are freed from dealing with cards, but you must learn to use an EDITOR.

Instead of sitting at the keypunch and putting cards in the card feed, you sit at the terminal and use the language of the editor to say "I am going to enter a program." The editor then allows you to key in lines and collects them in a file for you.

What happens if you make a mistake? Well, if you notice the error before you finish the line, you can erase back to the error and retype the line. If

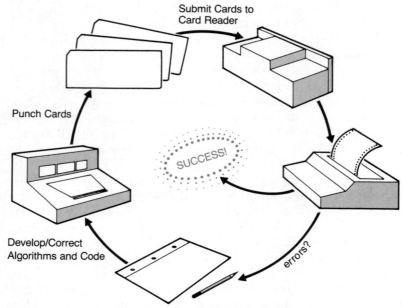

Figure 1-10. Batch Processing

you see the error after the line has been finished, you can use editor commands which allow you to go back and correct a line.

Most editors have two basic modes: creating a file and editing a file. A file is simply a place in memory where what you are inputting is being kept. It is like a file folder to keep your program in. You give it a name when you begin inputting the program and the editor remembers the name. When you need to correct something later you ask for your file and make corrections to it.

Editors allow you to perform such tasks as removing lines, inserting new lines, removing words or characters, or inserting new words or characters. We will not give a specific example because each editor has its own commands. Editors are not difficult to use. What they do is simulate what you do with your hands and a keypunch.

Once your program is in a file, you tell the operating system that you wish to compile this Pascal program file. For example, if you named your file PAYROLL, the command to the operating system might look like:

PRUN PASCAL PAYROLL L=PAYROLL.TXT

which means the Pascal compiler should translate the program in file PAYROLL. If there are errors, appropriate messages will appear on the screen. You can then print a copy of the program listing saved in file PAYROLL.TXT and determine which lines of your program must be corrected.

When your program is free of syntax errors, you can then execute the compiled code. Such a command might look like this:

PRUN PAYROLL.PCO

which means "run the program stored in the file named PAYROLL.PCO." How do you know the name of the file where the compiler will leave the code? Each compiler has a file name it uses to put the object code in. In the above example the code was left in the file named the same as the Pascal program but with a ".PCO" extension added.

The process from this point on is the same as with cards. Instead of correcting cards, you use the editor to make corrections in your program file. Remember, the editor simply simulates what is done by hand in a card system. (See Figure 1-11.)

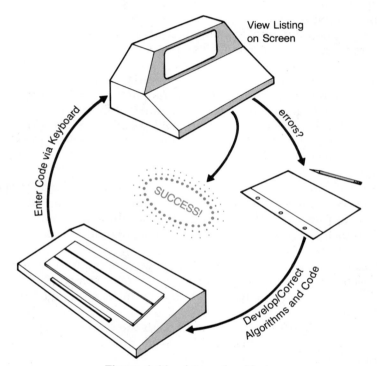

Figure 1-11. Interactive Mode

These examples of program preparation, entry, correction and execution are for two different computer systems. Your system may use different commands but the steps will be the same. Don't panic if you have trouble with this process at first. Everyone does; it comes easier with practice.

Summary

We think nothing of turning on a TV and sitting down to watch it. It's a communication tool we use to enhance our lives. Someday computers will be as widespread as television and just as normal a part of our lives. Computers of today, just like television, are based on complex principles, but they too are designed to be easy to use.

Computers are dumb—they must be told what to do. A true "computer error" is extremely rare (usually due to a component malfunction or an electrical fault). Since we tell the computer what to do, most errors in computer-generated output are really "human error".

As problem solvers, we use the computer to implement our solutions. Computer programming involves a problem-solving phase and an implementation phase. After analyzing a problem, we develop and test a general solution called an algorithm. This general solution becomes a specific solution, our program, when we write it in some convenient high-level programming language. This sequence of instructions to the computer (our program) is compiled into the language that the computer can execute. After correcting any errors or "bugs" that show up when testing, we can then use our program.

Computers are composed of five basic parts: memory, arithmetic/logic, control, input and output (I/O). The arithmetic/logic and control units together are called the central processing unit (CPU). Some I/O peripheral devices are the card reader, the line printer and the CRT terminal. Disk drives provide back-up storage for the memory unit. These physical parts are called hardware. A computer system is composed of both hardware and software.

System software improves the user/computer interface. The operating system obeys the system commands you enter. It can do things such as translate your program into machine code by calling the compiler and then run your translated-program and data. Other programs, such as the editor, provide further services.

A programming language reflects the range of operations a computer can perform. The basic control structures (sequence, selection, loop, procedure) of a programming language are based on these fundamental operations of a computer.

Users can communicate and interact with the computer by using an interactive system. On the other hand, a batch processing system allows no interaction during program execution.

Batch processing usually involves a card deck containing your program and control cards that tell the operating system what to do with your program. Cards are prepared on a keypunch. Interactive programming usually involves preparing your program at a terminal using an editor program. You can then enter directly at the terminal the commands to the operating system to compile and run your program.

Modern computer systems find wide usage in science, engineering, business and government. Learning to program in Pascal using top-down structured design (as shown in this book) will allow you to use this powerful tool effectively.

Problem Solving, Syntax/Semantics, and Pascal Programs 2

Goals

To be able to develop algorithms for solving problems.

To be able to read syntax diagrams in order to construct and identify legal Pascal statements and declarations.

To be able to create and/or recognize Pascal identifiers.

To be able to declare variables of type CHAR, INTEGER, BOOLEAN and REAL.

To be able to declare constants.

To be able to construct simple arithmetic expressions made up of variables, constants, and arithmetic operators (+, −, *, /, DIV, MOD).

To be able to evaluate simple Pascal arithmetic expressions.

To be able to construct a specified WRITE or WRITELN statement.

To be able to determine what would be printed, given a WRITE or WRITELN statement.

To be able to construct simple Pascal programs.

PROBLEM-SOLVING PROCESS

In Chapter 1 we described the programming process as being composed of a problem-solving phase and an implementation phase.

PROBLEM-SOLVING PHASE

Analyze—Understand (define) problem.

General Solution (Algorithm)—Develop a logical sequence of steps to be used to solve the problem.

Test—Follow the exact steps as outlined to see if the solution truly solves the problem.

IMPLEMENTATION PHASE

Specific Solution (Program)—Translate the algorithm into a programming language (code).

Test—Have the computer follow the instructions. Check the results and make corrections until the answers are correct.

Use—Use the program.

We solve problems every day, but we are often unaware of the process we are going through. In a learning environment we are usually given most of the information we need: a clear statement of the problem, the given input and the required output. In real life this is not always the case; we often must come up with the problem definition ourselves, decide what we have to work with and what the results should be.

After we have understood and analyzed the problem, we must come up with a solution—an algorithm.

ALGORITHM

A step-by-step procedure for solving a problem in a finite amount of time.

In Chapter 1 we discussed ordered logical sequences and the important role they play in our lives. We have given a name to a set of these ordered logical sequences when they allow us to perform a particular task or solve a particular problem. We call them algorithms.

Although we work with algorithms all the time, most of our experience with them is in the context of following them. We follow a recipe, play a game, assemble a toy, take medicine. We are all taught how to follow directions, i.e., execute an algorithm.

In the problem-solving phase of computer programming you will be designing algorithms, not following them. You will be given a problem and asked to devise the algorithm, to design the set of steps to be carried out in order to solve the problem. Actually, we do this kind of problem solving all the time at an unconscious level. We don't write down our solutions, however, we just execute them.

In learning to program you will have to make conscious some of your underlying problem-solving strategies in order to apply them to programming problems. Let's look at some of these strategies we all use every day.

Ask Questions If you are given a task verbally, you ask questions until what you are to do is clear. You ask when, why, where until your task is completely specified. If your instructions are written, you might put question marks in the margin, underline a word, group of words or a sentence, or in some other way indicate that the task is not clear. Perhaps your questions will be answered by a later paragraph, or you might have to discuss them with the person giving you the task.

If the task is one you set for yourself, this sort of questioning might not be verbal, but instead takes place on the subconscious level.

Some typical questions you will be asking in the programming context are as follows:

- What am I given to work with, i.e., what is my data?
- What does the data look like?
- How much data is there?
- How will I know when I have processed all the data?
- What must my output look like?
- How many times is the process I am doing to be repeated?
- What special error conditions might come up?

Look for Things that are Familiar We should never reinvent the wheel. If a solution exists, use it. If we have solved the same or similar problem before, we just repeat the successful solution. We don't consciously think, "I have seen this before, and I know what to do," we just do it. Humans are good at recognizing similar situations. We don't have to learn how to go to the store to buy milk, then to buy eggs, then to buy candy. We know that going to the store will be the same, and only what is bought is different.

In computing you will see certain problems again and again in different guises. A good programmer will immediately see a subtask that has been solved before and plug in the solution. For example, finding the daily high and low temperature is exactly the same problem as finding the highest and lowest grade on a test. You want the largest and smallest numbers among a set of numbers.

Divide and Conquer We constantly break up a large problem into smaller units that we can handle. The task of cleaning the house or apartment may seem overwhelming. The task composed of cleaning the living room, the dining room, the kitchen, the bedrooms, and the bathrooms seems more manageable. The same principle applies to programming. We break up a large problem into smaller pieces which we can solve individually. In fact the methodology we will outline in Chapter 3 for designing algorithms is based on this principle.

Now let's apply these strategies (called *heuristics*) to a specific problem.

Problem How can I get to the party?

Questions

Where is the party?
Where am I coming from?
What is the weather like (or likely to be like)?
Will I be walking? Driving a car? Taking a bus?

Once these questions have been answered, you can begin to design your algorithm.

If it is raining, your car is in the shop and the buses have stopped, your best solution (algorithm) might be to call a taxi and give the driver the address.

If you look at a map and see that where you are going is six blocks west of the building where you work, the first part of your algorithm might be to repeat what you do each morning to get to work (providing you are leaving from home). The next part would be to turn west and go six blocks. If you have trouble remembering how many blocks you have walked, you might take a pencil and make a hash mark on a piece of paper each time you cross a street.

Though hash marking might be stretching the human algorithm a little too much, this is a technique you will use frequently in your programs. If you wish to repeat a process 10 times, you will have to write the instructions to count each time you do the process and check to see when your count reaches 10. This is the repetition (looping) construct mentioned in Chapter 1.

If you wanted to write a set of directions for other people, some of whom would be leaving from one place and some from another, you would have to have two sets of instructions prefaced by a question. If you are coming from place A, follow the first set of directions; otherwise follow the second set of directions. This would be an example of the selection construct referred to in Chapter 1.

Coming up with a step-by-step procedure for solving a particular problem is not always cut and dried. In fact, it is usually a trial-and-error process requiring several attempts and refinements. Each attempt is tested to see if it truly solves the problem. If it does, fine. If it doesn't, we try again.

When designing algorithms for computer programs it is important to keep in mind that the computer manipulates data—that information which we have reduced to symbolic form. We have looked at some algorithms which require physical actions by a human being. These algorithms are not suitable for use on a computer. Our primary concern, then, is how the computer can transform, manipulate, calculate or process the input data to produce the desired output or results. We can analyze the content (what it is composed of) and the form (what the order or pattern is) of the input data as well as the required content and form of the output to help us develop an algorithm to process the data.

Program PAYROLL in Chapter 1 was coded from an algorithm that paralleled how the payroll was figured by hand. The algorithm for doing something by hand can very often be used with little or no modification as our general solution. Just keep in mind the things a computer can do. When writing an algorithm for a program, you know in the back of your mind the allowable instructions in a programming language. This awareness lets you avoid designing an algorithm that would be difficult or impossible to code.

Before writing a computer program to solve a problem, you go through the problem-solving phase and come up with a general solution (algorithm). When you have hand-tested your algorithm and feel that you have a working solution, you can proceed to translate your algorithm into a programming language. This implementation phase is similar to the problem-solving phase in that the program (algorithm) must be tested with input data to see that it produces the desired output. If it doesn't, you must locate the errors in the program. If your algorithm is faulty, you must go back to the problem-solving phase to see where you went wrong. Sometimes you have a correct algorithm, but have failed to translate it correctly into a programming language.

In this text, Pascal is the high-level language to be used to code your algorithms. We will now leave the general topic of programming and begin to look at the specifics of the Pascal language.

SYNTAX/SEMANTICS

A programming language is a set of rules, symbols and special words used to construct a program. There are rules for both syntax (grammar) and semantics (meaning).

SYNTAX

The formal rules governing the construction of valid constructs in a language.

SEMANTICS

The set of rules which give the meaning of a language construct.

We will discuss the syntax and semantics of Pascal throughout this text.

Syntax Diagrams

A useful tool for accurately describing syntax rules is the syntax diagram. The following is an example to explain how syntax diagrams work.

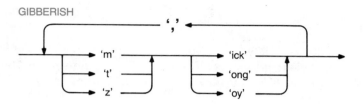

This syntax diagram shows how to form a piece of gibberish. By following the arrows from entry to exit, we can construct a syntactically correct piece of gibberish such as:

moy,toy,zick,zong,mick

There is no pattern for using the diagram other than beginning at the left and obeying the direction of the arrows. At a branching point, you may go either way. At the first branch you could take an 'm', 't', or 'z'. Then add 'ick', 'ong' or 'oy'. You could stop there or add a ',' and go back to the beginning and start again.

Another way of writing this diagram is as follows:

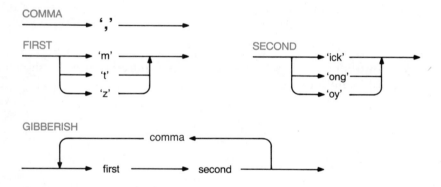

APPENDIX E is a collection of syntax diagrams used to describe the syntax rules of Pascal. You are urged to refer to these diagrams whenever you are in doubt concerning the syntax of a Pascal construct.

Identifiers

Identifiers are used in Pascal to name things. Some are defined in the language and reserved for specific uses. Any other names can be defined for your own use. These identifiers are formed using letters and digits.

IDENTIFIERS

Names that are associated with processes and objects and used to refer to those processes and objects. Identifiers are made up of letters (A–Z) and numbers (0–9) but must begin with a letter (A–Z).

Notice that an identifier must start with a letter.

IDENTIFIER

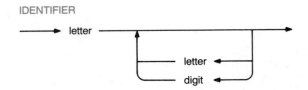

Examples of valid identifiers:

```
HELLO    J9    BOX22    GETDATA    BIN3    I    X
```

Identifiers are not limited in length but most compilers recognize only the first 8 characters as unique. The identifiers

```
DATAITEM1
DATAITEM2
```

are valid identifiers but may be treated as the same identifier by the compiler. Possible solutions might be:

```
DATA1
DATA2
```

or

```
DATA1ITEM
DATA2ITEM
```

and so on.

In the sample program at the end of Chapter 1, the user-defined identifiers listed at the top of the next page were used. Notice that the names were chosen to convey indications of their use. (The other identifiers in the program are pre-defined in Pascal.)

Data Types

Data are the physical symbols that represent information. We use different types of data in different ways. Musical notes are translated into sound from an instrument. Traffic signs are translated into steering, braking and other physical actions in our cars.

Identifier	How it is used
PAYROLL	the name of the program
PAYRATE	an employee's hourly pay rate
HOURS	the number of hours an employee worked
WAGES	weekly wages for an employee
TOTAL	sum of weekly wages for all employees
EMPNUM	employee ID number
PAYFILE	the output file (where the employee number, pay rate, hours and wages for each employee are written)

A computer program operates on data (whether stored internally in memory, stored on tape or disk, or input from terminal, card reader, electrical sensor, etc.) and produces an output. When we write a program, the data is our "given"; what we must process to produce desired results.

In Pascal, each item must be of a specific type. The data type affects the representation and processing of the piece of data. In addition to some basic built-in data types, Pascal also allows users to define new data types. These user-defined data types, declared by the programmer, will be discussed later in the text.

There are four simple types of data values which come up so often that Pascal has built-in rules about what they look like and what you can and cannot do with them. Three of them are already familiar to you. The fourth is so useful that it will soon become equally familiar to you.

Integer Integers are positive or negative whole numbers (no fractional part). They are made up of a sign and digits.

$$+22 \quad -16 \quad 1 \quad -426 \quad 0 \quad 4600$$

When the sign is omitted, positive is assumed. Commas are not allowed.

Theoretically, there is no limit on the size of integers, but the limitations of computer hardware and practical considerations do place a limit on the size an integer can be. Since this limit varies among machines, Pascal has a predefined identifier MAXINT whose value is set to the largest integer number that can be represented in that computer. If MAXINT were 32767, then the range of integers allowed would be:

$$-\text{MAXINT through MAXINT}$$

or

$$-32767 \text{ through } 32767.$$

MAXINT may be different for your machine, so you might print it to see how large it is. (This requires a Pascal program which you will be able to write by the end of this chapter.)

EMPNUM, the identifier for the employee number in Program PAY-ROLL in Chapter 1, is an INTEGER.

Real Real numbers are decimal numbers. They will be covered in detail in Chapter 8. What you need to know now are two things:

1. When writing them in your program or inputing them as data, always use a decimal point with at least one digit on either side. (Scientific notation explained in Chapter 8 is also acceptable.)

Valid	Not valid
3.1415	.42
−111.011	16.
76.43	.2
0.43	
−1.0	

2. Beware of comparing real numbers. Just as there is a limit on the size of an integer number, there is a limit on how accurate real numbers can be. For example, we know that 1/3 + 1/3 + 1/3 adds up to 1. Even though 1/3 is a repeating fraction, in a computer 0.333 stops when there are as many digits (3's) as that particular machine can represent. Therefore, if we summed three real numbers each containing the result of dividing 1 by 3 and asked if the sum were equal to 1.0, the answer would be "no." (0.333 + 0.333 + 0.333 = 0.999)

In Program PAYROLL, the identifiers PAYRATE, HRS, WAGES, and TOTAL are all REAL because they are identifiers for things which logically have decimal points.

Char The character data type describes data which is one alphanumeric character. Alphanumeric characters include letters, digits and special symbols.

'A'   'a'   '8'   '2'   '+'   '−'   '$'   '?'   '*'   ' '

Each machine has a set of alphanumeric characters which it can represent. This set is called the character set of the machine. (See APPENDIX N for some example character sets.) Your machine may not support both upper and lower case letters. If not, you will have to use upper case only. Notice that each character is enclosed in single quotes. The Pascal compiler needs the quotes to differentiate between the character data '8' or '+' and the integer 8 or the addition sign. Notice also that blank, ' ', is a character.

You can't add '8' and '3', but you can compare data values of type CHAR. The character set of a machine is ordered in what is known as the collating sequence. Although this sequence varies from one machine to another, 'A' is always less than 'B', 'B' less than 'C' and so forth. Also, '1' is less than '2', '3' is less than '4', etc. Later on we will discuss a program that will print out the collating sequence for your machine. None of the identifiers in Program PAYROLL is of type CHAR.

Boolean Boolean is a type with only two values: TRUE and FALSE. This type is associated with data created within your program and is used to represent the answers to questions. The importance of the type BOOLEAN will become clearer when we discuss conditions and how decisions are made by the computer. The ability to choose alternate courses of action (selection) is an important part of a programming language. (See Chapter 4.)

Boolean data cannot be read in as data, as the other three types can, but it can be printed out.

The B in Boolean is always capitalized because it is named after George Boole (1815–1864), an English mathematician who invented a system of logic using variables with only the two values, TRUE and FALSE.

Data Storage

Memory Memory is divided into a large number of separate locations, each of which can hold a piece of data. Each memory location has an address that can be used to refer to it when data is stored in it or retrieved from it. We can visualize memory as a set of post office boxes, with the box numbers as the addresses used to designate particular locations. (See Figure 2-1.)

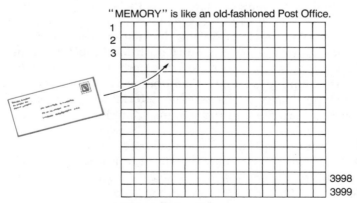

"MEMORY" is like an old-fashioned Post Office.

Figure 2-1. Memory

We could refer to memory locations by their addresses, as machine language programmers do. But how would you like to try to keep track of data stored in location 101101101? Or was it location 1011011001? Fortunately, higher level languages such as Pascal offer an alternative.

In Pascal we can use identifiers as the names of memory locations. The computer keeps track of the address corresponding to each name. It is as if we could put only the names on our letters and the post office would look up the addresses.

We can use identifiers for both variable and constant names. In other words, an identifier can be the name of a memory location whose contents changes or varies, or the name of a memory location whose contents never changes.

Besides variables and constants, the actual statements (instructions) of your program are also stored in various memory locations.

Variables Your program operates on data. This data may be of one of the simple types we have discussed: INTEGER, REAL, BOOLEAN, CHAR. Data is stored in memory. During execution of your program, different values may be stored in the same memory location at different times. We refer to the memory location as a "variable" and its contents as the "value of the variable." The symbolic name that we assign to this memory location (variable) is called a "variable name" or "variable identifier."

> **VARIABLE**
>
> A location in memory, referenced by a variable name (identifier), where a data value can be stored (this value can be changed).

We will refer to the variable name as the variable and say that its value changes. Actually, the memory location is the variable and its contents is what changes.

Variables must be declared in the declaration section of a Pascal program. (We discuss this in the Program Construction section of this chapter.) To declare a variable involves specifying both its name and its data type. This tells the compiler to name a memory location whose contents will be of a specific type. The type of a variable determines the operations that are allowed on that variable and the way its contents are represented in the machine.

Pascal is known as a strongly typed language. This means that only data values of the specified type may be stored in a variable. By checking for type compatibility, the compiler can also catch syntax errors such as adding a variable of type CHAR to an integer variable.

This is the syntax diagram of a variable declaration:

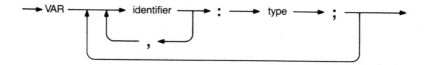

These would be valid variable declarations:

```
VAR A, B : INTEGER;
    PAYRATE : REAL;
    CH : CHAR;
```

The reserved word VAR denotes the variable declarations.
Now look at the VAR section of Program Payroll in Chapter 1.

```
VAR PAYRATE,          (*employee's pay rate*)
    HRS,              (*hours worked*)
    WAGES,            (*wages earned*)
    TOTAL:REAL;       (*total payroll*)
    EMPNUM:INTEGER;   (*employee ID number*)
    PAYFILE:TEXT;     (*company payroll file*)
```

This VAR section tells the compiler to set up locations in memory for four REAL variables, call them PAYRATE, HRS, WAGES and TOTAL and set up one location for an INTEGER variable. (Type TEXT is explained in Chapter 6.)

Constants   All the numbers, integer and real, are constants. So are characters and series of characters called strings.

16   32.3   'A'   'HOWDY BOYS'

We can use these constants in our program, wherever appropriate, as part of expressions. (See next section.) We can say "Add 5 and 6 and put that value in the variable SUM". The actual constant value stated in the program is called a literal constant.

Notice that the strings are in quotes. This is to differentiate between strings and identifiers. 'AMOUNT' (in quotes) is the character string made up of the letters A, M, O, U, N and T in that order. AMOUNT (without the quotes) is an identifier, the name of a place in memory. Since identifiers cannot begin with a digit, integers and reals do not have to be put in quotes because there is no ambiguity.

It makes the program more readable, however, to give a constant a name and use that name throughout your program. These are called named constants and are defined in the declaration section of your program. Using the constant identifier in place of the literal makes the meaning of the constant clearer. This is the syntax diagram of the constant definition section:

These would be valid constant definitions:

```
CONST STARS = '*******';
      BLANK = ' ';
      PI = 3.1416;
      INTERESTRATE = 0.12;
      TAXRATE = 0.001;
      MAX = 20;
      MESSAGE = 'ERROR CONDITION';
```

The constant definitions (if there are any) come before the variable declarations. If we had the following variable declaration after the above constant definitions

```
VAR RATE : REAL;
```

we could use the statements:

```
RATE := 0.12 + 0.001
```

or

```
RATE := INTERESTRATE + TAXRATE
```

and in both cases the value 0.121 would be stored in the variable RATE. Constant identifiers are just another way of representing the actual constant. In addition to readability, another advantage to using constant definitions is that if the value of a constant must be changed, it need be changed only in one place. For example, if you use TAXRATE throughout a program that you use on a daily basis, and one day the tax rate changes, you need change only the value of TAXRATE in the constant definitions and the new value would be used wherever TAXRATE appeared in the program. If, however, you used 0.001 as a literal, it would have to be changed in many places.

CONSTANT

A location in memory, referenced by a constant name (identifier), where a data value is stored (this value cannot be changed).

As a general rule, all identifiers in Pascal, including variables and constants, must be defined or declared before use. This is why, as you shall see, the declaration section comes before the main body of a Pascal program.

Assignment

Changing the value of a variable is done through an assignment statement. For example:

$$A := 10$$

assigns the value 10 to the variable A (puts 10 in the memory location called A). The syntax of the assignment statement is:

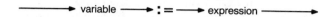

variable ⟶ := ⟶ expression ⟶

The assignment operator ":=" is read as "becomes"; the variable becomes the value of the expression.

Only one variable can be on the left-hand side of an assignment statement. Assignment is not like a math equation such as X + Y = Z + 4; the expression (what is on the right-hand side of the ':=') is evaluated and that value stored in the single variable on the left of the assignment operator. The value to be assigned to a variable must be of the same type as that variable. Given these declarations:

```
VAR I, J : INTEGER;
    RATE : REAL;
    TEST : BOOLEAN;
    CH : CHAR;
```

the following are valid assignments:

```
RATE := 0.36
TEST := TRUE
I := 2
CH := 'B'
```

These are not valid assignments:

```
I := 2.5          I is integer, 2.5 is real
CH := 3           3 is an integer constant, CH is CHAR
TEST := 'A'       TEST is Boolean, 'A' is a character constant
```

Variables keep their assigned values until changed by another assignment statement.

Expressions are made up of variables, constants and operators. The following are all valid expressions:

```
I + 2
RATE - 6.0
4 - I
RATE
TEST
I - J
```

The operators allowed in an expression depend on the data type of the constants and/or identifiers in the expression.

The arithmetic operators are:

+	addition
−	subtraction
*	multiplication
/	division
DIV	integer division (no fractional part)
MOD	modulus (remainder from integer division)

Since DIV and MOD are not operators you are familiar with, let's look at them more closely. When dividing one integer by another integer, you get an integer quotient and an integer remainder.

$$3 \Leftarrow 6 \text{ DIV } 2 \qquad 3 \Leftarrow 7 \text{ DIV } 2$$
$$2\overline{)6} \qquad\qquad 2\overline{)7}$$
$$\underline{6} \qquad\qquad \underline{6}$$
$$0 \Leftarrow 6 \text{ MOD } 2 \qquad 1 \Leftarrow 7 \text{ MOD } 2$$

More examples:

Expression	Value
3 + 6	9
3 − 6	−3
2 * 3	6
8 DIV 2	4
8 DIV 8	1
8 DIV 9	0
8 DIV 7	1
8 MOD 8	0
8 MOD 9	8
8 MOD 7	1
0 MOD 7	0

Be careful; 7 MOD 0 and 7 DIV 0 will give an error. You cannot divide by 0.

Since variables are allowed in expressions, the following are valid assignments:

```
I := J + 6
I := J DIV 2
J := I * 2
J := 6 MOD 3
I := I + 1
J := J + I
```

Notice that the same variable can appear on both sides of the assignment operator. In the case of

```
J := J + I
```

the value in J and the value in I are added together and the results stored back in J.

REAL values are added, subtracted, and multiplied just like INTEGER values. However, DIV and MOD have no meaning when applied to REAL values. To divide with REAL values use the '/' operator.

If one operand is a REAL and one is an INTEGER, the INTEGER value is converted to REAL before the operation is performed. If you use '/' between two INTEGER variables, both are converted to REAL before the division is done. The result is REAL.

It is valid to assign INTEGER values to REAL variables because it is clear what you want to have done. Any INTEGER value can be exactly represented in REAL form. For example, 2 can be 2.0, 42346 can be 42346.0. However, we cannot assign a REAL value to an INTEGER variable because it is not clear what you want done with the fractional part. If the REAL value is 1.7, what happens to the .7? If something is ambiguous, it is illegal.

Given the declarations:

```
VAR A, B : INTEGER;
      X : REAL;
```

the following statements are valid:

Statement	Result
A := B + 2	B + 2 gives an INTEGER result which is stored in an INTEGER place.
X := A + B	A + B gives an INTEGER result which is automatically converted to REAL to be stored in a REAL place.
X := A DIV B	Same as above.
X := A / B	A / B gives a REAL result. No conversion is necessary.
X := 2 + 2.3	An INTEGER plus a REAL gives a REAL which can be stored in a REAL place.

and the following statements are NOT valid:

Statement	Result
A := B + 2.0	An INTEGER plus a REAL gives a REAL which cannot be stored in an INTEGER place.
B := A + X	Same as above.
A := A / B	An INTEGER '/' an INTEGER gives a REAL which cannot be stored in an INTEGER place.
A := X DIV B	The variables on either side of DIV must be INTEGER.
B := A + 2 / B	The '/' gives a REAL result which cannot be stored in an INTEGER place.

The following chart summarizes what the resulting type will be, given the operator and the types of the operands.

	Type of operands			
Operator	Real Real	Real Integer	Integer Real	Integer Integer
+	Real	Real	Real	Integer
−	Real	Real	Real	Integer
*	Real	Real	Real	Integer
/	Real	Real	Real	Real
MOD	error	error	error	Integer
DIV	error	error	error	Integer

Remember that you can assign an INTEGER result to a REAL variable, but you *cannot* assign a REAL result to an INTEGER variable.

WRITE

Since computers rarely produce answers (output) just for other computers, programming languages always provide a way for the computer to return information in a form for human consumption. The WRITE statement is the Pascal instruction to produce this output.

→ WRITE → (→ parameter list →) →

The parameter list is a list of what you want printed. It can contain any expression. The following program segment produces the output shown. (Note that numeric values are printed right justified in a fixed field.)

Statements	What is printed ('☐' means blank)
`I := 2;`	
`J := 6;`	
`WRITE(I);`	`☐☐☐☐☐2`
`WRITE('I = ', I);`	`I☐=☐☐☐☐☐☐2`
`WRITE('SUM = ', I + J);`	`SUM☐=☐☐☐☐☐☐8`
`WRITE('ERROR MESSAGE');`	`ERROR MESSAGE`
`WRITE('ERROR#', I);`	`ERROR#☐☐☐☐☐2`
`WRITE('J:', J, 'I:', I);`	`J:☐☐☐☐☐6I:☐☐☐☐☐2`

String constants are used to generate text messages. Be sure to enclose them in quotes to differentiate them from variables. Each parameter in the list is separated by a comma.

All the parameters of successive WRITE statements are output on one line. In fact, the output of the above program segment is actually:

`☐☐☐☐☐2I☐=☐☐☐☐☐☐2SUM☐=☐☐☐☐☐☐8ERROR☐MESSAGEERROR#☐☐☐☐☐2J:☐☐☐☐☐6I:☐☐☐☐☐2`

You can cause output to be printed on different lines by using the WRITELN statement.

The WRITELN statement is similar to the WRITE statement, but it has the added feature of causing the *next* output to be printed on the next line. For example:

```
WRITE('HI');
WRITE(' THERE,');
WRITE(' LOIS LANE')
```

produces

```
HI THERE, LOIS LANE
```

whereas

```
WRITE('HI');
WRITELN(' THERE,');
WRITELN(' LOIS LANE')
```

produces

```
HI THERE,
LOIS LANE
```

You can use the WRITELN statement to generate blank lines.

```
WRITELN('HI THERE,');
WRITELN;
WRITELN('LOIS LANE')
```

produces

```
             HI THERE,

             LOIS LANE
```

The statement:

```
             WRITELN(A,B,C)
```

is equivalent to

```
             WRITE(A);
             WRITE(B);
             WRITE(C);
             WRITELN
```

Both the WRITE and WRITELN statements print what is specified on one line, but the WRITELN causes subsequent output to start on the next line (a line feed is generated).

Another way of saying this is that after printing, WRITE leaves the printing "pointer" under the last character it printed on a line. WRITELN moves its printing "pointer" to the beginning of the next line after printing. Given A=123, B=456, C=789, D=987, the following statements produce these results with the pointer left where indicated.

	print line			
	123	456	789	987
WRITE(A,B);		↑		
WRITE(C,D)				↑

and the following statements produce these results:

	print line	
WRITELN(A,B);	123	456
(next line) ↑		
WRITELN(C,D)	789	987
(next line) ↑		

In these examples each integer has been right justified in six columns. If you do not specify how many columns a number is to occupy on output, the default value for your particular system is used (six in this text). In Chapter 5 you will learn how to specify the number of columns.

If you want a blank to appear in your output, you must put it in quotes. For example:

```
         GRADE := 'A';
         WRITELN('THE GRADE IS', GRADE)
```

prints

```
THE GRADE ISA
```

The blanks before the identifier GRADE in the WRITELN statement are ignored. If you want a blank before the grade in the output line, you must insert it between the 'S' and the quote.

```
        WRITELN('THE GRADE IS ', GRADE)
```

Another way:

```
        WRITELN('THE GRADE IS', ' ', GRADE)
```

Some systems use the first character in each output line to control the vertical movement of the printer. If your system does this, you will have to make sure the first character in each line is one of the control characters below.

> '+' no line feed (overprinting)
> ' ' single space before printing
> '0' double space before printing
> '1' eject to a new page before printing

PROGRAM CONSTRUCTION

We can collect the statements we have learned into a program. Pascal programs are composed of a heading, a declaration section and a statement section. The outline looks like this:

> I. Heading
> II. Declarations
> III. Statements

The statements are the executable part of the program. They are set off with a "BEGIN-END" pair. Here is an example program:

```
PROGRAM EXAMPLE(INPUT,OUTPUT);            (* This example program
                          demonstrates the structure of a Pascal program. *)
CONST
    FREEZE = 32;
    BOIL = 212;
VAR
    TEMP : INTEGER;
BEGIN
    WRITELN('WATER FREEZES AT ', FREEZE,' DEGREES');
    WRITELN('WATER BOILS AT', BOIL,' DEGREES');
    TEMP := (FREEZE + BOIL) DIV 2;
    WRITELN('HALFWAY BETWEEN THEM IS ', TEMP,' DEGREES')
END.
```

Notice the heading composed of the reserved word PROGRAM, followed by a user-defined name for the program, followed by a list of the files used by the program. The files set up communication between your program and the outside world. (Files will be covered in Chapter 6.) INPUT is often your terminal keyboard or card reader and OUTPUT your terminal screen or printer. This is the syntax diagram for a program heading:

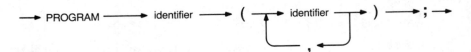

Next in the example program is a comment describing the program. Comments can appear anywhere in a program and are delimited by the "(* *)" pair. The compiler ignores anything within these pairs.

The declaration section defined both the constants FREEZE and BOIL and the variable TEMP. The declaration section gives information to the Pascal compiler to use in the translation phase. As a general rule, everything in Pascal must be defined before it is used.

The statement section is the executable part of the program. It is this section that gets translated, and during the execution phase these translated instructions get executed. Program EXAMPLE prints some messages about the freezing and boiling points of water and the average of the two.

Notice that the statements are separated by a semicolon (except before the END where it's not necessary). Semicolons are separators; they are not part of a statement. The Pascal program always ends with a period.

Program Formatting

Formatting refers to the place on a line or card where you begin a statement or declaration and the places where you insert extra blanks for readability. As far as the compiler is concerned, Pascal statements are free format: they may appear anywhere on a line (even more than one on a line). The compiler doesn't care; it only needs blanks to separate symbols and semicolons to separate statements. However, it is extremely important that your programs be readable, not only for your own sake but for the sake of anyone else who has to read them. Good formatting habits will help you in your programming.

Just as an outline for an English paper has certain indentation rules to make it readable, Pascal programs have recommended indentation and formatting rules. Use APPENDIX K: PROGRAM FORMATTING as a guideline when writing your programs.

The following is a copy of Program Payroll which does not conform to any formatting standards. Need we say more?

```
PROGRAM PAYROLL(INPUT,OUTPUT,PAYFILE); (*This program computes the
wages for each employee and the total payroll for the company*)
VAR PAYRATE,HRS,WAGES,TOTAL:REAL; EMPNUM:INTEGER;
PAYFILE:TEXT;
BEGIN REWRITE(PAYFILE); (*open file PAYFILE*)
TOTAL:=0; WRITE('ENTER EMPLOYEE #: '); (*prompting message on
screen*)
READLN(EMPNUM); (*read employee ID number*)
WHILE EMPNUM<>0 DO (*repeat until a zero emp. # is entered*)
BEGIN WRITE('ENTER PAYRATE: '); (*prompt on screen*)
READLN(PAYRATE); (*read hourly pay rate for emp.*)
WRITE('ENTER HOURS WORKED: '); (*prompt on screen*)
READLN(HRS); (*read hours worked by employee*)
IF HRS>40.00 (*check for overtime*)
THEN WAGES:=(40.0*PAYRATE)+(HRS-40.00)*PAYRATE*1.5
ELSE WAGES:=HRS*PAYRATE; TOTAL:=TOTAL+WAGES; (*add wages to
payroll*)
WRITELN(PAYFILE,EMPNUM,PAYRATE,HRS,WAGES);     (*put employee wage
                                                data in file PAYFILE*)
WRITE('ENTER EMPLOYEE #: '); (*prompt on screen*)
READLN(EMPNUM) END;
WRITELN('TOTAL PAYROLL IS ',TOTAL:10:2) (*print total on screen*)
END.
```

Compound Statements

The executable statement section of a program is actually called a compound statement. This is the syntax diagram for a compound statement:

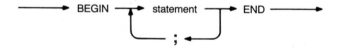

This is the syntax diagram for a statement:

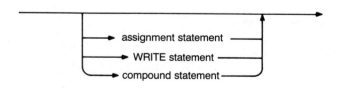

A statement can be the null statement or any of the other statements we have seen, even another compound statement. This is important because wherever a statement can be used, a compound statement may be used.

The "BEGIN-END" pair delimits a compound statement. You will have occasion to use compound statements often, especially as part of other statements. Leaving out a "BEGIN-END" pair can dramatically change the meaning as well as the execution of a program.

Blocks

The declaration and statement sections make up what is known as a block. The syntax diagram is:

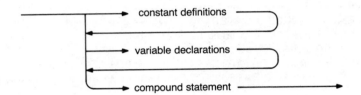

Notice that the declarations are optional, but if present the constant definitions must precede the variable declarations.

With the concept of the block we can now define a program as a heading and a block (followed by a period).

heading ⟶ ; ⟶ block ⟶ .

Check this syntax diagram against Program EXAMPLE in the Program Construction section in this chapter.

■ **SAMPLE PROBLEM**

Problem: What is the cost per square foot of my dream lot if the price is $20,000?

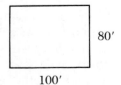

80′

100′

Discussion: Cost per square foot is calculated by dividing the price by the area. We know the price is $20,000. How do we find the area? Well, we are given the dimensions of the lot (100' by 80'). Since area is the product of these dimensions, we can calculate the area.

To execute this algorithm (or plan) by hand would involve multiplying two numbers together (the width and the length of the lot). The result (the area) would then be divided into the price of the lot to give the cost per square foot.

To express this algorithm or plan in a computer program will require two additional steps. We have to let the program know what we know, and we have to let it tell us what it knows. What we know is the size of the lot and the price. We will give this information to the program by setting constants equal to these values.

What the program will know that we don't is the answer. If we calculate the cost per square foot by hand or with a calculator, the answer is there for us to see. If this value is calculated by a program, the result must be written out.

Here is the solution expressed in Pascal. (Remember that anything enclosed in '(*...*)' is a comment and is ignored by the computer.)

```
PROGRAM COST(OUTPUT);          (* Program to calculate the cost per sq. ft. of a lot *)
CONST WIDTH = 100;                               (* set width to 100 feet *)
      LENGTH = 80;                               (* set length to 80 feet *)
      PRICE  = 20000;                       (* set price to 20000 dollars *)
VAR AREA : INTEGER;
    COSTSQFT : REAL;
BEGIN (*COST*)
  AREA := WIDTH * LENGTH;                            (* calculate the area *)
  COSTSQFT := PRICE/AREA;                  (* calculate cost per square foot *)
  WRITELN('COST PER SQUARE FOOT IS ',COSTSQFT) (* write answer *)
END. (*COST*)
```

Let's look at what each part of this program does. (See Figure 2-2.)

The CONST section causes three memory locations to be assigned the names WIDTH, LENGTH, and PRICE. It also causes the values 100, 80, and 20000 to be put into these locations.

Memory

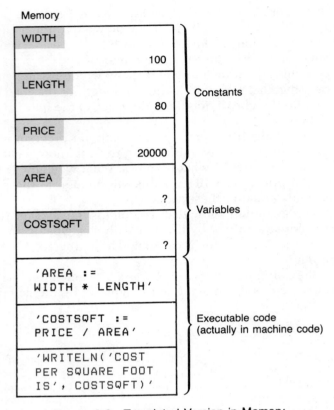

Figure 2-2 Translated Version in Memory

The VAR section causes the names AREA and COSTSQFT to be assigned to two memory locations, but no values are put into these places. The places are needed to hold the results of calculations.

The statements between the BEGIN and END are translated into the machine language the computer can execute. This will vary from machine to machine.

After the translated version of the program is in memory, control is turned over to the first statement after the BEGIN. In other words, what your program says to do is actually done. (See Figure 2-3.)

Pascal often uses scientific notation to print REAL numbers. Since COSTSQFT is a REAL variable, the answer was printed in scientific notation:

```
COST PER SQUARE FOOT IS 2.5000000000000E+000
```

This is discussed further in Chapter 8.

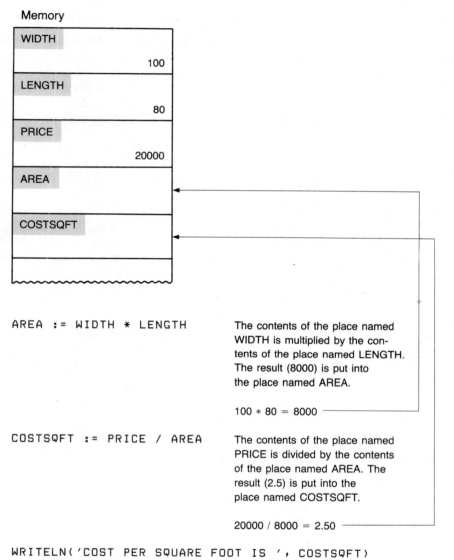

Memory

WIDTH	
	100

LENGTH	
	80

PRICE	
	20000

AREA	

COSTSQFT	

```
AREA := WIDTH * LENGTH
```

The contents of the place named WIDTH is multiplied by the contents of the place named LENGTH. The result (8000) is put into the place named AREA.

100 * 80 = 8000

```
COSTSQFT := PRICE / AREA
```

The contents of the place named PRICE is divided by the contents of the place named AREA. The result (2.5) is put into the place named COSTSQFT.

20000 / 8000 = 2.50

```
WRITELN('COST PER SQUARE FOOT IS ', COSTSQFT)
```

The sentence 'COST PER SQUARE FOOT IS ' is written out followed by the value in the place named COSTSQFT.

Figure 2-3. Execution of Translated Program

Summary

Writing a computer program involves a problem solving phase and an implementation phase. We analyze the problem and devise a workable algorithm. This algorithm is coded into a programming language and tested again. We go through this process until we get a correct program solution.

The syntax (grammar) of the Pascal language is defined by the syntax diagrams. Identifiers are used to name things in Pascal, those predefined as well as those user-defined.

The basic predefined data types of Pascal are INTEGER, REAL, BOOLEAN and CHAR. Variables and constants are defined to be one of these types and occupy a place in memory. Variables can be assigned different values of their defined type in the program during execution.

We have seen three symbols that are often confused: ":", "=" and ":=". The colon separates the variable name and its type in a variable declaration. The equal sign separates a constant name and its value in a constant definition. The assignment operator is used to change the value of a variable by assigning the value of an expression to that variable.

WRITE statements are used to display the output of a program. A WRITE statement will print the value of any expression in its parameter list.

Programs consist of a heading and a block. A block consists of optional declarations and a compound statement. By formatting our programs with proper indentation and spacing, we make them easier to read and understand.

Exercises

1. Mark the following as valid or invalid identifiers:

   a. ITEM#1   e. INVESTMENT
   b. DATA   f. BIN-2
   c. Y   g. NUM5
   d. 1SET   h. SQ FT

2. Given the following syntax diagrams:

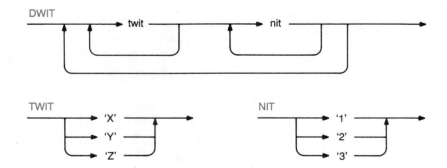

mark the following as valid or invalid "dwits":

		Valid	*Invalid*
a.	XYZ	____	____
b.	123	____	____
c.	X1	____	____
d.	23Y	____	____
e.	XY12	____	____
f.	Y2Y	____	____
g.	ZY2	____	____
h.	XY23X1	____	____

3. Write a constant definition for INCHESPERFOOT.

4. Write declarations for the REAL variables RATE and WEIGHT.

5. What is the value of the variable SUM after the following program segment is executed?

```
A  := 2;
B  := 7;
C  := B DIV A;
SUM := A + C;
```

6. Choose meaningful names and write a single VAR declaration for the following values:
   a. Your year of birth.
   b. Your grade point average.
   c. A variable indicating whether something is marked or not.
   d. A one-character grade code.
   e. A 10 digit ID number.

7. Write the statements that would print the following:
   ```
   ***DANGER***
   OVERVOLTAGE CONDITION
   ```

8. Good program formatting is important because it improves the readability of a program.   T   F

9. Circle any Pascal syntax errors in the following:
   a.   A+B=C;
   b.   Y=CONTENTS;
   c.   X:=*B;
   d.   PROGRAM ONE(INPUT,OUTPUT);
   e.   CONST X:=18;

10. A block consists of an optional declarations part and a compound statement.   T   F

11. Use a WRITELN statement to print both the value of an integer variable called AMOUNT and a description in English of AMOUNT (make one up).

12. Given the following program, determine what is printed.

```
PROGRAM EXERCISE (OUTPUT)
CONST LBS = 10;
VAR PRICE, COST : INTEGER;
    CH : CHAR;
BEGIN
  PRICE := 30;
  COST := PRICE * LBS;
  CH := 'A';
  WRITELN('COST IS ');
  WRITELN(COST);
  WRITELN('PRICE IS ', PRICE, 'COST IS ', COST);
  WRITE('GRADE ', CH, ' COSTS ');
  WRITELN(COST)
END.
```

Pre-Test

1. Which of the following are valid identifiers in Pascal?

	Valid	Not valid
R2D2	____	____
145R	____	____
R*2	____	____
TIME	____	____
X−Y	____	____

2. Syntax diagrams.

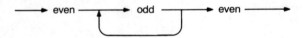

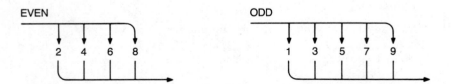

Given the above, which of the following are valid?

	Valid	Not valid
212	____	____
333	____	____
0330	____	____
6135798	____	____

3. Not formatting the program correctly will cause an error.

   T   F

4. Mark the following as either valid or not valid.

	Valid	Not valid
X × Y = C	___	___
Y := CON	___	___
CONST X = 10	___	___
VAR X : INTEGER	___	___
A := B MOD C	___	___

5. Use a WRITELN statement to print the value of an integer variable BALANCE preceded by the words 'YOUR BALANCE IS '.

6. Write a Pascal statement to create a constant called MAXUM which contains the number 100.

7. Write a Pascal statement to set up storage for an integer variable called ANSWER.

8. What are the values of the variables after the following program segment is executed?

```
PRICE := 10;
NOBOOKS := 12;
BILL := PRICE * NOBOOKS;
CHANGE := 150 - BILL
```

PRICE is ___   NOBOOKS is ___   BILL is ___   CHANGE is ___

9. Match each of the following terms to the correct definition. There is only one correct answer for each.

   _____program
   _____algorithm
   _____compiler
   _____identifier
   _____translation phase
   _____execution phase
   _____variable
   _____constant
   _____memory
   _____syntax
   _____semantics

   1. a place in memory where a data value can be stored

   2. a place in memory where a data value is stored which cannot be changed

   3. the part of a computer which holds both program and data

   4. an input device to a computer

   5. the time spent planning a program

   6. grammar rules

   7. a looping structure

8. meaning

9. a program which translates assembly language instructions into machine code

10. when the machine code version of a program is being run

11. symbolic names made up of letters and digits beginning with a letter

12. when a program in a high level language is translated into machine code

13. a program that takes a program written in a high level language and translates it into machine code

14. a step-by-step outline for solving a problem

15. a sequence of instructions to a computer to perform a particular task

More Syntax/Semantics and Design Methodology 3

Goals

To be able to construct a READ *or* READLN *statement to read in specified values.*

To be able to determine the contents of variables assigned values in a given READ *or* READLN *statement.*

To be able to evaluate expressions according to precedence rules.

To be able to distinguish between Pascal reserved words and user-defined identifiers, given a list of words.

To be able to follow a Pascal program, determining the values of the variables at the end of execution of each statement.

To be able to apply the top-down design methodology to solve a simple problem.

To be able to take a top-down design and code it in Pascal using self-documenting code.

MORE SYNTAX/SEMANTICS

There are two ways to assign a value to a variable. One is with the assignment statement which was discussed in Chapter 2; the other is by reading in the value as data. In this chapter we will examine how this is done and look at more complicated assignment statements.

In the latter part of this chapter we will set aside Pascal particulars and look at a general methodology for developing our algorithms: top-down design.

Read

A program needs data on which to operate. Data is separate from the program and can be input in Pascal using the READ statement.

```
──────▶ READ ──────▶ ( ──────▶ parameter list ──────▶ ) ──────▶
```

Input may be from a terminal, a punched card reader, or a tape or disk file.

The parameter list *must* be composed of variables. (You must have a place in which to put the data.) The input data must agree in type with the variable in which it is stored. The parameters are separated by commas.

The semantics of the READ where the parameters are REAL or INTEGER are as follows:

1. Get a number from the input data file or the terminal.
2. Store the number in memory in the first place named in the parameter list.
3. Is there another place still left in the parameter list? If so,
   - Get a number.
   - Store the number in the next place named in the parameter list.
   - Repeat 3.

   If not, READ is completed.

How do you separate numbers on a data card or the terminal keyboard? By putting one or more blanks between them.

Statement	Data	Contents after READ
(a) READ(X)	32	X:32
(b) READ(A, B, C)	3 4 60	A:3 B:4 C:60
(c) READ(D, E)	24 76	D:24 E:76
(d) READ(Y, Z)	(blank line) 46 32.4	Y:46 Z:32.4

NOTE: X, A, B, C, D, E, Y must have been declared INTEGER and Z must have been declared REAL.

What is the difference between the statements READ(A) followed by READ(B) and the statement READ(A, B)? Nothing, absolutely nothing. Using a list of variable identifiers is only a convenience for the programmer.

There is, however, a second input statement: READLN. READLN differs from READ in one major respect. After the variables in the parameter list have had values put into them, the READLN skips to the next line or card. If there are any numbers remaining on the line or card, they will never be read.

If there are two integer data items on each line of input:

```
10     20
15     16
22     21
```

then the following sets of statements are all equivalent:

(a) READ(A,B);
    READ(C,D);
    READ(E,F)

(b) READ(A);
    READ(B,C,D);
    READ(E,F)

(c) READ(A,B,C,D,E,F,)

(d) READLN(A,B);
    READLN(C,D);
    READLN(E,F)

(e) READLN(A,B,C,D,E,F)

Variable	Value read
A	10
B	20
C	15
D	16
E	22
F	21

Note that (a) and (d) are the same with READ and READLN interchanged; so are (c) and (e). What happens if the READs in (b) are replaced by READLNs? An error message occurs. Look what happens:

READLN(A);	10 is stored in A
READLN(B,C,D);	15 is stored in B
	16 is stored in C
	22 is stored in D
READLN(E,F)	There are no values to be put into E and F.

The second value on the first line or card is not read because, after reading a value into A, the balance of that card or line is skipped. The same is true of the second value on the third line or card.

READ leaves the reading "pointer" ready to begin with the next column. READLN performs the read and then moves the reading "pointer" to the beginning of the next line. Each input line has an end-of-line character <eoln> to tell the computer where one line ends and the next begins. The READ or READLN will cross line boundaries <eoln> to find as many values as there are identifiers in its parameter list.

Given three lines of input data:

```
123    456    789    <eoln>
987    654    321    <eoln>
888    777    666    <eoln>
```

and given that A, B, C and D are INTEGER variables, the following statements produce these results with the "pointer" left where indicated by " ↑ ". (Each example is independent.)

	Values read	Pointer position after READ/READLN
(a) READ(A,B);	A: 123 B: 456	123 456 789 <eoln> ↑
READ(C,D)	C: 789 D: 987	987 654 321 <eoln> ↑
(b) READLN(A,B);	A: 123 B: 456	987 654 321 <eoln> ↑
READLN(C,D)	C: 987 D: 654	888 777 666 <eoln> ↑
(c) READ(A,B);	A: 123 B: 456	123 456 789 <eoln> ↑
READLN(C,D)	C: 789 D: 987	888 777 666 <eoln> ↑
(d) READLN(A,B);	A: 123 B: 456	987 654 321 <eoln> ↑
READLN(C);	C: 987	888 777 666 <eoln> ↑
READLN(D)	D: 888	directly before next line
(e) READLN(A);	A: 123	987 654 321 <eoln> ↑
READ(B);	B: 987	987 654 321 <eoln> ↑
READLN(C);	C: 654	888 777 666 <eoln> ↑
READ(D)	D: 888	888 777 666 <eoln> ↑

Although we have used INTEGER data values in the above example, REAL data values are treated exactly the same way.

Look back at Program PAYROLL and examine the read statements. EMPNUM, PAYRATE, and HRS are each read in with a separate READLN. This implies that the data items are each on a separate line or card.

Character data is treated differently than numeric data. A CHAR variable holds *one* alphanumeric character. So when reading values into variables declared to be of type CHAR, only one character is read.

Given that X, Y, and Z are CHAR variables and the data:

```
A10<eoln>
BBB<eoln>
999<eoln>
```

the following sets of READs produce the results indicated. (Each example is independent.)

	Values read	Pointer position after READ/READLN
(a) READ (X,Y,Z)	X:'A' Y:'1' Z:'0'	A10 ↑
(b) READLN (X);	X:'A'	BBB ↑
READLN (Y);	Y:'B'	999 ↑
READ (Z)	Z:'9'	999 ↑
(c) READLN (X,Y);	X:'A' Y:'1'	BBB ↑
READLN (Z)	Z:'B'	999 ↑

Note that there are no quotes around the character data values shown. In our program we have to put quotes around character constants to differentiate them from identifiers or numeric constants. When reading in data values, there is no ambiguity. The type of the variable into which a value is to be stored determines how a value is interpreted.

Before the first READ in a program and after every READLN, the "pointer" is just before the first position on a line or card. After a READ, the "pointer" is just before the next character or number. This causes problems when reading numeric data followed by character data.

Look at what happens when numeric data and character data are mixed. CH1 and CH2 are CHAR, and P and Q are INTEGER. The data is:

24   36 A<eoln>

	Values read	Pointer position after READ/READLN
(a) READ (P,Q);	P:24 Q:36	24 36 A ↑
READ (CH1);	CH1:' '	24 36 A ↑
READ (CH2)	CH2:'A'	24 36 A ↑
(b) READ (CH1,CH2)	CH1:'2' CH2:'4'	24 36 A ↑

The thing to remember is that a READ involving a CHAR type variable always reads only one character and moves the "pointer" one character to the right. Since the INTEGER read in (a) left the pointer under the 6, the next character is a blank. Therefore, CH1 has a blank stored in it, and CH2 has the letter A. In (b), CH1 is a '2' and CH2 is a '4'. These are characters '2' and '4', not INTEGERs 2 and 4.

Where does the <eoln> come from? What *is* it? The first question is easy. If you are working at a terminal, you generate an <eoln> yourself when you hit the carriage return or new-line key. If you are using cards, the <eoln> character is inserted after each card when the cards are read.

The answer to the second question will vary from computer system to computer system. It is a special control character that a system recognizes. When your program is reading in values, the READ statement treats this character as a blank. Reading the <eoln> character into a variable of type CHAR results in a blank being stored in that variable.

When you use a WRITELN, you are actually writing an <eoln> character directly after the variables listed in the parameter list have been written. The printer or screen goes to a new line when it recognizes this character.

Precedence Rules

Expressions were defined as being made up of variables, constants and operators. Our examples showed constants and/or variables with one operator. Actually, expressions can be made up of many constants and/or variables and operators. For example:

```
I := I + J DIV 2
```

is valid if I and J are INTEGER variables (I could also be REAL). In an expression with more than one operator, it is not always clear in which order the operations are to be performed. Is I + J calculated first or is J DIV 2 calculated first? Pascal operators are ordered. This order is expressed in precedence rules.

*	/	DIV	MOD	highest precedence
+	−			lowest precedence

So in this example we divide J by 2 and add I. We could change the order of evaluating our example by the use of parentheses. The statement

```
I := (I + J) DIV 2
```

forces I and J to be added first and their sum divided by 2. (Here, I and J must both be INTEGER.) So subexpressions in parentheses are evaluated first and then the precedence of the operators is followed.

If A and B are REAL variables and we have the statement

```
A := (A + B) / A * 2
```

we evaluate the expression in the parentheses first. But do we divide the sum of A and B by the product of A and 2, or do we divide the sum of A and B by A and multiply this result by 2?

When there is more than one operator of the same precedence, we evaluate the expression from left to right. This means that in our example, after evaluating the overriding parentheses, we divide by A and multiply the result by 2.

Examples:
$$10 \text{ DIV } 2 * 3 = 15$$
$$10 \text{ MOD } 3 - 4 \text{ DIV } 2 = -1$$
$$5 * 2 / 4 * 2 = 5.0$$
$$5 * 2 / (4 * 2) = 1.25$$
$$5 + 2 / (4 * 2) = 5.25$$

These rules for defining how Pascal will evaluate an expression should not be new to you. They follow the way you would evaluate any arithmetic expression by hand.

Reserved Words, Standard Identifiers, User Names

The use of identifiers in Pascal is the way a programmer specifies variables, constants and processes. The identifiers a programmer can use are restricted to those not reserved by the Pascal language.

There are certain Reserved Words or keywords that are reserved by Pascal whose values or meanings are predefined. These identifiers *may not* be used for other than their intended purposes. Some examples are:

DIV   CONST   TYPE   VAR   BEGIN   END

See APPENDIX A for a complete list of Reserved Words.

Other identifiers are also predefined but may be redefined by the programmer. These are called Standard Identifiers and include:

READ   WRITE   ROUND   TRUNC   ABS

For example, the predefined functions TRUNC and ROUND will return an INTEGER value when given a REAL value.

ROUND(3.7) = 4   (rounds to nearest integer)
TRUNC(3.7) = 3   (truncates decimal part)

So, where it is invalid to assign a REAL value to an INTEGER variable, we can use ROUND or TRUNC to achieve an approximation. If J is an INTEGER variable, then

J := 16.3   is invalid,
J := ROUND(16.3)   is valid.

(The REAL constant 16.3 used as the parameter for the ROUND function could just as easily have been a REAL variable.) See APPENDIX B for a list of Standard Identifiers.

All valid identifiers that are not reserved in Pascal can be User Names. These user-defined identifiers may be used to specify variables, constants and program names. A good programmer chooses names that impart some meaning and aid in reading and understanding the program.

Tracing Program Variables

The computer is a literal device—it does exactly what we instruct it to do, not necessarily what we intend for it to do. We can try to make sure that our program does what we want by tracing the execution of instructions before we run the program (also useful during debugging). This technique is known by many names: "playing computer," "desk checking," doing a "dry run," or doing a code "walk-through."

We've listed a nonsense program as an example to explain the technique. Each line is numbered for reference purposes (the compiler does the same in order to refer to errors in specific lines). We keep track of the values of the program variables on the right-hand side. Variables with undefined values are indicated with a dash. When variables are assigned a value, that value is listed in its column on the right.

Line		A	B	C
1	PROGRAM TRACE(INPUT,OUTPUT);			
2	CONST X = 5;			
3	VAR A,B,C:INTEGER;	—	—	—
4	BEGIN	—	—	—
5	B := 1;	—	1	—
6	C := X + B;	—	1	6
7	A := X + 4;	9	1	6
8	A := C;	6	1	6
9	B := C;	6	6	6
10	A := A + B + C;	18	6	6
11	C := C MOD X;	18	6	1
12	C := C * A;	18	6	18
13	A := A MOD B;	0	6	18
14	WRITELN(A,B,C)	0	6	18
15	END.			

TOP-DOWN DESIGN

In Chapters 1 and 2 we discussed the programming process. This process consists of a problem-solving phase and an implementation phase.

You were warned not to try to by-pass the problem-solving phase even though small problems don't seem to require it and you are sure that you could write the program directly. There are good reasons for insisting on going through the complete process.

Even small problems have a large number of details to be taken care of, and a methodical approach is the best way to ensure that nothing is forgotten.

The practice of applying the following methodology to small problems will prepare you to tackle larger programming problems which you cannot solve directly. As a by-product, your programs will be readable, understandable, easily debugged and easily modified. We structure our approach to programming through a well-organized method or technique known as top-down design. Also called step-wise refinement and modular programming, this technique allows us to use a "divide and conquer" approach. In other words, a problem is divided into sub-problems that we can handle. After solving all the sub-problems we have a solution to the overall problem.

What we are doing in top-down design is working from the abstract (our description or specification of the problem) to the particular (our actual Pascal code).

If the problem description is a vaguely stated word problem, then the first step is to create a functional problem description. That is, a description which clearly states what the program is to do. In many cases, this means a dialogue between the person with the problem and the programmer. (We will attempt to make this unnecessary in this text!)

Modules

We start by breaking the problem into a set of sub-problems. Then, each sub-problem is divided into sub-problems. This process continues until each sub-problem cannot be further divided. We are creating a hierarchical structure, also known as a tree structure, of problems and sub-problems called functional modules. Modules at one level can call on the services of modules at a lower level. These modules are the basic building blocks of our program.

By dividing our problem into sub-problems, modules, or segments, we can solve each module fairly independently of the others. For example: one module could read data values, another could print values after processing. Various processing modules might keep a cumulative total, keep a count of data values, detect error conditions or do calculations.

Our design tree contains successive levels of refinement. (See Figure 3-1.) The top, or level 0, is our functional description of the problem, the lower levels are our successive refinements. How do you divide the problem into modules?

Well, let's think for a moment about how we humans usually approach any big problem. We spend some time thinking about the problem in an overall sort of way, then we jot down the major steps. We then examine each of the major steps, filling in the details. If we don't know how to accomplish a specific task, we go on to the next one, planning to come back and take care of the one we skipped later when we have more information.

This is exactly how you should approach a programming problem. Think about how you would solve the problem by hand. Write down the major steps. This then becomes your main module. Begin to develop the details of the major steps as level 1 modules. If you don't know how to do some-

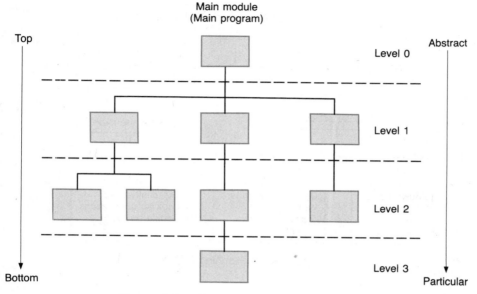

Main module
(Main program)

Top

Level 0

Abstract

Level 1

Level 2

Level 3

Bottom

Particular

Figure 3-1. Hierarchical or Tree Structure

thing, or feel yourself overwhelmed by details, give the task a name and go on. That name can be expanded later as a lower module.

This process continues for as many levels as it takes to expand every task to the smallest details. This might be called the Scarlett O'Hara technique. If a task is cumbersome or difficult, put off the problem to a lower level— don't think about it today, think about it tomorrow. Of course our tomorrows do come, but this whole process can then be applied to the troublesome sub-tasks. Eventually the whole problem is broken up into manageable units.

Let's apply this process to the pleasant task of planning a large party. A little thought will reveal that there are two main tasks: inviting the people and actually preparing the food.

One approach to inviting the people would be to reach for the phone book and start calling your friends. However, you would soon be confused as to whom you reached, whose line was busy, and who had said what. A much better approach would be to make a list of those you wished to invite, then put the list aside and check it over the next day to see which of your best friends you had forgotten.

Then, with the list in hand, you can go through and fill in the telephone numbers. Now you begin to call and mark down the responses. It may take a while to reach everyone, but you will know where you stand. By the time you have an estimate on numbers, you can start preparing the food.

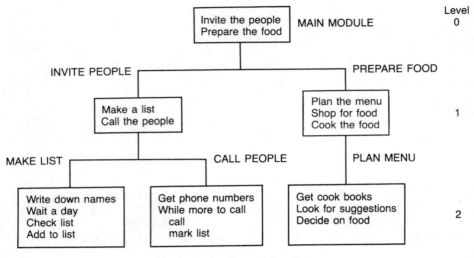

Figure 3-2. Planning a Party

Heaven help us if we just run in and start cooking! Without prior planning the job would be overwhelming. Instead, let's break down this task into planning the menu and preparing the food.

We can save a lot of time and effort in this task if we take advantage of what others have done and look at suggested menus in cookbooks. (In programming we would look in the literature to see if algorithms already exist to solve this sub-problem.) As we choose a menu, we can put off until later a careful examination of the recipes. The time to do that is when we are preparing the shopping list. (Defer details until later.)

The tree diagram in Figure 3-2 shows the process we have broken down so far.

Note that a module at each level expands a statement (task) at the level above. As humans we could probably take the level 2 modules and do them from this description. For a computer program we would have to break them down into much finer detail. For example, "Write down names" would have to be at the following level of detail:

Do you have paper?
No, get paper.
Do you have a pen?
No, get a pen.
Pick up pen.
Put pen to paper.
etc.

Your top-down design for giving a party might be quite different. Perhaps you have a great little delicatessen down the block, so you let them cater your party. Your main module would be:

```
Invite the people
Call the delicatessen
```

No two top-down designs will be exactly alike. There is no set way of writing a design. Your design will reflect your own individual style. However, a "good" design will be modular with tasks grouped into functional units.

Let's leave the social analogy now and look again at the process applied to computer programming problems. Remember, the domain is new but the process is one you have done all your lives.

The main module specifies the names of tasks. Each name of a task needs to be expanded at a lower level unless there is a one to one correspondence to a Pascal statement. This is true at each level. There will be as many modules at level 1 as there are names of tasks at level 0, and so on for each successive level.

If you make sure that each module works by using test data for that module, then your program should work when you put them all together. A little effort spent in testing each module can save a lot of effort spent in debugging your program.

THE IDEA IS TO DEFER DETAILS. Push the actual code to as low a level as possible. When you don't have to worry about actual implementation you can concentrate more on the functional divisions and algorithms. As you travel down the tree in your design you make a series of design decisions. If a decision proves awkward or incorrect (and it will many times!), it is easy to backtrack (go up the design tree to a higher level module) and try something else. At least you don't have to scrap your whole design; only that small part you are working on. There may be many intermediate steps and trial solutions before you reach your final design.

The bulk of your time should be spent analyzing and designing your solution. Coding will then take very little time and debugging should take even less.

Writing a top-down design is similar to writing an outline for an English paper. You can use English sentences or pseudo-code (a mixture of English and Pascal control structures) to describe each task or sub-task. The pseudo-code control structures are similar to the looping and selection statements discussed in Chapters 4 and 5. You will see examples of top-down designs using them as they are introduced. To demonstrate pseudo-code, here is a main module for the fairly simple problem of finding the average of a list of numbers.

```
initialize SUM and COUNT to zero
WHILE more data DO
    get data (read in a piece of data)
    add data to SUM
    increment COUNT (add one to COUNT)
AVERAGE = SUM / COUNT
print AVERAGE
```

The **WHILE-DO** is the looping control structure and the tasks

get data
add data to SUM
increment COUNT

are done over and over again until there is no more data (numbers in the list). Because this is such a simple problem, we can code from this module (each statement can be directly translated into a Pascal statement). This example demonstrates pseudo-code but doesn't really show off the beauty of top-down design: the reduction of problem complexity by the division of the problem into sub-problems (modules) that we can handle more easily.

"This was your first effort at TOP-DOWN design, wasn't it?"

Cartoon by M. Lad. Topolsky

What are the advantages of a program produced from a top-down design? It is easier to modify by parts; it is easier to understand because you can study it in functionally and logically organized pieces; and it is easier to test it.

Your program should reflect your top-down design. Any changes in the design should be easy to make in the program. Someone reading your program should be able to see your decomposition of the problem and the structure of your solution.

Methodology

The top-down design method can be broken down as follows:

(1) ANALYZE THE PROBLEM
(2) WRITE THE MAIN MODULE
(3) WRITE THE REMAINING MODULES
(4) RESEQUENCE AND REVISE AS NECESSARY

1. ANALYZE THE PROBLEM

Understand the problem. Understand what is given (INPUT) and what is required (OUTPUT). Specify INPUT and OUTPUT formats. List assumptions (if any). Think. How would you solve the problem by hand? Develop an overall algorithm or general plan of attack.

2. WRITE THE MAIN MODULE

Use English or pseudo-code to restate the problem in the main module. Use module names to divide the problem into functional areas. If this module is too long (more than 10 to 15 statements) you are at too low a level of detail. Introduce any control structures (such as looping or selection) that are needed at this point. Resequence logically if needed. Postpone details to lower levels. The main module may change during further refinement.

Don't worry if you don't know how to solve an unwritten module at this point. Just pretend you have a "smart friend" who has the answer and postpone it until later refinements have been made. All you have to do in the main module is to give the names of lower level modules that provide certain functions (solve certain tasks). Use meaningful module names.

3. WRITE THE REMAINING MODULES

There is no fixed number of levels. Modules at one level can specify more modules at lower levels. Each module must be complete although it references unwritten modules. Do successive refinements through each module until each statement can be directly translated into a Pascal statement.

4. RESEQUENCE AND REVISE AS NECESSARY

Plan for change. Don't be afraid to start over. Several attempts and refinements may be necessary. Try to maintain clarity. Express yourself simply and directly.

We will use the following outline for our top-down designs. The sample problem following the next section shows the use of this outline in a top-down design.

INPUT DESCRIPTION:
OUTPUT DESCRIPTION:
ASSUMPTIONS (IF ANY):
MAIN MODULE
REMAINING MODULES BY LEVELS

Documentation

As you create your top-down design, you are developing documentation for your program. Documentation consists of the written descriptions, specifications, development and actual code of a program.

Good documentation helps in reading and understanding and is invaluable when modifying (maintaining) software. If you haven't looked at your program for six months and need to haul it out and make some changes, you'll be happy that you documented it well. Of course, if someone else has to use and modify your program, the documentation is indispensable!

Documentation external to the program includes the specifications, development history and top-down design. Internal documentation includes program formatting, comments and self-documenting code. You can use the pseudo-code from your top-down design as comments in your program.

The documentation we have discussed is fine for the reader or maintainer of your programs. However, if a program is used in a production environment, you must provide a user's manual as well.

Documentation should be kept up to date. Any changes made in a program should be indicated in all of the pertinent documentation.

SELF-DOCUMENTING CODE

A program containing meaningful identifiers as well as judiciously used clarifying comments.

Using self-documenting code will make your programs more readable. Ideally, a Pascal program should be readable even by a non-programmer. APPENDIX J: PROGRAM DOCUMENTATION discusses some program documentation conventions.

As an aid in internal documentation it is good practice to use a meaningful constant identifier rather than the value of the constant itself in the body of your program. The statement:

```
AREA := PI * SQR(RADIUS)
```

is preferable to:

$$AREA := 3.1416 * SQR(RADIUS)$$

even though most people recognize that 3.1416 is PI.

■ SAMPLE PROBLEM

Problem: Find the weighted average of three test scores. The data will be in the form of an integer test score followed by its associated weight, each pair on a separate line.

Discussion: The concept of giving different weights to tests to arrive at a student's grade in a course is often used. For example, if there are two tests worth 30% each and a final exam worth 40%, we would take the first test grade and multiply it by 0.30, take the second test grade and multiply it by 0.30 and take the final and multiply it by 0.40. We would then add up these three values to get a weighted average. This "by hand" algorithm is exactly how we shall approach this problem.

Input: Three groups of data each composed of:
testscore (integer)   weight (real)

Output: Print input data with headings (Printing a copy of the input data as you read it is called echo printing.)
Print the weighted average with explanation

Assumptions: The three weights add up to one and the input data is correct (no error checking).

MAIN MODULE   Level 0

```
Get data
Print data
Find average
Print average
```

GET DATA   Level 1

```
READ TEST1, WT1, TEST2, WT2, TEST3, WT3
```

PRINT DATA

```
Print heading
WRITE TEST1, WT1
WRITE TEST2, WT2
WRITE TEST2, WT3
```

FIND AVERAGE

AVE = TEST1 * WT1 + TEST2 * WT2 + TEST3 * WT3

PRINT AVERAGE

WRITE ' WEIGHTED AVERAGE = ' AVE

PRINT HEADING   **Level 2**

WRITE ' TEST SCORE WEIGHT '

Design Tree Diagram:

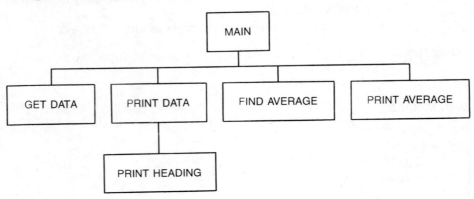

```
PROGRAM TESTAVE(INPUT,OUTPUT);          (* Program to find the weighted
                                            average of 3 test scores *)

VAR TEST1, TEST2, TEST3 : INTEGER;
    WT1, WT2, WT3, AVE : REAL;
BEGIN
    READ(TEST1, WT1, TEST2, WT2, TEST3, WT3);       (* get data *)
```

```
WRITELN(' TEST SCORE WEIGHT ');          (* print heading *)
WRITELN;                                 (* print a blank line *)
WRITELN(TEST1, WT1);                      (* print data *)
WRITELN(TEST2, WT2);                      (* print data *)
WRITELN(TEST3, WT3);                      (* print data *)
AVE := TEST1 * WT1 + TEST2 * WT2 + TEST3 * WT3;  (*find ave*)
WRITELN(' WEIGHTED AVERAGE = ', AVE)     (* print average *)
END.
```

The data for this program is separate and does not appear in the program itself. It might be input from cards, a data file, or even a terminal. If the following input data were used with this program:

```
90   0.3
85  0.25
78  0.45
```

then the output would look like this:

```
TEST SCORE WEIGHT

     90   3.0000000000000E-001
     85   2.5000000000000E-001
     78   4.5000000000000E-001
WEIGHTED AVERAGE =    8.3350000000000E+001
```

Remember that Pascal prints REAL numbers in scientific ("E") notation unless we specify otherwise. We will discuss how to suppress printing REAL numbers in scientific notation in Chapter 8.

■

STANDARD APPROACHES

As a programmer, you will develop many standard tools that you will use regularly in your programming. One tool is the top-down design methodology we have discussed. Other tools are the different ways of structuring statements such as sequentially, conditionally, repetitively and procedurally. Unlike some programming languages, Pascal already has these structures built-in.

You will develop a repertoire of standard approaches to common tasks that will come up again and again. Many problems will include at least one of the following tasks:

- keeping a cumulative total (summing)
- keeping a count (counting)
- finding the average of a set of values
- finding the minimum value in a set of values
- finding the maximum value in a set of values

For example, it is often necessary to keep a cumulative total of a variable during input or computation. The summing variable might be called SUM, TOTAL or AMT. You would initialize it to zero

```
SUM := 0
```

and then accumulate the value as follows:

```
READ(VALU);                    (* or other processing to get VALU *)
SUM := SUM + VALU
```

SUM is being changed each time by the contents of VALU. We know nothing about VALU, it could be negative or positive; it could be very large or very small.

Another common task is to keep track of the number of times something occurs. This counting variable might be called COUNT, N or CNTR. You would initialize it to zero

```
COUNT := 0
```

and then add one to it each time you wish to count:

```
COUNT := COUNT + 1
```

COUNT is increasing by one each time.

As you gain experience in problem solving, you will recognize these common tasks and plug in your standard approaches to solving them.

Summary

Programs operate on data. Data and programs are separate. (The same program can be run with many different sets of input data.) The READ statement inputs data from a file or a terminal and stores the input data in memory in the variables specified in its parameter list.

The precedence rules tell us how an arithmetic expression will be evaluated.

Tracing program variables lets us hand-simulate the execution of our code. This "playing computer" is a valuable tool in debugging programs. We often find that what we intended our program to do is not precisely what we specified. The computer is literal and does exactly what we say— not necessarily what we mean.

Top-down design provides a method for breaking down problems into pieces we can handle. It can be thought of as a modular or building-block approach.

If you do not know yet how to do a task, give it a name and go on. Later you can come back and fill in the details. If you are overwhelmed by details, step back and look at just what you are trying to do. Write down those tasks to be developed later at a lower level, and go on.

Top-down design results in highly structured and readable programs. Top-down design and program formatting and documentation are necessary for writing "good" programs.

Exercises

1. Modularization can be thought of as a building block approach to problem solving.   T   F

2. Compute the value of each expression if it is a legal expression. Indicate whether the value is REAL or INTEGER. If the expression is not legal, indicate why.
   a. 10 / 3 + 5 * 2
   b. 10 MOD 3 + 5 MOD 2
   c. 10 DIV 3 + 5 DIV 2
   d. 12.5 + (2.5 / (6.2 / 3.1))
   e. −4 * (−5 + 6)
   f. 13 MOD 5 / 3
   g. (10 / 3 MOD 2) / 3

3. Evaluate the following expressions to find the result:
   a. RESULT:=15 MOD 4
   b. RESULT:=7 DIV 3+2
   c. RESULT:=2+7 * 5
   d. RESULT:=45 DIV 8 * 4+2
   e. RESULT:=17+(21 MOD 6) * 2
   f. RESULT:=SQR(4 * 2+2)

4. Write input commands to read in the following data, using meaningful identifiers. You may assume variables predeclared. (A card is the same as one line of input.)
   a. A payroll identification card containing a social security number followed by a department number (integers). This is followed by a time card containing a deductions code (character), hours worked (integer) and overtime hours (integer).
   b. A grade card containing a student identification number (integer), a classification code (character), and four letter grades (character), all separated by one blank space.

5. Label each of the following identifiers as reserved words or user-defined identifiers. (R or U).

   TEMP
   VAR
   BEGIN
   CONST
   CONSTANT
   SIGNAL
   FLAG
   PROGRAM

6. If A = 5 and B = 2 show what each of the following statements produces:

```
WRITELN('A = ',A,' B = ',B);
WRITELN('SUM = ',A + B);
WRITELN(A DIV B);
WRITELN(B - A);
```

7. If the following input instructions were executed on the data shown, what values would the variables contain?

```
VAR A,B,C,D:INTEGER;
    READ(A);
    READLN(B,C);
    READ(D)
```

Data for this program: 24 72
                         46 55
                         18 4

(A) ——   (B) ——   (C) ——   (D) ——

8. Trace the values of the variables in the following program.

	X	Y	Z

```
PROGRAM TRACE(INPUT,OUTPUT);
VAR X,Y,Z:INTEGER;
BEGIN
    READ(X,Y,Z);
    X:=X+Y+Z;
    X:=X MOD Z;
    Z:=Y DIV 2;
    Y:=X * X+10;
    X:=(X-10) * 3;
    WRITELN(X,Y,Z);
END.
```

Data: 25 20
          2 10

9. Using correct syntax and program structure, and self-documenting code, write a top-down design and a Pascal program which reads an input line containing an invoice number, quantity ordered and unit price (all integers) and computes total price. Write out the invoice number, quantity, unit price and total price with identifying phrases.

10. Reserved words can be used as variable names.   T   F

Pre-Test

1. Compute the value of each of the following expressions. If the value is REAL, be sure to put in the decimal point.

   a.   10 MOD 3   ————
   b.   10 DIV 3   ————
   c.   16 MOD 8 + 16 DIV 8   ————
   d.   13/4   ————

e. 5 * 6 / 15   _____
f. 13 MOD 5 / 3   _____
g. 3 + 2 - 4 * 5 DIV 2 _____

2. Trace the values of the variables in the following program. Use a '?' if the value is undefined, repeat the value if it is the same.

```
                                    A        B        C
PROGRAM TEST3(INPUT,OUTPUT);
CONST N = 4;                        __       __       __
VAR A, B, C : INTEGER;              __       __       __
BEGIN                               __       __       __
   A := 5;                          ____     ____     ____
   B := A * N;                      ____     ____     ____
   C := A MOD N;                    ____     ____     ____
   A := C;                          ____     ____     ____
   B := A + C;                      ____     ____     ____
   WRITELN(A, B, C);                ____     ____     ____
END.
```

3. If the following input instructions were executed on the data shown, what values would the variables contain?

```
VAR A, B, C, D: INTEGER;
```

a. READLN(A);   A: _____
    READ(B,C);   B: _____
    READLN(D);   C: _____
                   D: _____

    Data: 24 72
           46 55
           18 4

b. READLN(A);   A: _____
    READLN(B);   B: _____
    READLN(C);   C: _____

    Data: 17 cost of gallon of paint
           14 width of room
           18 length of room

c. READ(A);   A: _____
    READ(B,C);   B: _____
    READ(D);   C: _____
                   D: _____

    Data: 24 17
           22 13
           12 14

4. Write input commands to read in the described data. You may assume the variables have been declared, but assume the identifiers are meaningful. A card is a line of data.
   a. A sales discount card containing the stock number of the item in columns 4–8, the original price in columns 20–27 (real), and the sale price in columns 29–36 (real).

   b. A card containing a service station identification number followed by a card
       containing a one-character code in column 1 (P for premium, L for lead-free,
       and R for regular) followed by the number of gallons of that type gas sold.

5. Name two things that contribute to the readability of programs.

6. Write the expression $\dfrac{A + B}{C}$ in Pascal

   a. when you want a real result
   b. when you want an integer result

7. Which of the following identifiers are RESERVED WORDS and which are
   USER-DEFINED?

	RESERVED	USER-DEFINED
PROGRAM	——	——
VAR	——	——
FLAG	——	——
CONST	——	——
THEEND	——	——

Selection 4

Goals

To be able to construct a simple BOOLEAN expression to evaluate a given condition.

To be able to construct a complex BOOLEAN expression to evaluate a given condition.

To be able to construct an IF-THEN statement to perform a specific task.

To be able to construct an IF-THEN-ELSE statement to perform a specific task.

To be able to construct a set of nested IF statements to perform a specific task.

To be able to debug a Pascal program with errors.

The order in which you enter your statements at the keyboard is the physical order of your program. So far the execution of your program has paralleled this physical order. The second statement is executed after the first, the third is executed after the second, etc. But what if you want to execute either one statement *or* another statement depending on what has happened before? What if you want to execute your statements in a logical order which is not the same as the physical order? To be able to do this we must have the capability to ask questions about what has happened so far in the execution of the program.

The IF statement is the statement that allows us to do this. This statement allows us to ask a question and do one thing if the answer is yes (TRUE) and do another thing if the answer is no (FALSE).

The first part of this chapter deals with how to ask questions, and the second part deals with the IF statement itself.

CONDITIONS AND BOOLEAN EXPRESSIONS

In Pascal, to ask a question, you make a statement. If the statement you make is true, the answer to the question is true. If the statement is not true, the answer to the question is false. So, asking questions amounts to making a statement (an assertion). We make our assertion in the form of a Boolean expression. The Boolean expression is then evaluated to either TRUE or FALSE giving us the answer to our question. BUT . . . What is a Boolean expression? How do we evaluate one?

A Boolean expression can be

(1) a Boolean variable

(2) an expression followed by a relational operator followed by an expression

(3) a Boolean expression followed by a Boolean operator followed by a Boolean expression

Let's look at each of these in detail.

(1) A Boolean variable is a variable declared to be of type BOOLEAN. This means the contents of this variable can be either TRUE or FALSE. Boolean variables differ from variables declared to be of type INTEGER, REAL or CHAR because values cannot be read into them; they must be set within the program by an assignment statement.

```
VAR TEST : BOOLEAN;
         .
         .
BEGIN
   TEST := TRUE;
         .
```

sets the variable TEST to TRUE and

```
TEST := FALSE;
```

sets the variable TEST to FALSE.

Evaluating a Boolean variable simply means determining its contents.

(2) We can assign values to Boolean variables by setting them equal to the result of an expression followed by a relational operator followed by an expression. For example:

```
VAR TEST : BOOLEAN;
    A, B : INTEGER;
         .
         .
BEGIN
   TEST := A < B;
         .
```

will assign TRUE to TEST if the answer to the question "Is A less than B?" is yes, otherwise TEST is assigned FALSE.

A relational operator is one of the following:

=	(equal to)
<>	(not equal to)
<=	(less than or equal to)
>=	(greater than or equal to)
>	(greater than)
<	(less than)

For example, if X is 5 and Y is 10, then the following expressions are all true:

$$X < Y$$
$$X <= Y$$
$$X <> Y$$
$$Y > X$$
$$Y >= X$$

If X is 'M' and Y is 'P', then the same expressions are true because '<', when referring to letters, means "comes before in the alphabet." Of course, we must be careful to compare like things, i.e., numbers with numbers (REAL or INTEGER) and characters with characters (CHAR).

(3) Relational operators compare things such as numbers and letters. Boolean operators are the special operators AND, OR and NOT which are defined only for Boolean expressions. Since Boolean expressions can only take on two values, TRUE or FALSE, the tables showing the result of applying operators to two expressions is quite small. (T stands for TRUE, F for FALSE.)

AND	T	F	OR	T	F	NOT	
T	T	F	T	T	T	T	F
F	F	F	F	T	F	F	T

What the AND table says is:

- If both expressions are TRUE, the result is TRUE.
- If one expression is TRUE and one expression is FALSE, the result is FALSE.
- If both expressions are FALSE, the result is FALSE.

What the OR table says is:

- If both expressions are TRUE, the result is TRUE.
- If either expression is TRUE, the result is TRUE.
- If both expressions are FALSE, the result is FALSE.

What the NOT table says is:

- If the expression is TRUE, the result is FALSE.
- If the expression is FALSE, the result is TRUE.

AND and OR are binary operators. That is, they go between two expressions. The NOT operator is a unary operator.

Just as there is an order of precedence in arithmetic operators, there is an order of precedence among Boolean operators. NOT has the highest precedence; AND, next; OR is third.

This means that if the following Boolean expression

A AND NOT B OR C

is evaluated, NOT B will be evaluated first. Then the result of that will be AND-ed with A. Then the result of that operation will be OR-ed with C.

Relational operators have the lowest precedence of all. This means that they are the last to be executed. This can cause problems.

For example, if you want to ask the question (make the statement) that A is equal to 24 and B is less than 10, you might write the expression:

$$A = 24 \text{ AND } B < 10$$

This statement however is syntactically incorrect. Since AND has higher precedence than "=", the expression 24 AND B will be evaluated first. AND is a Boolean operator and 24 and B are INTEGERS. This can be corrected by the use of parentheses.

$$(A = 24) \text{ AND } (B < 10)$$

In mathematics, we use the notation

$$X < Y < Z$$

to indicate that Y is greater than X and less than Z. This is illegal in Pascal. You must write out the expression as follows:

$$(X < Y) \text{ AND } (Y < Z)$$

If you leave off the parentheses, you again get a syntax error.

APPENDIX D: PRECEDENCE OF OPERATORS shows the order of precedence for all the operators: Boolean (logical), arithmetic, and comparison (relational). Remember, parentheses override the order of precedence of all operators.

$$A \text{ AND } B \text{ OR } C$$

is the same as

$$(A \text{ AND } B) \text{ OR } C$$

but not the same as

$$A \text{ AND } (B \text{ OR } C)$$

The following are some additional examples of valid assignments to a Boolean variable.

```
FLAG  := TRUE;
CHECK := FALSE;
TEST  := FLAG AND CHECK;
CHECK := I > 1;
FLAG  := J = I + 1;
FOUND := (X <= Y) OR (I = J + K * 6)
```

The first three are straightforward. Let's look at the last three with some actual values.

```
CHECK := I > 1
```

This will set CHECK to TRUE if the current value of I is greater than one and to FALSE for any value of I less than or equal to one.

```
FLAG := J = I + 1
```

This will set FLAG to TRUE for any pair of values for I and J where J is one more than I. For any other pair of values for I and J, FLAG will be set to FALSE.

```
FOUND := (X <= Y) OR (I = J + K * 6)
```

FOUND will be TRUE if either of the two expressions is TRUE. The first will be TRUE for any pair of values X and Y such that X is less than or equal to Y. The second expression will be TRUE for any set of values for I, J and K such that I is equal to J + K * 6. If neither expression is TRUE, FOUND will be FALSE.

SELECTION CONTROL STRUCTURE

The ability to make decisions, to execute instructions conditionally, is necessary for the practical application of computers. In Pascal, as in other programming languages, the structure that provides this control is called an IF statement.

IF STATEMENT

IF-THEN

Now that we have the capability to ask questions, we can use the answers to change the order in which program statements will be executed.

```
IF Boolean expression
    THEN statement1A;
statement2
```

means "If the Boolean expression is true, execute statement1A and continue with statement2. If the Boolean expression is false, skip statement1A and continue with statement2." Figure 4-1 illustrates the flow of control of the IF-THEN statement.

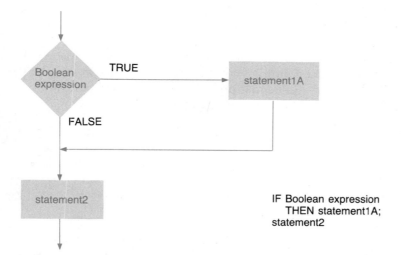

Figure 4-1. IF-THEN Structure Diagram

For example, if you want to test to see if a data value is positive and write an error message if it is not, the code would look as follows.

```
IF DATA < 0
    THEN WRITELN(' BAD DATA')
```

Figure 4-2 illustrates the flow of control of this statement.

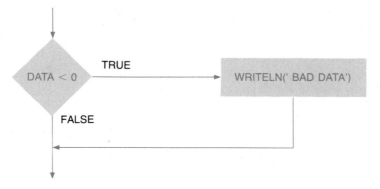

Figure 4-2.

As the program is executing, the Boolean expression "DATA < 0" will be evaluated. If the contents of the place named DATA is less than zero, the Boolean expression is true and the words "BAD DATA" are printed. If the contents of DATA is not less than zero, the expression is false and the WRITELN is not executed. In either case, execution continues with the statement following the WRITELN.

What if we needed to set the value of DATA to 0 whenever we print the error message? This would require two statements but the syntax says "statement1A". That's easy to fix. Just put a "BEGIN-END" pair around the two statements making them into one compound statement.

```
IF DATA < 0
   THEN
      BEGIN                              (*A single (compound) statement*)
         WRITELN(' BAD DATA');
         DATA := 0
      END
```

The test "DATA < 0" is made as before. If DATA does contain a negative value, the statements between the "BEGIN-END" pair are executed in sequence. After DATA has been set to 0, the program continues with the statement following the "END".

IF-THEN-ELSE

IF Boolean expression
    THEN statement1A
    ELSE statement1B;
statement2

The meaning of the IF-THEN-ELSE statement is "If the Boolean expression is true, execute statement1A and continue with statement2. If the Boolean expression is false, execute statement1B and continue with statement2." Figure 4-3 illustrates the flow of control for the IF-THEN-ELSE statement.

The following Pascal fragment would print either "TENNIS ANYONE?" or "TOO COLD FOR TENNIS" depending upon the value of the integer variable TEMPERATURE.

```
IF TEMPERATURE >= 50
   THEN WRITELN(' TENNIS ANYONE?')
   ELSE WRITELN(' TOO COLD FOR TENNIS')
```

Look back at Program PAYROLL in Chapter 1. The following IF-THEN-ELSE occurs.

```
IF HRS > 40.00
   THEN WAGES := (40.0 * PAYRATE) +
                 (HRS - 40.0) * PAYRATE * 1.5
   ELSE WAGES := HRS * PAYRATE
```

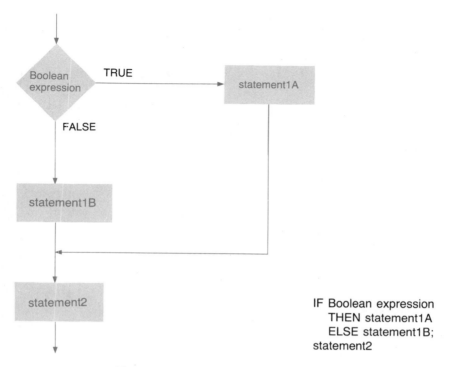

Figure 4-3. IF-THEN-ELSE Structure Diagram

The IF is used to determine if any overtime was worked (HRS > 40.0). If there is overtime, the hourly rate for the additional hours is time and a half (1.5 * PAYRATE).

■ **SAMPLE PROBLEM**

Problem: Read in three integer numbers. If the first is negative, print the product of all three. Otherwise, print the sum of all three.

Discussion: If you were asked to do this problem by hand, you would take the three numbers and examine the first to decide what to do. If the first number were negative you would multiply the three numbers together. If the first number were positive, you would add them up.

The process can be translated into a program directly. "Take the three numbers" will become a READ statement. We will use an IF statement to "examine the first" and decide whether to multiply or add the numbers. The last step will be to print the result and say whether the numbers were added or multiplied.

Input: 3 integer numbers (NUM1, NUM2, NUM3)

Output: Print the input (this is called echo printing)
Print 'The product is' PROD
or 'The sum is' SUM

MAIN MODULE   Level 0

> GET DATA
> IF first number < 0
>   THEN CALCULATE PRODUCT
>   ELSE CALCULATE SUM

GET DATA   Level 1

> READ NUM1, NUM2, NUM3
> PRINT NUM1, NUM2, NUM3

CALCULATE PRODUCT

> PRODUCT = NUM1 * NUM2 * NUM3
> PRINT PRODUCT

CALCULATE SUM

> SUM = NUM1 + NUM2 + NUM3
> PRINT SUM

Design Tree Diagram:

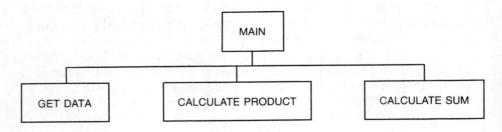

```
PROGRAM PRODSUM(INPUT, OUTPUT);
                (* This program reads in three integer numbers and prints the product *)
                    (* of the three numbers if the first number is negative and the *)
                    (* sum of the three numbers if the first number is not negative. *)
VAR
    NUM1,                                              (* first integer *)
    NUM2,                                             (* second integer *)
    NUM3,                                              (* third integer *)
    PRODUCT,                                 (* result of multiplication *)
    SUM : INTEGER;                              (* result of addition *)
BEGIN (* PRODSUM *)
    READ(NUM1, NUM2, NUM3);                              (* input data *)
    WRITELN(NUM1, NUM2, NUM3);                     (* echo print input *)
    IF NUM1 < 0                             (* test sign of first integer *)
        THEN                                       (* calculate product *)
            BEGIN
                PRODUCT := NUM1 * NUM2 * NUM3;
                WRITELN(' PRODUCT IS ', PRODUCT)
            END
        ELSE                                         (* calculate sum *)
            BEGIN
                SUM := NUM1 + NUM2 + NUM3;
                WRITELN(' SUM IS ', SUM)
            END
END.    (* PRODSUM *)
```

Given this input data:

333 777 200

the program produces this output:

```
       333          777         200
 SUM IS          1310
```

Given this input data:

-1 777 200

the program produces this output:

```
      -1          777         200
 PRODUCT IS       -155400
```

This program will be examined in more detail in the TESTING AND DEBUGGING section at the end of this chapter.

Nested IF Statements

There are no restrictions on what the statements in an IF statement can be. Therefore, an IF within an IF is okay. In fact, an IF within an IF within an IF . . . is legal. The limiting factor is that humans cannot follow such a structure if it gets too involved. A readable program is one of the marks of a "good" program.

■ **SAMPLE PROBLEM**

Problem: Read in a temperature and print out what sport is appropriate for that temperature using the following guidelines.

Sport	Temperature
swimming	> 85
tennis	70 < temp <= 85
golf	32 < temp <= 70
skiing	10 < temp <= 32
chinese checkers	<= 10

Discussion: The temperature must be compared with the limits of each sport. When the proper place is found, that sport is printed. This comparison can be done with the IF statement.

Input: Integer temperature (TEMPERATURE)

Output: Echo print temperature
Print the appropriate sport

MAIN MODULE   Level 0

```
GET TEMPERATURE
PRINT SPORT
```

GET TEMPERATURE   Level 1

```
READ TEMPERATURE
```

PRINT SPORT (next page) has five IF statements. However, it can actually be coded as a set of nested IF statements. The middle IFs look as if they should have compound Boolean conditions; however, the structure of the IF-THEN-ELSE makes this unnecessary because you know that you wouldn't be executing the ELSE branch unless one of the conditions wasn't satisfied.

PRINT SPORT

```
IF TEMPERATURE > 85
    THEN PRINT 'SWIMMING'
IF TEMPERATURE <= 85 AND > 70
    THEN PRINT 'TENNIS'
IF TEMPERATURE <= 70 AND > 32
    THEN PRINT 'GOLF'
IF TEMPERATURE <= 32 AND > 10
    THEN PRINT 'SKIING'
IF TEMPERATURE <= 10
    THEN PRINT 'CHINESE CHECKERS'
```

Design Tree Diagram:

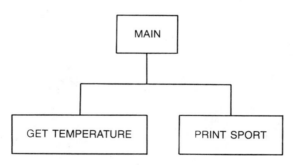

```
PROGRAM SPORT(INPUT, OUTPUT);          (* This program outputs an appropriate
                                          sport for a given temperature *)
VAR TEMPERATURE : INTEGER;
BEGIN (* SPORT *)
    READ(TEMPERATURE);
    WRITELN(TEMPERATURE);                        (* echo print input *)
    IF TEMPERATURE > 85
        THEN WRITELN(' SWIMMING')                (* temperature > 85 *)
    ELSE IF TEMPERATURE > 70                     (* temperature <= 85 *)
            THEN WRITELN(' TENNIS')           (* and temperature > 70 *)
    ELSE IF TEMPERATURE > 32                     (* temperature <= 70 *)
            THEN WRITELN(' GOLF')             (* and temperature > 32 *)
    ELSE IF TEMPERATURE > 10                     (* temperature <= 32 *)
            THEN WRITELN(' SKIING')           (* and temperature > 10 *)
            ELSE WRITELN(' CHINESE CHECKERS')    (* temp <= 10 *)
END.    (* SPORT *)
```

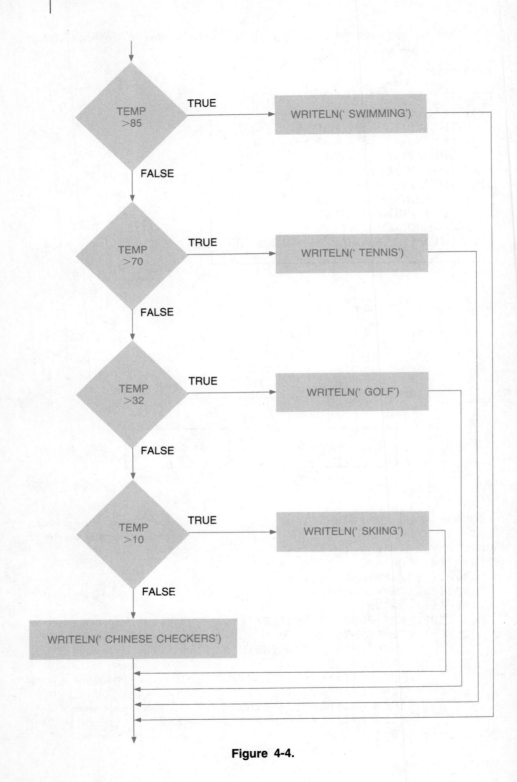

Figure 4-4.

For this input data:

-30

the output will be:

```
      -30
CHINESE CHECKERS
```

For this input data:

52

the output will be:

```
      52
GOLF
```

Figure 4-4 shows exactly how the flow of control works in this example.

■

■ SAMPLE PROBLEM

Problem: Many universities require that freshmen who are in danger of failing a class be sent a warning notice. You are to calculate the average of three test grades and print out the student ID number, the average and whether the student is passing or not. Passing is a 60 point average or better. If the student is passing but with less than a 70 average, indicate that he or she is marginal.

Discussion: To calculate the average we will have to read in the three test scores, add them up and divide by three.

To print the appropriate message we will have to determine whether the average is above or below 60. If it is above 60 we will have to determine if it is between 60 and 70.

In doing this calculation by hand you would probably notice if a test grade were negative and question it. If the semantics of your data imply that the values should be positive, then your program should test to be sure they are. Here we will test to be sure each grade is positive and use a Boolean variable to report the result of the test.

Input: Student ID (integer) followed by 3 test grades (integer).

Output: Echo print input data.
Message containing student ID, passing/failing, average grade, possible marginal indication or error message if any of the test scores are negative.

MAIN MODULE   Level 0

```
GET DATA
TEST DATA
IF DATAOK
   THEN
        CALCULATE AVERAGE
        PRINT MESSAGE
   ELSE
        PRINT ERROR MESSAGE
```

GET DATA   Level 1

```
READ  STUDENTID, TEST1, TEST2, TEST3
PRINT STUDENTID, TEST1, TEST2, TEST3
```

TEST DATA

```
IF (TEST1 < 0) OR (TEST2 < 0) OR (TEST3 < 0)
   DATAOK IS FALSE
OTHERWISE
   DATAOK IS TRUE
```

CALCULATE AVERAGE

```
AVE = (TEST1 + TEST2 + TEST3) / 3
```

PRINT MESSAGE

```
PRINT STUDENTID, AVERAGE
IF AVERAGE >= 60
   THEN
        PRINT PASSING,
        IF AVERAGE < 70
            PRINT MARGINAL
   ELSE PRINT FAILING
```

Design Tree Diagram:

```
PROGRAM NOTICES(INPUT, OUTPUT);          (* Program to determine a student's
                                         average and passing/failing status *)
VAR AVE : REAL;                          (* average of three test grades *)
    STUDENTID,                           (* student's identification number *)
    TEST1, TEST2, TEST3 : INTEGER;       (* three test grades *)
    DATAOK ): BOOLEAN;                   (* will be TRUE if data is correct *)
BEGIN (*NOTICES *)
  READLN(STUDENTID, TEST1, TEST2, TEST3);          (* get data *)
  WRITELN(STUDENTID, TEST1, TEST2, TEST3);   (* echo print input *)
  IF (TEST1 < 0) OR (TEST2 < 0) OR (TEST3 < 0)      (* test data *)
     THEN DATAOK := FALSE
     ELSE DATAOK := TRUE;
  IF DATAOK
     THEN                                           (* data is valid *)
        BEGIN
          AVE := (TEST1 + TEST2 + TEST3)/3;   (* compute average *)
          WRITELN(' STUDENT ', STUDENTID,
                  ' AVERAGE IS ', AVE);
          IF AVE >= 60.0
             THEN                                    (* print passing message *)
                BEGIN
                  WRITELN(' STUDENT IS PASSING ');
                  IF AVE < 70.0
                     THEN WRITELN('BUT MARGINAL ')
                END
             ELSE WRITELN(' STUDENT IS FAILING')  (* print failing
                                                      msg *)
        END
     ELSE WRITELN(' INVALID DATA ')               (* data is invalid *)
END.   (* NOTICES *)
```

■

In all three programs in this chapter so far, the input data has been printed out. This is called echo printing. It is good practice because it verifies the input data and documents what data was processed.

In Program NOTICES the test grades were tested to be sure they were positive. This type of data checking is important. If you know something must always be true about your data, put a test in your program to be sure that your data is valid.

There are three IF-THEN-ELSE statements and one IF-THEN statement in Program NOTICES. To test each branch, take the following sets of values for TEST1, TEST2, and TEST3 and hand-calculate what happens.

100	100	100
60	60	60
50	50	50
−50	50	50

The first set is valid and gives an average of 100 which is passing and not marginal. The second set is valid and gives an average of 60 which is passing but marginal. The third set is valid and gives an average of 50 which is failing. The fourth set has an invalid test grade and an error message would be printed.

There is one point of confusion when nesting IF statements: To which IF does an ELSE belong? For example, let's change the problem definition slightly for Program NOTICES. If a student's average is 70 or greater, print nothing. If it is between 60 and 70, print "PASSING BUT MARGINAL" and print "FAILING" if it is below 60.

Coding this slight change gives an IF-THEN-ELSE nested within an IF-THEN as follows.

```
IF AVE < 70
   THEN IF AVE < 60
           THEN WRITELN('FAILING')
           ELSE WRITELN('PASSING BUT MARGINAL')
```

How do we know that "PASSING BUT MARGINAL" will be written when average is between 60 and 70 and not for an average of 70 or above? In other words how do we know to which IF the last ELSE belongs? The rule is that an ELSE is paired with the closest IF. In this example we formatted the code to reflect this pairing. However formatting does not affect the code. If the ELSE had been lined up with the first THEN, it still would have belonged with the second IF.

Look at the existing IF-THEN-ELSE statement in Program NOTICES.

```
IF AVE >= 60.0
   THEN
      BEGIN
         WRITELN(' STUDENT IS PASSING ');
         IF AVE < 70.0
            THEN WRITELN('BUT MARGINAL ')
      END
   ELSE WRITELN(' STUDENT IS FAILING ')
```

We used a compound statement in the THEN branch because we want to execute two statements in that branch. However, even if we removed one of the statements, the WRITELN statement, we would still need the "BEGIN-END" pair! Why? Because we want the ELSE branch as part of the first IF statement, not the second. The "BEGIN-END" pair around the nested IF statement would indicate that that IF statement is complete, so the ELSE is matched up with the outside IF statement.

One other point we would like to make before leaving Program NO-TICES. We assigned a value to DATAOK in one statement before testing it in the next. We could have done this another way. We could simply have said

```
DATAOK := NOT ((TEST1 < 0) OR (TEST2 < 0) OR (TEST3 < 0))
```

In fact, we can reduce the code even more. How about

```
    IF (TEST1 >= 0) AND (TEST2 >= 0) AND (TEST3 >= 0)
```

in place of IF DATAOK? To convince yourselves that these two variations do work, try them by hand with the test data.

TESTING AND DEBUGGING

In Chapter 1 we discussed the problem-solving phase and the implementation phase. Both phases have testing as an integral part. Let's apply testing at both phases on the problem for Program PRODSUM developed earlier in this chapter.

Testing at the problem-solving phase involves looking at each level of our top-down design and saying, "If the levels below this are expanded correctly, will this level do what needs to be done?"

In this case, if (1) GET DATA correctly inputs three values, (2) CALCU-LATE PRODUCT correctly multiplies the three numbers together and prints the result, and (3) CALCULATE SUM correctly adds the three numbers and prints the result, then the main program is correct.

The next step is to examine each module at level 1 and ask the same question, "If the level 2 modules are assumed to be correct, will this module do what it is supposed to do?" In this example, there are no level 2 modules, so the level 1 modules must be complete. Note that there is no code in the top-down design. We could just as easily translate the design into FORTRAN (another widely used high-level language) as into Pascal.

GET DATA reads in three values NUM1, NUM2 and NUM3. (The next refinement is actually coding this instruction. Whether it is coded correctly or not is not the problem at this phase; that is determined at the implementation phase.)

CALCULATE PRODUCT assigns to variable PRODUCT the result of multiplying the contents of NUM1, NUM2 and NUM3. That is what the product means so this is correct and the calculated product is printed.

CALCULATE SUM assigns to the variable SUM the result of adding NUM1, NUM2 and NUM3. That is what the sum means so this is correct and the calculated sum is printed.

The algorithm has been desk checked and the translation of the top-down design into a programming language can begin.

Testing at the implementation phase is done at several different points. After the coding has been done you should go carefully over your code, checking to make sure that the top-down design has been faithfully reproduced. The code is then either entered at the console or punched on cards. At this stage you should take some actual values and hand calculate what the output should be by doing a code walk-through. In a later testing phase, use these same values as input and check the results.

In Chapter 1 we also discussed the compilation phase and the execution phase. The program you have coded is now ready for the compilation phase. The Pascal compiler takes the program coded in Pascal and translates it into a language which the machine we are using can execute.

There are two distinct outputs from the compilation phase: a listing of the program with error messages (if any) and the translated version of the program ready to be executed (if there are no errors). See APPENDIX G: SAMPLE PROGRAM LISTINGS WITH ERROR MESSAGES for an example of error messages in the program listing.

Now the translated version of your program is ready to be executed. Finally, at this stage, the tasks you wanted to be done are done, i.e., a line is read, a value is tested, etc.

You are now in the debug phase. This is where you locate and correct all errors (called bugs) in your program. Errors are of two types: syntactic or semantic. Syntactic errors are errors in Pascal syntax and are usually caught by the compiler. Semantic errors are more difficult to locate and usually surface at execution time. These are errors which give you the wrong answer. The error may be an undetected bug in your top-down design or a keying error which creates a syntactically correct but meaningless statement.

Figure 4-5 pictures the programming process we have just discussed. Where syntax and semantic errors occur, and at which phase they can be corrected, is indicated in the figure.

Each chapter of this book will end with a section on testing and debugging. As new Pascal constructs are introduced, we will point out common syntactic and semantic errors which occur with their use. We will also give you techniques to use in locating bugs.

Testing and Debugging Hints

1. Echo print all input data.

Immediately below each READ or READLN statement, put a corresponding WRITELN statement. This way you know your input data is what you thought it was.

2. Test for bad data in your program.

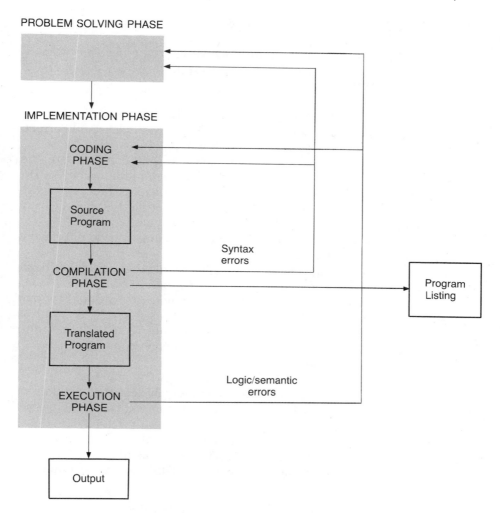

Figure 4-5. Programming Process

If a data value must be positive, put an IF statement in to test the value. If it is negative, print an error message, otherwise continue with the processing. For example, Program SPORT should have the following statement inserted after the first WRITELN (echo print):

```
IF (TEMPERATURE > 120) OR (TEMPERATURE < -25)
   THEN WRITELN(' TEMPERATURE DATA IS IN ERROR')
   ELSE
      BEGIN
         (* balance of program *)
      END
```

This tests the limits of reasonable temperatures and only continues if the data is reasonable.

Note that the parentheses are necessary. Otherwise the order of precedence would impose

```
TEMPERATURE > (120 OR TEMPERATURE) < -25
```

which would give a syntax error. This leads to the next hint.

3. Use parentheses to make your Boolean expression clear and correct.

4. Remember, semi-colons *separate* statements.

An IF-THEN-ELSE is one statement. A semi-colon before the ELSE would tell the translator that it had reached the end of an IF-THEN statement. The translator would then expect the next word, ELSE, to begin a new statement. Since it is not the first word in any statement and is a reserved word, an error occurs.

Always check each IF-THEN-ELSE to be sure you do not have a semi-colon before the ELSE!!

5. Check your declarations to be sure each variable name used has been declared.

6. Take sample data values and try them by hand as we did for Program NOTICES. (More on this in Chapter 5.)

7. If an answer produced by your program does not agree with the value you calculated by hand, try the following suggestions.

   a. Redo your arithmetic.

   b. Recheck your input data.

   c. Go carefully over the section of code which does the calculation. If in doubt about the order of operations, insert clarifying parentheses.

   d. Check for INTEGER overflow. The value of an INTEGER variable may have exceeded MAXINT during calculation. Many systems will give you an error message if this happens; however, some do not.

Summary

Chapter 4 has described a way of asking questions about the execution of a program as it runs. A Boolean expression is evaluated and is TRUE if the expression is true and is FALSE if the expression is not true.

The IF statement allows you to take different alternatives based on the value of a Boolean expression. The IF-THEN-ELSE allows you to choose between two courses of action. The IF-THEN allows you to choose whether or not to take one particular action.

The branches of an IF-THEN or IF-THEN-ELSE can be any statement—simple or compound. They can even be (or include) another IF statement.

Exercises

1. Boolean values are usually computed by a comparison. Is the following comparison legal in Pascal? If not, how can it be expressed properly?

```
MINIMUMAGE <= AGE < MAXIMUMAGE
```

2. Write a statement containing a comparison that sets the Boolean variable "AVAILABLE" to TRUE if NUMBERORDERED is less than or equal to NUMBERONHAND less NUMBERRESERVED. *AVAILABLE := NUMORD <= NUMONHAND - NUMRES*

3. Declare ELIGIBLE to be a Boolean variable. Assign it the value TRUE. *VAR ELIG : BOOLEAN   ELIG := TRUE*

4. Given the following values for Boolean variables A, B, C and D, evaluate the Boolean expressions.

   A=TRUE   B=FALSE   C=FALSE   D=TRUE

   a. (A AND B) OR (A AND D)
   b. NOT C AND D AND A
   c. NOT (A AND D) OR (C OR D)
   d. (A OR B) AND NOT (C OR D)

5. Write a statement containing a Boolean expression which assigns TRUE to the Boolean variable "CANDIDATE" if SATSCORE is greater than or equal to 1100, GPA is not less than 2.5, and AGE is greater than 15. CANDIDATE should be FALSE otherwise.

6. Given the following declarations,

```
VAR LEFTPAGE:BOOLEAN;
    PAGENUMBER:INTEGER;
```

write a statement that sets LEFTPAGE to TRUE if PAGENUMBER is even.

7. Simplify the following selection so that fewer comparisons are necessary.

```
IF AGE > 64
   THEN WRITE ('SOCIAL SECURITY');
IF AGE < 18
   THEN WRITE ('EXEMPT');
IF (AGE >= 18) AND (AGE < 65)
   THEN WRITE ('TAXABLE');
```

8. Write an IF-THEN-ELSE statement that assigns to the variable "LARGEST" the greatest value contained in variables A, B and C. Assume the three values are distinct.

9. What will the following program segment write in a case where:

   a. HEIGHT exceeds MINHEIGHT and WEIGHT exceeds MINWEIGHT.
   b. HEIGHT is less than MINHEIGHT and WEIGHT is less than MINWEIGHT.

```
IF HEIGHT > MINHEIGHT
   THEN IF WEIGHT > MINWEIGHT
      THEN WRITELN('ELIGIBLE TO SERVE')
      ELSE WRITELN('TOO LIGHT TO SERVE')
```

10. Use top-down design to write a Pascal program segment that reads three integer numbers corresponding to day, month and year of a person's birthdate, followed by three integer numbers corresponding to today's date. Compute the person's age in years (disregarding additional months and days). Write out the birthdate and age in years with identifying phrases.

11. Correct the syntax errors in the following program. You may rewrite it correctly, or mark your corrections clearly on this sheet.

```
PROGRAM EXERCISE(INPUT:OUTPUT)
CONST
      A = 10
      B = 5
      C = 6
VAR
      D;E;F:INTEGER
BEGIN
      READ(D,E F)
      IF (D > A) THEN D = A + D;
      ELSE D = A
      E:= D + F
      WRITE('THIS PROGRAM DOES NOT MAKE ANY SENSE,
            E,F D)
END;
```

Pre-Test

1. Boolean expressions a) and b) are logically equivalent, but only b) is legal in Pascal.   T   F
   a. TOTALINCOME >= NETINCOME > TAXAMOUNT
   b. (TOTALINCOME >= NETINCOME) AND (NETINCOME > TAXAMOUNT)

2. Given the following values for Boolean variables X, Y, and Z, evaluate the Boolean expressions and answer T if the result is TRUE and F if the result is FALSE.

$$X=TRUE \quad Y=FALSE \quad Z=TRUE$$

   a. (X AND Y) OR (X AND Z)   T   F
   b. (X OR NOT Y) AND (NOT X OR Z)   T   F
   c. X OR Y AND Z   T   F
   d. NOT (X OR Y) AND Z   T   F

3. Write an IF statement(s) that assigns to the variable BIGGEST the greatest value contained in variables I, J, K. Assume all three values are distinct.

4. Write a program that reads a package number followed by a weight in ounces. Write out the package number, followed by 'CLASS1' if the package weighs less than 32 ounces, 'CLASS2' for 32 up to 128 ounces, and 'CLASS3' for 128 ounces and over.

5. Correct the syntax errors in the following program. You may rewrite the program or mark your corrections clearly on this copy.

```
PROGRAM PRE-TEST(INPUT=OUTPUT);
CONST
      W = 5
VAR
      FOUR, ONE, ZERO := INTEGER;
BEGIN
      READ(FOUR; ZERO; ONE)
      FOUR = FOUR + ZERO + W
      IF FOUR =< ONE
          THEN FOUR = ONE
          ELSE ONE = FOUR
      IF ZERO < 0
          THEN WRITE(' ZERO IS NEGATIVE')
      WRITELN(' IT IS OVER')
BEGIN.
```

6. Using the corrected version of problem 5 and the following data, what are the values of the variables FOUR, ONE and ZERO at the end of execution, and what is written?

Data: 13 16 17

Looping 5

Goals

To be able to construct syntactically correct WHILE loops.

To be able to construct count controlled loops with a WHILE statement.

To be able to use EOF to control the inputting of data.

To be able to use EOLN to control the inputting of character data.

To be able to construct counting loops with a WHILE statement.

To be able to construct summing loops with a WHILE statement.

To be able to use flags to control the execution of a WHILE loop.

To be able to construct a correct WHILE loop of which another WHILE is a part.

To be able to format program output so that it is clear and readable.

To be able to choose data sets to test a program comprehensively.

LOOPING CONTROL STRUCTURE

In Chapter 4 the concept of the logical ordering of the program was introduced. The physical order of a program is the order in which the statements are entered from the terminal or from cards; the logical order is the order in which you want the statements to be executed.

The IF statement was presented as a way of making the logical order different from the physical order. IF a condition (or set of conditions) is TRUE, then one statement is executed. If the condition (or set of conditions) is not true, then another statement is executed. Note that in the abbreviated IF-THEN, no statement is executed if the condition (or set of conditions) is not true.

Two standard approaches that programmers use often were discussed in Chapter 3: summing and counting. In this chapter you will be given a statement called a WHILE statement which will allow you to implement these standard approaches by letting a statement be executed more than once.

WHILE a condition (or set of conditions) is TRUE, a statement will be executed. When the condition (or set of conditions) becomes FALSE, execution will continue with the statement following the WHILE statement.

With the introduction of the WHILE statement (looping control structure) you have all the control structures you will ever need. Pascal does have some additional control structures, but they are merely for convenience. The WHILE and IF are sufficient for any program.

Note that the IF statement is the Pascal equivalent of the conditional structure discussed in Chapter 1. The WHILE statement is the equivalent of the looping structure. Execution in physical order is equivalent to the sequential structure.

WHILE STATEMENT

The WHILE statement tests a condition just as the IF statement does.

> WHILE Boolean expression DO
> > statement1;
>
> statement2

means "If the Boolean expression is true, execute statement1. After the execution of statement1 go back and test the Boolean expression again." This process continues until the Boolean expression becomes false. At that time statement1 (could be a compound statement) is skipped and execution continues with statement2, the next statement outside the loop. Statement1 is often called the body of the loop. Figure 5-1 illustrates the flow of control of the WHILE statement.

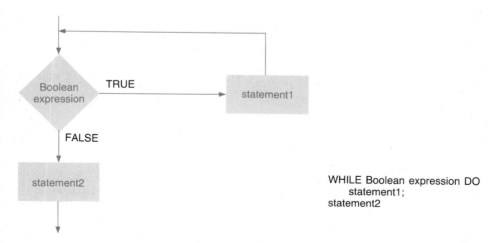

Figure 5-1. WHILE Structure Diagram

At first glance you might think the IF and the WHILE are alike. They do have similarities, but a careful examination shows their fundamental differences. (See Figure 5-2.) In the IF, either statement1A or statement1B will be executed exactly once. In the WHILE, statement1 will be executed zero or more times. (Zero times if the Boolean expression is FALSE to start with.)

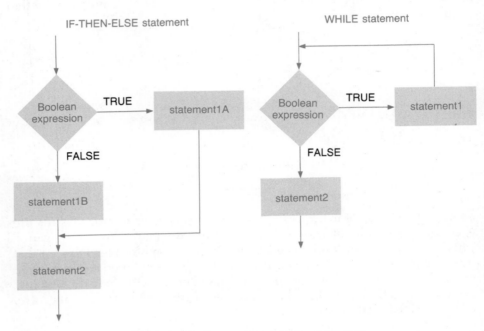

Figure 5-2. Comparison of IF and WHILE

The flow of control returns to test the Boolean expression in the WHILE; in the IF it does not. The IF is used to *choose between* two courses of action. The WHILE is used to *repeat* a course of action.

Note that statement1, statement1A, statement1B and statement2 can all be compound statements.

LOOPS USING THE WHILE STATEMENT

The concept of looping is so fundamental to programming that we will spend time now looking at typical types of loops and how to implement them with the Pascal WHILE statement. When you are analyzing your problems and doing your top-down design you will see these looping situations come up again and again.

Count Controlled Loops

A count controlled loop is a loop that executes a specified number of times. There are three parts to such a loop which makes use of a variable, called the loop control variable. The three parts are initialization, test and incrementation. The following code uses the WHILE statement to do the testing.

```
I := 1;                          (* initialization *)
WHILE I < 10 DO                        (* test *)
    BEGIN
      .
      .
      .
    I := I + 1               (* incrementation *)
    END
```

I is the loop control variable. It is set to 1 outside of the loop. The WHILE statement tests the expression I < 10 and executes the compound statement as long as the expression is true. The last statement in the compound statement increments I by adding 1 to it.

Notice that a WHILE statement always tests the condition first. If the condition is FALSE to begin with, the statement is never executed. It is the programmer's responsibility to see that the condition to be tested is set correctly (initialized) before the WHILE statement begins.

```
I := 1; ◄───────────── variable I must be initialized
WHILE I < 10 DO
    BEGIN
      .
      .
      .
    I := I + 1 ◄─────────── variable I must be incremented (changed)
    END
```

You must also make sure the condition is changed within the loop so that it will become FALSE at some point or you will never exit from the statement. (This situation is called an infinite loop.)

How many times will the previous loop be executed? Nine or ten? To determine the number of times, look at what the loop control variable (I in this case) was initialized to and look at the test. Here I starts out at 1 and the test is I < 10. Therefore the loop is executed nine times. If we had wanted to execute the loop ten times, we could have either set I to 0 to begin with, or changed the test to I <= 10. Be careful! If we changed both, the loop would be executed eleven times!

EOF Loops

EOF is a Boolean function provided in Pascal to ask the question "Have we read the last data value?" EOF becomes TRUE when the next character to be read is the special end-of-file character <eof>. This character is the last one in a data file. It follows the last end-of-line <eoln> character. (See Chapter 3.) You do not have to worry about putting the <eof> character after your data. The system will do this for you.

Example data file:

```
<value> <value> <value> . . . <eoln>
<value> <value> <value> . . . <eoln>
<value> <value> <value> . . . <eoln>
<value> <value> <value> . . . <eoln>
<eof>
```

We use the EOF function to control read loops where we do not know in advance how many sets of data values we have to read in. The code for such a loop follows.

```
WHILE NOT EOF DO
    BEGIN
        READLN(VALU1, VALU2, VALU3,...);
        .
        .
        .
    END
```

(Note that EOF is TRUE if there is no more data, so you have to use NOT EOF to control your loop.)

The READLN leaves the pointer ready to read the character at the beginning of each new line, which is the <eof> character when the data has all been read in.

Using a READLN implies that we know how our data is organized on lines or cards. There are times when this is not the case and a READ must be used. Look what happens if we simply replace the READLN with READ:

```
WHILE NOT EOF DO
    BEGIN
        READ(VALU);
        .
        .
    END
```

Sample data:

```
24 36 37<eoln>
<eof>
```

	VALU	Data line/ reading pointer
Before loop	?	24 36 37<eoln> ↑ <eof>
After 1st read in the loop	24	24 36 37<eoln> ↑ <eof>
After 2nd read in the loop	36	24 36 37<eoln> ↑ <eof>
After 3rd read in the loop	37	24 36 37<eoln> ↑ <eof>

Notice that the pointer is just before the <eoln>. EOF returns FALSE because the file is not empty (<eoln> is still to be read). The loop is executed again. Since there is no more data, VALU is undefined and the balance of the loop is executed using VALU. This will cause you to have incorrect results.

There is a technique called a "priming" read which solves the problem of reading numeric values in most systems. Read a value once outside of the loop. This value is processed in the loop, and the last statement in the loop is to read a new value. The READ looks for a value and stops trying when it sees the next character to be read is an <eof> character. Now when EOF is tested, it returns TRUE and you proceed with the statement following the WHILE loop.

```
READ(VALU);                    (* Initializes VALU for first time through loop *)
WHILE NOT EOF DO
   BEGIN
      .
      .
      READ(VALU)               (* Gets new input for next pass through the loop *)
   END
```

Sample data:

```
24 36 37<eoln>
<eof>
```

	VALU	Data line/ reading pointer
Before loop	24	24 36 37\<eoln\> ↑ \<eof\>
After 1st read in the loop	36	24 36 37\<eoln\> ↑ \<eof\>
After 2nd read in the loop	37	24 36 37\<eoln\> ↑ \<eof\>
After 3rd read in the loop	?	\<eof\> ↑

The last time the READ is executed, no data is found and the pointer is left before the \<eof\>. VALU is undefined, but since EOF is now TRUE, the loop is not executed and this undefined VALU isn't processed.

Notice, however, that reading and processing are "out of sync" when using this technique. The data for the first iteration is read outside the loop. The data that is read within the loop is used with the next iteration.

This solution will work on most systems. It is based on the fact that most systems will allow you to encounter an \<eof\> when attempting to read a data value, and give you an error only if EOF is TRUE when you issue your READ.*

The priming read is one solution for reading numeric values in a loop. However, it is not needed (or appropriate) when reading characters in a loop.

EOLN Loops

EOLN is a Boolean function provided in Pascal to ask the question "Have we read the last character in a line or card?" EOLN becomes TRUE if the next character to be read is the \<eoln\> character. This function is used to control a loop where we wish to process character data.

The following EOLN loop will read and print all the characters in a line or card. CH is of type CHAR.

```
WHILE NOT EOLN DO
    BEGIN
        READ(CH);
        WRITE(CH)
    END
```

---

* Some systems consider an \<eof\> encountered while trying to READ a value a fatal error. Processing stops with the message "TRIED TO READ PAST EOF." If your system does this, one way to input integer or real values with an unknown number of values on a line is to read them as characters and convert them to integer or real values yourself. Believe it or not, you will be able to do this by the time you read Chapter 13. (Another solution, the use of a sentinel in the data, is discussed in a following section.)

This loop will continue until the next character to be read is the <eoln> character. At that time EOLN will become TRUE, NOT EOLN will then be FALSE and the loop will not be executed. Since character reads are always one character at a time, a priming read is not necessary. In fact, if you use a priming read you will not process your last character. After you read the last character, EOLN would become TRUE, and you would not execute the loop with that last character.

If the <eoln> character itself is read, it is converted into a blank before it is stored.

In all of our discussions of <eof> and <eoln> we have talked about them as if they were explicit characters. This is not true in some systems. However, whatever technique a system uses to separate lines (cards) and files, the functions EOF and EOLN operate as we have described.

Sentinel Controlled Loops

To avoid the problems caused by EOF, reading may be controlled by a sentinel or special data value. For example, if all the data values are non-zero, a zero value could be used to signal the end of the data. The following loop fragment continues to read data until a zero value is read. This is another form of the priming read, using a predetermined data value instead of <eof>.

```
READ (VALU);
WHILE VALU <> 0 DO
    BEGIN
        .
        .
        READ (VALU)
    END
```

What would happen if you forgot to put in a zero value at the end of the data? Right: 'TRIED TO READ PAST EOF'.

Counting Loops

A common subtask is to keep track of how many times the loop is executed. Note that this is different from a count controlled loop. The Boolean expression does not depend on the count. For example, the following program fragment reads, counts and prints characters until a period is encountered. (CH is of type CHAR.)

```
COUNT := 0;                    (* initialize count *)
READ(CH);          (* reading into a CHAR variable inputs one character only *)
WHILE CH <> '.' DO
   BEGIN
      WRITE(CH);
      COUNT := COUNT + 1;             (* increment count *)
      READ(CH)
   END
```

The loop continues until a period character is read. At the termination of the loop, COUNT contains the number of characters written, one less than the number read. Note that if a period is the only character, nothing is printed and COUNT contains a zero—which it should.

Summing Loops

If you know how many data values you have (say 10) and want to sum them, the following code would work. Note this is also a count controlled loop.

```
SUM := 0;                         (* initialize the sum *)
I := 0;                       (* initialize control variable *)
WHILE I < 10 DO
   BEGIN
      READ(VALU);                  (* input a value *)
      SUM := SUM + VALU;       (* add the value to sum *)
      I := I + 1             (* increment control variable *)
   END
```

If you initialize I to 1 instead of 0, your test should be "I <= 10" not "I < 10". When this fragment has been executed, SUM will contain the sum of the 10 values read in, I will contain a 10 (if initialized to 0) or an 11 (if initialized to 1), and VALU will contain the last number read in.

In this example, the count control variable is being increased by one each time through the loop. For each new value for I, there is a new value for VALU. Does this mean we can decrement I by one and get the previous value of VALU? NO!! Because I is a counter you are incrementing by one, its previous value is known. Once a new value for VALU has been read in, the previous one is gone forever. If you will need a previous value, then you must explicitly save it.

Let's look at another example. We want to sum the first ten even numbers in a set of data. It looks quite like the last problem except that we need to test each number to see if it is even or odd. If it is odd, we do nothing. If it is even, we increment our counter and add the value to our sum.

```
I := 1;                              (* Initialize loop control variable *)
SUM := 0;
WHILE I <= 10 DO
   BEGIN
      READ(VALU);                    (* Get next value *)
      IF (VALU MOD 2) = 0            (* Test for even *)
         THEN
            BEGIN
               I := I + 1;           (* Increment counter *)
               SUM := SUM + VALU     (* Increment sum *)
            END
   END
```

In this example there is no relation between the value of the loop control variable and the number of numbers being read in. I is only incremented when an even number is read. The counter in this example is called an event counter because it is incremented only when a certain event occurs. The counter in the previous example is called an iteration counter because it is incremented during each iteration of the loop.

Flag Controlled Loops

The use of flags refers to the technique of using a Boolean variable to control the logical flow of your program. You can set a Boolean variable to TRUE before a WHILE, and when you wish to stop executing the loop you set it to FALSE. For example, the following segment of code would let you continue reading and summing values until the data contained a negative value. (POSITIVE is of type Boolean.)

```
SUM := 0;
POSITIVE := TRUE;                    (* initialize flag *)
WHILE POSITIVE DO
   BEGIN
      READ(VALU);
      IF VALU < 0                    (* test input value *)
         THEN POSITIVE := FALSE      (* set flag *)
         ELSE SUM := SUM + VALU      (* add to sum *)
   END
```

Note that sentinel controlled loops can be coded with flags. In fact, the above code is using a negative value as a sentinel.

The looping structure in Program PAYROLL in Chapter 1 is a sentinel controlled loop. It uses a zero employee number (EMPNUM) to stop the reading and processing cycle. It could have been coded using a flag as follows. (MOREDATA is a Boolean variable.)

```
READLN (EMPNUM);
MOREDATA := EMPNUM < > 0; (* MOREDATA is TRUE if EMPNUM is non-zero *)
WHILE MOREDATA DO
   BEGIN
      .
      .
      .
      READLN (EMPNUM);
      MOREDATA := EMPNUM < > 0
   END
```

Now let's look at the case where we want to count how many INTEGER numbers there are in a set of data, and print out that count and the last two data values. We will again use a negative value as a sentinel. In order to remember the last two values we will have to remember the current value and the previous one. We read the next one in. If it is negative we are finished reading. If it is positive, the current value becomes the previous value and this new value becomes the current value.

```
POSITIVE := TRUE;                             (* Initialize flag *)
I := 1;                                       (* Initialize counter *)
READ(CURRENT);                                (* Initialize current value *)
WHILE POSITIVE DO
   BEGIN
      READ(NEXT);                             (* Get next value *)
      IF NEXT < 0                             (* Test input value *)
         THEN POSITIVE := FALSE               (* Set flag *)
         ELSE
            BEGIN
               I := I + 1;                    (* Increment counter *)
               PREVIOUS := CURRENT;   (* Set next to last value read *)
               CURRENT := NEXT             (* Set last value read *)
            END
   END
WRITELN('NUMBER OF DATA VALUES READ ', I,
        ' LAST VALUE READ ', CURRENT,
        ' NEXT TO THE LAST VALUE READ ', PREVIOUS)
```

Study this routine carefully. There will be many times when you will need to keep track of the last value read in addition to the current value. By the way, what will happen if there are no data values? Right: 'TRIED TO READ PAST EOF'. What happens if there is only one data value and the sentinel? PREVIOUS will be undefined.

■ SAMPLE PROBLEM

Problem: Take hourly outdoor temperature readings for one 24-hour period.
Find the average temperature for the
day and the day's high and low temperatures.

Discussion: To do this task without the use of a computer is easy. Each hour
we would read the thermometer and write down the temperature. At the
end of the 24-hour period, we would add up the numbers and divide by
24 to get the average.

We know how to program that. We will use a count controlled and
summing loop.

To find the day's high by hand, we would scan the list of numbers
looking for the largest. To find the day's low, we would scan the list for
the smallest number. How can we simulate scanning the list looking for
the largest or smallest? Well, let's look a little more carefully at what we
are actually doing.

To find the largest number in a list of numbers, we compare the first
with the second and remember which number is the largest. This number is then compared with the third one. Again the largest number is
remembered and compared with the fourth. This process continues until
we run out of numbers on our list. The one we remember is the largest.

The process of finding the smallest number is the same, only we remember the smaller not the larger one. Now that we understand the process in detail, we can design an algorithm to do it. We will declare two
variables, HIGH and LOW, in which we will save ("remember") the
largest and smallest we have seen so far. As we look at each new temperature, we will compare it to HIGH and LOW.

Now we are ready to write the design for the program. We will assume
that someone else has already recorded the temperatures and they are
ready to be input to our program. We will read and process each temperature.

Input: 24 integer numbers representing hourly temperatures.

Output: echo print the temperatures
the average temperature
the day's high temperature
the day's low temperature

MAIN MODULE   Level 0

```
WHILE more data DO
    GET TEMP
    add TEMP to SUM
    SMALLEST SO FAR?
    LARGEST SO FAR?
COMPUTE AVERAGE
PRINT
```

GET TEMP   Level 1

```
READ(TEMP)
PRINT(TEMP)
```

SMALLEST SO FAR?

```
IF TEMP < LOW
    THEN LOW = TEMP
```

LARGEST SO FAR?

```
IF TEMP > HIGH
    THEN HIGH = TEMP
```

COMPUTE AVERAGE

```
AVERAGE = SUM / 24
```

PRINT

```
PRINT ('AVERAGE TEMPERATURE IS ', AVERAGE)
PRINT ('HIGH TEMPERATURE IS ', HIGH)
PRINT ('LOW TEMPERATURE IS ', LOW)
```

Design Tree Diagram:

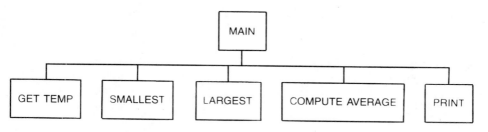

```
PROGRAM TEMPSTAT(INPUT,OUTPUT);        (* This program calculates the average
                                    temperature, the high temperature and the low temperature
                                         from 24 hourly temperature readings *)
CONST NUMHRS = 24;                        (* number of hours in time period *)
VAR  TEMP,                                (* an hourly temperature reading *)
     HIGH,                                (* highest temperature seen so far *)
     LOW,                                 (* lowest temperature seen so far *)
     SUM,                                 (* running sum of temperatures *)
     HOUR,                          (* loop control variable for hours in a day *)
     AVERAGE : INTEGER;                      (* average temperature *)
BEGIN (* TEMP *)
   HIGH := -MAXINT;               (* initialize HIGH to impossibly low value *)
   LOW := MAXINT;                 (* initialize LOW to impossibly high value *)
   HOUR := 1;                       (* initialize loop control variable *)
   SUM := 0;                          (* initialize running sum *)
   WHILE HOUR <= NUMHRS DO
      BEGIN
         READ(TEMP);                                   (* get temp *)
         WRITELN(TEMP);
         SUM := SUM + TEMP;                         (* add temp to sum *)
         IF TEMP < LOW                             (* check for new low *)
            THEN LOW := TEMP;
         IF TEMP > HIGH                            (* check for new high *)
            THEN HIGH := TEMP;
         HOUR := HOUR + 1           (* increment loop control variable *)
      END;
   AVERAGE := SUM DIV NUMHRS;                   (* compute average *)
   WRITELN('AVERAGE TEMPERATURE IS ', AVERAGE:4);        (* print *)
   WRITELN('HIGH TEMPERATURE IS ', HIGH:7);
   WRITELN('LOW TEMPERATURE IS ', LOW:8)
END. (* TEMP *)
```

The ':' followed by a digit in the WRITELN statements are for formatting the output. They are explained in the last section of this chapter. Given this input data:

```
45 47 47 47 50 50 55 60 70 70 72 75
75 75 75 74 74 73 70 70 69 67 65 50
```

the output would look like this:

```
45
47
47
47
50
50
55
60
70
70
72
75
75
75
75
74
74
73
70
70
69
67
65
50
AVERAGE TEMPERATURE IS    63
HIGH TEMPERATURE IS       75
LOW TEMPERATURE IS        45
```

There are several things to note about the code. The initialization of SUM to 0 and COUNT to 1 is self-explanatory. The initialization of HIGH to −MAXINT and LOW to MAXINT is not. HIGH and LOW must be given starting values. These starting values must be assured of being changed immediately. So HIGH was set to the largest negative number possible, and LOW was set to the largest positive number possible. Therefore the first temperature read in will be lower than LOW and higher than HIGH and would replace each.

What would happen if we made the two IF-THEN statements into one IF-THEN-ELSE statement like this?

```
IF TEMP < LOW
    THEN LOW := TEMP
    ELSE IF TEMP > HIGH
            THEN HIGH := TEMP
```

At first glance it looks more efficient. Why should you ask if it is larger than HIGH if you know it is lower than LOW? Logically you shouldn't have to, but because of the way HIGH and LOW have been initialized, you would get the wrong answer if the highest temperature were the first value read in.

Exercise 7 asks you to redo this program using another initialization scheme which removes this data dependent bug. (Hint: Use a priming read and set HIGH and LOW to that first value.)

∎

NESTED LOGIC

In Chapter 4 we described nested IF statements. Both the WHILE and IF statements contain statements and are themselves statements. So the body of a WHILE statement or the branch of an IF statement can contain other WHILE and/or IF statements. Remember that any statement can be replaced with a compound statement. This nesting can be extended to create complex control structures.

How could we extend the previous algorithm to calculate daily temperature statistics for a year? Simply put a count controlled loop around the body of Program TEMPSTAT.

WHILE more days DO

> WHILE more data DO
>   GET TEMP
>   add TEMP to SUM
>   SMALLEST SO FAR?
>   LARGEST SO FAR?
> COMPUTE AVERAGE
> PRINT

The two loops would be coded as follows. Note we are assuming it is not a leap year!

```
DAY := 1;
WHILE DAY <= 365 DO
    BEGIN
        .
        .
        HOUR := 1;
        WHILE HOUR <= 24 DO
            BEGIN
                .
                .
                HOUR := HOUR + 1
            END;
        .
        .
        DAY := DAY + 1
    END
```

Notice that each loop has a counter which is initialized to 1 and is incremented at the end of the loop. This is a useful pattern. Let's take a closer look at the general pattern of a nested loop. The pattern looks as follows: where INCTR is the counter for the inner loop, OUTCTR is the counter for the outer loop, and LIMIT1 and LIMIT2 are the number of times each loop is to be executed.

```
OUTCTR := 1;                          (* initialize outer loop counter *)
WHILE OUTCTR <= LIMIT1 DO
   BEGIN
         .
         .
      INCTR :=1;                       (* initialize inner loop counter *)
      WHILE INCTR <= LIMIT2 DO
         BEGIN
               .
               .
            INCTR := INCTR + 1         (* increment inner loop counter *)
         END;
      OUTCTR := OUTCTR + 1             (* increment outer loop counter *)
   END
```

Although both of these loops are count controlled loops, the same pattern can be used with any type of loop. The following program fragment shows an example of an EOLN loop nested within an EOF loop where characters are read and printed. The number of lines in the input is printed at the end.

```
NOLINES := 0;                     1
WHILE NOT EOF DO                  2
   BEGIN
      WHILE NOT EOLN DO           3
         BEGIN
            READ(CH);             4
            WRITE(CH)             5
         END;
      READLN;                     6
      NOLINES := NOLINES + 1;     7
      WRITELN                     8
   END
```

Notice that there are two WHILE loops: an EOLN loop within an EOF loop. Let's look at exactly what happens at execution time with a specific set of data values. We will need to keep track of the contents of the variables CH and NOLINES as well as the results of the Boolean EOLN and EOF expressions. Let's introduce some simple notation here. Number each line, omitting the BEGINs and ENDs as above. As we go through the program we will indicate the first time line 1 is executed by 1.1, the second by

Data: T☐<eoln>
D2<eoln>
<eof>

NOTE: There are two characters on
the first line: a 'T' and
a blank.

Statement	Variables		Expressions		Output
	NOLINES (integer)	CH (char)	EOLN	EOF	
1.1	0	—	—	—	—
2.1	0	—	—	F	—
3.1	0	—	F	—	—
4.1	0	T	—	—	—
5.1	0	T	—	—	T
3.2	0	T	F	—	—
4.2	0	☐	—	—	—
5.2	0	☐	—	—	☐
3.3	0	☐	T	—	—
6.1	0	☐	—	—	—
7.1	1	☐	—	—	—
8.1	1	☐	—	—	<eoln>
2.2	1	☐	—	F	—
3.4	1	☐	F	—	—
4.3	1	D	—	—	—
5.3	1	D	—	—	D
3.5	1	D	F	—	—
4.4	1	2	—	—	—
5.4	1	2	—	—	2
3.6	1	2	T	—	—
6.2	1	2	—	—	—
7.2	2	2	—	—	—
8.2	2	2	—	—	<eoln>
2.3	2	2	—	T	—

Output: T☐<eoln>
D2<eoln>

Figure 5-3. Code Walk-through

1.2, etc. (See Figure 5-3.) We will use a box to stand for a blank. The iterations of the loops are bracketed on the left.

This is called a code walk-through, similar to what we did in Chapter 3 when we traced program variables. It is an extremely useful technique when debugging your program. We are using it here to point out several interesting things.

Since NOLINES and CH are variables, their values remain the same until explicitly changed. This is indicated by the repeating values. The values of the Boolean expressions EOLN and EOF, however, exist only when the test is made. This is indicated by a dash in that column at all times except the test.

The data itself is made up of two lines of characters, each with two characters. Notice three things: a blank (□) is a character; the 2 in the data is a character; but the number 1 in statement 7 is an integer 1 and can be added to NOLINES. Although the 1 and the 2 both look like numbers to us, they are represented in memory in two entirely different ways. How does Pascal know which you mean? Because you tell it which it is. Statement 7 is an arithmetic assignment statement where you add a 1 to the integer variable NOLINES. Since CH is of type CHAR, the 2 read into CH is character data.

FORMATTING INTEGER AND CHARACTER OUTPUT

You can control what your output looks like by indicating how many *columns* you want a variable or constant to occupy in the printed output or on the screen. You do this by putting a ':' followed by an integer value after the variable or constant in the parameter list of a WRITE statement. The integer following the ':' says how many columns (character positions) on the line the printed value of the variable or constant is to occupy.

The value of the variable or constant will be printed right-justified with blanks filled in to the left to fill up the proper number of columns. Let's look at an example:

$$ANS = 33 \text{ (integer)}$$
$$NUM = 7132 \text{ (integer)}$$
$$CH = \text{'Z' (char)}$$

WRITE statement parameters	Output ('□' stands for blanks)
(1) (ANS:4,NUM:5,CH:3)	□□33□7132□□Z
(2) (ANS:4,NUM:4,CH:1)	□□337132Z
(3) (ANS:6,CH:2,NUM:5)	□□□□33□Z□7132
(4) (CH:6,NUM:4)	□□□□□Z7132
(5) (ANS:1,NUM:5)	33□7132

In (1) the value 33 is printed with two blanks to the left; the value 7132 is printed with one blank to the left; and 'Z' is printed with two blanks to the left.

In (2) the values 33 and 7132 and Z all run together and are therefore difficult to read. In (3) there are extra blanks for readability, in (4) there are not. In (5) the number of columns (called field width) is not large enough for the number. In that case the field width is automatically extended so that all the digits will print.

In addition to lining up the output, you must be sure to explain each item of output. That is, put in column headings or explanatory statements to identify each output value.

The same spacing convention holds true for literals. For example:

WRITE *statement parameters*	*Output*
(1) ('THE ANSWER IS':16)	◌◌◌THE◌ANSWER◌IS

16 columns

| (2) (' ':5, 'X':4) | ◌◌◌◌◌◌◌◌X |

9 columns

In (1) three blanks are inserted at the left to make up the 16 character positions. In (2) the first five blanks come from ' ':5 and the next three are filled in to make 'X':4 cover four positions.

The number of character positions to be used to print a value is called the fieldwidth specification. We have used examples with integer constants as the fieldwidth specification, but integer variables and expressions can also be used. This can be useful. For example, the following program segment would plot a graph of an item's sales history.

```
READ(UNITSALES);              (* input the number of unit sales *)
WHILE NOT EOF DO
   BEGIN
      WRITELN('*':UNITSALES);  (* print UNITSALES-1 blanks followed
                                            by an asterisk *)
      READ(UNITSALES)
   END
```

Of course, if UNITSALES is larger than the number of columns on a page, an appropriate scaling function should be used. If the data were as follows,

5 7 8 9 10 9 8 9 10 9 <eof>

the graph would look like this.

```
   *
    *
     *
      *
       *
      *
     *
      *
       *
      *
```

A combination of WRITEs and WRITELNs can be used to center headings, line up columns, and make your output clear and readable. Just as comments in the program document the code, your headings and explanatory material document your output.

The first step is to decide exactly what is to be printed. We will use the temperature data problem to illustrate the process by setting up the WRITE and WRITELN statements to create a table with a year's worth of daily high, low and average temperatures. The table should contain a heading describing what is in the table, column headings describing what temperature values are being printed, and the temperature values themselves.

The next step is to take a pencil and paper and make a sketch of how the table might look. Line up headings and put in some actual values. Graph paper is useful here. After several tries, you might come up with the layout in Figure 5-4. Notice that we have added a column which shows to which day of the year the corresponding temperatures refer. Once you have it lined up the way you want it, you need to mark off the number of character positions associated with each heading or data value.

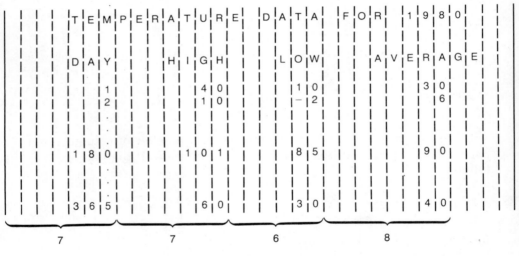

Figure 5-4. Output Formatting

The table heading takes up 25 character positions and the column headings take up 26. If we want 4 blanks before each heading line, we would use field specifications of ':29' and ':30' respectively. To line up the values in each column, you count the number of character positions from the end of the previous column to the last character position in the column whose field width you are determining. This count becomes the field width. In this case, ':7', ':7', ':6', and ':8' respectively.

The following is our complete program with the WRITE statements set up as we have described.

```
PROGRAM YEARTEMP(INPUT,OUTPUT);          (* This program calculates daily
                                         temperature statistics for a year *)
CONST NUMHRS = 24;                       (* number of hours in time period *)
      NUMDAYS = 365;                     (* number of days in year *)
VAR TEMP,                                (* an hourly temperature reading *)
    HIGH,                                (* highest temperature seen so far *)
    LOW,                                 (* lowest temperature seen so far *)
    SUM,                                 (* running sum of temperatures *)
    HOUR,                                (* loop control variable for hours in a day *)
    DAY,                                 (* loop control variable for days in year *)
    AVERAGE : INTEGER;                   (* average temperature *)
BEGIN (* YEARTEMP *)
   DAY := 1;                             (* initialize loop control variable *)
   WRITELN('TEMPERATURE DATA FOR 1980':29);
   WRITELN;
   WRITELN;
   WRITELN('DAY    HIGH    LOW    AVERAGE':30);
   WRITELN;
   WHILE DAY <= NUMDAYS DO
     BEGIN
        HIGH := -MAXINT;                 (* initialize HIGH to impossibly low value *)
        LOW := MAXINT;                   (* initialize LOW to impossibly high value *)
        SUM := 0;                        (* initialize running sum *)
        HOUR := 1;
        WHILE HOUR <= NUMHRS DO
          BEGIN
             READ(TEMP);                 (* get temp *)
             SUM := SUM + TEMP;          (* add temp to sum *)
             IF TEMP < LOW               (* check for new low *)
                THEN LOW := TEMP;
             IF TEMP > HIGH              (* check for new high *)
                THEN HIGH := TEMP;
             HOUR := HOUR + 1
          END;
        AVERAGE := SUM DIV NUMHRS;       (* compute average *)
        WRITELN(DAY:7, HIGH:7, LOW:6, AVERAGE:8);    (* print *)
        DAY := DAY + 1
     END
END. (* YEARTEMP *)
```

Notice that the table heading and the column headings are printed before entering the nested loops. The values to be printed in the columns are computed within the inner loop and then printed at the bottom of the outer loop.

■ SAMPLE PROBLEM

Problem: Play the children's game "rock, paper and scissors."

This is a game where two people simultaneously say or gesture with their hands either rock, paper or scissors. Whether you win or lose depends not only upon what you say, but what your opponent says. The rules are as follows:

paper covers rock ⟹ paper wins
scissors cut paper ⟹ scissors win
rock breaks scissors ⟹ rock wins

The winner is the player who wins the most individual games.

Discussion: We will assume that everyone has played this game and understands it. (If not, ask a sister, brother, child or classmate.) Therefore, our discussion will center on how to represent the game in a program.

Since input must be in the form of alphanumeric characters, not words or gestures, we will have to simulate the input by using letters to stand for 'scissors', 'paper' and 'rock'. The characters 'S', 'P' and 'R' seem appropriate.

How do we indicate which player made which choice? Let's assume each player writes down a series of plays which are then input from the console (or cards) in pairs: the first character representing player one's move and the second character representing player two's move. When there are no more plays, the game is over.

Input: A set of ordered pairs of characters ('S', 'P', 'R'). The first character represents the first player's move and the second character represents the second player's move.

Output: 'First' or 'Second' to indicate which player wins each individual game.
The total number of wins for the first player.
The total number of wins for the second player.
Which one wins the most games.

MAIN MODULE

Level 0

```
WHILE more games DO
    GET PLAY
    IF NOT LEGAL
        THEN PRINT ('PLAY NOT LEGAL')
        ELSE
            FIND WINNER
            PRINT GAMENUM AND WINNER
PRINT BIG WINNER
```

GET PLAY

Level 1

```
READLN FIRST, SECOND
WRITELN FIRST, SECOND
IF ((FIRST = 'S') OR (FIRST = 'P')
    OR (FIRST = 'R')) AND ((SECOND = 'S')
    OR (SECOND = 'P') OR (SECOND = 'R'))
        THEN LEGAL = TRUE
        ELSE LEGAL = FALSE
```

FIND WINNER

```
IF (FIRST = 'P') AND (SECOND = 'R')
    THEN WIN1 is incremented
    ELSE
      IF (FIRST = 'S') AND (SECOND = 'P')
          THEN WIN1 is incremented
          ELSE
            IF (FIRST = 'R') AND (SECOND = 'S')
            THEN WIN1 is incremented.
```

PRINT BIG WINNER

```
PRINT WIN1 AND WIN2
IF WIN1 > WIN2
    THEN PRINT ('FIRST PLAYER WINS')
    ELSE PRINT ('SECOND PLAYER WINS').
```

Design Tree Diagram:

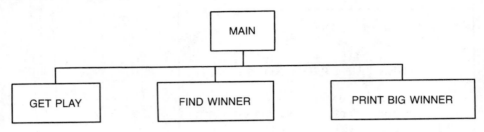

Let's walk through this algorithm and see if it works. The main loop continues until there are no more games. GET PLAY reads in the play of each participant and tests to make sure the first player's choice is either an 'S', 'P' or 'R' and the second player's choice is either an 'S', 'P' or 'R'. The result of the test is kept as a Boolean variable LEGAL.

The main program level tests this variable and writes an error message if the play is not legal. If the play is legal a winner is determined and the game number and winner of that game is printed. OOPS! Where is the game number determined? This must be a counting loop where we count the number of moves (input pairs). This count is the game number. We will have to add this to the design.

GET PLAY reads in the two moves and echo prints them. Each move is tested to be sure it is an 'S', 'P' or 'R'. If one (or both) is not legal, a Boolean variable is set to FALSE. This looks all right.

We continue our walk-through with FIND WINNER. Even as we begin we notice something peculiar. WIN1 is incremented in each case. When does the second player win? The IF that looks for the winner is only half completed! We will have to fix this too. We must now check to see if SECOND has a 'P' to FIRST's 'R', an 'S' to FIRST's 'P' or an 'R' to FIRST's 'S'.

That seems a very complicated set of IFs. Is there some fact we may have overlooked which would shorten it? What do we know when we reach the end of FIND WINNER as originally coded? We know the input plays are legal and FIRST has not won. Is this evidence enough to simply add an "ELSE increment WIN2" to the end? Probably. If FIRST doesn't win, then SECOND must.

PRINT BIG WINNER prints the number of games each player has won, compares these scores and prints which player won the most games.

The revised top-down design is as follows.

MAIN MODULE   Level 0

```
GAMENUM is 0
WHILE more games DO
      increment GAMENUM
      GET PLAY
      IF NOT LEGAL
          THEN PRINT ('PLAY NOT LEGAL')
          ELSE
              FIND WINNER
              PRINT GAMENUM AND WINNER
PRINT BIG WINNER
```

GET PLAY (same as before)   Level 1

FIND WINNER

```
IF (FIRST = 'P') AND (SECOND = 'R')
    THEN WIN1 is incremented
    ELSE
        IF (FIRST = 'S') AND (SECOND = 'P')
            THEN WIN1 is incremented
            ELSE
                IF (FIRST = 'R') AND (SECOND = 'S')
                    THEN WIN1 is incremented
                    ELSE WIN2 is incremented
```

PRINT BIG WINNER (same as before)

Now the top-down design is ready to be coded in Pascal.

TESTING AND DEBUGGING

We will use this program to illustrate this chapter's testing and debugging hints. During the coding of the program an awkward construction came to light:

```
ELSE
    FINDWINNER
    PRINT GAMENUM AND WINNER
```

If we code the top-down design directly, we find ourselves at the stage to print the winner and we don't know which it was! The obvious solution would be to print where the winning total is incremented, but that involves creating a compound statement for each simple statement in that big IF statement. This poses no conceptual problem but adds greatly to the length and our program will not conform to our design. Another solution is to set a Boolean variable FIRSTWIN to TRUE at the beginning of the loop. Then if SECOND does win, you can set FIRSTWIN to FALSE in only one place. Then the printing is based on FIRSTWIN. The following code corresponds to the second solution.

```
PROGRAM GAME(INPUT,OUTPUT);          (* This program simulates the children's
                                    game "rock, paper and scissors." Each game consists of inputs from
                                    2 players. A winner is determined and printed. Individual scores are kept
                                    and the overall winner is printed when there are no more games. *)
VAR
    FIRST,                                          (* first player's move *)
    SECOND : CHAR;                                  (* second player's move *)
    WIN1,                               (* number of games the 1st player has won *)
    WIN2,                               (* number of games the 2nd player has won *)
    GAMENUM : INTEGER;                                      (* game count *)
    LEGAL,                                          (* TRUE if input is correct *)
    FIRSTWIN : BOOLEAN;          (* if 1st player wins game, FIRSTWIN is TRUE *)

BEGIN
    WIN1 := 0;                                               (* initialization *)
    WIN2 := 0;
    GAMENUM := 0;
    WHILE NOT EOF DO
        BEGIN
            GAMENUM := GAMENUM + 1;
            FIRSTWIN := TRUE;
            READLN(FIRST, SECOND);                          (* get play *)
            WRITELN(FIRST, SECOND);
            IF ((FIRST = 'S') OR (FIRST = 'P') (*check for legal plays*)
                OR (FIRST = 'R')) AND ((SECOND = 'S')
                OR (SECOND = 'P') OR (SECOND = 'R'))
                THEN LEGAL := TRUE
                ELSE LEGAL := FALSE;
            IF NOT LEGAL
                THEN WRITELN('PLAY NOT LEGAL')          (* play illegal *)
                ELSE
                    BEGIN                                   (* play legal *)
                        IF (FIRST = 'P') AND (SECOND = 'R')     (* find
                                                               winner *)
                            THEN WIN1 := WIN1 + 1
                            ELSE IF (FIRST = 'S') AND (SECOND = 'P')
                                THEN WIN1 := WIN1 + 1
                                ELSE IF (FIRST = 'R') AND
                                    (SECOND = 'S')
                                    THEN WIN1 := WIN1 + 1
```

```
                               ELSE
                                 BEGIN
                                   WIN2 := WIN2 + 1;
                                   FIRSTWIN := FALSE
                                 END;
                      IF FIRSTWIN                          (* print winner *)
                        THEN WRITELN('FIRST PLAYER WINS GAME ',
                                       GAMENUM:7)
                        ELSE WRITELN('SECOND PLAYER WINS GAME ',
                                       GAMENUM:6)
                  END;
            END;
      IF WIN1 > WIN2                                (* print big winner *)
        THEN WRITELN('FIRST PLAYER IS THE OVERALL WINNER')
        ELSE·WRITELN('SECOND PLAYER IS THE OVERALL WINNER')
END.
```

This program is the longest we have done so far. There are many places for possible errors. There are seven ELSEs, any one of which could have had a semi-colon before it. There are a lot of parentheses in the program, all of which are either syntactically or semantically necessary.

Once the program is free of syntax errors, the testing begins. You must choose test data to run through your program which tests each possible path through the program. In this case, this is easy to do. We know all the combinations of plays so we can try all possible data values. The test data then is:

```
SP
SR
SS
PP
PR
PS
RP
RR
RS
SK←——————— Error to test the check for legal data.
```

And the output is as follows:

```
SP
FIRST PLAYER WINS GAME        1
SR
SECOND PLAYER WINS GAME       2
SS
SECOND PLAYER WINS GAME       3
PP
SECOND PLAYER WINS GAME       4
PR
FIRST PLAYER WINS GAME        5
PS
```

```
SECOND PLAYER WINS GAME      6
RP
SECOND PLAYER WINS GAME      7
RR
SECOND PLAYER WINS GAME      8
RS
FIRST PLAYER WINS GAME       9
SK
PLAY NOT LEGAL
SECOND PLAYER IS THE OVERALL WINNER
```

Each of the possible outputs is printed but it looks strange. Why did the second player win so many more games? In particular, why did the second player win each tie game? TIES!!! The way the code is written, all the ties go to the second player.

Taking care of ties should have been considered when doing the top-down design. However, since programmers are human, this logic bug wasn't caught until the program was tested. Now a design decision must be made. What should we do with ties? We can ignore them, divide them or simply count them. The last seems the most reasonable.

We need to declare an integer variable TIECOUNT, initialize it to zero, and add the following IF-THEN-ELSE as the first test under the BEGIN commented with "play legal".

```
IF FIRST = SECOND
   THEN TIECOUNT := TIECOUNT + 1
   ELSE
```

We should also print out the tie count. In addition, the last IF which tests for the overall winner must be expanded to a nested IF to print a message if WIN1 and WIN2 are equal. That is, if the set of games ends in a tie.

In this case, we could test all possible combinations of input data. How do we test a program when this isn't possible? There isn't an easy answer for this, but the minimum you should test are the limits and several values in between. If a value can range between 0 and 100, test the program using 0, 100 and several numbers in between. Be sure to test the code that checks for input errors by giving the program bad data.

Testing and Debugging Hints

1. Plan your test data carefully to test all sections of your program.
2. Beware of infinite loops.

   An infinite loop is a loop where the expression in the WHILE statement never becomes false. The symptom is that your program doesn't stop. If you are at a terminal, nothing happens. Your program just keeps going and doesn't terminate. If you are on a system which monitors the amount of time a program is taking and stops it if it goes too long, the message would be "TIME LIMIT EXCEEDED."

If this occurs, check your logic and your syntax on your loops. Check to be sure there is no semi-colon immediately after the DO in the WHILE loop. This will cause an infinite loop. Make sure the control variable has been incremented within the loop in a counting loop. In a flag controlled loop, make sure the flag is changed eventually within the loop.

3. Treat EOF with great respect.

If you know what your data looks like (i.e., how it is organized on lines or cards) use READLN to avoid possible EOF errors. If READs must be used, plan your input statements carefully using a priming read outside of the loop.

4. If all else fails use debug WRITE statements.

Debug WRITE statements are WRITE statements inserted in a program to aid in debugging. They provide an output message indicating the flow of execution in the program. They are also useful in reporting the value of variables at a certain point in the program.

For example, if you wanted to know the value of variable SUM at a certain point in a program, you could insert the statement

```
WRITELN('SUM = ', SUM)
```

at that point. If this debug WRITE statement is in a loop, you will get as many values of SUM printed as the number of times the body of the loop is executed.

After you have debugged your program you can remove the debug WRITE statements.

Summary

The WHILE statement is a looping construct giving us the facility to repeat a statement as long as an expression is TRUE. When the expression is FALSE, the statement is skipped and execution continues with the statement following the loop.

There are several distinct types of loops which can be constructed using the WHILE which you will use again and again.

Count controlled loops are loops where a statement is repeated a specified number of times. You initialize a variable to be used as a counter immediately before the WHILE statement. (This variable is often called LCV for "loop control variable".) The LCV is tested against the limit in the expression of the WHILE. The last statement in the WHILE loop's compound statement must increment the LCV.

EOF loops are loops which continue to input (and process) data values until there is no more data. To implement them with a WHILE statement, the expression must be NOT EOF since EOF becomes TRUE when there are no more data values.

EOLN loops are used to input (and process) character data until there are no more characters on the line.

Sentinel controlled loops are input loops which use a data value not in the possible range of valid data values as a signal to stop reading.

Counting loops are loops which keep track of how many times they are repeated. An EOF loop can also be a *counting* loop if you have a variable that is initialized outside of the loop and is incremented within the loop. Note that a *counting* loop just keeps a count of how many times it is executed. That count is not used to control the loop. The variable that is used to keep this count is not used in the expression of the WHILE.

Summing loops are loops in which a running sum is being kept. It is like a *counting* loop in that a variable is initialized outside the loop. The *summing* loop, however, adds up unknown values, whereas the *counting* loop adds a one to the counter each time.

A *flag* is a variable which is set in one part of a program and tested in another to control the logical flow. In the context of the WHILE loop, a flag is set before the WHILE, tested in the expression, and changed somewhere in the body of the loop.

A *counter* is a variable which is used for counting. It may be a loop control variable, an iteration counter in a *counting* loop or an event counter which counts the number of times a particular condition occurs in a loop.

All output should be annotated and placed on the page for ease of reading. You can control where your output appears on a page by indicating the number of columns a variable or literal is to occupy.

Testing takes place at many levels. After completing your top-down design, you should go through it step-by-step to see that if you follow it exactly you will arrive at the correct answer.

After your solution has been coded in Pascal (or whatever language you are using) and the syntax bugs have been removed, you must run your program with a set of test data. This test data must be carefully chosen to test your program thoroughly.

Exercises

1. Write a program to read in integers from a card, count and print out the number of positive integers and the number of negative integers. If a value is zero, do not count it. Continue the process until EOF becomes TRUE.

2. Write a program segment which adds up the even integers from 16 to 26.

3. Write a program segment which processes 6 data lines (cards). Each data line contains 5 values. You are to write out which data line it is and the sum of the 5 values.

4. Write a program segment which reads in 10 data values or until a negative value is read, whichever comes first.

5. Use top-down design to write a Pascal program that finds the average of N integers, with the value of N being the first number of the data followed by N integers.

6. Write a program segment that sets a Boolean variable OVERFLOW to TRUE and stops reading in data if LEVEL (a real variable being read in) exceeds 200.0. Use OVERFLOW as a flag to control the loop.

7. Rewrite program TEMPSTAT using a different initialization scheme. Read one temperature outside of the loop and initialize all values (except HOUR) to the first temperature.

8. Write a program segment which reads in pairs of integers and prints out each pair in ascending order. Use EOF to control your loop. You do *not* know how the data is organized on lines or cards.

9. a. Write a statement to create the following headings.

```
        SALES
WEEK1    WEEK2    WEEK3
```

b. Write a statement to print values lined up under each week. The values are stored in WEEK1, WEEK2, WEEK3. The last digit of each number should fall under the '1', '2' and '3' of the respective column headings.

Pre-Test

1. Write a program segment that sets a Boolean variable DANGER to true and stops reading in data if PRESSURE (a real variable being read in) exceeds 510.0. Use DANGER as a flag to control the loop.

2. Write a program segment that counts the number of times the integer 28 occurs in a file of 100 integers.

3. Write a program segment that will read a file of grades for a class (any size) and find the class average.

4. Write a program segment that reads a file of integers until either a zero value is found or EOF is true. After leaving the loop, print either 'ZERO OCCURRENCE FOUND' or 'NO ZERO OCCURRENCE', whichever is the case.

5. a. What are the contents of SUM and VALU at the end of the execution of the following program.

```
PROGRAM PRETEST(INPUT,OUTPUT);
CONST N = 8;
VAR I, SUM, VALU : INTEGER;
        FLAG : BOOLEAN;
BEGIN
    SUM := 0;
    I := 1;
```

```
        FLAG := FALSE;
        WHILE (I <= N) AND NOT FLAG DO
            BEGIN
                READ(VALU);
                IF VALU > 0
                    THEN SUM := SUM + VALU
                    ELSE IF VALU = 0
                            THEN FLAG := TRUE;
                I := I + 1
            END;
        WRITELN(' END OF TEST ' , SUM, VALU)
    END.
```

Assume this data: 5 6 -3 7 -4 0 5 8 9

b. Does this data fully test this program? Explain your answer.

Procedures 6

Goals

To be able to write a program which reflects the structure of your top-down design.

To be able to write a module of your design as a procedure.

To be able to correctly define a procedure to do a specified task.

To be able to invoke that procedure correctly.

To be able to use formal *and* actual *parameters correctly.*

To be able to define and use local variables correctly.

To be able to declare and use external files of type TEXT.

TOP-DOWN STRUCTURED DESIGN WITH PROCEDURES

One of the exercises in Chapter 5 was to read and process 6 sets of data. The output was to be the sum of the 5 values in each data set along with the number of the data set (Exercise 3). Let us do a top-down design for this problem.

■ SAMPLE PROBLEM

Problem: Write a program segment which processes 6 data lines (cards). Each data line contains 5 values. You are to write out which data line it is and the sum of the 5 values.

Discussion: The input is in terms of "data sets". It doesn't matter whether they are input lines from the terminal or punched cards.

We must read 5 values from a line, sum them up and print out the data set number and the sum. A summing loop will work for this.

We also have to repeat the above for each of the 6 data sets. Nesting the above solution for a data set within a count controlled loop allows us to repeat the process for all 6 data sets.

Input: 6 sets of data with 5 values (integer) in each set

Output: 6 lines of output, each line containing 2 values, the data set number and the sum of the values in that set

MAIN MODULE   Level 0

```
WHILE more data sets DO
       PROCESS DATA SET
       PRINT RESULT
```

PROCESS DATA SET   Level 1

```
WHILE more data values DO
    GET VALU
    ADD VALU TO SUM
```

PRINT RESULT

```
WRITELN' DATA SET ', data set number,' SUM = ', sum
```

Level 0   Control Structure

WHILE Loop: A count controlled loop going from 1 to 6, where the counter variable will also be used as the DATA SET number.

Level 1   Control Structure

WHILE Loop: A summing loop going from 1 to 5.

Design Tree Diagram:

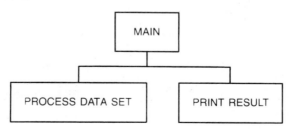

At this point we are ready to write our complete Pascal program. The declarations and definitions must be done and the actual code generated.

```
PROGRAM EXERCISE (INPUT,OUTPUT);
VAR COUNTER1,                              (*Level 0 loop control variable*)
    COUNTER2,                              (*Level 1 loop control variable*)
    VALU,                         (*variable into which the data values are read*)
    SUM : INTEGER;                            (*the summing variable*)
BEGIN (* MAIN PROGRAM *)
    COUNTER1 := 1;
    WHILE COUNTER1 <= 6 DO                      (* process 6 data sets *)
        BEGIN
            SUM := 0;
            COUNTER2 := 1;
            WHILE COUNTER2 <= 5 DO               (* process 5 values *)
                BEGIN
                    READ(VALU);
                    SUM := SUM + VALU;            (* add value to sum *)
                    COUNTER2 := COUNTER2 + 1
                END;
            READLN;                    (* this sets up for the next data set *)
            WRITELN(' DATA SET ', COUNTER1,' SUM = ', SUM);
                                                          (* print *)
            COUNTER1 := COUNTER1 + 1
        END
END.  (* MAIN PROGRAM *)
```

■

If you gave this code to someone and asked for a description of the program, you would get something like:

> "Well, you have a counting loop and then another counting loop—no, the second one is a summing loop—."

The beautiful explanatory top-down structure is no longer readily apparent. Wouldn't it be nice if you could write your main program as follows?

```
BEGIN
    COUNTER1 := 1;
    WHILE COUNTER1 <= 6 DO
        BEGIN
            PROCESS DATA SET
            PRINT RESULT
            COUNTER1 := COUNTER1 + 1
        END
END.
```

The structure is now evident in the code: 6 data sets are being processed. We have preserved the top-down design in our main program, thus making it more readable and understandable. If PROCESS DATA SET could be a complete program that returns the SUM to be printed to another complete program, PRINT RESULT, then this code describes the problem.

Such a facility does exist in Pascal if you name your modules with only one word. PROCESS DATA SET would have to be PROCESSDATASET and PRINT RESULT would have to be PRINTRESULT. You can define and name complete subprograms, or mini-programs, which do a specific task, and use them by putting that name as a statement in your main program.

These subprograms are called PROCEDURES. A procedure looks just like the programs you have been writing except that the PROGRAM heading is replaced by a PROCEDURE heading, and the last END has a semicolon following it instead of a period.

The PROGRAM heading names the program and lists the files where its input is coming from and where its output is going to. In analogous fashion the PROCEDURE heading names the subprogram and lists the variables (called parameters) that serve as its "input" and "output".

Let's rewrite our program using procedures to illustrate what we mean. Let's begin by writing module PROCESS DATA SET as procedure PROCESSDATASET.

```
PROCEDURE PROCESSDATASET(VAR SUM: INTEGER);          (*the procedure
                                               will leave the sum in SUM*)
VAR
    COUNTER2,                               (*Level 1 loop counter*)
    VALU : INTEGER;            (*variable into which data values will be read*)
BEGIN  (*PROCESSDATA*)
    SUM := 0;
    COUNTER2 := 1;
    WHILE COUNTER2 <= 5 DO
       BEGIN
          READ(VALU);
          SUM := SUM + VALU;
          COUNTER2 := COUNTER2 + 1
       END;
    READLN
END;   (*PROCESSDATA*)
```

PRINT RESULT can be turned into a procedure as follows:

```
PROCEDURE PRINTRESULT(VAR NUMBER, SUM : INTEGER);
BEGIN  (*PRINTRESULT*)
    WRITELN(' DATA SET ', NUMBER,' SUM = ', SUM);
END;   (*PRINTRESULT*)
```

Now what does the actual body of our program look like?

```
BEGIN
    COUNTER1 := 1
    WHILE COUNTER1 <= 6 DO
       BEGIN
```

```
        PROCESSDATASET(SUM);
        PRINTRESULT(COUNTER1, SUM);
        COUNTER1 := COUNTER1 + 1
      END
END.
```

This is now very similar to the main module of our top-down design. The names of the procedures appear as statements with the names of variables in parentheses beside them.

Just as variables are declared in the VAR section and used in the executable part of the program, procedures are declared in the PROCE-DURE section and used when their names appear as part of an executable portion of the program.

How does all this get put together? How do the procedures get executed? What are those variables in parentheses? PROCESSDATASET has SUM in its PROCEDURE heading and that matches SUM in the call to PROCESSDATASET in the main program. But PRINTRESULT has NUM-BER and SUM, not COUNTER1 and SUM.

Let's take these questions one at a time.

When the whole program is typed in at the console or punched on cards, the physical order of the lines will look as follows.

```
PROGRAM SUMDATA(INPUT,OUTPUT);
VAR SUM, COUNTER1 : INTEGER;

(***********************************************************)

PROCEDURE PROCESSDATASET(VAR SUM: INTEGER);
VAR
    COUNTER2, VALU : INTEGER;
BEGIN (* PROCESSDATASET *)
    SUM := 0;
    COUNTER2 := 1;
    WHILE COUNTER2 <= 5 DO              (* process 5 values *)
      BEGIN
        READ(VALU);
        SUM := SUM + VALU;
        COUNTER2 := COUNTER2 + 1
      END;
    READLN
END; (* PROCESSDATASET *)

(***********************************************************)

PROCEDURE PRINTRESULT(VAR NUMBER, SUM : INTEGER);
BEGIN (* PRINTRESULT *)
    WRITELN(' DATA SET ', NUMBER,' SUM = ', SUM);
END; (* PRINTRESULT *)
```

```
( ******************************************************** )

BEGIN (* MAIN PROGRAM *)
    COUNTER1 := 1;
    WHILE COUNTER1 <= 6 DO                   (* process 6 data sets *)
        BEGIN
            PROCESSDATASET(SUM);
            PRINTRESULT(COUNTER1, SUM);
            COUNTER1 := COUNTER1 + 1
        END
END.   (* MAIN PROGRAM *)
```

Note that the procedures go physically before the main program or level 0 module. So the physical order is different from the logical order. What then is the logical order in which these statements are executed? There are many "BEGIN-END" pairs but only one "BEGIN-END." pair. That period is very important because it tells the system to begin execution at the first statement in this "BEGIN-END" pair. The procedures and the main program get translated in this physical order during compilation, but when the translation phase is completed and the execution phase begins, it is to the first statement in the "BEGIN-END." pair that control is transferred. This statement is executed first and execution continues in logical sequence. Figure 6-1 illustrates this physical versus logical ordering of procedures.

When the name of a procedure is encountered as a statement, logical control is passed to the first statement in the first "BEGIN-END" pair (body) of the procedure. Therefore the logical order of the revised program is identical with the logical order of our original version. The difference is that the structure of the top-down design is maintained in the second version. The semantics of the problem solution itself are clear from looking at the code for the main program. As your problems get more complex, this clarity of design will become increasingly more important.

Remember that a program was defined as a program heading and a block. We can expand our definition of a block from Chapter 2 to include procedures. This is our expanded syntax diagram for a block.

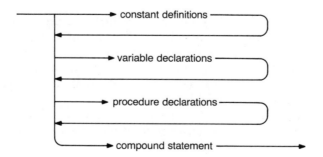

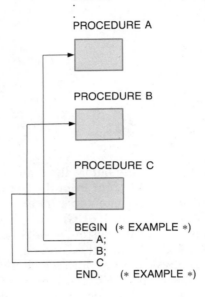

PROGRAM EXAMPLE(INPUT,OUTPUT);

PROCEDURE A

PROCEDURE B

PROCEDURE C

BEGIN (* EXAMPLE *)
    A;
    B;
    C
END.   (* EXAMPLE *)

Design Tree Diagram

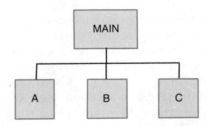

Figure 6-1. Physical versus Logical Order of Procedures

By definition, a program can contain procedures. A procedure is also defined as a procedure heading and a block. This means that we can declare a procedure within a procedure within a procedure . . . However, we will not consider nesting of procedures until later. It is mentioned here only to show that even very complicated top-down designs can be coded without losing the structure of the problem.

What are those identifiers in parentheses after the procedure names? They represent the way the main program and the procedures (or procedures and other procedures) communicate.

The procedure PROCESSDATASET is reading and summing values. The main program does not care what values are read, only what their sum is. Therefore it tells the procedure where to leave the sum by giving it the location (the variable SUM) when it turns control over to the procedure. PRINTRESULT needs two pieces of information: the data set number and the sum. The calling program gives it this information. The fact that the calling program calls them COUNTER1 and SUM and the procedure calls them NUMBER and SUM isn't important. The procedure expects to be given two integer numbers to work with and takes the first as NUMBER and the second as SUM because that is the order in the procedure heading. The calling program follows this convention and gives the procedure two integers in order. It is the position of the variable in the parameter list that is important, not the name.

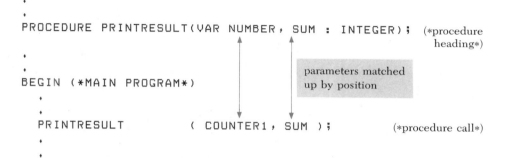

Before we formally define all the terms we have been using, let's leave the world of computing and draw an analogy from the world of entertainment. There is going to be a super concert on Friday night, and, since no programming assignments are due on Saturday, you decide to go.

You call the box office and tell the reservation clerk that you want two balcony tickets to Friday's performance. The clerk puts you on hold while she checks to see if seats are available and calculates what the cost will be if they are. Five minutes later she comes back on the line with the information that you have your seats, the price is $20 and you should pick up the tickets no later than 5 PM on Thursday. You hang up and go about your business.

This everyday happening describes how procedures work. The clerk is like a procedure. To do her job she must know how many tickets you want, where you want to sit and for which night you want the tickets. Your telephone call is like a procedure call. You give her the actual values she needs to operate with. You are put on hold until she completes her task. She then gives you the information she calculated for you and her job is finished.

She does this task all day long with different "input" values. Each telephone call activates this process. The caller holds until the clerk returns with "output" information based on that caller's specific "input".

The mechanism used to pass this input data from the caller to the procedure, and to return the output data from the procedure to the caller, is a pair of lists of variable names. The list the procedure uses is called the *formal parameter* list. These are the names it (she) always uses.

Each caller has a list of variable names, called the *actual parameter* list. These names may or may not be the same. The clerk (procedure) knows, however, that the first name in the *actual parameter* list is your synonym for the first name in her parameter list. The second name in the *actual parameter* is your name for the second in her list. That is, the names are matched up by their positions on the respective lists.

Now that we have covered procedures intuitively through an example and looked at them through an analogy, we will formally define the terms we have been using.

PROCEDURE DECLARATIONS

A procedure is defined as a heading and a block. The heading has the following form (simplified version of syntax diagram):

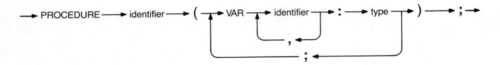

The identifiers listed in the heading (the parameter list) are the *formal parameters* of the procedure. They are the "input" to the procedure (a list of variables that the procedure needs to use) and the "output" from the procedure (a list of variables that the procedure is to calculate or read in for the calling program). A variable (parameter) is listed only once in the heading, even if it is both an "input" and an "output" parameter. Within the body of the procedure these parameters are treated like any other variable. Note that the type of each parameter is given.

Procedures are declared after the variable declarations and before the main body of the program. They must physically appear in the program before they are called from either the main body or another procedure.

PROCEDURE CALL (INVOCATION)

A procedure is called (or invoked) by using the name of the procedure as a statement in the main program or the body of another procedure, with the variables it is to use in parentheses following the name. This is the syntax diagram of a procedure call:

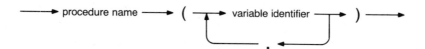

A procedure call results in the execution of the body of the called procedure. Control then continues with the statement following the call. As in our analogy, once the caller gets back the information he needs, he hangs up and goes on to other things.

PARAMETERS

The variables given to the procedure in the call are called *actual parameters*. The procedure is written using variable names, called *formal parameters*, listed in its heading.

When the procedure is executed, it uses the variables (*actual parameters*) given to it. How is this done? Remember, a variable identifier is assigned a location in memory. When a procedure is invoked, a list of the locations in the order in which they appear in the actual parameter list is given to the procedure. You might think of it as writing the list on a message board. (See Figure 6-2.) Procedures are written so that when one of the formal parameters is used in a statement in the procedure body, the proce-

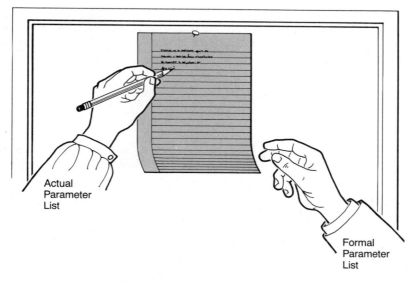

Figure 6-2. Parameter Passing

dure knows where to go to find the address. That is, the message board is queried for the correct location. How does it find the correct one? It does it by position. When a formal parameter is used, the procedure looks to see whether it is the first, second, etc. on its formal parameter list and then gets the first, second, etc. location from the message board.

These positional parameters must match in data type. An actual parameter must match the data type of the formal parameter in that position. Also there must be the same number of actual parameters in the call as there are formal parameters in the procedure heading. It is because the formal and actual parameters are matched by position that the names don't have to be the same. The usefulness of this positional matching will become apparent when a procedure is called more than once, but with different actual parameters used in each call.

These formal parameters are called variable or VAR parameters because addresses or locations are left on the message board. In Chapter 7 we will look at a second type of parameter, a value parameter, where only a copy of the value of a variable is given to the procedure, not the address of the variable.

Note that in the formal parameter list of the procedure, the type of each parameter must be listed. It is essential that the actual parameters agree in type with that specified for the formal parameters. The data type the procedure expects to find must be exactly what is actually there. This becomes increasingly important later when we look at more involved data types.

It is up to the programmer to be sure that the *formal* and *actual* parameter lists match up semantically. For example, if the call to PRINTRESULT had been

```
PRINTRESULT(SUM,COUNTER1);
```

the lists match up in type and number of parameters so there would be no syntax error, but the output would be incorrect. This is because the wrong parameters are matched up.

LOCAL VARIABLES

In PROCESSDATASET we needed a counter and a place to read in a value before adding it to the sum. These were defined in a VAR declaration within the procedure itself. These are called local variables. They are known only within the block in which they are declared. As far as the calling program is concerned, they don't exist. If you tried to print the contents of VALU from the main program, you would get a compile time error: UNDEFINED IDENTIFIER. The values of local variables are not saved when you leave a procedure, so every call to a procedure is independent of every other call to that same procedure. What this means is that local variables must be initialized each time within the procedure itself.

In our concert reservation analogy, any information that the clerk needed which didn't come from you and wasn't passed back to you would be a local variable.

program parameters - external files

```
PROGRAM TERMS(INPUT,OUTPUT);
VAR GLOBAL1,GLOBAL2 : INTEGER;
    GLOBAL3 : CHAR;
```

formal parameter list

```
PROCEDURE ONE(VAR POSITION1,POSITION2:INTEGER;
              VAR POSITION3:CHAR);
VAR LOCAL1 : INTEGER;
BEGIN    (* ONE *)
   .
   .
   .
END;     (* ONE *)

BEGIN    (* MAIN *)
   .
   .
   ONE(GLOBAL1,GLOBAL2,GLOBAL3);          (* procedure call to ONE *)
   .
   .
END.     (* MAIN *)
```

actual parameter list

EXTERNAL FILES

Up to now we have used the standard external files INPUT and OUTPUT. In interactive programs both INPUT and OUTPUT are defined as the terminal. In batch processing INPUT is often defined as the card reader and OUTPUT as the line printer. We listed these external files as parameters in the program heading.

```
PROGRAM EXAMPLE(INPUT,OUTPUT);
```

The standard functions and procedures EOF, EOLN, READ and READLN are used with input files, and WRITE and WRITELN are used with output files. Normally the external file must be explicitly indicated, such as

```
EOF(INPUT)
EOLN(INPUT)
READ(INPUT, parameters)
WRITE(OUTPUT, parameters).
```

Since INPUT and OUTPUT are used so frequently, if the filename is missing from these standard functions and procedures, then INPUT and OUTPUT are assumed (used by "default"). For example:

EOF	is equivalent to	EOF(INPUT)
READ(parameters)	is equivalent to	READ(INPUT,parameters)
WRITE(parameters)	is equivalent to	WRITE(OUTPUT,parameters)

All of our programs so far have used INPUT and OUTPUT by default.

INPUT and OUTPUT are predeclared files of type TEXT. In other words,

```
VAR INPUT , OUTPUT : TEXT;
```

is done automatically, so do not put these declarations in your programs. The type TEXT is also defined as FILE OF CHAR.

We can have many input and output files in our programs. Files are important in that they can provide permanent storage of data (usually on tape or disk). The amount of data stored can be greater than the memory space available to a program.

While a program is running, it can input (or output) a data value from (or to) a file. The file itself is not in memory. Since memory may be used for other programs after a program terminates, the output results can be saved in external files.

We are not limited to just one input and one output file. For example, we might want a program to combine the data in several files into one output file. This output file might then be used as an input file for another program.

In order to use other external files besides INPUT and OUTPUT, just list the filename in the program heading and declare the filename to be of type TEXT in the VAR declaration section. For example:

```
PROGRAM TEST(FILE1 , FILE2);
VAR FILE1 ,FILE2 : TEXT;
```

File names can be any legal identifier.

Before you use a file, it must be "opened" in the main body of the program. That is, the file must be initialized so the reading "pointer" (for an input file) or the writing "pointer" (for an output file) is positioned at the beginning of the file. The standard procedures that do this are RESET and REWRITE. (The system "opens" INPUT and OUTPUT for you automatically.)

RESET(filename)	—	opens an input file
REWRITE(filename)	—	opens an output file

INPUT is always an input file; OUTPUT is always an output file. Any other file that you use is what you last declared it to be. For example, you can write out intermediate results to a file and later read those results back in.

```
REWRITE(FILE1)                (* FILE1 is now an output file. You can only write to it *)
```

(* some process that writes to file FILE1 *)

```
RESET(FILE1)                                      (* move pointer to beginning of the file.
                                                     FILE1 can only be read from *)
```

(* some process that reads from FILE1 *)

```
REWRITE(FILE1)                          (* FILE1 is now an output file again *)
```

What happens if we RESET(INPUT)? Well, it is redundant at the beginning of the program since the system does it for you. If you do it after you have already read some data from INPUT, the pointer is just returned to the beginning of the file. Therefore you can read any file including INPUT as many times as you wish by just resetting the file each time. You *cannot* REWRITE(INPUT) or RESET(OUTPUT).

The following program reads all of the data values from the file INPUT and writes them to the file OUTPUT, and then does the same with the files DATA and RESULTS.

```
PROGRAM EXAMPLE(INPUT,OUTPUT,DATA,RESULTS);
VAR I,J:INTEGER;
    DATA,RESULTS:TEXT;                      (* declare file variables *)
BEGIN
  RESET(DATA);                                   (* open file DATA *)
  REWRITE(RESULTS);                              (* open file RESULTS *)
  WHILE NOT EOF DO
    BEGIN
      READLN(I);                             (* reading from INPUT *)
      WRITELN(I)                             (* writing to OUTPUT *)
    END;                              (* until EOF encountered in INPUT *)
  WHILE NOT EOF(DATA) DO
    BEGIN
      READLN(DATA,J);                        (* reading from DATA *)
      WRITELN(RESULTS,J)                     (* writing to RESULTS *)
    END                       (* until EOF encountered in DATA *)
END.
```

In the above example the first WHILE loop uses INPUT and OUTPUT (by default) and the second WHILE loop uses the files DATA (as an input file) and RESULTS (as an output file). Notice that the files INPUT and OUTPUT are automatically opened for reading and writing. Any other input files must be opened for reading by RESET(filename) and output files must be opened for writing by REWRITE(filename).

Here is a word of caution. In the above example, if the second WHILE loop had been

```
WHILE NOT EOF DO
   BEGIN
      READLN(DATA,J);
      WRITELN(RESULTS,J)
   END
```

then the EOF would have referred to the file INPUT. Consequently, we would have attempted to read past the end-of-file of file DATA because we never tested EOF(DATA). (This is a very common error.)

Look again at Program PAYROLL in Chapter 1 (for the last time, we promise!). Three files are used for input and output: INPUT, OUTPUT and PAYFILE. Only PAYFILE had to be declared in the VAR section and opened with the REWRITE statement. INPUT and OUTPUT are automatically declared and opened.

Program PAYROLL is an interactive program. INPUT and OUTPUT are the terminal. PAYFILE is an external file that is created and saved for listing on a printer at a later time.

As the program is executing, it WRITEs a prompt on the screen asking for what is to be keyed in at the console. The READLN statement following each WRITE reads those values in. Because the reads are READLNs, the person at the console must hit the <RETURN> key to signify the end-of-line.

This is called interactive computing because the program and the human are carrying on a conversation. The programmer has built into the program a prompt for the person at the console. The program prints on the screen

ENTER EMPLOYEE #:

The person at the console types in an identification number. The program compares the number just read in to zero (this is the condition in the WHILE loop). If it is greater than zero, the program prints on the screen

ENTER PAYRATE :

The person then types in a REAL value representing the hourly rate of pay. This interactive process continues until an identification number of zero is entered.

Within the loop, a copy of each employee identification number, rate of pay, hours and wages is written to file PAYFILE.

■ SAMPLE PROBLEM

Problem: Rewrite the program which simulated the game "Rock, paper and scissors" from Chapter 5 using procedures. There will be the following change: the input will come from two external files named FILE1 (first player's moves) and FILE2 (second player's moves).

Discussion: In order to show that there are many possible top-down solutions to a given problem, we will decompose this problem a little differently this time.

Input: A set of pairs of characters ('S', 'P', 'R'); one character from file FILE1; one character from file FILE2.

Output: For each pair of inputs: the game number and whether it is won by the first player, the second player or is a tie. Error message if a play is illegal.

MAIN MODULE   Level 0

```
GAMENUM is 0
WHILE more games DO
    Increment GAMENUM
    GETPLAY
    IF LEGAL
        THEN PROCESSPLAY
        ELSE PRINT 'PLAY NOT LEGAL'
PRINTOVERALLWINNER
```

GETPLAY   Level 1

```
READ FIRST
READ SECOND
PRINT FIRST, SECOND
CHECK FOR LEGAL PLAY
```

Note FIRST will come from file FILE1, SECOND will come from file FILE2

PROCESSPLAY

```
IF (FIRST = SECOND) THEN PRINT TIE MESSAGE
    ELSE IF (FIRST = 'P') AND (SECOND = 'R')
        THEN FIRSTWINS
        ELSE IF (FIRST = 'S') AND (SECOND = 'P')
            THEN FIRSTWINS
            ELSE IF (FIRST = 'R') AND (SECOND = 'S')
                THEN FIRSTWINS
                ELSE SECONDWINS
```

PRINTOVERALLWINNER

> IF WIN1 = WIN2
>   THEN PRINT 'GAME ENDS IN A TIE'
>   ELSE IF WIN1 > WIN2
>   THEN PRINT 'FIRST PLAYER WINS'
>   ELSE PRINT 'SECOND PLAYER WINS'

FIRSTWINS   **Level 2**

> increment WIN1
> PRINT 'FIRST PLAYER WINS GAME NUMBER ', GAMENUM

SECONDWINS

> increment WIN2
> PRINT 'SECOND PLAYER WINS GAME NUMBER ', GAMENUM

Design Tree Diagram:

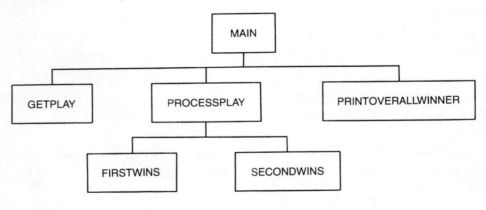

Let's examine in detail the interfaces among these modules. What values does the main program have that each module at level 1 needs? What values does each module at level 1 have that are needed elsewhere?

Module	Needs	Returns
GETPLAY		FIRST SECOND LEGAL
PROCESSPLAY	FIRST SECOND GAMENUM	WIN1 WIN2
PRINTOVERALLWINNER	WIN1 WIN2	
FIRSTWINS	GAMENUM	WIN1
SECONDWINS	GAMENUM	WIN2

Therefore, the *actual parameter* list for each procedure looks like this:

```
GETPLAY(FIRST, SECOND, LEGAL)
FIRSTWINS(GAMENUM, WIN1)
SECONDWINS(GAMENUM, WIN2)
PROCESSPLAY(GAMENUM, FIRST, SECOND, WIN1, WIN2)
PRINTOVERALLWINNER(WIN1, WIN2)
```

Note that PROCESSPLAY does not actually use WIN1 and WIN2. However, PRINTOVERALLWINNER needs these values which are calculated in FIRSTWINS and SECONDWINS. Therefore, WIN1 and WIN2 are returned to PROCESSPLAY from FIRSTWINS and SECONDWINS (see design tree diagram). PROCESSPLAY in turn returns WIN1 and WIN2 to the main program to be used in the call to PRINTOVERALLWINNER. These parameters are pass-through parameters. Their only purpose is to allow information to pass through them to another procedure.

Now the program can be coded. Remember, the *formal parameter* list of each procedure can use the same names or names different from the *actual parameter* list, as long as the names match the correct variable according to position.

```
PROGRAM GAME(OUTPUT, FILE1, FILE2);        (*This program simulates the
                children's game "rock, paper and scissors." Each game consists of inputs from
                two players. A winner is determined and printed. Individual scores are kept
                    and the overall winner is printed when there are no more games.*)
VAR FIRST, SECOND : CHAR;                           (*players' moves*)
    WIN1, WIN2,                                     (*players' wins*)
    GAMENUM : INTEGER;                              (*game count*)
    LEGAL : BOOLEAN;                                (*validity of moves*)
    FILE1, FILE2 : TEXT;                       (*files containing player moves*)

(*************************************************************)
```

```
PROCEDURE GETPLAY(VAR FIRST, SECOND : CHAR;
                    VAR LEGAL : BOOLEAN);
BEGIN   (*GETPLAY*)
   READLN(FILE1, FIRST);
   READLN(FILE2, SECOND);
   IF ((FIRST = 'S') OR (FIRST = 'P')        (* check for valid data *)
      OR (FIRST = 'R')) AND ((SECOND = 'S')
      OR (SECOND = 'P') OR (SECOND = 'R'))
      THEN LEGAL := TRUE
      ELSE LEGAL := FALSE
END;    (*GETPLAY*)


(*********************************************************)


PROCEDURE FIRSTWINS(VAR GAMENUM, WIN1 : INTEGER);
BEGIN   (*FIRSTWINS*)
   WIN1 := WIN1 + 1;
   WRITELN('FIRST PLAYER WINS GAME  ', GAMENUM:6)
END;    (*FIRSTWINS*)


(*********************************************************)


PROCEDURE SECONDWINS(VAR GAMENUM, WIN2 : INTEGER);
BEGIN   (*SECONDWINS*)
   WIN2 := WIN2 + 1;
   WRITELN('SECOND PLAYER WINS GAME ', GAMENUM:6)
END;    (*SECONDWINS*)


(*********************************************************)


PROCEDURE PROCESSPLAY(VAR GAMENUM : INTEGER;
                      VAR FIRST, SECOND : CHAR;
                      VAR WIN1, WIN2 : INTEGER);
BEGIN (*PROCESSPLAY*)
  IF (FIRST = SECOND)                        (* check for tie *)
     THEN WRITELN('GAME NUMBER ', GAMENUM:1, ' IS A TIE')
     ELSE IF (FIRST = 'P') AND (SECOND = 'R')      (* check
                                                for winner *)
           THEN FIRSTWINS(GAMENUM, WIN1)
           ELSE IF (FIRST = 'S') AND (SECOND = 'P')
                THEN FIRSTWINS(GAMENUM, WIN1)
                ELSE IF (FIRST = 'R') AND (SECOND = 'S')
                     THEN FIRSTWINS(GAMENUM, WIN1)
                     ELSE SECONDWINS(GAMENUM, WIN2)
END; (*PROCESSPLAY*)


(*********************************************************)


PROCEDURE PRINTOVERALLWINNER(VAR WIN1, WIN2 : INTEGER);
BEGIN  (*PRINTOVERALLWINNER*)
```

```
    IF WIN1 = WIN2                         (* check for overall tie *)
        THEN WRITELN('GAME ENDS IN A TIE')
        ELSE IF WIN1 > WIN2                (* check for overall winner *)
                THEN WRITELN('FIRST PLAYER WINS')
                ELSE WRITELN('SECOND PLAYER WINS')
END;   (*PRINTOVERALLWINNER*)

(*************************************************************)
BEGIN   (* GAME *)
    RESET(FILE1);                          (* open FILE1 *)
    RESET(FILE2);                          (* open FILE2 *)
    WIN1 := 0;
    WIN2 := 0;
    GAMENUM := 0;
    WHILE NOT EOF(FILE1) AND NOT EOF(FILE2) DO      (* while more
                                                        moves *)
        BEGIN
            GAMENUM := GAMENUM + 1;
            GETPLAY(FIRST, SECOND, LEGAL);          (* get moves *)
            IF LEGAL                    (* check if data is valid *)
                THEN PROCESSPLAY(GAMENUM, FIRST, SECOND,
                                   WIN1, WIN2)
                ELSE WRITELN(' PLAY ILLEGAL')
        END;
    PRINTOVERALLWINNER(WIN1, WIN2)
END.   (* GAME *)
```

Note that the expression in the WHILE loop had to be a compound condition. We want to stop if either file runs out of data. If we check only one, and the other file is shorter because of an error, then we would encounter a run-time read error: TRIED TO READ PAST EOF.

Note also that the fieldwidth specifications for GAMENUM are not all the same. In FIRSTWINS and SECONDWINS a fieldwidth of 6 is specified (a game number greater than 999999 is not expected). Both the strings 'FIRST PLAYER WINS GAME ' and 'SECOND PLAYER WINS GAME ' have one blank added at the end for spacing. The first string has a second blank embedded at the end to make them the same length. This results in the game numbers in these output messages being in columnar form. (See example output below.) In PROCESSPLAY a fieldwidth of 1 is used for GAMENUM to force the game number to be evenly spaced in the output message. Any game number greater than one digit in length will automatically get the number of columns it needs.

```
FIRST PLAYER WINS GAME      2
SECOND PLAYER WINS GAME     3
GAME NUMBER 4 IS A TIE
SECOND PLAYER WINS GAME     5
  •
  •
```

```
GAME NUMBER 120 IS A TIE
SECOND PLAYER WINS GAME    121
FIRST PLAYER WINS GAME     122
   ◆
   ◆
```

TESTING AND DEBUGGING

The errors that occur with the use of procedures are usually due to incorrect interfaces between the main program and a procedure or between two procedures. This section shows how to design these interfaces in order to avoid bugs.

For each module listed in the main program make a list of the following items:

1. What information (data values) the main program has that the procedure needs.
2. What information (data values) the procedure will produce that the main program will need later.

The identifiers used to reference the values in (1) and (2) become the items in the *actual parameter* list in the procedure call. The *formal parameter* list for the procedure should list the same items in the same order. Usually the identifiers used to reference the items in the two lists will be the same. This makes it easier for humans to read the code. However, the items are actually matched up by their position in the *formal* and *actual parameter* lists, not by spelling.

The *actual parameters* have been declared in the CONST or VAR sections of the main program or the calling procedure. The procedure must also know the type of the variables it is to work with, so this information must be included in the procedure heading. All other variables or constants that the procedure needs to use are local and must be declared in the CONST or VAR section of the procedure itself.

Now repeat the process for each module (procedure) which references a module at a lower level. Notice that the module at the higher level should specify the interfaces for each module it references at the next level (higher level meaning higher level in the design tree, even though that level will have a lower number).

Testing and Debugging Hints

1. Follow the documentation guidelines carefully when writing procedures. As your programs get more complex, it is increasingly important to adhere to the documentation and formatting standards. Label the main "BEGIN-END" pair of each procedure with the procedure

name. If the procedure name does not completely define the process being done, describe that process in comments. Use comments to explain the purpose of all local variables.*

2. Be sure to put a semi-colon following the procedure heading.
3. Be sure the *formal* parameter list gives the types of each parameter.
4. Be sure the *formal* parameter list matches the *actual* parameter list in number, type of variables and order.
5. If you are using external files other than INPUT and OUTPUT, be sure to include the file name with all input and output statements. Remember that all references to reading in values (READ, READLN, EOF, EOLN) refer to INPUT if you do not put the file name as a parameter. You may be reading from a file you have called DATA, but if you use EOF or EOLN without DATA as a parameter, it is the file INPUT which is tested.

Summary

Pascal has the facility to let you write your program in functional modules. Therefore the structure of your program can parallel your top-down design. Your main program (what is between the BEGIN-END. pair) can look exactly like the Level 0 of your top-down design. You do this by writing each functional module as a procedure. Your main program simply executes these procedures in logical sequence.

Communication between the calling program and the procedure is handled by the use of two lists of identifiers: the *formal parameter* list (which includes the type of each identifier) which is in the PROCEDURE heading, and the *actual parameter* list which is in the calling statement. These lists of identifiers must agree in length, position and type.

Part of the top-down design process is determining what data must be given to a lower level module and what information must be received back. The module interfaces defined become the formal and actual parameter lists and the module name becomes a call to the procedure.

External files are the way our programs communicate with the outside world. INPUT and OUTPUT are predefined files of type TEXT. When we don't specify a file name in a READ or WRITE statement, INPUT and OUTPUT are assumed. We can define and access other files which allows us to get input from more than one source and write output which does not go to the printer or screen. This means, for example, output from one program can be input to another in the form of a file.

---

* We have chosen not to comment procedures as much as good style dictates because the discussion of the top-down design directly precedes the code. In addition, we wished to make the programs as compact as possible for the purposes of this book.

Exercises

1. Write a top-down design for exercise question 1 from Chapter 5. Convert your design into a structured Pascal program using procedures.

2. a. Write a procedure which adds up the even integers from N to M. The result is left in ANSWER.
   b. Write a statement to invoke your procedure which sums the integers from 16 to 26.

3. a. Write a procedure which reads and sums ten positive values. If a negative value is encountered, stop the process and set ALLPOSITIVE to FALSE.
   b. Write an invoking statement for the procedure of a.

4. Define the following:

   procedure call
   parameter list
   positional parameter
   formal parameter
   actual parameter
   variable parameter
   local variable

5. Show what is printed by this program. Use this data: 2 4 6 8

```
PROGRAM EXER(INPUT,OUTPUT);
VAR A,B,C,SUM:INTEGER;

PROCEDURE ADD(VAR X,A,Z,SUM:INTEGER);
BEGIN
   READ(X,A,Z);
   SUM := X + A + Z
END;

BEGIN
   ADD(A,B,C,SUM);
   WRITELN(A,B,C,SUM)
END.
```

Pre-Test

1. Since a procedure is a subprogram contained within a Pascal program, it may not contain input or output instructions and may not contain other subprograms. T F

2. The parameters listed in the procedure heading are called FORMAL parameters. The parameters listed in the invoking statement are called ACTUAL parameters. T F

3. Write a procedure named INCREMENT, with one variable parameter of type INTEGER, which adds 15 to the value received in the parameter and returns the new value to the calling program.

4. a. Write a procedure that reads in data values (integer HEARTRATEs), until a NORMAL heartrate (between 60 and 80) is read or EOF becomes TRUE. NORMAL is a parameter that returns TRUE if a normal heartrate is read or FALSE if <eof> is encountered.

   b. Write the invoking statement for your procedure. (Use the same variable names as in the procedure).

5. a. Write a procedure that reads grades and counts the number of failing grades (SCORE <= 59) in a set of N grades. N is an input parameter, and the number of failing grades is an output parameter of the procedure.

   b. Write an invoking statement for your procedure. (Use NP and NFAIL as your ACTUAL parameters.)

6. Show what is printed by the following program.

```
PROGRAM PRETEST(INPUT,OUTPUT);
        CONST TEN = 10;
        VAR   A, B, C : INTEGER;

        PROCEDURE TEST(VAR  Z,X,A : INTEGER);
        BEGIN
          READLN(Z,X,A);
          A := Z * X + A
        END;

        BEGIN
          TEST(A,B,C);
          B := B + TEN;
          WRITELN(' THE ANSWERS ARE ', B, C, A, TEN)
        END.
```

Assume this data: 3 2 4

Parameters 7

Goals

To be able to do the following tasks, given a Pascal program with procedures:
- *determine whether each parameter is a VAR or VALUE parameter*
- *determine whether a variable is being referenced globally*
- *determine which variables are local variables*
- *determine which variables are defined in each block*

To be able to do the following tasks, given a top-down design of a problem:
- *determine what the* formal *and* actual *parameter lists should be for each module*
- *determine which* formal parameters *should be* VAR *parameters and which should be* VALUE *parameters*
- *determine what local variables should be declared for each module*
- *to be able to code the program correctly*

To be able to determine the scope of each variable in a program.

To be able to determine the contents of variables during execution of a program containing procedures.

To understand and avoid undesirable side effects.

MULTIPLE CALLS TO THE SAME PROCEDURE

In Chapter 6 procedures were introduced as a way of making your program reflect your top-down design. There is a second major reason for using procedures. If there is a task which must be done in more than one place in your program, you can make it a procedure and call it wherever you need it. Let's look at an example which illustrates this use of procedures.

■ SAMPLE PROBLEM

Problem: The regional sales manager for the Greenley Department Stores has just come into town. He wants to see the department-by-department comparison of the two Greenley stores in town. These comparisons are to be generated monthly in the form of bar graphs for use as a management tool. The daily sales for each department are kept on each store's accounting files. Data on each store file is in the form

Department ID#
N—number of business days for the department
Daily sales for day 1
Daily sales for day 2

.

.

.

Daily sales for day N
Department ID#
N—number of business days for the department
Daily sales for N days

and the required output is in the form

```
STORE SALES IN 1,000s OF DOLLARS
  #    0          5          10          15          20          25
       |· · · · · · · · ·|· · · · · · · · ·|· · · · · · · · ·|· · · · · · · · ·|· · · · · · · · ·|
       DEPT 1030
  1    ***********************
       DEPT 1030
  2    ************************************************
       DEPT 1210
  1    ****************************************************************
       DEPT 1210
  2    ********************************************************
       DEPT 2040
  1    ************************************************************
       DEPT 2040
  2    *****************************
```

Discussion: Reading the input data from both files is straightforward. We need to RESET the files (let's call them FILE1 and FILE2) and read a department ID, the number of business days and the following daily sales for that department. After processing each department, we can read the data for the next department and so on until we run out of departments (EOF becomes TRUE). Since the process is the same for reading FILE1 and FILE2, we can use one procedure for reading both files. All we have to do is pass the filename as a parameter to the procedure. We want total sales for each department, so this procedure will have to sum the daily sales for a department as they are read in.

A procedure can be used to print the output heading. Another procedure can print out each department's sales for the month in graphic form.

Input: 2 data files (FILE1,FILE2) each containing

> ID   - department ID# (integer)
> N   - # of business days (integer)
> SALES - daily sales (real)

repeated for each department.

Output: Bar graph showing total sales for each department.

Assumptions: Each file is in order by department IDs.
There are the same departments in each store.
There is one piece of data per line.

MAIN MODULE   **Level 0**

```
PRINTHEADER
WHILE more data DO
    GETDATA for FILE1
    GETDATA for FILE2
    PRINTDATA for store 1 dept.
    PRINTDATA for store 2 dept.
```

'more data': an EOF loop.
Read and sum dept. sales.

Print dept. sales in graph form

PRINTHEADER   **Level 1**

```
WRITELN title
WRITELN head
WRITELN scale
```

GETDATA

```
READ department ID
READ N
WHILE more daily sales DO
    READ sales
    Add sales to dept. sales
```

GETDATA receives a filename and returns the dept. sales for the month and the dept. ID.

'more daily sales': a count controlled loop.

PRINTDATA

```
WRITELN dept. ID
WRITE store number
WHILE more dept. sales DO
    WRITE '*'
    Decrement sales by $500
```

PRINTDATA receives the dept. ID, the store number and the dept. sales.

'more dept. sales': count controlled loop. (Notice it's a different sort of count.) Each star, '*', represents $500 on the bar graph.

This top-down design required several passes through the design process and several mistakes to arrive at the design you see here. So don't think that you should be able to come up with a perfect top-down design every time, first try. Here is the tree diagram for this design.

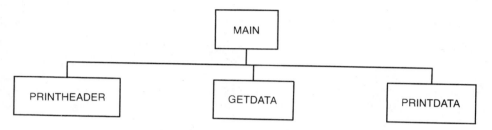

The following is the Pascal program which parallels our design.

```
PROGRAM GRAPH(FILE1,FILE2,OUTPUT);  (* Program to generate bar graphs
                                       of monthly sales by department *)
VAR ID : INTEGER;                            (* dept. ID# *)
    SALES1,SALES2 :REAL;                     (* dept. sales *)
    FILE1,FILE2 : TEXT;                      (* data files *)


(*************************************************************)

PROCEDURE PRINTHEADER;
BEGIN   (*PRINTHEADER*)
   WRITELN('BAR GRAPH COMPARING DEPARTMENTS OF STORE#1 AND',
           ' STORE#2');
   WRITELN;
   WRITELN('STORE   SALES IN 1,000s OF DOLLARS');
   WRITELN('  #     0          5          10          15',
           '         20          25');
   WRITELN('        I..........I..........I..........I',
           '..........I..........I')
END;    (*PRINTHEADER*)


(*************************************************************)

PROCEDURE GETDATA(VAR DATAFILE:TEXT;VAR DEPTID:INTEGER;
                  VAR DEPTSALES:REAL);
VAR  N,I : INTEGER;                  (* N is the number of business days *)
     SALE : REAL;
BEGIN   (*GETDATA*)
  READ(DATAFILE,DEPTID,N);
  DEPTSALES := 0.0;
  I := 1;
  WHILE I <= N DO                    (* WHILE more daily sales *)
     BEGIN                           (* READ and sum sales *)
        READ(DATAFILE,SALE);
```

```
        DEPTSALES := DEPTSALES + SALE;
        I := I + 1
     END;
  READLN(DATAFILE)
END;    (*GETDATA*)
```

(***)

```
PROCEDURE PRINTDATA(DEPTID,STORENUM:INTEGER;
                    DEPTSALES:REAL);
BEGIN  (*PRINTDATA*)
  WRITELN('       DEPT ',DEPTID:1);
  WRITE(STORENUM:3,'        ');
  WHILE DEPTSALES > 250 DO
     BEGIN
        WRITE('*');                        (* print a '*' for each $500 of sales*)
        DEPTSALES := DEPTSALES - 500
     END;
  WRITELN
END;   (*PRINTDATA*)
```

(***)

```
BEGIN  (*GRAPH*)
  RESET(FILE1);
  RESET(FILE2);
  PRINTHEADER;
  WHILE NOT EOF(FILE1) AND NOT EOF(FILE2) DO
     BEGIN
        GETDATA(FILE1,ID,SALES1);
        GETDATA(FILE2,ID,SALES2);
        WRITELN;
        PRINTDATA(ID,1,SALES1);
        PRINTDATA(ID,2,SALES2)
     END
END.   (*GRAPH*)
```

The main program of GRAPH not only reflects our top-down design, but calls both GETDATA and PRINTDATA twice. The result is a shorter and more readable program than one in which the code for each procedure is repeated.

■

VAR/VALUE PARAMETERS

In Chapter 6 we described a VAR parameter as a parameter whose *location* is put on the message board. (VAR parameters are said to be passed by reference or address.) On the other hand, a *value* parameter is a parameter where a *copy* of the value of the *actual parameter* is put on the message board. This means that a procedure cannot change the contents of an actual parameter passed as a *value* parameter; it can only use the copy. If a procedure does contain a statement which redefines the value, the copy is changed, not the original.

Value parameters are distinguished from VAR parameters by not having the VAR before the identifier in the *formal parameter* list. The syntax diagram for a procedure heading is expanded to the following form.

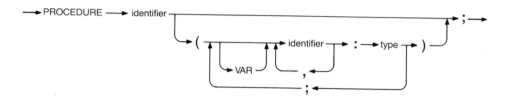

The *actual parameter* for a VAR parameter can only be a variable. The *actual parameter* for a value parameter can be an expression (which includes variables, constants and arithmetic operators). The expression will be evaluated and the result put on the message board.

Imagine what would happen, however, if the expression A*B were passed as a VAR parameter. What location would you put on the message board?

Program GRAPH uses both VAR and *value* parameters. The communication interface of a procedure's parameter list conveys more information to the reader when VAR parameters are used for input/output and only *value* parameters are used for input.

Let's examine the interfaces to the procedures of program GRAPH.

```
PROCEDURE PRINTHEADER;
```
       PRINTHEADER needs no parameters. It is self-contained.

```
PROCEDURE GETDATA(VAR DATAFILE:TEXT;VAR DEPTID:INTEGER;
                  VAR DEPTSALES:REAL);
```
       Since GETDATA receives a filename, it can be used to read from any appropriate file. (Note that a file parameter *must be passed as a VAR parameter.*) DEPTID is read in and returned to the main program so it must be a VAR parameter. The department sales are read in, summed in DEPTSALES, and returned to the main program, so DEPTSALES must be a VAR parameter.

```
PROCEDURE PRINTDATA(DEPTID,STORENUM:INTEGER;
                    DEPTSALES:REAL);
```
       PRINTDATA only needs certain values for printing, so all of its parameters are *value* parameters. VAR parameters must have a variable

for an actual parameter, but *value* parameters can have any expression for an actual parameter. In the call to PRINTDATA, variables were used to pass the values of DEPTID and DEPTSALES, but a constant (a 1 or a 2 in this case) was passed as the value for STORENUM.

Use the following rules when determining if a parameter should be VAR or *value*.

1. If the procedure reads in values or calculates values that the invoking procedure (or program) needs to use, these parameters should be VAR parameters.
2. If the procedure reads in values or calculates values that the invoking procedure (or program) needs to give to another procedure, these parameters need to be VAR parameters.
3. File names passed as parameters must be VAR parameters.
4. All other parameters should be *value*. (One more exception will be given in Chapter 9.)

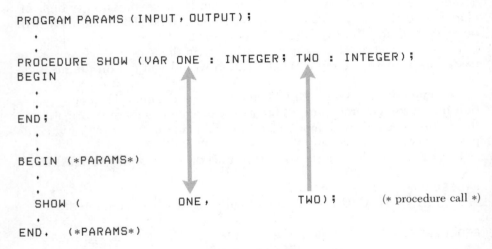

```
PROGRAM PARAMS (INPUT, OUTPUT);
   .
   .
PROCEDURE SHOW (VAR ONE : INTEGER; TWO : INTEGER);
BEGIN
   .
   .
END;
   .
   .
BEGIN (*PARAMS*)
   .
   .
   SHOW (           ONE,          TWO);      (* procedure call *)
   .
END.   (*PARAMS*)
```

VAR parameters return a value, *value* parameters do not. If the invoking program needs to have access to values read in or computed in a procedure, either for itself or to pass to another procedure, the parameters must be VAR parameters. Otherwise they should be *value* parameters.

■ SAMPLE PROBLEM

Problem: Write a program that reads in names in the form of first name, blank(s), last name and prints them out last name, comma, blank, first initial, period. There may be leading blanks and any number of blanks between the first name and last name in your input.

Discussion: This would be an easy task to do by hand. We would read the two names and write down the second one, followed by a comma. We would then go back and write down the first letter of the first name, followed by a period. This is basically how we will program the problem. The hard part comes in trying to simulate "reading the two names." The program will have to read one character at a time, examine it and decide what to do with it.

Let's analyze this process by going character by character through the input by hand. Starting from left to right we are going to see a blank or a letter. If it is a blank, we skip over it and get another character. If it is a letter, we need to save it since it is the first initial.

Once we have the first initial, we are not interested in the rest of the first name. So we just continue to read until we reach the last name. How do we recognize the beginning of the last name? Well, it is the first letter after the blank(s) following the first name. Once we find the last name, we continue reading a character and printing it until we find a blank. Then we print a comma followed by a blank and the initial of the first name, which we saved, followed by a period.

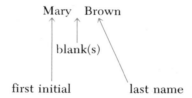

Here is an example of possible input/output:

Input data: Mary   Brown
            John   Smith
Output: Brown, M.
        Smith, J.

Now that we have analyzed the problem, we can do our top-down design.

Input: First name '▢' Last name

Output: Last name ',' '▢' First initial '.'

Assumptions: Input data is valid and has one name per line

MAIN MODULE   **Level 0**

```
WHILE more data DO
    GETINITIAL
    PRINTLAST
    PRINTINITIAL
```

The first letter of the first name
must be returned from GETINITIAL and
given to PRINTINITIAL.

GETINITIAL   **Level 1**

```
SKIPBLANKS
SAVEINITIAL
```

SKIPBLANKS will recognize the first
letter and return it to be saved.

PRINTLAST

```
FINDLAST
PRINT
```

FINDLAST will recognize first
letter of last name and return
it to PRINT.

PRINTINITIAL

```
WRITE(INITIAL)
```

SKIPBLANKS   **Level 2**

```
GETCH
WHILE CH = BLANK
    GETCH
```

CH is the name of the character
we are looking at.

FINDLAST

```
SKIPFIRST
SKIPBLANKS
```

PRINT

```
WHILE CH <> BLANK
    WRITE(CH)
    GETCH
```

SAVEINITIAL

```
INITIAL = CH
```

SKIPFIRST   **Level 3**

```
WHILE CH <> BLANK
    GETCH
```

GETCH

```
READ(CH)
```

When Pascal is reading into a CHAR
variable, one character only is read.
Note that a blank is a character.

This design goes to four levels. SAVEINITIAL, PRINTINITIAL and
GETCH are only one line of code each. Let's not make them procedures
but instead put that line of code in the level above. The tree diagram would
look like this:

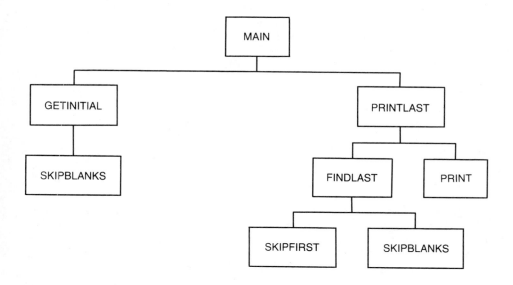

Before coding this problem, we need to spell out clearly the module or
procedure interfaces.

MAIN PROGRAM: Must receive back from GETINITIAL the first letter of the
first name.

GETINITIAL: Must receive back from SKIPBLANKS the first non-blank character.

PRINTLAST: Returns nothing to MAIN PROGRAM but must get from FINDLAST the first character of the last name.

FINDFIRST: Returns to PRINTLAST the first non-blank character after the blanks between the first and last names.

SKIPFIRST Just reads until a blank is found, so needs nothing and produces no output.

SKIPBLANKS: Needs no input but does send back the first non-blank it encounters.

PRINT: Needs as input first letter of last name but does not send anything back.

Now we can begin to code our program. Does it matter in what physical order the procedures go? Yes, a procedure must be declared before it is used or referenced by another procedure. Therefore, the lowest level modules should be declared first. Within this constraint however, it improves readability to have them in logical order. A good ordering here would be:

> SKIPBLANKS
> GETINITIAL
> PRINTLAST
>> FINDLAST
>>> SKIPFIRST
>> PRINT

The following is the Pascal program which parallels our design.

```
PROGRAM TRANSPOSE(INPUT,OUTPUT);        (* This program reformats names
                      to be in the form of last name, comma, blank, first initial, period. *)
CONST BLANK = ' ';
VAR INITIAL : CHAR;
(*****************************************************)
PROCEDURE SKIPBLANKS(VAR CH : CHAR);
BEGIN   (*SKIPBLANKS*)
    READ(CH);
    WHILE CH = BLANK DO
        READ(CH)
END;    (*SKIPBLANKS*)
(*****************************************************)
```

```
PROCEDURE GETINITIAL(VAR INITIAL : CHAR);
VAR CH : CHAR;
BEGIN  (*GETINITIAL*)
    SKIPBLANKS(CH);
    INITIAL := CH
END;   (*GETINITIAL*)
(*********************************************************)
PROCEDURE PRINTLAST;
VAR CH : CHAR;

  PROCEDURE FINDLAST(VAR CH : CHAR);

    PROCEDURE SKIPFIRST;
    VAR CH : CHAR;
    BEGIN  (*SKIPFIRST*)
        READ(CH);
        WHILE CH <> BLANK DO
            READ(CH)
    END;   (*SKIPFIRST*)

  BEGIN  (*FINDLAST*)
      SKIPFIRST;
      SKIPBLANKS(CH)
  END;   (*FINDLAST*)

  PROCEDURE PRINT(CH : CHAR);
  BEGIN  (*PRINT*)
      WHILE CH <> BLANK DO
          BEGIN
              WRITE(CH);
              IF NOT EOLN
                  THEN READ(CH)
                  ELSE CH := BLANK
          END
  END;   (*PRINT*)

BEGIN  (*PRINTLAST*)
    FINDLAST(CH);
    PRINT(CH)
END;   (*PRINTLAST*)
(*********************************************************)
BEGIN  (*TRANSPOSE*)
    WHILE NOT EOF DO
        BEGIN
            GETINITIAL(INITIAL);
            PRINTLAST;
            WRITELN(', ', INITIAL,'.');
            READLN
        END;
END.   (*TRANSPOSE*)
```

Notice that Program TRANSPOSE has several procedures nested within procedures: SKIPFIRST nested in FINDLAST; PRINT and FINDLAST nested in PRINTLAST. This is a matter of style in this program, and more will be said about nesting procedures later in this chapter.

This problem may seem too simple to need such an involved structure. However, we have set it up this way to illustrate several concepts.

Let's look at each procedure heading in this example and analyze its *formal parameter* list.

`PROCEDURE SKIPBLANKS(VAR CH : CHAR);`
   Since SKIPBLANKS returns the first non-blank character it sees, it must have a VAR parameter.

`PROCEDURE GETINITIAL(VAR INITIAL : CHAR);`
   INITIAL is sent back to the MAIN PROGRAM so it must be a VAR parameter.

`PROCEDURE PRINTLAST;`
   PRINTLAST has no parameters at all. It needs no input and sends back no output.

`PROCEDURE FINDLAST(VAR CH : CHAR);`
   CH must be a VAR parameter because it locates the first letter of the last name. This letter will be given to PRINT.

`PROCEDURE SKIPFIRST;`
   SKIPFIRST skips over the characters of the first name looking for a blank. Since it returns only when it finds a blank, it needs no parameters.

`PROCEDURE PRINT(CH : CHAR);`
   PRINT needs CH because it contains the first letter of the last name at the time the procedure is called. CH is redefined within the procedure. The calling program, however, does not need to know what its last value is, so it is made a *value* parameter.

Here is a helpful technique for learning to use VAR/*value* parameters. You can embed comments in the *formal* parameter lists indicating if a parameter is strictly an input parameter or an output parameter, or if it is both an input and output parameter. For example, the procedure headings in Program TRANSPOSE would look as follows:

```
PROCEDURE SKIPBLANKS(VAR CH (*OUT*) : CHAR);
PROCEDURE GETINITIAL(VAR INITIAL (*OUT*) : CHAR);
PROCEDURE FINDLAST(VAR CH (*OUT*) : CHAR);
PROCEDURE PRINT( CH (*IN*) : CHAR);
```

Of course, *value* parameters are always input parameters. The VAR parameters are used as output parameters in Program TRANSPOSE, but VAR parameters can also be both input *and* output parameters. Here is another example:

```
PROCEDURE EXAMPLE( CH (*IN*) : CHAR; VAR A (*IN/OUT*),
                   B (*IN/OUT*), SUM (*OUT*) : INTEGER);
```

LOCAL/GLOBAL VARIABLES

Local variables are those variables defined in the VAR section of a procedure. These are variables the procedure needs for itself. Counter variables are examples of variables often needed only within a procedure.

In Program TRANSPOSE, GETINITIAL needed a place to read a character into, so a local variable CH was defined. Procedure PRINTLAST also needed a place to read a character into. A local variable CH was defined here also. The fact that they both used the same identifier causes no problem because the compiler associates that identifier with the local variable inside the procedure.

When a procedure is called, local variables (if any) are defined; i.e., a location or cell is associated with an identifier. When the procedure has finished, immediately before returning control to the calling program, those cells are marked as available again. Since a cell for a local variable is arbitrarily assigned each time a procedure is called, there is no guarantee that a local variable will be assigned the same location the next time it is called. Therefore, local variables must be initialized within the procedure itself.

So much for local variables. What are *global* variables? Any variable or constant declared in the MAIN PROGRAM is known by any procedure which does not declare a variable or constant with the same name. In Program TRANSPOSE, BLANK is a *global* constant. It is defined in the MAIN PROGRAM and used in SKIPBLANKS, SKIPFIRST and PRINT.

```
PROGRAM EXAMPLE(INPUT,OUTPUT);
VAR  A,B : INTEGER;

PROCEDURE ONE;
VAR  B : REAL;
BEGIN
  B := 2.3;
```

```
      WRITELN('A = ',A);
      WRITELN('B = ',B)
END;

BEGIN   (*EXAMPLE*)
  A := 4;
  ONE
END.    (*EXAMPLE*)
```

In this example, Procedure ONE references the global variable A but redefines B as a local variable, thus "hiding" the global B. Here is a diagram of parameter and local variable use:

PROCEDURE EXAMPLE(A,B:INTEGER;VAR LIMIT:BOOLEAN;X:REAL;

VAR C1,C2:CHAR);

VAR I,CT1:INTEGER;
    SUM:REAL;

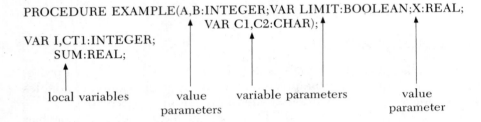

| local variables | value parameters | variable parameters | value parameter |

SCOPE RULES

Any variable or constant defined in a block is known (called global) to any procedure within that block. Let's look at Program TRANSPOSE in terms of blocks defined (Figure 7-1), and see just what this means.

In this example INITIAL is a variable known or available to every procedure since it is defined in the MAIN PROGRAM. The local variable CH defined in PRINTLAST is global to FINDLAST, SKIPFIRST and PRINT since FINDLAST, SKIPFIRST and PRINT are defined within Procedure PRINTLAST. The rules that govern what identifiers are known where are called *scope* rules. The *scope* of the variable CH defined in PRINTLAST includes FINDLAST, SKIPFIRST and PRINT.

Why, then, do we use parameter lists? Because good programming practice dictates that communication between modules of our program should be explicitly stated. This limits the possibility of one module accidentally interfering with another. In other words, each procedure is given only what it needs to know. "Good" programs are written using this principle. There are a few cases where globally referenced constants and variables are okay. The use of the constant BLANK in Program TRANSPOSE is one such example. In later chapters we will point out other cases where global referencing is acceptable.

If the same identifier is declared in a procedure and in the main program, there is no confusion. The declaring of a *local* variable keeps the procedure from knowing about the *global* variable with the same name. We call this "name precedence".

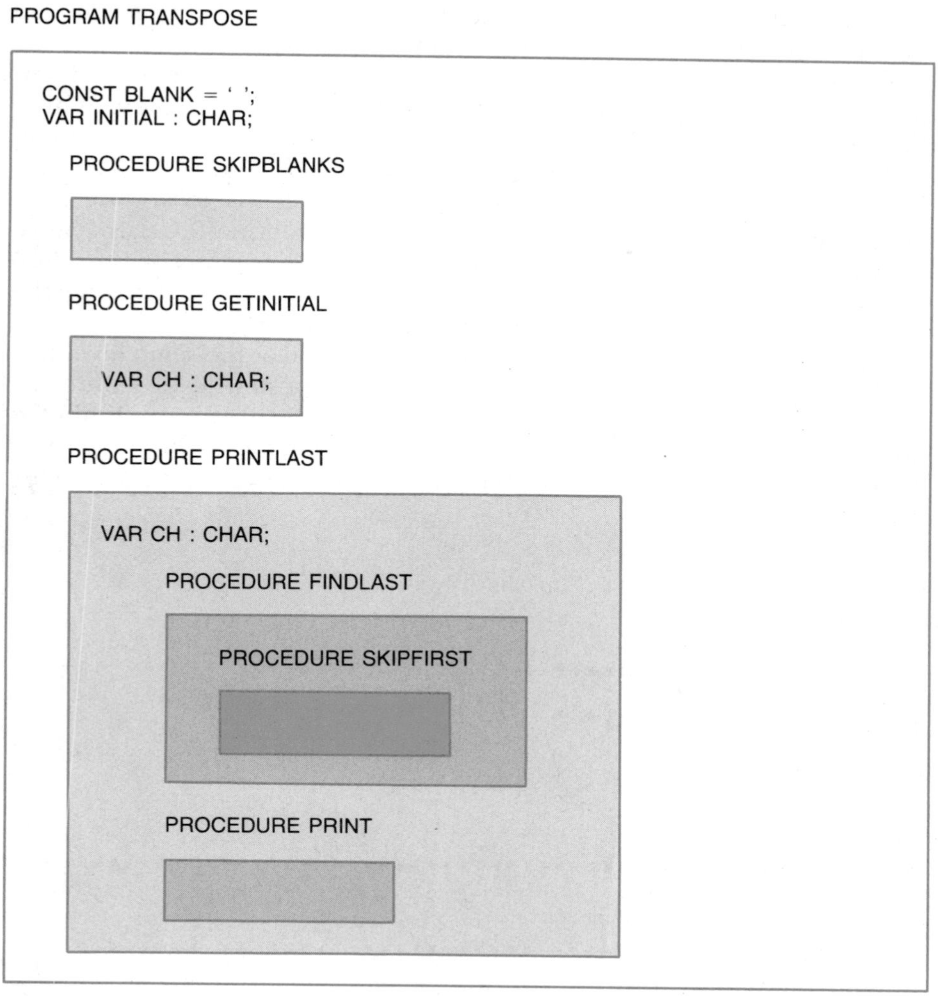

PROGRAM TRANSPOSE

Figure 7-1. Scope Diagram

For example, Program SUMDATA in Chapter 6 needed two counter variables. We called them COUNTER1 and COUNTER2. We could have called them both simply COUNTER because the identifier COUNTER in the MAIN PROGRAM has been assigned to a memory cell before the program begins executing. When a procedure is executed, the first thing that happens is the assignment of local variables to locations or addresses in memory. The Procedure PROCESSDATASET would use the local variable COUNTER and not even know that another one existed.

When an identifier is used in a procedure, the compiler first looks to see if the identifier is a local variable, then looks to see if it is a *formal* parameter. Only if it doesn't find the identifier listed in either place does it look to see if it is declared in the MAIN PROGRAM. If procedures are nested, the compiler works upward through each level of nesting, looking for the identifier declaration, until the compiler either finds it or gives the compile-time error: UNDECLARED IDENTIFIER. (Note: The scope rules apply to any identifier—variables and constants as well as procedure names.)

In Program TRANSPOSE the identifier CH is used as a local variable in both Procedure GETINITIAL and Procedure PRINTLAST. CH is a separate variable in each procedure, and neither CH has any effect on the other. Also, the scope rules prohibit a procedure from being able to reference the variables local to another procedure at the same level.

Multiple declarations of an identifier are not legal at the same level in a block, but an identifier can be redefined at any nested level within the block. The scope rules tell us that an identifier can be used only within the block where it is declared, and it is not known outside of that block.

Here is an example to demonstrate the scope rules.

```
PROGRAM EXAMPLE(INPUT, OUTPUT);
VAR A1 : INTEGER;
    A2 : BOOLEAN;
(**********************************************************)
PROCEDURE BLOCK3(P1 : INTEGER; VAR P2 : BOOLEAN);
VAR D1, D2 : INTEGER;
BEGIN (*BLOCK3*)
    .
    .
END;   (*BLOCK3*)
(**********************************************************)
PROCEDURE BLOCK1;
VAR B1 ,B2 : INTEGER;
    (**********************************************************)
    PROCEDURE BLOCK2;
    VAR C1, C2 : INTEGER;
    BEGIN (*BLOCK2*)
        .
        .
    END;   (*BLOCK2*)
    (**********************************************************)
BEGIN (* BLOCK1 *)
    .
    .
END;   (*BLOCK1*)
(**********************************************************)
BEGIN (*MAIN*)
    .
    .
END.   (*MAIN*)
```

PROGRAM EXAMPLE

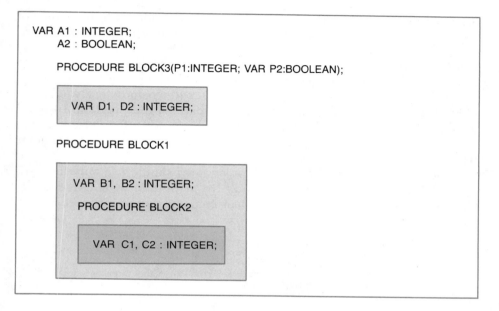

VAR A1 : INTEGER;
    A2 : BOOLEAN;

PROCEDURE BLOCK3(P1:INTEGER; VAR P2:BOOLEAN);

VAR D1, D2 : INTEGER;

PROCEDURE BLOCK1

VAR B1, B2 : INTEGER;

PROCEDURE BLOCK2

VAR C1, C2 : INTEGER;

Figure 7-2.

The following are comments relating to scope within Program EXAM-PLE. (See Figure 7-2.)

A1 and A2 are global variables, accessible to all parts of Program EXAM-PLE. However, the identifiers A1 and A2 can be redefined in any block within the program such as BLOCK1, BLOCK2 or BLOCK3 (or all three).

BLOCK2 can access any global variable or block in the program. BLOCK2 can call BLOCK3, but BLOCK3 cannot call BLOCK2 (it is hidden in BLOCK1). In addition, BLOCK3 cannot call BLOCK1 because BLOCK1 is declared after BLOCK3.

EXAMPLE, BLOCK1 and BLOCK3 cannot reference C1 or C2 in BLOCK2 (C1 and C2 only exist when BLOCK2 is called). BLOCK2 can reference A1 or A2 or B1 or B2 but not D1 or D2 or P1 or P2. (The variables in BLOCK3 only exist when it is called.)

B1 and B2 are local to BLOCK1 but are global to BLOCK2.

When BLOCK3 is called, P1 is actually a local variable with an initial value passed through the parameter list. P2 can be thought of as a "synonym" for its actual parameter.

SIDE EFFECTS

Since procedure parameter lists can be so complicated with the choice of VAR and *value* parameters, you will be tempted to reference *global* variables directly instead of passing them through the parameter list. *Don't!* It is a bad habit. It can lead to program bugs which are extremely hard to locate. If communication between program modules is confined to the parameter lists, and all non-output variables are *value* parameters, each module is isolated from what happens in other parts of the program. In other words, the code in one procedure should not have side effects elsewhere in the program, except through the well-defined interface of the parameter list. (See Figure 7-3.)

Another way of saying this is that procedures should use only the variables defined in their *formal* parameter list or in their own VAR section. Create stand-alone modules with a clear communication interface.

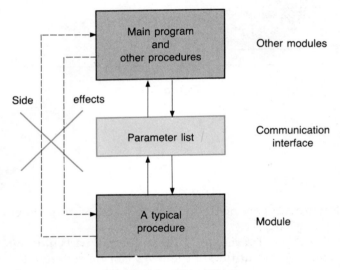

Figure 7-3. Side Effects

You should avoid side effects because it is often hard to keep track of the results.

> "I shot an arrow into the air,
> It fell to earth I know not where.
> I looked here, I looked there.
> I sure lose a lot of arrows that way!"
> Anonymous

Here is a short example of a program that runs but produces incorrect results because of side effects.

```
PROGRAM TROUBLE(INPUT, OUTPUT);
VAR CT : INTEGER;
    CH : CHAR;
(*********************************************************)
PROCEDURE CHARCT;                        (* Counts the number of characters in a line
                                              of input and prints the count *)
BEGIN (*CHARCT*)
    CT := 0;                                            (* side effect *)
    WHILE NOT EOLN DO
        BEGIN
            READ(CH);                  (* direct reference to global variable *)
            CT := CT + 1                           (* side effect *)
        END;
    WRITELN(' NUMBER OF CHARACTERS ON LINE ', CT)
END;  (*CHARCT*)
(*********************************************************)
BEGIN (*TROUBLE*)
    CT := 0;
    WHILE NOT EOF DO
        BEGIN
            CT := CT + 1;
            CHARCT
        END;
    WRITELN('NUMBER OF LINES OF INPUT ', CT)
END.  (*TROUBLE*)
```

Program TROUBLE is supposed to count and print the number of characters on each line of input. After the last line has been processed, it should print the number of lines. Strangely enough, each time you run the program, the number of lines of input is the same as the number of characters in the last line of input!

If you declare a local variable CT in Procedure CHARCT, the program works correctly. There is no conflict between the local CT and the global CT—they are separate variables known only to the blocks they are local to. CH, of course, should be declared locally in the procedure, since it is used only in the procedure.

TESTING AND DEBUGGING

In Program GRAPH we made several assumptions: each file is in order by department IDs; there are the same departments in each store; there is one piece of data per line. What if there is an error in the data files? We have not paid too much attention to error checking in our programs, yet in the "real world" errors do occur. Let's redo our main module for Program GRAPH and add some error checking. This is what the original design looked like:

MAIN

```
PRINTHEADER
WHILE more data DO
    GETDATA for FILE1
    GETDATA for FILE2
    PRINTDATA for store 1 dept.
    PRINTDATA for store 2 dept.
```

And this is a possible redesign with some error checking added.

MAIN

```
PRINTHEADER
WHILE more data DO
    GETDATA for FILE1
    GETDATA for FILE2
    IF EOF for one file only OR dept. IDs not equal
        THEN error
        ELSE PRINTDATA for store 1 dept.
                PRINTDATA for store 2 dept.
```

In the call to GETDATA, we will now have to keep track of the ID for each department so that we can see if they are the same for each store. Here is the recoding of the main program for Program GRAPH:

```
BEGIN  (*GRAPH*)
   RESET(FILE1);
   RESET(FILE2);
   PRINTHEADER;
   WHILE NOT EOF(FILE1) AND NOT EOF(FILE2) DO
      BEGIN
         GETDATA(FILE1,ID1,SALES1);
         GETDATA(FILE2,ID2,SALES2);
         WRITELN;
         IF (EOF(FILE1) <> EOF(FILE2)) OR (ID1 <> ID2)
            THEN WRITELN('ERROR IN DATA FILES')
            ELSE
               BEGIN
                  PRINTDATA(ID1,1,SALES1);
                  PRINTDATA(ID2,2,SALES2)
               END
      END
END.  (*GRAPH*)
```

If either file ends prematurely or the department IDs are not the same for both stores, then the error message 'ERROR IN DATA FILES' would be printed. (More error checking could be added to this program—this is just an example.) We took advantage of the fact that a *value* parameter can have an expression for an actual parameter by using a constant in the call to PRINTDATA. If you used a constant as the actual parameter for a VAR parameter, you would get the compile-time error: ACTUAL PARAMETER MUST BE A VARIABLE. This is because a VAR parameter must have a place in which to return a value.

Many program bugs are the result of unintentional side effects. If you reference global variables only through the parameter list of your procedures, you will save yourself a lot of headaches during debug time. Confusing and spurious effects of your procedures will be avoided.

In Program GRAPH there is no nesting of procedures. We could just as easily have written Program TRANSPOSE without nesting of procedures, but we did so as a tool for teaching scope rules. Whether or not you nest your procedures is a matter of style and what your top-down design calls for. It is perfectly all right to list all your procedures sequentially without nesting, as long as you declare a procedure before you call it. Since most programs will change during design, testing and maintenance, it might be better not to nest your procedures.

For example, if in Program TRANSPOSE we decide that we want another procedure to call SKIPFIRST, we might have to rewrite our program or even our design—because SKIPFIRST is nested in FINDLAST which is nested in PRINTLAST. The scope rules prevent a procedure at the same level as PRINTLAST from calling the nested SKIPFIRST. Of course we may want this nesting just for the purpose of preventing any other procedure from calling SKIPFIRST. If you think that you may want to call a procedure from more than one place, don't nest it. If one procedure is an integral part of another and has no functional meaning of its own, nest it. Otherwise it doesn't matter. Nesting does sometimes allow your program to reflect your top-down design more accurately.

Testing and Debugging Hints

1. Make sure that variables used as *actual* parameters are declared in the block where the procedure call is made.
2. Declare a procedure before any calls to that procedure are made.
3. When using *formal* and *actual* parameters, be aware that they are matched by position in the parameter list and their types must be the same.
4. A VAR parameter requires a variable as an *actual* parameter to hold the value that is returned. A *value* parameter can have any expression that supplies a value (variables and/or constants and operators) as an *actual* parameter.

5. VAR parameters return a value, *value* parameters do not. Use *value* parameters unless you need to return a value.
6. Avoid side effects from procedures. Use the well-defined interface of the parameter list to communicate with the calling block. Variables used only in a procedure should be declared as local variables. DO NOT reference global variables directly from inside a procedure.
7. The symbol "VAR" must precede each VAR parameter in the *formal* parameter list. When no symbol is used, the parameter is a *value* parameter. Given:

```
PROCEDURE ONE(A, B : INTEGER; VAR C : BOOLEAN;
              D : BOOLEAN; E, F : REAL;
              VAR G, H : INTEGER);
```

C,G,H are VAR parameters; A,B,D,E,F are *value* parameters.
8. You can't reference from within a block an identifier (variable, constant, procedure, etc.) which is outside the scope of that block.

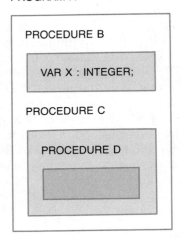

PROGRAM A

PROCEDURE B

VAR X : INTEGER;

PROCEDURE C

PROCEDURE D

Procedure C, procedure D and program A cannot reference the local variable X of procedure B. Procedure B cannot call procedure D.
9. If necessary, use debug WRITE statements to indicate when a procedure is called and if it is executing correctly. The value of the variables in the *actual* parameter list can be shown by WRITE statements immediately before (to show the values of the input parameters) and immediately after (to show the values of the output parameters) the call to the procedure. You may want to use debug WRITE statements in the procedure itself to indicate every time it is called.

Summary

Pascal has two types of parameters: VAR and *value*. VAR parameters have the word "VAR" before them in the *formal parameter* list. *Value* parameters do not have the word "VAR" before them. Parameters which are output parameters from the procedure should be VAR parameters. All others should be *value* parameters. This minimizes side effects since the procedure is given a copy of a *value* parameter and can change only the copy, not the original.

Anything declared in the MAIN PROGRAM is known to all procedures and is called *global*. However, it is not good programming practice to reference *global* variables directly. All communication between modules of your program should be done through the use of *formal* and *actual* parameter lists.

The *scope* of a variable refers to where it is known. The rule says a variable is defined in the block in which it is declared and in all of the blocks within that block.

Exercises

1. Using a variable parameter (passing by reference), a procedure can obtain the initial value of an actual parameter as well as change the value of the actual parameter in the calling program.

T   F

2. Using a value parameter, the value of a variable can be passed to a procedure and used for computation there, without any modification to the value of the variable in the main program.

T   F

3. A particular procedure can be an inner block relative to the program that contains it, and an outer block to any procedures declared within it.

T   F

4. Identifiers declared at the beginning of a block are accessible to all executable statements that are part of that block, including statements belonging to inner blocks.

T   F

5. If we declare a local variable in a procedure with the same name as a variable in an outer block, no confusion will result because references to variables in procedures are first interpreted as references to local variables.

T   F

6. Given the following procedure declaration and procedure call:

```
PROCEDURE PARAMETERS(X:INTEGER; VAR Y:INTEGER);
    .
    .
    .
PARAMETERS (A,B);
```

a. When the procedure is called, a storage location is created for X and it is initialized to the value of A.   T F
b. Since Y is a variable parameter, no new storage location is created. Y stands for the variable B itself and any change in Y will constitute a change in B.   T F
c. X would be initialized to the value of A because their positions correspond in the parameter list.   T F
d. X and Y could both be used to receive values from the main program but only X, the value parameter, can be used to return a value to the main program.   T F

7. Given the following block structure:

```
PROGRAM SCOPERULES(INPUT,OUTPUT);
VAR A,B:INTEGER;

PROCEDURE BLOCK1;
VAR A1,B1:INTEGER;

  PROCEDURE BLOCK2;
  VAR A,A2,B2:INTEGER;
  BEGIN
      .
      .
      .
  END;

BEGIN (* BLOCK1 *)
    .
    .
    .
END;

PROCEDURE BLOCK3;
VAR A3,B3:INTEGER;
BEGIN
    .
    .
    .
END;

BEGIN   (* MAIN PROGRAM *)
    .
    .
    .
END.
```

a. A and B are global variables, accessible to all parts of program SCOPE-RULES, including procedure BLOCK2.   T   F

b. Since SCOPERULES is the outer block, statements in its body can reference all variables declared in inner blocks, including procedure BLOCK2.   T   F

c. Since procedure BLOCK2 is the innermost block, its local variables can be accessed by all other blocks.   T   F

d. Variable A1 is global to procedure BLOCK2.   T   F

e. Variable B2 is local to procedure BLOCK1.   T   F

f. The statement A1:=A would be legal in procedure BLOCK1.   T   F

g. The statement A3:=A1 would be legal in procedure BLOCK3.   T   F

h. Variables A2 and B2 are not defined in any of the outer blocks.   T   F

i. The statement A:=B2 in procedure BLOCK2 would assign the value of B2 to the local variable A, and the global A would not be affected.   T   F

j. Variables A1 and B1 are global to procedure BLOCK2, local to procedure BLOCK1, and not defined for the program outer block.   T   F

8. Define the following:

> value parameter
> variable parameter
> local variable
> global variable
> scope
> name precedence
> side effects

9. Read the following program containing procedure CHANGE. Fill in the values of all variables when the procedure is called. Then fill in the values of all variables after returning to the main program. (Let 'u' indicate undefined value.)

```
PROGRAM SAMPLE(INPUT, OUTPUT);
VAR A, B : INTEGER;

PROCEDURE CHANGE(X :INTEGER; VAR Y : INTEGER);
VAR B : INTEGER;
BEGIN (*CHANGE*)
   B := X;
   Y := Y + B;
   X := Y
END;   (*CHANGE*)

BEGIN   (* MAIN *)
   A := 10;
   B := 7;
   CHANGE(A, B);
   WRITELN(A, B)
END.    (* MAIN *)
```

SAMPLE variables when CHANGE is called:

    A＿＿＿

    B＿＿＿

CHANGE variables when CHANGE is called:

    X＿＿＿

    Y＿＿＿

    B＿＿＿

SAMPLE variables after return from CHANGE:

    A＿＿＿

    B＿＿＿

10. Read the following program containing procedure TWO. Fill in the values of all variables when the procedure is called. Then fill in the values of all variables after returning to the main program. (Let 'u' indicate undefined value.)

```
PROGRAM ONE(INPUT, OUTPUT);
VAR A, B : INTEGER;

PROCEDURE TWO(VAR X : INTEGER; Y : INTEGER);
VAR B : INTEGER;
BEGIN (*TWO*)
  B := X;
  Y := Y + B;
  X := Y
END; (*TWO*)

BEGIN  (* MAIN *)
  A := 5;
  B := 4;
  TWO(A, B);
  WRITELN(A, B)
END.  (* MAIN *)
```

ONE variables when TWO is called:

    A＿＿＿

    B＿＿＿

TWO variables when TWO is called:

    X＿＿＿

    Y＿＿＿

    B＿＿＿

ONE variables after return from TWO:

    A＿＿＿

    B＿＿＿

11. Read the following program containing procedure CAT. Fill in the values of all variables when the procedure is called. Then fill in the values of all variables after returning to the main program. (Let 'u' indicate undefined value.)

```
PROGRAM DOG(INPUT, OUTPUT);
VAR A, B : INTEGER;
```

```
PROCEDURE CAT(X : INTEGER; Y : INTEGER);
BEGIN (*CAT*)
  B := X;
  Y := Y + B;
  X := Y
END;  (*CAT*)

BEGIN  (* MAIN *)
  A := 7;
  B := 10;
  CAT(A, B);
  WRITELN(A, B)
END.    (* MAIN *)
```

DOG variables when CAT is called:

   A＿＿＿

   B＿＿＿

CAT variables when CAT is called:

   X＿＿＿

   Y＿＿＿

   B＿＿＿

DOG variables after return from CAT:

   A＿＿＿

   B＿＿＿

12. Draw a scope diagram for the block structure in exercise 7.

Pre-Test

1. When writing procedures we must be aware of the declarations for all other blocks, because if we declare a local variable with the same name as a global variable in an outer block, we may accidentally modify the global variable in our procedure.

T   F

2. Read the following program containing procedure ALTER. Fill in the values of all variables when ALTER is called. Then fill in the values of all variables after returning to the main program. (Let 'u' indicate an undefined value).

```
PROGRAM TEST7(INPUT,OUTPUT);
VAR X,Y : INTEGER;

PROCEDURE ALTER(VAR A : INTEGER; B : INTEGER);
VAR Y : INTEGER;
BEGIN  (*ALTER*)
  Y := B;
  A := A + Y;
  B := A
END;    (*ALTER*)
```

```
BEGIN  (*MAIN*)
   X := 12;
   Y := 2;
   ALTER(Y,X);
   WRITELN(X,Y)
END.  (*MAIN*)
```

TEST7 variables when ALTER is called:

    X_____

    Y_____

ALTER variables when ALTER is called:

    A_____

    B_____

    Y_____

TEST7 variables after return from ALTER:

    X_____

    Y_____

3. a. Write a procedure that returns the sum of the squares of 3 numbers (integers) and returns a Boolean TRUE if all three numbers are positive, otherwise a FALSE. Use variable and value parameters as required.

   b. Write the calling statement for your procedure if the 3 numbers are A, B and C.

4. Given the following block structure:

```
PROGRAM SCOPETEST(INPUT,OUTPUT);
VAR X, Y : INTEGER;


PROCEDURE BLOCK1(X1 : INTEGER);
VAR X, Y1 : INTEGER;
BEGIN   (*BLOCK1*)
    .
    .
END;    (*BLOCK1*)


PROCEDURE BLOCK2(X2,Y2 : INTEGER);

    PROCEDURE BLOCK3(Y3 : INTEGER);
    VAR X3 : INTEGER;
    BEGIN   (*BLOCK3*)
        .
        .
    END;    (*BLOCK3*)


BEGIN   (*BLOCK2*)
    .
    .
END;    (*BLOCK2*)
```

```
BEGIN       (*MAIN*)
        .
        .
END.        (*MAIN*)
```

answer the following as either true or false.

1. X and Y are global variables, accessible to all parts of the program, including procedure BLOCK3.   T   F
2. Since procedure BLOCK3 is the innermost block, its local variables can be accessed by all other blocks.   T   F
3. Variable Y1 is local to procedure BLOCK1 and global to procedure BLOCK2.   T   F
4. The statement X := X1 in procedure BLOCK1 would change local variable X of procedure BLOCK1, and leave global variable X of program SCOPETEST unaffected.   T   F
5. The statement Y2 := X3 in procedure BLOCK2 would be legal.   T   F

5. Write the output produced by execution of the following program. (This program is not intended to make any sense, only to test your knowledge of scope rules and side effects.)

```
PROGRAM SCOPEOUT(INPUT,OUTPUT);
VAR A, B, C : INTEGER;

PROCEDURE ONE(X, Y : INTEGER; VAR Z : INTEGER);
VAR A : INTEGER;
BEGIN (*ONE*)
     A := 1;
     B := 7;
     X := Y;
     Z := A + X
END;   (*ONE*)

BEGIN   (*MAIN*)
     A := 4;
     B := 5;
     C := 12;
     ONE(A,B,C);
     WRITELN(A,B,C)
END.    (*MAIN*)
```

Functions, Real Numbers, and Additional Control Structures

8

Goals

To be able to determine where it is appropriate to use a function.

To be able to code and invoke a function correctly for a specified task.

To be able to define and use REAL numbers.

To be able to format REAL output.

To be able to use a REPEAT statement correctly.

To be able to use CASE statements for multi-way selection.

To be able to determine whether to use a REPEAT or a WHILE to perform a specific task.

Pascal has two types of subprograms, PROCEDURES and FUNCTIONS. We have spent two chapters on PROCEDURES. This chapter deals with FUNCTIONS, real numbers and two additional control structures: the REPEAT-UNTIL statement and the CASE statement.

FUNCTIONS

Everything we have said about PROCEDURES is also true about FUNCTIONS. Their main use is in a situation where you wish to return only one value to the calling program. In a FUNCTION, the actual name of the FUNCTION is the variable identifier which transmits the value back.

For example, in Program SUMDATA in Chapter 6 there was a procedure named PROCESSDATASET which returned the sum of five values in a VAR parameter SUM. This procedure could just as easily have been a function.

```
FUNCTION SUM : INTEGER;
VAR COUNTER2, TSUM, VALU : INTEGER;
BEGIN
   TSUM := 0;
   COUNTER2 := 1;
   WHILE COUNTER2 <= 5 DO
      BEGIN
         READ(VALU);
         TSUM := TSUM + VALU;
         COUNTER2 := COUNTER2 + 1
      END;
   READLN;
   SUM := TSUM
END;
```

The word FUNCTION has now replaced the word PROCEDURE in the heading.

Since the function for this particular case needs no inputs from the calling program, there is no *formal* parameter list. Note that following the name of the function is a ':' and a type. Since the value to be returned is stored in the name of the function, it must have a type associated with it. If a function has a *formal* parameter list, the ':' and type follow the ')' which ends the *formal* parameter list. This is the syntax diagram of a function heading:

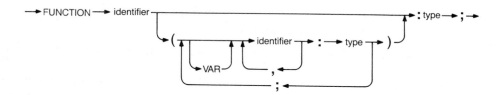

The value to be returned must be stored in the function name (SUM in our example). This is usually accomplished by the last logical statement in the function (SUM := TSUM).

How are functions invoked? By using the function name (along with the *actual* parameter list, if it exists) in an expression. The body of the program in Chapter 6 using Function SUM would look as follows:

```
BEGIN
    COUNTER1 := 1;
    WHILE COUNTER1 <= 6 DO
        BEGIN
            WRITELN(' DATA SET ', COUNTER1, 'SUM = ', SUM);
            COUNTER1 := COUNTER1 + 1
        END
END.                                            function call
```

Since PRINTRESULT was only one statement, it was put in the main program. The WRITELN statement causes the words " DATA SET " followed by the value stored in COUNTER1 followed by the words "SUM = " to be written out. When it encounters the identifier SUM, it recognizes it as a function call and transfers control to the function SUM. The value returned in the identifier SUM is then printed.

Notice that the identifier used as a function name has two roles. It identifies the function so that it can be called, and it acts as a parameter through which a value is passed back to the point of the call.

Another place a function would have been appropriate was in Program GAME. In PROCESSPLAY the plays were read in and tested to see if they were 'S', 'R', or 'P'. The procedure returned the two plays, FIRST and

SECOND, and a Boolean variable LEGAL which was TRUE if the plays were valid and FALSE if they were not. This test for legality could have been removed from PROCESSPLAY and written as a Boolean function. The heading would look as follows:

```
FUNCTION LEGAL(FIRST, SECOND : CHAR) : BOOLEAN;
```

Then the statement which tested the Boolean variable LEGAL would test the Boolean function as follows:

```
IF LEGAL(FIRST, SECOND)
    THEN . . .
```

Are there any rules for when to use a procedure and when to use a function? No, but there are a few guidelines:

1. If there is more than one output from your module, *do not use a function.*
2. If there is only one output from the module, and it is a Boolean value, a function is probably called for.
3. If there is only one output and that value is to be used immediately, a function is probably called for.
4. When in doubt, use a procedure. Any function can be recoded as a procedure with the function name becoming an output parameter of the procedure.
5. If both are acceptable, use the one you feel the most comfortable with.

Functions were included in Pascal to provide a way to simulate mathematical entities called functions. Pascal also provides a set of built-in commonly used mathematical functions. A list of these is in APPENDIX B.

RECURSION

In the function SUM, why did we use the local variable TSUM instead of just using the identifier SUM? On the surface this looks redundant, but it is necessary because SUM is a function name, not a variable name. Pascal allows a function or procedure to call itself. If SUM had been used in an expression (on the right-hand side of an assignment statement or in a Boolean condition), the logical order of execution would be to turn over control to SUM again. The ability of a function or procedure to call or invoke itself is called recursion.

Recursion is a very powerful feature of Pascal and will be used in more advanced work. For the beginner, it simply means that you must not use the name of your function in an expression in the body of that function. You therefore must define and use a local variable and set the name of the function to the value of the local variable before you exit the function. This is why we used the local variable TSUM. If the function name will never appear in an expression in the body of the function, you don't need a local variable such as TSUM. Note that the function name may appear any number of times on the left-hand side of assignment statements in the body of the function.

For those of you whose curiosity has been piqued, we include one recursive example. Pascal does not have an exponentiation operator, so let's write a function to calculate:

$$X^n$$

where X and n are both non-zero, positive integers. The formula is:

$$X^n = \underbrace{X * X * X * \cdots * X}_{n \text{ times}}$$

Another way of writing this relationship would be:

$$X^n = X * \underbrace{(X * X * \cdots * X)}_{(n - 1) \text{ times}}$$

If we know what X^{n-1} is, we can calculate X^n since $X^n = X(X^{n-1})$. In like manner we can reduce X^{n-1} further:

$$X^n = X * (X * \underbrace{(X * \cdots * X)}_{(n - 2) \text{ times}})$$

If we know what X^{n-2} is, we can calculate X^{n-1} and thus calculate X^n since $X^n = X(X(X^{n-2}))$. We can continue this process until the innermost expression becomes X^1. We know what X^1 is, it's X.

We express this reasoning in the following recursive Function POWER which has two parameters, X and N.

```
FUNCTION POWER(X, N : INTEGER) : INTEGER;
BEGIN  (*POWER*)
    IF  N = 1
        THEN POWER := X
        ELSE POWER := X * POWER(X, N - 1)
    END;  (*POWER*)
```

Each call to Function POWER puts the actual parameters on the message board for the version being called to use. The value for X will be the same for each version of POWER, but the value for N will be decreasing by 1 for each call until N − 1 becomes 1. The call to Function POWER where N is 1 stops the calling chain because POWER can now be given a value. POWER is assigned a value (X to be exact) which is passed back to the version of Function POWER which made the last call. The value of POWER for that version can now be calculated and passed back to the version which made that call. This continues until the value of POWER can be passed back to the original call.

Let's see what a call to POWER with X = 2 and N = 3 does. The statement:

```
NUM := POWER(2,3)
```

in the body of the program assigns the value returned by the call to the variable NUM. The value returned by POWER and assigned to NUM should be 8 (2 to the third power or 2*2*2).

For illustrative purposes let's assume that each call to POWER creates a complete version of POWER. Each box in the following diagram represents the code for POWER listed above, along with the values of the actual parameters for that version. Use the diagram and the code to satisfy yourself that the POWER function does what it is supposed to do. Each version of POWER goes to the message board to get the values left for it. There is no confusion as to which N is being used because N is a formal parameter. (See Figure 8-1.)

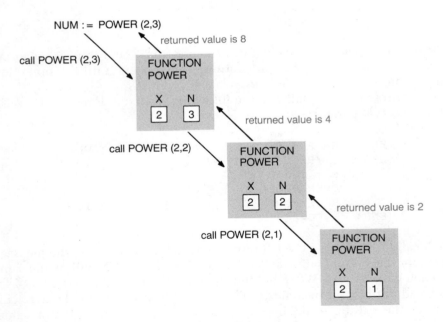

Figure 8-1.

To those of you who find this example not only crystal clear, but obvious, go ahead and use recursion. It is a powerful technique. The rest of you should not feel intimidated, however. Understanding recursion is not one of the goals of this chapter. Should you continue in computing, you will undoubtedly study recursion in depth in later work.

SIDE EFFECTS

Functions are designed to be used where a single value is to be returned. However, if a function has VAR parameters in the *formal* parameter list, the corresponding *actual* parameters can indeed be changed. The sending back or changing of more than one value in a function call is called a side effect of the function, and should be avoided.

A good rule of thumb is: Never have VAR parameters in the *formal* parameter list of a function. If you must have them, then you should be using a procedure and not a function. Of course you can use *value* parameters as you need them.

Another example of a side effect is when a procedure or function references a global variable directly, not through its *formal* parameter list. Remember, communication between program modules should be confined to the *actual* and *formal* parameter lists.

The following example illustrates the two types of side effects.

```
PROGRAM UNEXPECTED(INPUT, OUTPUT);
VAR  A, B : INTEGER;

FUNCTION SIDE(VAR X, Y : INTEGER) : INTEGER;
BEGIN (*SIDE*)
    X := X + Y;
    A := X + 1;
    SIDE := X + A
END;   (*SIDE*)

BEGIN (*MAIN*)
    A := 0;
    B := 1;
    WRITELN(SIDE(A, B));
    WRITELN(SIDE(A, B));
    WRITELN(SIDE(B, A));
    WRITELN(SIDE(B, A))
END.   (*MAIN*)
```

You would expect the first two WRITELN statements to produce the same output and the second two WRITELN statements to produce the same output. That is, you would expect a function to return the same result from duplicate inputs. Unfortunately, Function SIDE has side effects and does not return the same value from two successive identical calls. Let's do a code walk-through and see what happens.

Statement	A	B	X	Y	SIDE	
(initial values)	0	1	?	?	?	
SIDE(A, B) (when entered)	0	1	0	1	?	
X := X + Y	1	1	1	1	?	
A := X + 1	2	1	2	1	?	
SIDE := X + A	2	1	2	1	4 ←— what is printed	
SIDE(A, B) (when entered)	2	1	2	1	?	
X := X + Y	3	1	3	1	?	
A := X + 1	4	1	4	1	?	
SIDE := X + A	4	1	4	1	8 ←— what is printed	
SIDE(B, A) (when entered)	4	1	1	4	?	
X := X + Y	4	5	5	4	?	
A := X + 1	6	5	5	6	?	
SIDE := X + A	6	5	5	6	11 ←— what is printed	
SIDE(B, A) (when entered)	6	5	5	6	?	
X := X + Y	6	11	11	6	?	
A := X + 1	12	11	11	12	?	
SIDE := X + A	12	11	11	12	23 ←— what is printed	

Because the first parameter is a VAR parameter, when the *formal* parameter is changed, the *actual* parameter is changed also. Since A is being referenced globally, the function is changing it each time as well. As you can see by the output of Function SIDE (values marked with an arrow), not only are different values returned with the same input, but there is no pattern.

DESIGN AND PROGRAM STRUCTURE

Our top-down design represents a structured approach to programming. Procedures and functions allow us to easily modularize our programs to create a hierarchical ordering (tree structure). This leads to better organization, reduces control complexity and makes programs easy to read, understand and modify.

Because procedures and functions allow modular design, we can independently create and test the building blocks of our program. (We can use the informal method of the code walk-through.) If each module tests correctly and the module interfaces are clear and accurate, then the entire program should work. This is another reason to avoid side effects by using the parameter list as the only communication interface to a module.

Using modules also allows us to call the same block of code from more than one place in our program. The parameters provide this flexibility since the actual parameters can be different in each call. In the following design tree, module G is called by both module D and module F.

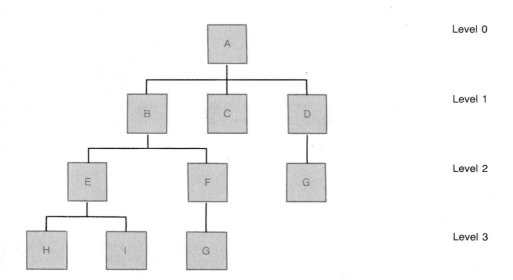

We have discussed developing our top-down designs level by level. However, this is a matter of style. You may be more comfortable developing one branch of the design tree at a time. For example, after writing module A you might then write modules B, E, H and I. Then you might finish modules F and G followed by C and D. The problem itself may dictate the approach you use. Whatever style you adopt, you will still need several passes through the design to develop each module to the point where you are satisfied. All of the top-down designs in this book required several passes to fully develop each module.

Pascal provides structure for our programs in addition to procedures and functions. In Chapter 1 we listed the four basic statement structures: sequence, selection, loop and procedure. These are "built-in" in Pascal. As a result, we benefit from this structuring at the lowest level of our code. Other programming languages do not have such clear-cut control structures, and programs written in them are sometimes hard to follow.

We have said that top-down design reduces complexity—the sheer weight of details as well as control complexity. For example, a typical main module might contain:

```
WHILE more data DO
   GETDATA
   PROCESSDATA
PRINTRESULTS
```

Even if all the other modules contain their own looping control structures, we have only concerned ourselves with one WHILE loop. We don't worry about the complexity of nested loops. We have pushed the details of other control structures to a lower level. This can be done at any point in our design. After developing lower level details, we may decide to move some of those details to a higher level module. It's up to us. After all, it is our design and we can develop it any way we see fit.

ADDITIONAL CONTROL STRUCTURES

Pascal contains the four basic ways of structuring statements. You have seen sequential code, the IF statement for selection, the WHILE statement for looping, and procedures and functions. These are all the control structures you need to write a program, but Pascal does have several more for convenience: the REPEAT and FOR statements for looping, and the CASE statement for multi-way selection. We'll cover the FOR statement in the next chapter.

REPEAT Statement

The REPEAT statement is actually the REPEAT-UNTIL statement. It is a looping control structure with the loop condition tested at the end of the loop after the reserved word UNTIL. Because UNTIL delimits the statement, a "BEGIN-END" pair is not necessary for the body of the loop.

REPEAT STATEMENT

A looping control structure similar to a WHILE statement except that there will always be at least one execution of the loop since the loop condition is tested after the body of the loop.

```
REPEAT
    A := A + 1;
    B := C MOD A
UNTIL B = 0;
```

is equivalent to

```
A := A + 1;
B := C MOD A;
WHILE B <> 0 DO
    BEGIN
        A := A + 1;
        B := C MOD A
    END;
```

This example assumes that you will always want to execute the body of the loop at least once because this is the effect of using a REPEAT loop.

Because the WHILE statement tests the loop condition before executing the body of the loop, it is called a pre-test loop. The REPEAT statement does the opposite and is known as a post-test loop. Note that the tests are reversed. The body of the WHILE loop is executed as long as the expression is TRUE. The body of the REPEAT loop is executed as long as the expression is FALSE.

The following compares a counting loop constructed using both the WHILE and the REPEAT statements. Figure 8-2 compares the structure diagrams of counting loops using the WHILE and REPEAT statements.

Counting loop going from 1 to 10 using WHILE

```
COUNTER := 1;
WHILE COUNTER <= 10 DO
    BEGIN
        PROCESS;
        COUNTER := COUNTER + 1
    END
```

Counting loop going from 1 to 10 using REPEAT

```
COUNTER := 1;
REPEAT
    PROCESS;
    COUNTER := COUNTER + 1
UNTIL COUNTER > 10
```

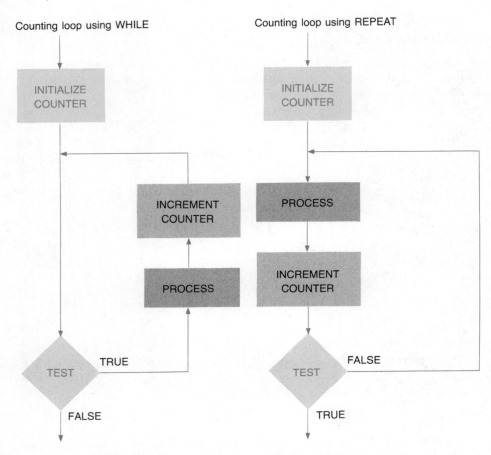

Figure 8-2. Comparison of WHILE and REPEAT.

A REPEAT-UNTIL would be the natural choice in the task of skipping blanks that was coded as Procedure SKIPBLANKS in Program TRANS-POSE in Chapter 7.

```
PROCEDURE SKIPBLANKS(VAR CH : CHAR);
BEGIN
    REPEAT
        READ(CH)
    UNTIL CH <> ' '
END;
```

CASE Statement

The CASE statement is a selection control structure that allows you to list several alternate courses of action and choose one to be executed at run-time. The selection is done by matching up the value of an expression (case selector) with a label attached to a course of action.

CASE STATEMENT

A selection control structure that provides for multi-way selection of different courses of action; a generalization of the IF statement equivalent to nested IF-THEN-ELSE statements.

```
CASE I OF
   1  :  A := A + 1;
   2  :  B := B + 1;
   3,4 :  C := C + 1
   END;  (*CASE*)
```

has the same effect as

```
IF I = 1
   THEN A := A + 1
   ELSE IF I = 2
      THEN B := B + 1
      ELSE IF (I = 3) OR (I = 4)
         THEN C := C + 1;
```

CASE SELECTOR

The expression or scalar variable (except for type REAL) whose value determines the case label list selected.

CASE LABEL LIST

A list of constants of the same type as the case selector appearing in the body of a CASE statement.

In the boxed example, I is the case selector and each of the following

$$1$$
$$2$$
$$3,4$$

are case label lists.

The following program fragment would print the appropriate comment based on a student's grade.

```
CASE GRADE OF
    'A', 'B' : WRITE(' GOOD WORK');
         'C' : WRITE(' AVERAGE WORK');
    'D', 'F' : WRITE(' POOR WORK')
END  (*CASE*)
```

GRADE is the CASE selector and 'A', 'B', 'C', 'D' and 'F' are the constants in the CASE label lists. If GRADE contains an 'A' or a 'B', 'GOOD WORK' will be printed. If GRADE contains a 'C', 'AVERAGE WORK' will be printed. If GRADE contains a 'D' or an 'F', 'POOR WORK' will be printed.

What if we wish to execute more than one statement in a course of action? For example, we might also want to keep a count of students doing poor work. The following program fragment contains a compound statement so the NUMPOOR counter could be added.

```
CASE GRADE OF
    'A', 'B' : WRITE('GOOD WORK');
         'C' : WRITE('AVERAGE WORK');
    'D', 'F' : BEGIN
                   WRITE('POOR WORK');
                   NUMPOOR := NUMPOOR + 1
               END
END  (*CASE*)
```

What happens if GRADE does not contain one of these five letters? The result is undefined; you cannot predict what will happen.*

Notice several things about the syntax of the CASE statement. The labels are separated from the action by a ':'. The action can be a simple statement or a compound statement. The type of the case selector expression must be the same as the type of the case label constants. INTEGER, CHAR, BOOLEAN and other types that we will discuss in Chapter 9 can be used; REAL cannot.

Figure 8-3 shows the flow of control for a CASE statement.

---

* Some Pascal implementations just skip the entire statement if there is no match between the selector and a label; some give you a run-time error. There is discussion of adding an OTHERWISE clause to the CASE statement to handle this problem.

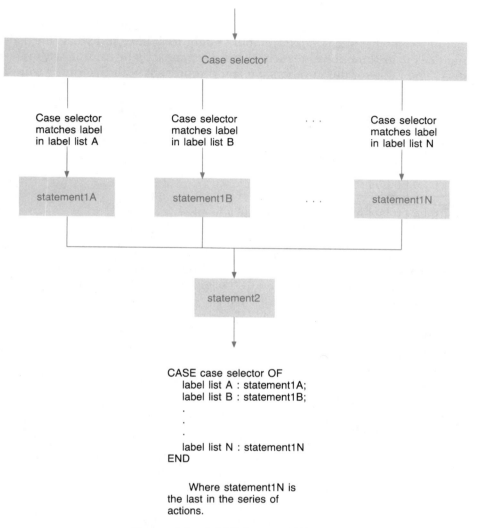

Figure 8-3. CASE Structure Diagram

MORE ON REAL NUMBERS

Representation of Numbers

Let's assume we have a computer where each word (location) in memory is divided up into a sign plus five decimal digits.

This means that when a variable or constant is defined, the cell or location assigned to it consists of five digits and a sign. When an INTEGER variable or constant is defined, the interpretation of the number stored in that place is quite straightforward. When a REAL variable or constant is defined, the number stored there has both a whole number part and a fractional part. It must be coded in some way to represent both parts.

Let's see what such coded numbers might look like, and what this coding does to arithmetic values within our programs, by beginning with integers. The range of the numbers we could represent with five digits would be:

−99999 to +99999

| + | 9 | 9 | 9 | 9 | 9 | Largest positive number

| + | 0 | 0 | 0 | 0 | 0 | Zero

| − | 9 | 9 | 9 | 9 | 9 | Largest negative number

Our precision (number of digits that can be represented) would be 5 digits, and each number within that range could be represented exactly.

What happens if we allow one of those digits (the left-most one, for example) to represent an exponent? Thus,

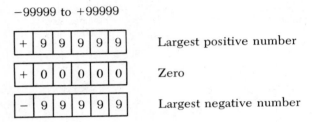

exponent

represents the number $+2345 * 10^1$. The range of numbers we can now represent is much larger:

$$-9999 * 10^9 \text{ to } 9999 * 10^9$$

or

$$-9,999,000,000,000 \text{ to } +9,999,000,000,000$$

However, our precision is now only 4 digits. That is, we can represent only 4 significant non-zero digits of the number itself. This means that any 4-digit number can be represented exactly in our system. What happens to larger numbers? The 4 left-most digits are correct and the balance of the digits are assumed to be 0. You lose the right-most, or least significant, digits. The following table shows what happens.

Number	Power of ten notation	Coded representation						Value
		Sign	Exp.					
+99,999	$9999 * 10^1$	+	1	9	9	9	9	+99,990

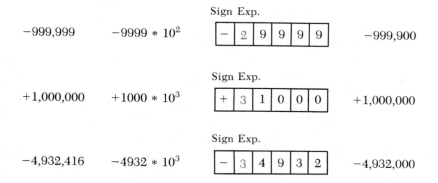

Note that 1,000,000 can be represented exactly, but $-4,932,416$ cannot. This coding scheme limits us to 4 significant (non-zero) digits, so the digits which cannot be represented are assumed to be zero.

To extend our coding scheme to represent real numbers we need to be able to represent negative exponents. For example:

$$4394 * 10^{-2} = 43.94$$

or

$$22 * 10^{-4} = .0022$$

Since our scheme does not allow for a sign for the exponent, we shall have to change the scheme slightly. We will let the sign that we have be the sign of the exponent and add a sign to the far left to be the sign of the number itself.

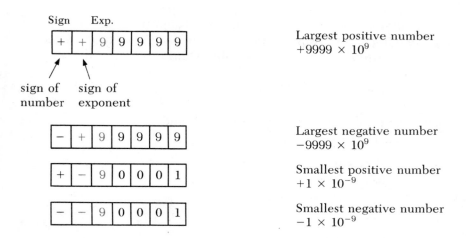

All of the numbers between 9999×10^9 and 1×10^{-9} can now be represented accurately to 4 digits. Adding negative exponents to our scheme has allowed us to represent fractional numbers.

The following table shows how we could encode some numbers.

Number	Power of ten notation	Coded representation							Value
		Sign	Exp.						
0.1032	$1032 * 10^{-4}$	+	−	4	1	0	3	2	0.1032
−5.4060	$-5406 * 10^{-3}$	−	−	3	5	4	0	6	−5.406
−0.003	$-3000 * 10^{-6}$	−	−	6	3	0	0	0	−0.0030
476.0321	$4760 * 10^{-1}$	+	−	1	4	7	6	0	476.0
1,000,000	$1000 * 10^{3}$	+	+	3	1	0	0	0	1,000,000

Note that we still have only 4 digits precision. The numbers 0.1032, 5.406 and 1000000 can be represented exactly. The number 476.0321 has 7 significant digits, but since only 4 can be represented, the "321" cannot be represented.

Although most modern computers do not use decimal arithmetic, real numbers in binary machines are encoded in a scheme similar to the one outlined here, except that the digits are binary digits, not decimal digits.

When using integer arithmetic our results are exact. Real arithmetic, however, cannot be exact. Let's examine this by adding three real numbers X, Y and Z together.

First we will add X to Y and then add Z to the result. Second, we will add Y to Z and then add X to that result. The associative law of arithmetic says that the two answers should be the same—but are they?

The computer limits the precision (number of significant digits) of a real number. We will continue our coding scheme of 4 significant digits and an exponent. Let's use the following allowable values of X, Y and Z.

$$X = -1324 * 10^3 \qquad Y = 1325 * 10^3 \qquad Z = 5424 * 10^0$$

Here is the result of adding Z to the sum of X and Y.

$$
\begin{array}{ll}
\text{(X)} & -1324 * 10^3 \\
\text{(Y)} & \underline{1325 * 10^3} \\
& 1 * 10^3 = 1000 * 10^0
\end{array}
$$

$$
\begin{array}{ll}
\text{(X + Y)} & 1000 * 10^0 \\
\text{(Z)} & \underline{5424 * 10^0} \\
& 6424 * 10^0 \longleftarrow \text{(X + Y) + Z}
\end{array}
$$

Here is the result of adding X to the sum of Y and Z.

$$
\begin{array}{ll}
\text{(Y)} & 1325000 * 10^0 \\
\text{(Z)} & \underline{\quad\ 5424 * 10^0} \\
& 1330424 * 10^0 = 1330 * 10^3 \text{ (truncated to 4 digits)}
\end{array}
$$

$$
\begin{array}{ll}
\text{(Y + Z)} & 1330 * 10^3 \\
\text{(X)} & \underline{-1324 * 10^3} \\
& \quad\ 6 * 10^3 = 6000 * 10^0 \longleftarrow X + (Y + Z)
\end{array}
$$

These answers are the same in the thousands place but are different thereafter. This is called representational error. The result of adding Y to Z gives a number with 7 digits of precision, but only 4 digits can be stored.

Real Numbers

Now let's formally define some of the terms we have used informally in the previous section.

> **REAL NUMBER**
>
> One of the numbers that has a whole and a fractional part and no imaginary part.

The type REAL is limited to the range and precision defined in a specific implementation of Pascal. This is because the number of digits used to represent the exponent and the number of digits used for the number itself (mantissa) vary from machine to machine.

> **RANGE**
>
> Largest and smallest allowable values.

> **PRECISION**
>
> Maximum number of significant digits.

SIGNIFICANT DIGITS

Those digits that begin with the first non-zero digit on the left and end with the last non-zero digit on the right (or a zero digit that is exact).

REPRESENTATIONAL ERRORS

Arithmetic errors caused by the fact that the precision of the result of our arithmetic operations is greater than the precision of our machine.

REAL is a standard type in Pascal. When you declare a variable to be of type REAL, the value stored in that place is interpreted as a floating point number (the name given to the coding scheme described previously). That is, the left-most part of the word in memory is assumed to be the exponent and the number itself is assumed to be in the balance of the word. It is called floating representation because the number of significant digits is fixed and the decimal point floats. In our coding scheme example, every number is stored as 4 digits with the left-most one being non-zero and the exponent adjusted accordingly.

1,000,000 was stored as
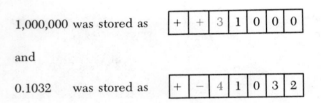

and

0.1032   was stored as

This allowed for the maximum precision possible.

There are two ways of expressing real numbers in Pascal, whether they are constants or data. One way is by using a decimal point, the other way is by using power of 10 notation. Since the keyboard or keypunch cannot do superscripts, an 'E' is used before the exponent. The syntax diagram is shown below.

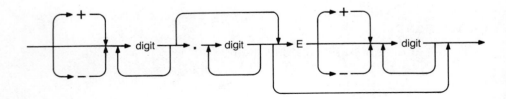

Valid reals	Invalid reals	
1.1	.032	(no digit before '.')
55E5	1.	(no digit after '.')
56.3E+01	5.E−32	(no digit after '.')
1000.0E42	1000	(no 'E' or '.')
21E−36	21.0E	(no digit after 'E')

Two standard functions used with real numbers which are quite useful are ROUND and TRUNC. They take a real parameter and return an integer value.

Value of I	ROUND(I)	TRUNC(I)
3.41	3	3
3.56	4	3
−5.02	−5	−5
−5.52	−6	−5

There are two problems to watch out for in real arithmetic: underflow and overflow.

Underflow is where the value of a calculation gets too small to represent. Going back to our decimal representation, let's look at a calculation involving very small numbers:

$$\begin{array}{r} 4210 \times 10^{-8} \\ \times\ 2000 \times 10^{-8} \\ \hline 8420000 \times 10^{-16} = 8420 \times 10^{-13} \end{array}$$

This value cannot be represented in our scheme because an exponent of −13 is too large. Our maximum was −9. Therefore the result of this calculation would be set to 0. This is called underflow. Any value too small to be represented is set to 0. Your answer would therefore not be exact.

Overflow is a more serious problem, because there is no logical thing to do when it occurs. For example, the results of this calculation

$$\begin{array}{r} 9999 \times 10^9 \\ \times\ 1000 \times 10^9 \\ \hline 9999000 \times 10^{18} = 9999 \times 10^{21} \end{array}$$

cannot be stored, so what should you do? To be consistent with underflow, you could set the result to 9999×10^9, MAXINT in this case. Yet this seems intuitively wrong and the alternative is to stop with an error message.

Pascal does not define what should happen in the case of overflow. You might try it with your compiler and see what happens.

Another error that can occur with real numbers is called cancellation error. This happens when numbers of widely differing sizes are added or subtracted giving a representational error. Let's look at an example:

$$(1 + .00001234) - 1 = .00001234$$

The laws of arithmetic say this should be true. But is it, if the computer does the arithmetic?

$$
\begin{array}{r}
100000000 \times 10^{-8} \\
+ \quad 1234 \times 10^{-8} \\
\hline
100001234 \times 10^{-8}
\end{array}
$$

With 4 digits accuracy, this becomes 1000×10^{-3}. Now we subtract 1

$$
\begin{array}{r}
1000 \times 10^{-3} \\
- \ 1000 \times 10^{-3} \\
\hline
0
\end{array}
$$

The result is 0 not .00001234.

We have been discussing problems with real numbers, but integer numbers can overflow both negatively and positively. To see how your compiler handles the situation you should try adding a one to MAXINT and a negative one to −MAXINT. On one system we have used, adding a one to MAXINT sets the results to −0!

The moral of this discussion is twofold. (1) The results of real calculations often will not be what you expect. (2) If you are working with very large numbers or very small numbers, you need more information than this book provides.

"It gives the answer as 12,621,859.007. But, it says it's just a hunch."

Colossal Computer

Formatting Real Output

If you do not indicate how many columns a real value is to take up on output, the value will be printed in E notation with one digit before the decimal point. Twenty-two columns is used by some systems as the default value for the number of columns.

To indicate the number of columns to be used (fieldwidth specification), you put a ':' followed by the number of columns (just as with integers) in a WRITE statement. A blank or a minus sign is always put before a real number and is included in the column count.

Here is an example. Remember, your machine may have a different range and use more or fewer digits for the exponent.

Value of I	WRITE statement	Output ('□' is a blank)
310.0	(I:10)	□3.10E+002
310.0	(I:9)	□3.1E+002
310.0	(I:12)	□3.1000E+002
310.0	(I:1)	□3.1E+002 (uses 9 columns)
0.0112	(I:10)	□1.12E−002
0.0112	(I:12)	□1.1200E−002
0.0112	(I:2)	□1.12E−002 (uses 10 columns)

With REALs, Pascal gives you a second option. If you specify a second ':' followed by an integer value, the output will be in decimal notation. The first number still specifies the total number of columns to be used; the second specifies the number of digits to print after the decimal point.

Value of I	WRITE statement	Output
310.0	(I:10:2)	□□□□310.00
310.0	(I:10:5)	□310.00000
310.0	(I:9:5)	□310.00000 (uses 10 columns)
32.76	(I:8:3)	□□32.760
0.012	(I:8:3)	□□□0.012
0.012	(I:8:2)	□□□□0.01 (last digit not printed)

As with integers the total number of columns is expanded, if necessary, so no significant digits are lost. However, the number of columns for fractional digits can be limited by the second field specification. This would be useful, for example, if you wanted the output in dollars and cents.

TESTING AND DEBUGGING

Since this chapter covers several different topics, no general discussion of testing and debugging will be included, only hints associated with each topic.

Testing and Debugging Hints

1. The FUNCTION heading must include a type.

   Since the function name will be assigned a value, it must be typed. (Don't forget to assign a value to the function name.) This is done by putting a ':' and type after the *formal* parameter list, or after the function name if there is no *formal* parameter list.

2. Do not use the function name in an expression within the function unless you are deliberately writing a recursive function.

   If you do this by mistake, it will probably cause a syntax error because you have no *actual* parameter list. If, however, the function has no parameters and you use the function name in an expression in the function, you will get a run-time error saying something about 'STACK OVERFLOW'.

3. Avoid comparisons of REALs when possible. When not possible, consider testing for "close equality" rather than exact equality.

   Not only does 1/3 + 1/3 + 1/3 not equal 1.0, but .1 + .1 + .1 + .1 + .1 + .1 + .1 + .1 + .1 + .1 does not equal 1.0 on computers that use binary arithmetic!

   We are familiar with this problem in decimal. We know that some numbers never stop, like 2/3 or PI (as in area of a circle). However, what is a simple fraction like 1/10 in decimal, cannot be represented exactly in binary. Since numbers are represented in binary in most machines, this means our tests might not be exact. This is another example of representational error.

   One way of handling this problem is to put in a tolerance. For example, if you wanted to see if A = B, test ABS(A − B) < 0.01. This would test if they were equal to at least two decimal places. The size of this tolerance depends upon the data and the situation.

4. Use INTEGERs if you know you are dealing with whole numbers only.

   Any integer can be represented exactly in any base. This means there is no loss of accuracy in converting a decimal integer to binary. Also, on most machines, integer arithmetic is faster.

5. Be aware of round off and/or truncation errors.

6. Remember the REPEAT statement will always execute at least once.

   The WHILE tests the expression at the beginning of the loop and does not execute the body of the loop if the expression is FALSE. The REPEAT tests the expression *after* it has executed the loop body.

Note also that the WHILE stops when the expression becomes FALSE; the REPEAT stops when the expression to be tested becomes TRUE.

7. Use the CASE statement with caution.

Remember that if the selector expression does not match one of the label constants, the results are undefined. This means that your program may run and produce an answer which looks reasonable but is wrong.

The label constants cannot be combined into an expression. If you want to take one action if a value is between 1 and 5, you must list 1, 2, 3, 4 and 5.

Summary

A function is a special type of procedure which sends back its answer in the name of the function. The function therefore has to have a type.

A function is invoked by using its name in an expression: all the rules about VAR and *value* parameters apply to both procedures and functions.

REAL numbers are those with a fractional part. They are encoded in a floating point format where the exponent is carried separately. The range for REALs is much wider than for INTEGERs, but the accuracy may be much less.

The REPEAT statement is a post-test loop where the expression is not tested until the loop has been executed at least once.

The CASE statement is a multi-way selection statement. The logical order is determined by matching a selector expression with a label.

Exercises

1. Write a function, P5, which returns the fifth power of its REAL parameter.

2. Write a function, MIN, which returns the minimum of its three INTEGER parameters.

3. A function call is always a component of an expression, but a procedure call is always a statement in itself.

T F

4. Both procedures and functions must have type.

T F

5. VAR parameters are illegal in the FORMAL parameter list of a function.

T F

6. Rewrite exercises 1 and 4 from Chapter 5 using a REPEAT loop.

7. Write a CASE statement which does the following:
   If the value of GRADE is 'A' add 4 to SUM
                             'B' add 3 to SUM
                             'C' add 2 to SUM
                             'D' add 1 to SUM
                             'F' print 'Student is on probation'

8. Write a case statement which does the following:
   If the value of ERROR is 1 print 'Invalid input'
                             2 print 'Results out of range'
                             3 print 'Error type 3'
                             4,5 print 'Undefined error'

9. Mark true if a valid REAL constant and false if not.

   a. +0.472   T   F
   b. −6.0E7   T   F
   c. 3.   T   F
   d. .057   T   F
   e. −2.4E2.5   T   F
   f. 3.141592   T   F
   g. +0.029   T   F
   h. 47   T   F
   i. 7E5   T   F
   j. −7.4E−16   T   F

10. Given AREA = 749.7434126 show the WRITE statements which would format this value in the following ways:
    a. 7.497434126E+002
    b. 74.97E+002
    c. 749.7434126
    d. 749.74

11. Given the following program structure,

```
PROGRAM MODULAR(INPUT, OUTPUT);
VAR A, B, C : INTEGER;
    Q : BOOLEAN;
(*********************************************************)
FUNCTION ONE (Q1 : BOOLEAN; A1 : INTEGER): INTEGER;
VAR B : INTEGER;
BEGIN (*ONE*)
    .
    .
END;  (*ONE*)
(*********************************************************)
PROCEDURE BUZZ(VAR A2 : INTEGER; B2 : INTEGER);
VAR Q2 : BOOLEAN;

    FUNCTION TWO(B3 : INTEGER; Q3 : BOOLEAN): BOOLEAN;
    BEGIN (*TWO*)
       .
       .
    END;  (*TWO*)
```

```
BEGIN (*BUZZ*)
    +
    +
END;   (*BUZZ*)
(***********************************************)
BEGIN (*MAIN*)
    +
    +
END.   (*MAIN*)
```

answer the following as True or False. Read them carefully.

1. The statement ONE (Q, A) in the body of program MODULAR would invoke function ONE, initializing Q1 and A1 with the values of Q and A.   T   F

2. The statement B := A1 in function ONE would assign the value of A1 to the local variable B of ONE, and global variable B of program MODULAR would be unaffected.   T   F

3. The statement A2 := TWO (B2, Q2) in the body of procedure BUZZ would invoke function TWO and assign the result to A2.   T   F

4. The statement Q1 := TWO (B, Q) in the body of function ONE would invoke TWO and assign the BOOLEAN result to Q1.   T   F

5. The statement BUZZ (A, B) in the body of program MODULAR would invoke procedure BUZZ, initialize A2 and B2 to the values of A and B, and any changes in variable parameter A2 will be returned to the main program in A.   T   F

12. Write a recursive function which computes the factorial of its positive integer parameter.

Pre-Test

1. Value parameters allow values to be passed into a function but do not return values to the main program, so the only way a function can return a value to the main program is through a variable parameter.

T   F

2. Given the following declaration:
```
VAR : INCOME, DEDUCTIONS: INTEGER;
        +
        +
FUNCTION HIGHTAXBRACKET(INC, DED : INTEGER) : BOOLEAN;
        +
        +
```
the following statement is legal in the main program:
```
        IF HIGHTAXBRACKET(INCOME, DEDUCTIONS)
           THEN WRITELN(' UPPER CLASS');
```
T   F

3. Declare a Pascal function REBATE of type BOOLEAN which will receive the integer day, month, and year of a car sale and return TRUE if the sale occurred on or before an 8/9/80 deadline.

4. The basic difference between a REPEAT loop and a WHILE loop is that the REPEAT loop is a pre-test loop and the WHILE loop is a post-test loop.

T   F

5. Convert the following into a CASE statement.

```
IF (COUNT=1) OR (COUNT=2) OR (COUNT=3)
    THEN WRITELN(' LOW COUNT')
    ELSE IF (COUNT=4) OR (COUNT=5)
        THEN WRITELN(' PASS')
        ELSE IF COUNT=6
            THEN WRITELN(' PASS')
            ELSE IF COUNT=7
                THEN
                    BEGIN
                        WRITELN(' HIGH COUNT');
                        OK := OK + 1
                    END;
```

6. Given the following program structure:

```
PROGRAM PRETEST(INPUT, OUTPUT);
VAR A, B, C : INTEGER;
        Q : BOOLEAN;

FUNCTION TASK1(Q1:BOOLEAN; A1 : INTEGER):INTEGER;
VAR B : INTEGER;
BEGIN  (*TASK1*)
    .
    .
END;   (*TASK1*)

PROCEDURE TASK2(VAR A2:INTEGER; B2:INTEGER);
VAR Q2 : BOOLEAN;

    FUNCTION TASK3(B3:INTEGER;Q3:BOOLEAN):BOOLEAN;
    BEGIN  (*TASK3*)
        .
        .
    END;    (*TASK3*)

BEGIN  (*TASK2*)
    .
    .
END;   (*TASK2*)

BEGIN  (*MAIN*)
    .
    .
END.   (*MAIN*)
```

answer the following as True or False. Read them carefully.

1. Function TASK3 cannot be invoked from the body of program PRE-TEST. T F
2. A2 := TASK3(A2,Q2) would be legal in the body of procedure TASK2. T F
3. B := TASK1 (A) would invoke function TASK1 in the body of program PRETEST. T F
4. TASK2(B,A) in the body of program PRETEST would invoke TASK2, initialize A2 to B, and B2 to A. During execution of TASK2, any assignments to B2 would change the value of A in the main program. T F
5. A1 := B in the body of function TASK1 would assign the value of the local variable B to A1. T F

7. For each of the following, answer True if it is a valid REAL constant and False if it is not.

a. 6.42E−7.5   T F
b. .41325   T F
c. +7E16   T F
d. 257.5415   T F
e. −47.9E−10   T F

8. Write a program segment which would produce the following output. (VALUE is real and FREQ is integer.) ('□' indicates a blank.) Be sure to write both lines of output.

```
□□□□□VALUE□□□□□□□FREQ
     26.33564        7
```

Data Types and Data Structures **9**

Goals

To be able to define and use scalar variables for handling both numeric and non-numeric data.

To be able to define and use subrange variables to take advantage of range-checking and improve readability.

To be able to use FOR loops when the number of repetitions is known.

To be able to define a one-dimensional array type to handle collections of data objects of the same type.

To be able to declare an array variable.

To be able to process (access) elements in a one-dimensional array.

SCALAR TYPES

The TYPE of a simple variable or constant determines what it can look like. That is, what allowable values it can assume. If a variable is declared to be INTEGER, only an integer can be stored in that variable. If a variable is declared to be BOOLEAN, only TRUE or FALSE can be stored there. If a variable is declared to be CHAR, only one character can be stored there. If a variable is REAL, only a real number can be stored there. These four standard data types are *scalar* data types. A *scalar* type is one in which the set of values is ordered.

> **SCALAR DATA TYPE**
>
> A set of distinct values (constants) that are ordered.

For example, values of the type CHAR exhibit an ordering so that 'A'<'B'<'C'<'D' . . . is true. Values of the type INTEGER are ordered so that 1<2<3<4 . . . is true.

ORDINAL TYPES

All of the scalar data types are called *ordinal* with the exception of REAL. In *ordinal* data types, each value (except the first) has a unique predecessor and each value (except the last) has a unique successor.

There are two predeclared functions in Pascal, PRED and SUCC, which will return these unique values. (Note that the SUCC(I) where I is MAXINT and the PRED(I) where I is −MAXINT are undefined and would result in an error.)

PRED('B') returns 'A'.
SUCC(4) returns 5.
If I is 10,
      PRED(I) returns 9,
      SUCC(I) returns 11.

REALs are not ordinal because there is not an unambiguous predecessor or successor. Add one more digit of precision and you change what the predecessor and successor of a real number are.

Pascal allows the user to define new ordinal types. These are called enumerated types because they are defined by listing the constants that make up the type. These constants are separated by the comma, and the set of them is enclosed in parentheses.

> **USER-DEFINED (ENUMERATED) TYPE**
>
> The ordered set of distinct values (constants) defined as a data type in a program.

The variable declarations

```
VAR ANIMAL : (MOUSE, CAT, DOG, BUFFALO, ELEPHANT);
    CAR : (FORD, CHEVROLET, PLYMOUTH, FIAT, DATSUN,
           TOYOTA);
```

create two new enumerated types. MOUSE is now a constant in a data type made up of five constants. Notice that MOUSE is *not* a variable name. MOUSE is one of the "things" that the variable ANIMAL can contain.

Look at the following assignment statement.

```
              ANIMAL := MOUSE
```

ANIMAL does not contain the character string 'MOUSE'; it does not contain the contents of the place MOUSE. It contains the value MOUSE. The following statement would be valid provided ANIMAL had been assigned a value.

```
IF ANIMAL = MOUSE
   THEN WRITELN(' SET TRAP')
   ELSE IF ANIMAL <= DOG
           THEN WRITELN(' PET')
           ELSE WRITELN(' RUN')
```

Enumerated types can be used in CASE statements as well.

```
CASE CAR OF
   FORD,
   CHEVROLET,
   PLYMOUTH  : BEGIN
                 TAX := PRICE * 0.10;
                 WRITELN(' DOMESTIC TAX ', TAX)
              END;
   FIAT      : BEGIN
                 TAX := PRICE * 0.20;
                 WRITELN(' EUROPEAN TAX ', TAX)
              END;
   DATSUN,
   TOYOTA    : BEGIN
                 TAX := PRICE * 0.25;
                 WRITELN(' FAR EAST TAX ', TAX)
              END
END  (*CASE*)
```

User-defined scalar types are ordinal because an ordering is defined by the order in which they are listed. Therefore PRED(CAT) returns MOUSE, SUCC(DATSUN) returns TOYOTA.

The constants that make up an enumerated type must be unique—they cannot be used to define another enumerated type. For example,

```
VAR VOWEL : ('A', 'E', 'I', 'O', 'U');
```

is not valid because the constants that make up the type are part of the standard type CHAR. In like manner,

```
VAR FOOD : (CORN, FISH, BEAN, SQUASH);
    GRAIN : (WHEAT, CORN, RYE, BARLEY, SORGHUM);
```

is not valid because CORN is used in two different type definitions.

Since user-defined types have meaning only within the program, we cannot read them in or write them out. We have to use some sort of a code. For example, the following program fragment reads in an animal represented by its first letter.

```
READ(CH);
IF CH = 'M' THEN ANIMAL := MOUSE
   ELSE IF CH = 'C' THEN ANIMAL := CAT
        ELSE IF CH = 'D' THEN ANIMAL := DOG
             ELSE IF CH = 'B' THEN ANIMAL := BUFFALO
                  ELSE IF CH = 'E'
                          THEN ANIMAL := ELEPHANT
```

If we wish to output an enumerated type we could use the following fragment:

```
CASE CAR OF
    FORD : WRITELN('FORD');
       .
       .
       .
    TOYOTA : WRITELN('TOYOTA')
END (* CASE *)
```

As with enumerated values, a Boolean value cannot be read in. However, unlike enumerated values, Boolean values can be printed (prints 'TRUE' or 'FALSE').

There is an additional predefined function to be used with *ordinal* types. ORD takes as a parameter an *ordinal* value and returns an INTEGER which represents the parameter's place in the ordering. For example,

ORD(MOUSE) is 0
ORD(CAT) is 1
ORD(ELEPHANT) is 4
ORD(FIAT) is 3

Note that the ORD of the first element in a type is zero.

The ORD function can be used to determine the lexicographic ordering of the character set for any particular machine. That is, all the characters (letters, digits and special symbols) recognized by a machine (called the character set of that machine) are ordered. This ordering varies from machine to machine. The only thing you can count on is that the letters are in order and the digits are in order. However, letters come before digits in some machines and after digits in others. Also, in some character sets the letters are not contiguous—there are unprintable "control characters" embedded in the ordering of the letters. (See APPENDIX N: CHARACTER SETS.) To simplify the examples in this text, we assumed the character set to be ASCII in which the letters are contiguous.

The following program reads in characters and prints the characters along with the ordinal position of each.

```
PROGRAM CHARSET(INPUT, OUTPUT);
VAR CH : CHAR;
BEGIN
    WHILE NOT EOF DO
        BEGIN
            READ(CH);
            WRITELN(CH, ORD(CH))
        END
END.
```

For type CHAR only, there is a function CHR which takes an INTEGER value and returns the corresponding character if it exists. Therefore, the lexicographic ordering can actually be found with no input at all—as demonstrated by the following program.

```
PROGRAM CHARSET2(OUTPUT);
CONST NUMCHAR =  (number of characters in character set of your machine);
VAR COUNTER : INTEGER;
BEGIN
    COUNTER := 0;
    WHILE COUNTER < NUMCHAR DO
        BEGIN
            WRITELN(COUNTER, CHR(COUNTER):3);
            COUNTER := COUNTER + 1
        END
    END.
```

The digits are contiguously ordered in all character sets, so that

$$ORD(`4') - ORD(`0') = 4$$

is true. Therefore, the expression

$$ORD(\text{digit character}) - ORD(`0')$$

can be used to convert a digit character into its actual numeric value. The expression

$$CHR(\text{number} + ORD(`0'))$$

can be used to convert a number into its actual character.

SUBRANGE TYPES

Sometimes a new data type is not needed, only a portion of an already existing type. Pascal allows us to define a subrange data type that is a specified range of either a standard or user-defined ordinal type (any scalar type except REAL).

For example, we may need a variable, TESTSCORE, which can contain an integer value in the range of 0 to 100. If we limit TESTSCORE to values in this subrange, we can use it as an integer variable within the range but not allow it to contain invalid scores such as −10 or 560.

> **SUBRANGE TYPE**
>
> A data type composed of a specified range of any standard or user-defined ordinal type.

Subrange types can be defined in the VAR section by specifying the first value and the last value with two periods in between. (First value must be a predecessor of last value.) For example,

Subrange type	Values included
VAR NUM : 5 . . 10;	(* 5, 6, 7, 8, 9, 10 *)
LETTER : 'A' . . 'D';	(* 'A', 'B', 'C', 'D' *)
SMALAML : MOUSE . . DOG;	(* MOUSE, CAT, DOG *)
SMALCAR : FIAT . . TOYOTA;	(* FIAT, DATSUN, TOYOTA *)

The subrange type can also be given a name in the TYPE section (see next section) and that name used in the VAR section.

Subrange types improve the readability of a program. By telling a reader the range of values a variable can take, you have conveyed something about its use. Subrange types also take advantage of automatic range-checking, which can be invaluable during debugging. That is, when you assign a value to a variable, the system checks to see if that value is within the specified range. If it is not, a run-time error message is returned: VALUE OUT OF RANGE. For example, given the above declarations,

```
NUM := 0
```

will generate an error.

RANGE-CHECKING

The automatic detection of an out-of-range value being assigned to a variable.

TYPE DECLARATIONS

Pascal has the facility to create new data types for simple variables by listing the allowable values a variable or constant can contain. As we have shown, this can be done in the VAR section, by enumerating the allowable values in parentheses following the ':'. This can also be done in a TYPE declaration by giving the allowable list a name and using that name (the created data type) in the VAR section.

TYPE DEFINITION

A definition of a data type in the TYPE declaration of a block, with the type identifier on the left of the equal sign ("=") and the definition on the right.

```
TYPE COLOR = (RED,GREEN,BLUE);
     LIMITS = -10..10;
     POSINT = 0..MAXINT;
```

Figure 9-1 shows where the TYPE definitions fit into the declaration section of a Pascal program. Remember that procedures and functions can have their own declaration sections which can contain TYPE definitions.

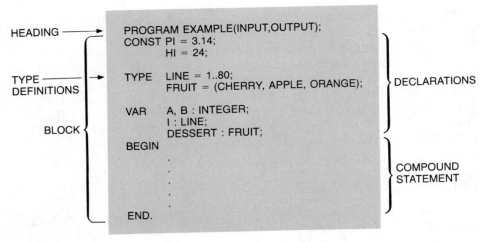

HEADING ⟶

PROGRAM EXAMPLE(INPUT,OUTPUT);
CONST PI = 3.14;
      HI = 24;

TYPE
DEFINITIONS ⟶

TYPE   LINE = 1..80;
        FRUIT = (CHERRY, APPLE, ORANGE);

VAR   A, B : INTEGER;
        I : LINE;
        DESSERT : FRUIT;

BLOCK

BEGIN
    .
    .
    .
    .
END.

DECLARATIONS

COMPOUND
STATEMENT

Figure 9-1. Program Shell

The following two examples produce the same results:

```
TYPE RANGE = 2..25;
VAR   TALLY : RANGE;
```

or

```
VAR TALLY : 2..25;
```

Note that defining a type merely says what something can look like; it does not create a place in memory which looks like that. Declarations of variables of that type in the VAR section create storage space in memory.

Since we can put the subrange or enumerated type right next to the variable name in the VAR section, why would you ever want to put it in the TYPE section? Because subrange and enumerated type declarations are not allowed in the formal parameter list of a procedure or function. The types used in the formal parameter list of a function or a procedure must be globally defined. That is, they must be one of the standard scalar types, or a user-defined type defined in the TYPE section of the main program or a block global to the function or procedure.

Acceptable	Not acceptable

```
.
.
TYPE RANGE = 1..15;
     PET = (CAT,DOG,BIRD,FISH);         .
.                                        .
.                                        .
.                                        .
PROCEDURE PASS(I:RANGE);        PROCEDURE PASS(I:1..15);
.                                        .
.                                        .
.                                        .
PROCEDURE EAT(ANIMAL : PET);    PROCEDURE EAT(ANIMAL:(CAT,
.                                      DOG,BIRD,FISH));
.                                        .
.                                        .
```

Notice that enumerated types are enclosed in parentheses, but subrange types are not.

```
TYPE WEATHER = (RAIN, FOG, SLEET, HUMID, COLD, HOT, DRY);
     WETWEATHER = RAIN..SLEET;
```

FOR STATEMENT

In this chapter we discuss data types and data structures. The only looping control structure we haven't discussed is the FOR statement, and as it is useful for processing data structures such as arrays, we introduce it here.

The FOR statement is designed to be used for count controlled loops. The statement

```
FOR I := 1 TO N DO
    statement
```

is functionally equivalent to but easier to write than

```
I := 1;
WHILE I <= N DO
    BEGIN
        statement;
        I := I + 1
    END
```

FOR STATEMENT

A looping control structure similar to a WHILE statement, but with predefined initial and final values for the loop control variable, as well as automatic incrementing (or decrementing) of the loop control variable.

```
FOR I := 1 TO 10 DO
    BEGIN
        READLN(VALU);
        WRITELN(VALU);
        SUM := SUM + VALU
    END;
                -----*-----
FOR COLOR := RED TO BROWN DO
    WRITELN(' PROCESSING COLOR #', ORD(COLOR));
                -----*-----
FOR J := 5 DOWNTO 0 DO
    WRITELN(' COUNTDOWN ', J);
```

FOR statements are very convenient and many students tend to overuse them. *Be warned:* FOR loops are not general-purpose. They are designed exclusively for *count controlled* loops. To use them intelligently, you should know and remember the following facts about FOR loops:

1. The loop control variable (LCV) may not be changed within the loop. Its value may be used but not changed. That is, the LCV may appear in an expression but not on the left side of an assignment statement.
2. The LCV is incremented or decremented by one, automatically. If you need to increment or decrement by another value, you should use a WHILE or REPEAT.
3. The LCV is undefined at the end of the loop. If you try to use the LCV in an expression in the statement following the FOR, you may get a run-time error message (depending on the implementation of Pascal). You might expect the LCV to be the final value plus one, but it is not. It is undefined.
4. The LCV of a FOR statement used in a procedure or function must be a local variable.
5. The LCV can be any *ordinal* type. In cases where the LCV is not an integer, incrementing is just the SUCC function and decrementing is the PRED function. For example,

```
FOR CH := 'A' TO 'K' DO
    statement
```

The initial and final values must be of the same type as the LCV.
6. The loop is executed with the LCV at the initial value, the final value

and all values in-between. If the initial value is greater than the final value, the FOR statement is not executed. If the initial value is equal to the final value, the FOR statement is executed once.

7. *You cannot put an additional termination condition in the loop.* The heading must be exactly like the following:

> FOR name := initial value TO final value DO
> or FOR name := initial value DOWNTO final value DO

where name must be a variable, and initial value and final value can be any valid expressions (variables and/or constants and operators).

8. FOR statements are useful for processing arrays; that is why they are being introduced in this chapter.

Figure 9-2 illustrates the flow of control of the FOR statement. As in the other looping control structures, the body of the loop, statement1, can be a compound statement.

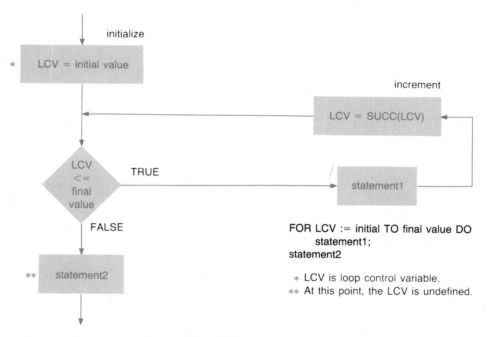

Figure 9-2. FOR Structure Diagram

Here is an example program using a FOR statement.

```
PROGRAM CLASSAVERAGE(INPUT, OUTPUT);       (* This program calculates the
                                              average of a set of 30 grades. *)
CONST N = 30;
VAR SUM, STUDENT, GRADE, AVG : INTEGER;
BEGIN (*MAIN*)
```

```
    WRITELN(' CLASS GRADES ');                (*print heading*)
    SUM := 0;                                 (*initialize sum*)
    FOR STUDENT := 1 TO N DO          (*process 30 student grades*)
       BEGIN
          READ(GRADE);                         (*input grade*)
          WRITELN(GRADE);                      (*print grade*)
          SUM := SUM + GRADE             (*add grade to "sum"*)
       END;
    AVG:= SUM DIV N;                       (*find class average*)
    WRITELN(' CLASS AVERAGE IS ', AVG)   (*print the class average*)
END. (*MAIN*)
```

NOTE: This program does not check for errors in input data.

Given this input data:

80 90 50 90 100 70 30 20 90 80 90 90 8 20 10 100
100 90 90 80 80 70 70 30 60 50 40 30 20 100

Program CLASSAVERAGE produces the following output:

```
CLASS GRADES
        80
        90
        50
        90
       100
        70
        30
        20
        90
        80
        90
        90
         8
        20
        10
       100
       100
        90
        90
        80
        80
        70
        70
        30
        60
        50
        40
        30
        20
       100
CLASS AVERAGE IS        64
```

DATA STRUCTURES

So far we have discussed simple scalar data types. Sometimes it is necessary to show a relationship among different variables or to store and reference variables as a group. For these reasons, Pascal provides data structures composed of simple scalar data types. These data structures can be built up into more and more complex structures, but ultimately they are all composed of some simple type. (See Figure 9-3.)

> **DATA STRUCTURE**
>
> A composition of scalar types characterized by a particular structuring method.

Since the lowest level component must be of some simple scalar type, it can be manipulated like a simple variable. The built-in data structures of Pascal are ARRAYS, RECORDS, SETS and FILES.

Pascal is known as a strongly typed language, and its type checking feature also extends to structured types. Assignment between two variables, whether they are simple variables or structured variables (data structures), is allowed only if they are both of the same type. FILES are the exception; they can't be assigned to each other because *files are external to memory.* We have access to and can store (or retrieve) only one component of a file at a time. On the other hand, *all other data structures, just like simple vari-*

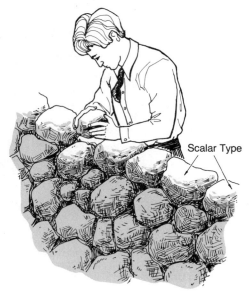

Scalar Type

Figure 9-3. Building a Data Structure

ables, are stored in memory and are destroyed when the program termi-nates. Keep this in mind as you program.

Data structures allow us to write programs to manipulate data more easily.

ARRAYS

An ARRAY is a group of elements given a common name. Each element is accessed by its position within the group. The component type says what can be stored in each cell (element) of the array. The index type says what type the variable, constant, or expression must be which will be used to specify the cell we are referring to at any one time. The range of the index type specifies how big (how many cells) the array is.

ARRAY

A structured data type composed of a fixed number of components of the same type, with each component directly accessed by the index.

index type (also called subscript)   component type (also called base type)

```
VAR GRADE : ARRAY[1..25] OF CHAR;
            -----*-----
VAR A : ARRAY['A'..'Z'] OF INTEGER;
            -----*-----
TYPE DRINK = (ORANGE,COLA,LEMON);
VAR AMT : ARRAY[ORANGE..LEMON] OF REAL;
    or
VAR AMT : ARRAY[DRINK] OF REAL;
            -----*-----
TYPE OCCUPANT = 0..5;
     ROOMS = ARRAY[1..350] OF OCCUPANT;
VAR BUILDING : ROOMS;
```

Note that the index type can be any ordinal type and does not have to be the same type as the component type.

To declare an array type you use the following syntax:

ARRAY[range of index type] OF component type

To access a particular cell in the array you use the following syntax:

array name[constant or variable of the index type]

Note that '[]'s are used, not '()'s.

Let's look in detail at each of the ARRAY examples in the preceding colored box. The declaration

```
VAR GRADE : ARRAY[1..25] OF CHAR;
```

sets up 25 cells each of which can contain a character. Each cell is accessed by its position in the group of 25.

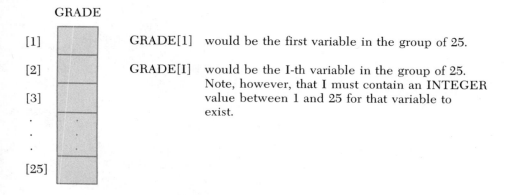

GRADE

[1]   GRADE[1]   would be the first variable in the group of 25.

[2]   GRADE[I]   would be the I-th variable in the group of 25.
                       Note, however, that I must contain an INTEGER
[3]   value between 1 and 25 for that variable to
                       exist.

[25]

The declaration

```
VAR A : ARRAY['A'..'Z'] OF INTEGER;
```

sets up 26 cells each of which can contain an INTEGER value. Each cell can be accessed by A['A'] to A['Z']. To process the array cell by cell you could use a loop such as:

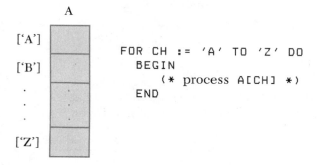

A

```
['A']
              FOR CH := 'A' TO 'Z' DO
['B']            BEGIN
                    (* process A[CH] *)
                 END
['Z']
```

Note that A is the name of a group of elements (an array) and bears no relation to the character 'A'. A['A'] is the first in the group of 26 and A['Z'] is the last.

The declaration

```
TYPE DRINK = (ORANGE, COLA, LEMON);
VAR AMT : ARRAY[ORANGE..LEMON] OF REAL;    (*or ARRAY [DRINK] OF
                                                           REAL*)
```

creates a group of 3 REAL elements called AMT. These three cells can be processed sequentially by the code:

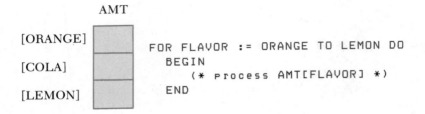

```
FOR FLAVOR := ORANGE TO LEMON DO
    BEGIN
        (* process AMT[FLAVOR] *)
    END
```

The declaration

```
TYPE OCCUPANT = 0..5;
     ROOMS = ARRAY[1..350] OF OCCUPANT;
VAR BUILDING : ROOMS;
```

creates a group of 350 elements called BUILDING. Each cell can contain an INTEGER between 0 and 5. These 350 cells can be processed sequentially as follows:

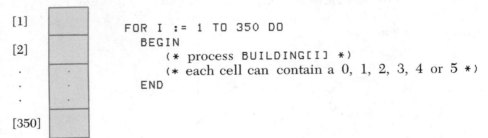

```
FOR I := 1 TO 350 DO
    BEGIN
        (* process BUILDING[I] *)
        (* each cell can contain a 0, 1, 2, 3, 4 or 5 *)
    END
```

GRADE, A, AMT and BUILDING are all called array variables. The following chart summarizes these variables as we defined them.

Array variable	Index type	Component type	# cells
GRADE	1..25	CHAR	25
A	'A'..'Z'	INTEGER	26
AMT	DRINK	REAL	3
BUILDING	1..350	OCCUPANT	350

Figure 9-4 shows these arrays with some sample contents.

GRADE		A		AMT		BUILDING	
[1]	'B'	['A']	23	[ORANGE]	0.60	[1]	2
[2]	'A'	['B']	1032	[COLA]	0.45	[2]	1
[3]	'C'	['C']	1	[LEMON]	0.60	[3]	1
[4]	'C'	['D']	0			[4]	0
[5]	'F'	['E']	82			[5]	0
[6]	'D'	['F']	−16			[6]	3

Figure 9-4.

When working with arrays we use a variable to help us find the cell we are looking for.

$$GRADE[I]$$

Name of group of elements each of which has the same type called component type or base type.

A variable which allows us to specify one of the group of elements. This is called an index or subscript and the type is the index type or subscript type.

In our examples of processing (accessing) each element (cell) in an array, we used a FOR loop. However, if we had wanted either to process all of the cells or to quit if a certain condition became true, we would have had to use a WHILE loop.

For example, if our task is to see if all the students in a class are passing, we can stop looking if we find just one 'F'. The following program fragment would do this.

```
PASSING := TRUE;
I := 1;
WHILE (I <= 25) AND PASSING DO
    IF GRADE[I] = 'F'
        THEN PASSING := FALSE
        ELSE I := I + 1
```

The program on page 248 reads values into an array, sums these values, prints the average, and prints the values in the array. (It does not check for valid data.)

Using an Array

Let's assume these declarations in the main program:

```
TYPE GRADES = 'A'..'F';
VAR  STUDENTS : ARRAY[1..10] OF GRADES;
     ID : 1..10;
```

The array variable STUDENTS is pictured below. Values are shown for each of the cells, which implies that some processing of the array has already taken place. Following the illustration are some simple examples showing how the array may be used.

STUDENTS

[1]	'F'
[2]	'B'
[3]	'C'
[4]	'A'
[5]	'F'
[6]	'C'
[7]	'A'
[8]	'A'
[9]	'C'
[10]	'B'

```
READ(STUDENTS[2]);
```
Assigns the next character in file INPUT to the cell in array STUDENTS indexed by 2.

```
STUDENTS[4] := 'A';
```
Assigns the character 'A' to the cell in array STUDENTS indexed by 4.

```
ID := 6;
STUDENTS[ID] := 'C';
```
Sets the index variable ID to 6. Assigns the character 'C' to the cell of array STUDENTS indexed by ID; i.e., by 6.

```
FOR ID := 1 TO 10 DO
   WRITE(STUDENT[ID]);
```
This loop prints all the values in array STUDENTS. In this case the output would be:

```
FBCAFCAACB
```

```
FOR ID := 1 TO 10 DO
   WRITELN('STUDENT ',ID:1,
          ' GRADE ',
          STUDENTS[ID])
```
This loop also prints all the values in array STUDENTS, but in a more readable form. ID is used as the index, but it also has semantic content—it is the student's identification number. Output would be:

```
STUDENT 1 GRADE F
STUDENT 2 GRADE B
  .
  .
  .
STUDENT 10 GRADE B
```

```
PROGRAM CLASSAVERAGE(INPUT, OUTPUT);
CONST N = 20;
VAR GRADE : ARRAY[1..N] OF INTEGER;
    SUM, STUDENT, AVG : INTEGER;
BEGIN (*MAIN*)
    SUM := 0;                                  (*Initialize SUM*)
    FOR STUDENT := 1 TO N DO                    (*Process 20 student grades*)
        BEGIN
            READ(GRADE[STUDENT]);               (*Input grade into array*)
            SUM := SUM + GRADE[STUDENT];        (*Add grade to SUM*)
        END;
    AVG := SUM DIV N;                           (*Find the class average*)
    WRITELN(' CLASS AVERAGE IS ', AVG);         (*Print the class average*)
    WRITELN;                                    (*Skip a line*)
    WRITELN(' INDIVIDUAL GRADES ');             (*Print heading*)
    FOR STUDENT := 1 TO N DO                    (*Print list of grades*)
        WRITELN(GRADE[STUDENT])
END. (*MAIN*)
```

A loop is used to fill the array: the array index variable STUDENT is incremented by one for each iteration of the loop, causing the READ statement
to store values in successive cells of the array. Given this input data,

```
80 90 50 90 100 70 30 20 90 80 90
90 8 20 10 100 100 90 80 80
```

the output would look like this:

```
CLASS AVERAGE IS          68

INDIVIDUAL GRADES
        80
        90
        50
        90
       100
        70
        30
        20
        90
        80
        90
        90
         8
        20
        10
       100
       100
        90
        80
        80
```

Special Note on Passing Arrays as Parameters

The data type of a variable (including array variables) used as a *formal* parameter must be globally defined.

```
PROCEDURE PASS(VAR LIST:ARRAY[1..20] OF INTEGER); Invalid
PROCEDURE PASS(VAR LIST:LISTSTRUCTURE); Valid, assuming that
                                        LISTSTRUCTURE was
                                        defined in the main
                                        program.
```

It is also a good idea to pass large data structures as VAR parameters. This saves memory space by not making copies of the large data structure during the procedure call. Of course if you made any changes to an array passed as a VAR parameter, this would change the global array. If you want to make changes in the passed array without changing the global array, then pass it as a value parameter.

TESTING AND DEBUGGING

Because Pascal is a strongly typed language, every variable must be declared in a VAR section with its type explicitly stated. When an assignment statement is compiled in your program, the type of the value to be computed is checked against the type of the variable into which it is to be stored. If the types do not match, there is a compile-time error. The only exception to this is that an INTEGER value can be stored into a REAL variable. At execution time the INTEGER value is converted into REAL form before the value is stored.

A further check on values is allowed by the use of subrange types. If the variable name on the left of an assignment statement is a subrange type, before a value is put in that location during execution, the value is checked to be sure it is within the proper range. If it is not, an error occurs.

This is particularly useful with arrays. Since the index type of an array is usually a subrange type, you cannot access places which do not exist. If you try to access the 0th or 21st element of an array whose index type is 1..20 you would get the error message: INDEX OUT OF RANGE.

Testing and Debugging Hints

1. Use a subrange type if you know the bounds or the values of a variable.
2. Use enumerated types to make your programs more readable.
3. Use the TYPE section.
   Define types in the TYPE section rather than the VAR section. For example, if you change a subrange, you only have to change one line

in the TYPE section, not each line where you used it in the VAR section.

4. Variables cannot be used in the declaration part of a type.

Information in the CONST, TYPE and VAR sections is used by the computer at compile time. Variables do not get values until execution time. So declaring a subrange type 1..N makes no sense unless N was defined in the CONST section.

5. Use the same type definition for *formal* and *actual* parameters.

Formal and actual parameters must have the same type definition. You cannot define a type in the formal parameter list. Use the same global definition for both the actual and the formal parameter.

6. Be sure you don't apply SUCC to the last element of a type, or PRED to the first.

7. Do not use the LCV from a FOR loop outside of the loop unless you redefine it.

The LCV from a FOR loop is undefined after exiting the loop.

Summary

Pascal has four standard scalar types: INTEGER, REAL, CHAR and BOOLEAN. User-defined scalar types are also allowed. The subrange type is a subset of a scalar type (except REAL). It is valuable in improving the readability of a program as well as taking advantage of automatic range-checking.

The FOR statement is useful when we know the number of times we want to repeat a loop. The FOR statement is often used in processing arrays when the number of elements is known.

Pascal allows you to define an array variable. An array variable is a structured data type where a name is given to a group of elements. You access each one by giving the array name and an index. The index (variable or constant) indicates which one of the group of elements you want.

Arrays are a convenient way to handle a related collection of data. Since the index can be a variable, this allows random access to any component of the array. This data structure simplifies the design of many algorithms.

Exercises

1. Define an enumerated type for each of the following:
   a. The local area high schools.
   b. The positions on a baseball team.
   c. The members of your immediate family.

2. Define a subrange type for each of the following:
   a. The numerals '0' to '9'.

b. The integers between −4 and 24 (including −4 and 24).

c. A subrange of Problem 1.b.

3. Declare array variables for each of the following:

    a. A 24 element REAL array where the index goes from 1 to 24.

    b. A 26 element INTEGER array where the index goes from 'A' to 'Z'.

    c. A 10 element character array where the index goes from −5 to 4.

4. Write a program fragment which does the following processing for the corresponding array in Problem 3.

    a. Initialize each value to 0.0

    b. Initialize each value to 0

    c. Read 2 characters into the array with the first character going into the cell whose index is −5

5. Write a program fragment which reverses the order of elements of an array LIST.

```
VAR LIST : ARRAY[1..10] OF THING;
```

6. Write a program fragment which finds the number of vehicles in-service.

```
VAR INSERVICE : ARRAY[1..83] OF BOOLEAN;
```

7. Scalar data types are ordered so that every variable must be less than, equal to or greater than any other variable of that type.

T   F

8. INTEGER, CHAR and enumerated types are ordinal so it is possible to declare a subrange type based on them.

T   F

9. Given the following type declaration

```
TYPE MEMBERS = (SMITH,JONES,GRANT,WHITE);
```

the expression GRANT < SMITH would be true.

T   F

10. The following type declaration segment would be legal.

T   F

```
TYPE FAMILY = (JOHN,JOE,EVELYN,BURT);
     FRIENDS = (BILL,ALICE,EVELYN,JOHN);
```

11. The following declaration section contains no errors.

T   F

```
TYPE RAINTOTALS = ARRAY[1..NUMCOUNTIES] OF INTEGER;
VAR RAINFALL : RAINTOTALS;
     NUMCOUNTIES : INTEGER;
```

Pre-Test

1. The type integer is a scalar type, but a subrange type is not.

    T F

2. The type of the predeclared ordinal function ORD must be an integer since it returns the internal integer representation of a character.

    T F

3. The range of subscripts for an array is fixed at declaration, and every element of the array must have the same fixed type. But during execution an array of 50 elements might only contain 10 meaningful data items, leaving the other 40 elements with undefined values.

    T F

4. What values would result from the following functions?
    a. PRED(12) ⎯⎯⎯⎯
    b. SUCC('B') ⎯⎯⎯⎯
    c. SUCC(MONDAY) where MONDAY is an element of type DAYS.
        DAYS = (MONDAY,TUESDAY,WEDNESDAY,THURSDAY,FRIDAY)
        ⎯⎯⎯⎯
    d. ORD('C') where CHR(1)='A' ⎯⎯⎯⎯
    e. CHR(5) where ORD('A')=1 ⎯⎯⎯⎯

5. Define a scalar type or subrange type (as appropriate) for each of the following.

    a. The CROPS consisting of rice, beans, corn and peas.
    b. All the days of the week.
    c. The WORKDAYS of Monday through Friday from the type in part b.
    d. The RANGE of −10 to +200 inclusive.
    e. The characters 'B' through 'K'.
    f. A column counter of the range 1 to 72.

6. Mark true or false for the legality of the following declaration segments.

    a. TYPE COLOR = (RED,YELLOW,BLUE);
        SHADE = (LIGHT,DARK);

        T F
    b. TYPE SIZE = (SMALL,MEDIUM,LARGE,GIANT);
        CREATURES = (DWARF,DRAGON,GIANT,KNIGHT);

        T F
    c. TYPE LIST = ARRAY[1..200] OF CODE;
        CODE = 1..10;
        VAR CODELIST : LIST;

        T F
    d. TYPE CODE = 1..5;
        LIST = ARRAY[CODE] OF INTEGER;
        VAR CODELIST : LIST;

        T F
    e. VAR CODELIST : ARRAY[1..5] OF INTEGER;

        T F
    f. VAR COLOR : (RED,YELLOW,BLUE);

        T F

g. TYPE CODE = (FIXED,VARYING,MIXED);
    RUNTYPE = ARRAY[1..15] OF CODE;
    VAR LIST : RUNTYPE;
    MIXED : INTEGER;

                    T F

7. Write a function called POSARRAY that receives an array variable name as a parameter and returns FALSE if any of the elements of the array are negative. (Return TRUE otherwise.) Assume this declaration in the main program:

```
TYPE ARRAYTYPE = ARRAY[1..50] OF INTEGER;
```

8. Write a procedure called SUMARRAY that will receive an array variable name as a parameter, sum the values in that array and return the total to the calling program. Assume these declarations in the main program.

```
CONST TOTALIMIT = 200;
TYPE TOTALS = ARRAY[1..TOTALIMIT] OF INTEGER;
```

Note: Other declarations will have to be made before the function in Problem 7 or the procedure in Problem 8 can be called, but this is not part of your problem.

Typical Problems Using Arrays 10

Goals

To be able to follow the development of the top-down design of a specific problem which includes one of the following typical types of array processing

■ *searching*
■ *using parallel arrays*
■ *indexes with meaning*
■ *merging*
■ *working with only a portion of the array*

To be able to read the code which implements each of the above top-down designs.

To gain experience in reading programs.

In Chapter 9 we introduced the concept of a one-dimensional array: a data structure made up of a group of locations given a common name. Each individual location is accessed by its position (index) in the group. There are two types associated with each location: the type of what can be stored in each location (the component type) and the type of the variable, constant, or expression which specifies a particular location within the group (the index type).

Chapter 10 is designed to give you more experience with the use of one-dimensional arrays. Described below are five kinds of processing that are done again and again in programs using one-dimensional arrays. We will demonstrate these typical processes in the context of specific problems. (Another common task, ordering or sorting the elements of an array, will be covered in Chapter 12.)

SEARCHING: Looking systematically through the elements of an array for a specific value is called searching. There are two classes of searching. One is used when you only want to know if the value is in the array; the other is used when you want to know its position in the array (if it is even there).

PARALLEL ARRAYS: In many problems there are several pieces of information which go together. For example, you might have social security numbers and grades. You set up one INTEGER array for the social security numbers and one CHAR array for the grades. A particular social security number goes with a particular grade because they have the same position in their respective arrays (i.e., they have the same index).

INDEXES WITH MEANING: This type of processing refers to problems in which the index has meaning beyond simple position (i.e., it has semantic content). For example, the employees in a company might be given identification numbers ranging from 100 to 500. If a one-dimensional array variable of social security numbers were defined

```
VAR SSNO : ARRAY[100..500] OF INTEGER;
```

then the index of a specific social security number would be the corresponding employee identification number.

MERGING: Taking two arrays where the values are ordered in some fashion, and producing a third array (or a listing) which contains the elements of both arrays ordered in the same fashion, is called merging.

SUB-ARRAY: There are times when you want to process some of the elements in an array, but not all of them. To do this, you might keep track of two specific indexes which represent the range you are interested in at any one time. In our example problem we are concerned only with the last four elements of an array.

Before we present these five processes in the concrete form of particular examples, a word should be said about choosing the size of an array. Storage for an array must be allocated at compile-time. That is, the number of locations for an array must be known in advance. Since the exact number of locations to be used is often dependent on the data itself, a safe maximum number is chosen to use in the definition of the array type. As values are actually put into the elements of the array, a count is kept of how many locations are used. This count is used to ensure that only those locations into which we have stored values are processed later.

For example, if there are 250 students in a class, a program to do a statistical analysis of grades would have to set aside 250 locations to hold test grades. However, for each test there would probably be fewer than 250 test grades. So in the processing, the number of test grades would be counted and that number, rather than 250, would be used to control the processing of the array.

Procedures and functions which have array parameters should also have a parameter which tells how many of the locations have values in them to be processed. For example, the following procedure will sum the test grades for a given class. NUMGRADES is the number of array elements to be processed.

```
TYPE GRADES = ARRAY[1..250] OF INTEGER;
     .
     .
     .
PROCEDURE SUMGRADES(VAR TEST : GRADES; NUMGRADES :
                    INTEGER; VAR SUM : INTEGER);
VAR LCV : INTEGER;
BEGIN
  SUM := 0;
  FOR LCV := 1 TO NUMGRADES DO
      SUM := SUM + TEST[LCV]
END;
```

This is a typical example of sub-array processing.

The data structures (arrays) used in each of the following examples are used to represent the "lists" we would use if we were solving the problems by hand. (Unlike paper and pencil lists, the data structures stored in memory don't exist after program termination, so we stored the input data and output results in files external to memory. Of course, the file INPUT may be on cards or from the terminal, and the file OUTPUT may be the line printer or the terminal.) Being able to structure our data simplifies algorithm design and reduces program complexity.

SEARCHING

■ SAMPLE PROBLEM

Problem: A dress manufacturing company wants a printed list of designs which were ordered during a particular week. They are interested not in how many of a particular design were ordered—only in which designs were ordered. To prepare this list you are provided with a week's worth of sales receipts on a file. Each sales receipt (line of data) contains the design number, the quantity of that design ordered, the unit cost and the total cost of the order.

Discussion: How would you do this job if you were to do it by hand? One algorithm might be to start going through the stack of orders one by one. If you have not seen that design number before, write it down. If you have, simply go on to the next order. How would you determine if you had seen it before? Scan (search) the list of those you have written down. If it isn't there, write it down; this is the first time you have seen an order with that design number. The list you have written down would be the list of designs sold that week.

This sounds promising. Writing the design number on a piece of paper can be translated into putting the value in the next open location in an array. Scanning the list can be translated into comparing each value already in the array with the design number on the order. If it matches you have seen this design number before. The problem is now understood well enough to begin the top-down design.

Input: A sales file containing sets of the following:

design number	(integer)	(DESIGN)
quantity ordered	(integer)	(NUMORD)
unit cost	(real)	(PRICE)
total sale	(real)	(SALE)

Output: A list of the designs which were ordered

Data Structures: A one-dimensional array, DESIGNLST, to hold design numbers

Note that this is the first time we have had a section in our top-down design called DATA STRUCTURES. Until now we have dealt only with simple variables (scalar types). If you are using a data structure, specify it in your design (and define it in the program). The DESIGNLST array can be pictured like this:

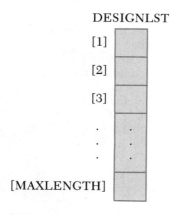

DESIGNLST

MAIN   Level 0

```
WHILE more data DO
    GETDATA
    PROCESSDATA
PRINT DESIGNLST
```

GETDATA   Level 1

```
READ DESIGN, NUMORD, ...... ?
```

DESIGN is the only value we are interested in. Why bother to input the other values simply because they are there? How do we by-pass them? By using a READLN.

GETDATA (revised)

```
READLN DESIGN
```

PROCESSDATA

> IF NOT BEFORE
>   THEN add to LIST

If we haven't seen the design before, add it to the list.

BEFORE   Level 2

> FOUND is FALSE
> WHILE more values AND NOT FOUND
>   IF DESIGN = DESIGNLST[CURRENT]
>   THEN FOUND is TRUE
>   ELSE increment CURRENT

Scan the list of design numbers we've seen so far.
CURRENT is the loop control variable that points to the current element in the array DESIGNLST. Note that a FOR loop cannot be used here.

ADDTOLIST

> Increment LENGTH
> DESIGNLST[LENGTH] = DESIGN

Adding the design # to the list.

GETDATA, PROCESSDATA, and ADDTOLIST are each only one simple statement long and do not need to be procedures. BEFORE should be a Boolean function.

Our design tree diagram now looks like this:

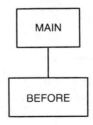

```
PROGRAM DESIGNCT (ORDERS, OUTPUT);          (* Program to list different
                                               designs for weekly orders *)
CONST MAXLENGTH = 500;                      (*total number of designs is 500*)
TYPE LIST = ARRAY[1..MAXLENGTH] OF INTEGER;
VAR  DESIGNLST : LIST;                      (*list of designs ordered*)
     LENGTH : INTEGER;                      (*number of items in DESIGNLST*)
```

```
          COUNT : INTEGER;                          (*loop control variable*)
          DESIGN : INTEGER;                         (*dress design number*)
          ORDERS : TEXT;                   (*file in which the orders are recorded*)


(*************************************************************)

FUNCTION BEFORE (DESIGNLST : LIST; LENGTH, DESIGN :
                    INTEGER): BOOLEAN;
VAR   CURRENT : INTEGER;                        (*loop control variable*)
      FOUND : BOOLEAN;                      (*will be TRUE if there is a match*)
BEGIN   (*BEFORE*)
  FOUND := FALSE;
  CURRENT := 1;
  WHILE (CURRENT <= LENGTH) AND NOT FOUND DO      (* search list *)
     IF DESIGN = DESIGNLST[CURRENT]      (* check if design seen before *)
        THEN FOUND := TRUE
        ELSE CURRENT := CURRENT + 1;
  BEFORE := FOUND
END;    (*BEFORE*)


(*************************************************************)

BEGIN    (*MAIN*)
  LENGTH := 0;
  RESET(ORDERS);
  WHILE NOT EOF(ORDERS) DO               (* while more orders to check *)
     BEGIN
       READLN(ORDERS, DESIGN);
       IF NOT BEFORE(DESIGNLST,LENGTH,DESIGN)           (*check if
                                                       design in list*)
          THEN
            BEGIN
              LENGTH := LENGTH + 1;
              DESIGNLST[LENGTH] := DESIGN      (* add design to list *)
            END
     END;
  WRITELN (' THE FOLLOWING DESIGN NUMBERS WERE ORDERED');
  FOR COUNT := 1 TO LENGTH DO                   (* print out list *)
      WRITELN (DESIGNLST[COUNT]);
END.   (*MAIN*)
```

Note that LENGTH is initialized to zero, so the first time BEFORE is executed, CURRENT=1, LENGTH=0 and the body of the WHILE loop in BEFORE is not executed.

Using this input:

```
22 70 3.00 210.00
30 1900 1.00 1900.00
25 100 2.50 250.00
450 1000 0.50 500.00
```

```
250 100 3.50 350.00
450 500 0.50 250.00
22 1500 5.00 7500.00
```

produces the following output:

```
THE FOLLOWING DESIGN NUMBERS WERE ORDERED
        22
        30
        25
       450
       250
```

In this example, the search routine is coded as a Boolean function since we need to know only if the DESIGN number is in the list, not where it is. Let's now recode this routine as a procedure and also send back where in the array the value is found, if it is. To make it more general, let's replace the problem-dependent variable names with general ones.

Let's call the array being searched SETOFVALUES and the value being searched for VALU. LENGTH can remain the same. We will need two VAR parameters: FOUND which will return the result of the search and INDEX which will contain the contents of the LCV if the match occurred or LENGTH + 1 if a match did not occur. Yes, the two output parameters are redundant. INDEX would be sufficient because the calling routine could check INDEX> LENGTH rather than checking FOUND. For clarity, however, let's have this redundancy.

```
PROCEDURE SEARCH (VAR SETOFVALUES : LIST; LENGTH : INTEGER;
                  VALU : LISTCOM; VAR INDEX : INTEGER;
                  VAR FOUND : BOOLEAN);
BEGIN  (*SEARCH*)
  FOUND := FALSE;
  INDEX := 1;
  WHILE (INDEX <= LENGTH) AND NOT FOUND DO
   IF VALU = SETOFVALUES[INDEX]
      THEN FOUND := TRUE
      ELSE INDEX := INDEX + 1
END;  (*SEARCH*)
```

Notice that VALU is not of type INTEGER but rather of some globally defined type LISTCOM (list component). The assumption is that the following TYPE definitions will be in the Main Program.

```
CONST    MAXLENGTH = maximum possible number of elements needed;
TYPE     LISTCOM = some scalar type;
         LIST = ARRAY[1..MAXLENGTH] OF LISTCOM;
```

This procedure will now search an array of any type (LISTCOM) for a value of that type. (See Figure 10-1.) We can use this generalized linear search procedure in any program requiring an array search.

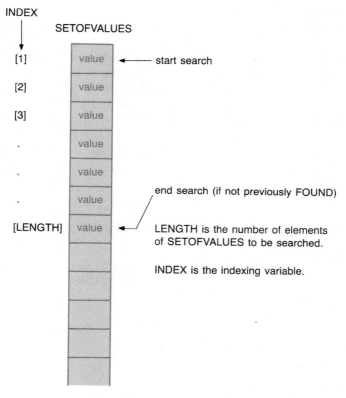

Figure 10-1. Array Search

PARALLEL ARRAYS

■ SAMPLE PROBLEM

Problem: Count the frequency of occurrence of certain characters in a sample of text.

Discussion: If you were to do this by hand, you would probably make a list of the characters whose frequency you want to count. Then you would start processing the text character-by-character. You would take each character and look for it in your list. If it is there, you would make a hash mark beside it.

This algorithm can be used directly. The list of characters whose frequency we wish to count can be read into an array of CHAR. This is analogous to making a list of the characters. To look for a character in the list, we can use the generalized search routine we wrote for the previous problem.

To simulate making a hash mark, we use a second array that is the same size as the one containing the characters. This second array will be of type INTEGER. Since the search routine returns the place in the array where the character was found, we will use that position as an index into the second array and add a one at that position (i.e., make a hash mark). For example, if the first character in our list is an 'A', then each time we find an 'A' the first slot in the integer array will be incremented by one. Using two (or more) separate arrays, containing related information in corresponding positions, is called using parallel arrays. (See Figure 10-2.)

Input: A list of the characters to be counted (in INPUT)

Text is to be processed character-by-character (CH) from file TXT

Output: The characters looked for and their frequency of occurrence

Data Structures: A one-dimensional CHAR array to hold the characters being looked for (CHARLIST)

A one-dimensional INTEGER array to hold the frequencies (FREQ)

MAIN   Level 0

```
GETCHARLIST
ZEROFREQ
WHILE more characters DO
    GETCH
    SEARCH
    INCREMENTFREQ
PRINT CHARLIST and FREQ
```

GETCHARLIST   Level 1

```
COUNTER = 0
WHILE more characters DO
    Increment COUNTER
    READ CHARLIST[COUNTER]
```

Characters will be read from INPUT.

ZEROFREQ

```
FOR LCV going from 1 to LENGTH DO
    FREQ[LCV] = 0
```

GETCH

```
READ CH from TXT
```

SEARCH

```
WHILE NOT FOUND AND more cells in list DO
    IF value = list[INDEX]
        THEN FOUND = TRUE
```

We search for the character in the list, sending back the location in INDEX. We can use the generalized search procedure from the previous problem.

INCREMENTFREQ

```
increment FREQ[INDEX]
```

The corresponding position in FREQ is incremented.

PRINT

```
FOR LCV going from 1 to LENGTH DO
    WRITELN CHARLIST[LCV], FREQ[LCV]
```

Since INCREMENTFREQ and GETCH are only one simple statement they will be coded directly in the main module. Let's look at the interfaces of the other procedures.

Procedure	Needs	Returns	Comments
GETCHARLIST		COUNTER CHARLIST	The last value of COUNTER is the number of characters being looked for.
ZEROFREQ	LENGTH	FREQ	LENGTH is called COUNTER in GETCHARLIST.
SEARCH	CHARLIST CH	FOUND INDEX	
PRINT	FREQ CHARLIST LENGTH		

Remember that any variables in the "Returns" column must be VAR parameters. Those listed only in the "Needs" column should be value parameters. The exception is when you have a *large* data structure which is an input parameter only. In that case, the amount of extra storage needed to copy the data structure may take up more memory space than is available.

Our design tree diagram looks like this:

```
PROGRAM CHARCOUNT (INPUT, TXT, OUTPUT);          (*Program to count
                                      frequency of occurrence in text of specified characters*)
CONST MAXLENGTH = 256;          (*maximum number of different characters to be
                                                                          searched for*)
TYPE LISTCOM = CHAR;                      (*the implementation character set*)
     LIST = ARRAY[1..MAXLENGTH] OF LISTCOM;
     LISTINT = ARRAY[1..MAXLENGTH] OF INTEGER;
VAR  CHARLIST : LIST;                             (* character list *)
     FREQ : LISTINT;                              (* frequency list *)
     LENGTH, INDEX : INTEGER;
     FOUND : BOOLEAN;
     TXT : TEXT;
     CH : CHAR;


(********************************************************)

PROCEDURE GETCHARLIST (VAR CHARLIST : LIST; VAR COUNTER :
                            INTEGER);
VAR  CH:CHAR;
BEGIN  (*GETCHARLIST*)
  COUNTER := 0;
  WHILE NOT EOF DO
    BEGIN
      COUNTER := COUNTER + 1;
      READ(CH);
      CHARLIST[COUNTER] := CH;
      IF EOLN THEN READLN            (* skip over <eoln> character *)
    END
END;    (*GETCHARLIST*)


(********************************************************)

PROCEDURE ZEROFREQ (VAR FREQ : LISTINT; LENGTH : INTEGER);
VAR  LCV : INTEGER;                          (*loop control variable*)
BEGIN  (*ZEROFREQ*)
```

```
   FOR LCV := 1 TO LENGTH DO
        FREQ[LCV] := 0
 END;    (*ZEROFREQ*)


(*********************************************************)

PROCEDURE SEARCH (VAR SETOFVALUES : LIST; LENGTH : INTEGER;
                  VALU : LISTCOM; VAR INDEX : INTEGER;
                  VAR FOUND : BOOLEAN);
BEGIN  (*SEARCH*)
  FOUND := FALSE;
  INDEX := 1;
  WHILE (INDEX <= LENGTH) AND NOT FOUND DO       (* search list *)
    IF VALU = SETOFVALUES[INDEX]                  (* check if found *)
       THEN FOUND := TRUE
       ELSE INDEX := INDEX + 1
 END;    (*SEARCH*)


(*********************************************************)

PROCEDURE PRINT (FREQ : LISTINT; CHARLIST : LIST;
                 LENGTH : INTEGER);
VAR  LCV : INTEGER;                            (*loop control variable*)
BEGIN  (*PRINT*)
  FOR LCV := 1 TO LENGTH DO
       WRITELN (CHARLIST[LCV],' OCCURRED ',
                FREQ[LCV]:3,' TIMES')
 END;    (*PRINT*)


(*********************************************************)

BEGIN  (*MAIN*)
  RESET(TXT);
  GETCHARLIST (CHARLIST, LENGTH);
  ZEROFREQ (FREQ, LENGTH);
  WHILE NOT EOF(TXT) DO                    (* while more characters in text *)
    BEGIN
      WHILE NOT EOLN(TXT) DO                        (* for each line *)
         BEGIN
           READ (TXT, CH);
           SEARCH (CHARLIST, LENGTH, CH, INDEX, FOUND);
           IF FOUND                                 (* increment freq. *)
              THEN FREQ[INDEX] := FREQ[INDEX] + 1
         END;
      READLN(TXT)
    END;
  PRINT (FREQ, CHARLIST, LENGTH)                (* print frequencies *)
END.    (*MAIN*)
```

Let's do a partial code walk-through of this program with the following data. The characters to be counted are:

```
AEIOU
```

and the text is

```
PASCAL IS A STRUCTURED LANGUAGE,
AS STRUCTURED AS CAN BE.
I USED IT TO STRUCTURE MY PROGRAM,
AND NOW IT'S STRUCTURING ME!
```

The contents of the data structures after procedures GETCHARLIST and ZEROFREQ are executed are as follows:

CHARLIST[1] = 'A'	FREQ[1] = 0	LENGTH = 5
[2] = 'E'	[2] = 0	
[3] = 'I'	[3] = 0	
[4] = 'O'	[4] = 0	
[5] = 'U'	[5] = 0	

We will assume the control structures of the reading loops in the main program are correct and look at the three inner statements:

```
1. READ (TXT, CH)
2. SEARCH (CHARLIST, LENGTH, INDEX, FOUND)
3. IF FOUND
     THEN FREQ[INDEX] := FREQ[INDEX] + 1
```

The following table shows our partial code walk-through.

	CH	INDEX	FOUND	FREQ
1.1	P	?	FALSE	—
2.1	P	6	FALSE	—
3.1	P	6	FALSE	—
1.2	A	6	FALSE	—
2.2	A	1	TRUE	—
3.2	A	1	TRUE	FREQ[1] is 1
1.3	S	1	TRUE	—
2.3	S	6	FALSE	—
3.3	S	6	FALSE	—
1.4	C	6	FALSE	—
2.4	C	6	FALSE	—
3.4	C	6	FALSE	—
1.5	A	6	FALSE	—
2.5	A	1	TRUE	—
3.5	A	1	TRUE	FREQ[1] is 2
1.6				

The output from the program using this data would be as follows:

```
A OCCURRED   10 TIMES
E OCCURRED    7 TIMES
I OCCURRED    5 TIMES
O OCCURRED    3 TIMES
U OCCURRED   10 TIMES
```

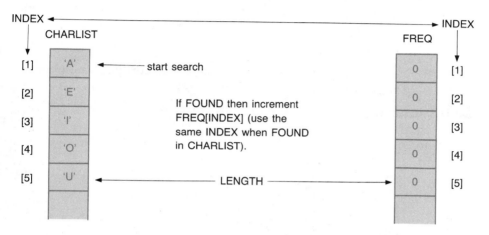

Figure 10-2. Using Parallel Arrays

INDEXES WITH SEMANTIC CONTENT

Program CHARCOUNT (previous example) is the implementation of an algorithm which not only uses parallel arrays but parallels the way a human would do the problem by hand. There is nothing wrong with this solution except that we are not taking advantage of all the information we have. Let's change the problem statement slightly and approach the solution from another angle, this time keeping in mind the features of Pascal.

■ SAMPLE PROBLEM

Problem: Count the frequency of occurrence of all the characters in a sample of text.

Discussion: Pascal already has a built-in list of all the characters it recognizes. They are the values in type CHAR. Pascal also allows us to use any ordinal type as an index type. So instead of searching a list of characters for a value and counting the frequency in a parallel array, we will let Pascal do all that for us. How? By using the characters themselves as the indexes into the frequency list.

The number of characters in a character set will vary and can be 64, 128 or 256 characters. This is machine dependent and must be given to the program as a constant. However, the character codes actually go from 0 to 63, 0 to 127, or 0 to 255. That is, the ORD of the first character is 0 and the ORD of the last is either 63, 127, or 255. Therefore, it is either 63, 127, or 255 which is defined as the size (MAXCHAR) of our frequency list.

Let's look at how the problem is simplified by the fact that the index itself has meaning.

Input: A file of text (TXT)

Output: Each character in the character set followed by the number of times it occurred

Data Structures: An array of frequencies (FREQ)

The frequency array can be pictured like this:

FREQ

[CHR(0)]

[CHR(1)]

[CHR(2)]

.
.
.

[CHR(MAXCHAR)]

The actual values of the indexes are dependent on the character set for the machine being used.

MAIN PROGRAM   **Level 0**

```
ZEROFREQ
WHILE more data DO
     READ CH from TXT
     Increment FREQ[CH] by one
PRINT characters and frequencies
```

ZEROFREQ   **Level 1**

```
FOR LCV = 0 TO MAXCHAR
    FREQ[CHR(LCV)] = 0
```

PRINT

```
FOR LCV going from 0 to MAXCHAR
    PRINT CHR(LCV), FREQ(CHR(LCV))
```

Design Tree Diagram:

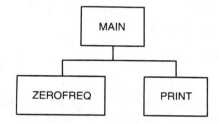

If we know the first and last characters in the collating sequence, LCV could be a CHAR variable and we could print LCV, FREQ (LCV). This, however, would make our program less general.

```
PROGRAM COUNTALL (TXT, OUTPUT);          (*Program to count frequency
                                            of occurrence of characters in text*)
CONST MAXCHAR = 255; (*maximum number of characters less one in character set*)
TYPE    LIST = ARRAY[CHAR] OF INTEGER;
VAR     FREQ : LIST;
        CH : CHAR;
        TXT : TEXT;

(****************************************************************)

PROCEDURE ZEROFREQ (VAR FREQ : LIST; MAXCHAR : INTEGER);
VAR LCV : INTEGER;
BEGIN   (*ZEROFREQ*)
  FOR LCV := 0 TO MAXCHAR DO
      FREQ[CHR(LCV)] := 0
END;    (*ZEROFREQ*)
```

```
(*********************************************************)

PROCEDURE PRINT (FREQ : LIST; MAXCHAR : INTEGER);
VAR LCV : INTEGER;                           (*loop control variable*)
BEGIN   (*PRINT*)
  FOR LCV := 0 TO MAXCHAR DO
      IF FREQ[CHR(LCV)] <> 0
         THEN WRITELN (CHR(LCV):2,' OCCURRED ',
                          FREQ[CHR(LCV)]:3,' TIMES ')
END;    (*PRINT*)


(*********************************************************)

BEGIN   (*MAIN*)
  RESET(TXT);
  ZEROFREQ (FREQ, MAXCHAR);
  WHILE NOT EOF(TXT) DO                    (* while more characters in text *)
    BEGIN
      READ(TXT, CH);
      FREQ[CH] := FREQ[CH] + 1             (* increment frequency *)
    END;
  PRINT (FREQ, MAXCHAR)                    (* print frequencies *)
END.    (*MAIN*)
```

So by taking advantage of the fact that an index can have meaning in itself, this program is considerably simplified. It is left as an exercise (Exercise 5 at the end of this chapter) to modify this program to handle the previous problem. Note that the <eoln> was read as a character. When <eoln> is read it appears as a blank.

Using the same input file as in the previous problem:

```
PASCAL IS A STRUCTURED LANGUAGE,
AS STRUCTURED AS CAN BE.
I USED IT TO STRUCTURE MY PROGRAM,
AND NOW IT'S STRUCTURING ME!
```

the output from Program COUNTALL will be:

```
A OCCURRED   10 TIMES
B OCCURRED    1 TIMES
C OCCURRED    6 TIMES
D OCCURRED    4 TIMES
E OCCURRED    7 TIMES
G OCCURRED    4 TIMES
I OCCURRED    5 TIMES
L OCCURRED    2 TIMES
M OCCURRED    3 TIMES
N OCCURRED    5 TIMES
O OCCURRED    3 TIMES
P OCCURRED    2 TIMES
```

```
R OCCURRED    10  TIMES
S OCCURRED    10  TIMES
T OCCURRED    11  TIMES
U OCCURRED    10  TIMES
W OCCURRED     1  TIMES
Y OCCURRED     1  TIMES
  OCCURRED    22  TIMES
, OCCURRED     2  TIMES
. OCCURRED     1  TIMES
' OCCURRED     1  TIMES
! OCCURRED     1  TIMES
```

MERGING

■ SAMPLE PROBLEM

Problem: Your friend is running for City Council. It is getting down to the wire, and you want to call all those people who showed an interest in your friend and remind them to vote. The problem is that you have two different lists of telephone numbers. You don't want to annoy someone by calling twice, so you decide to put the two lists together, removing any duplicates. Fortunately, the two lists are each sorted in ascending numerical order.

Discussion: How would you do this process if you had two sets of index cards and had to do it by hand? You would probably take the top one from each set and compare them. If they were the same, you would put one in a new set and throw the other card away. If they weren't the same, you would put the card with the lower number in the new set and take a replacement card.

You would repeat this process until the end of one of the sets, and you would then move the rest of the other set to the new one. Of course the lists may both end at the same time with a duplicate number (see previous paragraph).

This is exactly how we can solve the problem. Rather than having two sets of index cards, we have information in two files. We will read them into two one-dimensional arrays. (Note: Although we can read and merge directly from the two files, we are using two arrays to demonstrate merging with arrays.) Incrementing an index will be equivalent to "take another card from that set". We can use two separate index variables to tell us where we are in each array.

Input: A list of phone numbers (integers) from file ONE
A list of phone numbers (integers) from file TWO

Output: A listing of all the numbers in order with duplicates removed
Data Structures: A one-dimensional array for the numbers in file ONE (LIST1)
A one-dimensional array for the numbers in file TWO (LIST2)

Assumptions: No hyphens in the phone numbers (single integer values)

The phone number lists can be pictured like this:

LIST1   LIST2

[1] ▢   [1] ▢
[2] ▢   [2] ▢
[3] ▢   [3] ▢
[4] ▢   [4] ▢
.   .
.   .
.   .

MAIN   **Level 0**

```
GETLIST                                   For first list.
GETLIST                                   For second list
INDEX1 AND INDEX2 set to 1
WHILE INDEX1 and INDEX2 are both OK DO
    PROCESSPAIR
    INDEXTEST
FINISHUP
```

GETLIST   **Level 1**

```
COUNT=0                    This procedure can be used to
WHILE more data DO         input both lists. You simply
    COUNT=COUNT + 1        pass the file name, list name and
    READ LIST[COUNT]       counter as parameters.
```

PROCESSPAIR

```
IF LIST1[INDEX1] < LIST2[INDEX2]
   THEN PRINT LIST1[INDEX1]
           INCREMENT INDEX1
   ELSE IF LIST2[INDEX2] < LIST1[INDEX1]
           THEN PRINT LIST2[INDEX2]
                   INCREMENT INDEX2
           ELSE PRINT LIST1[INDEX1]
                   INCREMENT INDEX1 and INDEX2
```

INDEXTEST What are the possible conditions which the indexes describe?

1. LIST1 and LIST2 both still have more items.
2. LIST1 is finished but LIST2 still has more items.
3. LIST2 is finished but LIST1 still has more items.
4. Both are finished.

One approach is to define an enumerated type with four possible values (which will correspond to these four cases) and have INDEXTEST return (in a VAR parameter of that type) which case has occurred. That is,

```
TYPE CONDITION = (BOTHOK, LIST1OUT, LIST2OUT, BOTHOUT);
VAR TEST : CONDITION;
```

If we take this approach, INDEXTEST could look like this:

```
IF INDEX1 <= LENGTH1 and INDEX2 <= LENGTH2
   THEN TEST = BOTHOK
   ELSE IF INDEX1 > LENGTH1 and INDEX2 > LENGTH2
           THEN TEST = BOTHOUT
           ELSE IF INDEX1 > LENGTH1
                   THEN TEST = LIST1OUT
                   ELSE TEST = LIST2OUT
```

FINISHUP

```
CASE TEST OF
    LIST1OUT : PRINT balance of LIST2
    LIST2OUT : PRINT balance of LIST1
    BOTHOUT : do nothing
```

PRINT

```
FOR LCV = INDEX TO LENGTH
    PRINT LIST[LCV]
```

GETLIST, PROCESSPAIR, INDEXTEST, and PRINT are all complex enough to be procedures. Since FINISHUP is only one statement, it can be coded in-line.

Procedure	Needs	Returns	Comments
GETLIST		PHONENUM	A list of phone numbers
		LENGTH	The length of the list
	FILENO	FILENO	and the file name.
PROCESSPAIR	LIST1		1st list of phone numbers
	LIST2		2nd list of phone numbers
	INDEX1	INDEX1	Pointer to LIST1
	INDEX2	INDEX2	Pointer to LIST2
INDEXTEST		TEST	
	INDEX1		
	LENGTH1		
	INDEX2		
	LENGTH2		
PRINT	PHONENUM		A list to print
	LNGTH		Number of elements in list
	INDEX		Where to begin printing

The design tree diagram now looks like this:

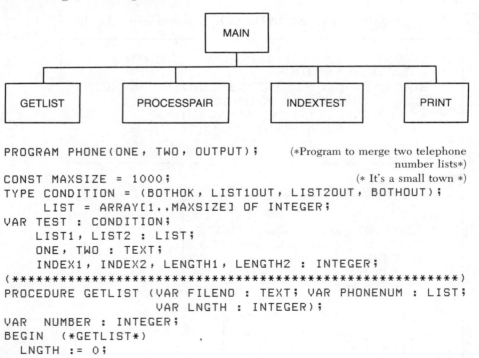

```
PROGRAM PHONE(ONE, TWO, OUTPUT);        (*Program to merge two telephone
                                                number lists*)
CONST MAXSIZE = 1000;                   (* It's a small town *)
TYPE CONDITION = (BOTHOK, LIST1OUT, LIST2OUT, BOTHOUT);
     LIST = ARRAY[1..MAXSIZE] OF INTEGER;
VAR TEST : CONDITION;
    LIST1, LIST2 : LIST;
    ONE, TWO : TEXT;
    INDEX1, INDEX2, LENGTH1, LENGTH2 : INTEGER;
(**************************************************************)
PROCEDURE GETLIST (VAR FILENO : TEXT; VAR PHONENUM : LIST;
                   VAR LNGTH : INTEGER);
VAR  NUMBER : INTEGER;
BEGIN  (*GETLIST*)
  LNGTH := 0;
```

```
    READ (FILENO, NUMBER);
    WHILE NOT EOF(FILENO) DO
      BEGIN
        LNGTH := LNGTH + 1;
        PHONENUM[LNGTH] := NUMBER;
        READ (FILENO, NUMBER)
      END
END;   (*GETLIST*)
(***********************************************************)
PROCEDURE PROCESSPAIR(VAR INDEX1, INDEX2 : INTEGER;
                         LIST1, LIST2 : LIST);
BEGIN  (* PROCESSPAIR *)
  IF LIST1[INDEX1] < LIST2[INDEX2]
      THEN
        BEGIN
          WRITELN (LIST1[INDEX1]);
          INDEX1 := INDEX1 + 1        (* remove number from first list *)
        END
      ELSE IF LIST2[INDEX2] < LIST1[INDEX1]
              THEN
                BEGIN
                  WRITELN (LIST2[INDEX2]);
                  INDEX2 := INDEX2 + 1     (*remove number from
                                                   second list*)
                END
              ELSE                        (* duplicate found *)
                BEGIN
                  WRITELN (LIST1[INDEX1]);
                  INDEX1 := INDEX1 + 1;    (* remove number *)
                  INDEX2 := INDEX2 + 1     (* from both lists *)
                END
END;   (* PROCESSPAIR *)
(***********************************************************)
PROCEDURE INDEXTEST (INDEX1, INDEX2, LENGTH1, LENGTH2 :
                     INTEGER; VAR TEST : CONDITION);
BEGIN  (*INDEXTEST*)
  IF (INDEX1 <= LENGTH1) AND (INDEX2 <= LENGTH2)    (*check for
                                                     empty list*)
     THEN TEST := BOTHOK
     ELSE IF (INDEX1 > LENGTH1) AND (INDEX2 > LENGTH2)
             THEN TEST := BOTHOUT
             ELSE IF INDEX1 > LENGTH1
                     THEN TEST := LIST1OUT
                     ELSE TEST := LIST2OUT
END;   (*INDEXTEST*)
(***********************************************************)
PROCEDURE PRINT (PHONENUM : LIST; LNGTH, INDEX : INTEGER);
VAR LCV : INTEGER;
BEGIN  (*PRINT*)
  FOR LCV := INDEX TO LNGTH DO
```

```
             WRITELN (PHONENUM[LCV])
END;   (*PRINT*)
(******************************************************)
BEGIN   (*MAIN*)
  RESET (ONE);                              (* open file for LIST1 *)
  RESET (TWO);                              (* open file for LIST2 *)
  GETLIST (ONE, LIST1, LENGTH1);
  GETLIST (TWO, LIST2, LENGTH2);
  INDEX1 := 1;
  INDEX2 := 1;
  TEST := BOTHOK;
  WHILE TEST = BOTHOK DO            (* while neither list is empty *)
    BEGIN
       PROCESSPAIR (INDEX1, INDEX2, LIST1, LIST2);
       INDEXTEST (INDEX1, INDEX2, LENGTH1, LENGTH2, TEST)
    END;
  CASE TEST OF
    LIST1OUT : PRINT (LIST2, LENGTH2, INDEX2);
    LIST2OUT : PRINT (LIST1, LENGTH1, INDEX1);
    BOTHOUT  : ;
  END (*CASE*)
END.   (*MAIN*)
```

SUB-ARRAY PROCESSING

▪ SAMPLE PROBLEM

Problem: There is a solitaire game you have played on
rainy days all your life. The only problem is that you
have won the game only twice in all that time. Your
assignment in your computer class is to write a program that simulates a game. You decide to write a program to play that solitaire game and run it 1000 times to
see whether it really is a most difficult game to win or
whether you have just been unlucky.

Game: Although this card game is played with a regular poker or bridge
deck, the rules deal with suits only; the face values are ignored. The
rules are as follows. (Rules 1 and 2 are initialization.)

1. Take a deck of playing cards and shuffle it.
2. Place four cards face up side by side from left to right.
3. (a) If the last four cards are of the same suit, remove them to a discard
   pile.

Initialize with the first 4 cards.

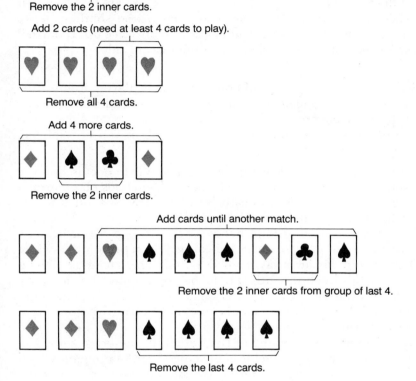

Remove the 2 inner cards.

Add 2 cards (need at least 4 cards to play).

Remove all 4 cards.

Add 4 more cards.

Remove the 2 inner cards.

Add cards until another match.

Remove the 2 inner cards from group of last 4.

Remove the last 4 cards.

Add cards until another match.

Remove the 2 inner cards from group of last 4.

Add cards until another match.

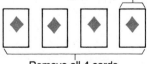

Remove all 4 cards.

Figure 10-3. Solitaire Game

(b) Otherwise, if the first one and the fourth one (of the last four cards) are of the same suit, remove the ones in between (second and third) to the discard pile.

(c) If any cards have been removed you repeat (a) and (b) with the right-most four cards until you cannot remove any more cards. To make a move, there must always be at least four cards face up.

4. Take the next card from the shuffled deck and place it face up to the right of those already there. Repeat this step if there are less than four cards face up (assuming there are cards left in the shuffled deck).

5. Repeat 3 and 4 until you have no more cards to turn face up. You win if all of the cards have been removed to the discard pile.

Let's walk through an example of how the game is played. Figure 10-3 shows part of a typical game. All we are interested in is the suit of each card. We start by placing four cards face up from left to right. Note that if the number of cards facing up is less than four, nothing can be removed.

Discussion: In a simulation such as this, the first step is to decide how we can represent in a program the things we need to keep track of. For example, we must represent a "deck of cards" and a "cards face up". At first you might think that a "discard pile" must be represented. Since the cards which are discarded are not needed again, this is not necessary.

A one-dimensional array seems a logical way to represent a deck of cards. There could be an array named DECK and an array named FACEUP. So a full deck of cards would be represented by the array DECK with 52 locations in it. The array named FACEUP would begin with nothing in it and would hold a maximum of 52 cards (if none were ever removed during the game).

How do you represent "nothing in it"? Set all the values to zero? No. There is an easier way with a technique we used in the program which created a list of dress designs ordered. We keep a count of how many cards we have showing (in FACEUP). If this count is zero, the pile is empty. This count tells us the part (sub-array) of the array we are using.

How can we simulate "placing the first four cards side by side"? Take DECK[52] and put it into FACEUP[1]; DECK[51] into FACEUP[2]; DECK[50] into FACEUP[3] and DECK[49] into FACEUP[4]. The LENGTH (count) of FACEUP is now 4.

Let's see what these two arrays would look like with the given example after placing the first four cards face up. (See Figure 10-4.) We will use the following abbreviations for the suits:

H — HEART
C — CLUB
D — DIAMOND
S — SPADE

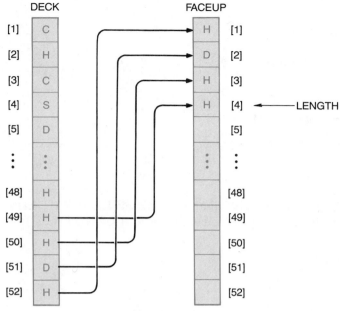

Figure 10-4.

Let's look back at the algorithm and see how we can represent the scheme which compares and removes cards. Notice that at any one time, we are looking only at the last four cards which were put face up. That is, we are looking only at the last four cards in the array FACEUP. That last one put down (most recent) would be FACEUP[LENGTH]; the one before that would be FACEUP[LENGTH − 1]; etc.

Now if all four of the cards are of the same suit, all we have to do to remove them is to subtract 4 from LENGTH. If the last card matches the first of the last four, we need to remove the 2 inner cards FACEUP [LENGTH − 1] and FACEUP[LENGTH − 2]. We can do this by putting the last one, FACEUP[LENGTH], into FACEUP[LENGTH − 2] and subtracting 2 from LENGTH. We must, however, remember to keep LENGTH at 4 or greater until the end. If we don't, we will be accessing a place in the array that doesn't exist (for example, LENGTH − 3 when LENGTH is 2 evaluates to a −1 which gives an index out-of-range error).

As an example, let's look at FACEUP and LENGTH after the first ten cards have been put face up:

FACEUP

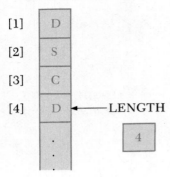

[1] D

[2] S

[3] C

[4] D ◄——————LENGTH

. 4

.

.

FACEUP[LENGTH] is equal to FACEUP[LENGTH − 4] so the middle two are removed leaving FACEUP and LENGTH as follows:

FACEUP

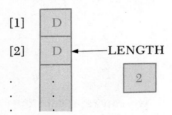

[1] D

[2] D ◄——————LENGTH

. . 2

. .

. .

Now that we understand how to represent the items in our simulation, we can do a top-down design for the program.

Input: None

Output: Number of games won in 1000 games played

Data Structures: One-dimensional array DECK which represents the initial deck of cards
One-dimensional array FACEUP which represents the cards which have been placed face up

MAIN   **Level 0**

```
FOR LCV going from 1 to 1000 DO
     SHUFFLE DECK
     PLAYGAME
     IF WON THEN increment NUMWON
PRINT NUMWON
```

SHUFFLE   **Level 1**

This is a hard one. Let's come back to this.

PLAYGAME

```
FOR LCV going from 52 DOWNTO 1 DO
    TURNUPCARD
    TRYREMOVE
```

WON

```
IF LENGTH = 0 THEN WON = TRUE
```

TURNUPCARD   Level 2

```
Increment LENGTH
FACEUP[LENGTH] = DECK[LCV]
```

TRYREMOVE

```
IF LENGTH >= 4
    THEN TRY = TRUE
    ELSE TRY = FALSE
WHILE TRY DO
    IF ALLMATCH
        THEN LENGTH is decremented by 4
        ELSE IF MATCH2
                THEN FACEUP[LENGTH − 2] = FACEUP[LENGTH]
                    LENGTH is decremented by 2
                ELSE TRY = FALSE
    IF LENGTH < 4
        THEN TRY = FALSE
```

Notice that by checking LENGTH at the beginning we do not have to explicitly turn the first four cards face up. The first 3 times TRYREMOVE is executed, the WHILE statement will not be executed.

ALLMATCH   Level 3

```
IF (FACEUP[LENGTH] = FACEUP[LENGTH − 1])
    AND (FACEUP[LENGTH − 1] = FACEUP[LENGTH − 2])
    AND (FACEUP[LENGTH − 2] = FACEUP[LENGTH − 3])
    THEN ALLMATCH is TRUE
    ELSE ALLMATCH is FALSE
```

MATCH2

```
IF (FACEUP[LENGTH] = FACEUP[LENGTH − 3])
   THEN MATCH2 is TRUE
   ELSE MATCH2 is FALSE
```

Let's return to module SHUFFLE now. What we want to do here is to put the cards into random order. After all, that is what you do when you shuffle a deck of cards. Since we can't physically rearrange the cards, we must simulate this process. Therefore, shuffling the deck becomes a simulation within a simulation (the game)—like *The Taming of the Shrew*, which is a play within a play.

We want to begin at DECK[1] and go through all 52 cards (52 locations in DECK) and set each one to either a HEART, CLUB, DIAMOND, or SPADE. We will do this by using a random number generator. Most computer systems have one of these built into the system software. We will assume our system has a function called RAN which will return a random number between 0.00 and 1.00 each time it is executed.

How does that help us? We need a HEART, CLUB, DIAMOND, or SPADE. If we can convert the random number into an integer between 0 and 3, we can use a CASE statement to store a HEART, CLUB, DIAMOND, or SPADE in DECK. (Remember, we don't care about the face value of the card, only the suit.)

To convert the real number between 0.00 and 1.00 returned by the RAN function into an integer (DIGIT) between 0 and 3, we can use the following conversion formula:

$$\text{DIGIT} = \text{TRUNC}(\text{RAN} * 100) \bmod 4$$

Rather than assigning the value of the expression to a variable, we can use it directly in a CASE statement.

```
CASE (TRUNC(RAN * 100) MOD 4) OF
    0 : set a HEART
    1 : set a CLUB
    2 : set a DIAMOND
    3 : set a SPADE
END (*CASE*)
```

We must also put in a mechanism to make sure we do not get 14 HEARTS and 12 DIAMONDS. To do this, we keep count of how many of each suit we generate and skip setting that suit after 13 have been set. So this is what the SHUFFLE module would look like:

SHUFFLE

```
LCV = 1
WHILE LCV <= 52 DO
    CASE (TRUNC(RAN * 100) MOD 4) OF
        0 : IF HCOUNT < 13
               THEN DECK[LCV] = HEART
                    Increment HCOUNT
                    Increment LCV
        1 : IF CCOUNT < 13
               THEN DECK[LCV] = CLUB
                    Increment CCOUNT
                    Increment LCV
        2 : IF DCOUNT < 13
               THEN DECK[LCV] = DIAMOND
                    Increment DCOUNT
                    Increment LCV
        3 : IF SCOUNT < 13
               THEN DECK[LCV] = SPADE
                    Increment SCOUNT
                    Increment LCV
```

WON and TURNUPCARD can be coded in-line, and since PLAYGAME is so short, TRYREMOVE can be coded in-line in PLAYGAME. There is a lot of repetitive code in the CASE statement in SHUFFLE so we can add a nested procedure, PLACE, to process each suit.

Procedure	Needs	Returns	Comments
SHUFFLE		DECK	SHUFFLE must be a procedure.
PLAYGAME	DECK	LENGTH	PLAYGAME could be a function since 1 value is returned.
ALLMATCH	LENGTH FACEUP		Boolean function
MATCH2	LENGTH FACEUP		Boolean function
PLACE	COUNT CARD DECK LCV	DECK COUNT LCV	

A tree diagram with parameters should make this clearer. Note that any parameter with an arrow going *up* the tree must be a VAR parameter.

```
PROGRAM SOLITAIRE (OUTPUT);        (*Program to simulate a game of solitaire*)
CONST MAXGAMES = 1000;
TYPE SUIT = (HEART, CLUB, DIAMOND, SPADE);
     CARDS = ARRAY[1..52] OF SUIT;
VAR  DECK : CARDS;                               (*deck of playing cards*)
     LENGTH : 0..52;                   (*will be 0 if you win the game*)
     NUMWON : 0..MAXGAMES;                  (*number of games won*)
     GAMECTR : 1..MAXGAMES;        (*counter for number of games played*)
(*********************************************************)
PROCEDURE SHUFFLE (VAR DECK : CARDS);             (*shuffle the deck*)
VAR  CARDCTR,                            (*counter for number of cards*)
     HCOUNT,                         (*number of HEARTS generated*)
     CCOUNT,                          (*number of CLUBS generated*)
     DCOUNT,                       (*number of DIAMONDS generated*)
     SCOUNT : INTEGER;                (*number of SPADES generated*)

   PROCEDURE PLACE (VAR DECK:CARDS; VAR CARDCTR, COUNT :
                    INTEGER; CARD:SUIT);
   BEGIN  (*PLACE*)
     IF COUNT < 13
        THEN
           BEGIN
             DECK[CARDCTR] := CARD;
             COUNT := COUNT + 1;
             CARDCTR := CARDCTR + 1
           END
   END;    (*PLACE*)

BEGIN  (*SHUFFLE*)
  HCOUNT := 0;
  CCOUNT := 0;
  DCOUNT := 0;
```

```
    SCOUNT := 0;
    CARDCTR := 1;
    WHILE CARDCTR <= 52 DO
      CASE TRUNC(RAN * 100) MOD 4 OF
        0 : PLACE(DECK, CARDCTR, HCOUNT, HEART);
        1 : PLACE(DECK, CARDCTR, CCOUNT, CLUB);
        2 : PLACE(DECK, CARDCTR, DCOUNT, DIAMOND);
        3 : PLACE(DECK, CARDCTR, SCOUNT, SPADE)
      END   (*CASE*)
END;   (*SHUFFLE*)
(**********************************************************)
PROCEDURE PLAYGAME (VAR DECK : CARDS; VAR LENGTH :
                    INTEGER);
VAR  CARDCTR : INTEGER;                    (*loop control variable*)
     FACEUP : CARDS;                       (*cards placed face up*)
     TRY : BOOLEAN;                   (*if TRUE apply removal algorithm*)

  FUNCTION ALLMATCH (FACEUP : CARDS; LENGTH : INTEGER) :
                     BOOLEAN;
  BEGIN   (*ALLMATCH*)
    IF (FACEUP[LENGTH] = FACEUP[LENGTH - 1]) AND
       (FACEUP[LENGTH - 1] = FACEUP[LENGTH - 2]) AND
       (FACEUP[LENGTH - 2] = FACEUP[LENGTH - 3])
       THEN ALLMATCH := TRUE
       ELSE ALLMATCH := FALSE
    END;    (*ALLMATCH*)

  FUNCTION MATCH2 (FACEUP : CARDS; LENGTH : INTEGER) :
                  BOOLEAN;
  BEGIN   (*MATCH2*)
    IF FACEUP[LENGTH] = FACEUP[LENGTH - 3]
       THEN MATCH2 := TRUE
       ELSE MATCH2 := FALSE
    END;    (*MATCH2*)

BEGIN   (*PLAYGAME*)
  LENGTH := 0;
  FOR CARDCTR := 52 DOWNTO 1 DO
     BEGIN
        LENGTH := LENGTH + 1;
        FACEUP[LENGTH] := DECK[CARDCTR];
        IF LENGTH >= 4
           THEN TRY := TRUE
           ELSE TRY := FALSE;
        WHILE TRY DO
          BEGIN
             IF ALLMATCH(FACEUP, LENGTH)
                THEN LENGTH := LENGTH - 4
                ELSE IF MATCH2(FACEUP, LENGTH)
```

```
                              THEN
                                BEGIN
                                  FACEUP[LENGTH - 2] :=
                                            FACEUP[LENGTH];
                                  LENGTH := LENGTH - 2
                                END
                              ELSE TRY := FALSE;
                    IF LENGTH < 4
                        THEN TRY := FALSE
                END
            END
END;     (*PLAYGAME*)
(*******************************************************)
BEGIN     (*MAIN*)
   NUMWON := 0;
   FOR GAMECTR := 1 TO MAXGAMES DO              (*play 1000 games*)
        BEGIN
           SHUFFLE(DECK);
           PLAYGAME(DECK, LENGTH);
           IF LENGTH = 0
              THEN NUMWON := NUMWON + 1
        END;
   WRITELN ('THE NUMBER OF GAMES WON IN 1000 GAMES IS ',
            NUMWON)
END.     (*MAIN*)
```

■

TESTING AND DEBUGGING

Let's go back over each of the five problems we have programmed in this chapter, look at problems that might arise and determine what would constitute adequate testing.

Program DESIGNCT

In the Dress Design problem, the solution involved creating a list of all the dress designs ordered over a period of time. The algorithm was to search the list for each order number read in. If the order number was not there, it was added at the end of the list.

The design number (called DESIGN in the program) is the only input. There were no constraints on the size of the number. A logical assumption might be that an order number should be positive. Before putting in such a test on the data, however, you should go back to the customer and make sure. If indeed it should be positive, find out what the customer wants to have done in the case of bad data.

MAXLENGTH, the maximum number of designs possible, was set at 500. Since MAXLENGTH is used to set the size of the array DESIGNLST which holds the designs ordered, it should be equal to the total number of designs possible. Although it is unlikely that all of the designs would be ordered during that time period, it is possible. If you set the size to 250 and 251 were ordered, the attempt to store the 251st design would cause a run-time error: 'VALUE OUT OF RANGE'.

In testing this program, how many times must the program be run with different data values? What are the possible cases?

1. There were no orders.
2. Every design was ordered.
3. There were no duplicate designs ordered.
4. Only one design was ordered but it was ordered many times.
5. Some designs were ordered many times, some only once, and some not at all.

Data sets reflecting each of these 5 cases must be run. In order to test condition 2, MAXLENGTH could be lowered for that run to save having to create a test file of 500 numbers.

Program CHARCOUNT

The second problem was to count the frequency of occurrence of certain characters in a sample of text. To do this, parallel arrays were defined. CHARLIST holds the characters to be counted and FREQ holds the corresponding frequency counts. The characters to be counted come in from the console or standard input device, and the text comes in from a text file named TXT. The only possible error in the data would be a character that your particular machine doesn't recognize. A run-time error 'ILLEGAL CHARACTER IN TEXT' would result. There is no way to test for this, since the error occurs when you are trying to read a character.

There is data coming in from the standard input file and file TXT. The cases which must be tested are as follows.

1. No characters to be counted.
2. No text to count.
3. Input data in both files.

Program COUNTALL

This problem expanded the counting of characters to every character in the character set of a particular computer. Rather than having an array to hold the characters and an array to hold the frequency, the character itself was the index into the frequency array.

Note that in Program CHARCOUNT, MAXLENGTH was set to 256, the maximum number of characters you might want to count. In COUNTALL, MAXCHAR is 255. They are each used as the upper limit of the subrange defining one-dimensional arrays. One is indexed 1..256 and the other is 0..255. This was not done to confuse you. In each case we have the possibility of counting 256 characters. It is more natural for humans to count from 1 to 256. This is reflected in Program CHARCOUNT. In Program COUNTALL the index is the character itself, and the ORD of the characters goes from 0 to 255.

To adequately test this program, a data file should be created which contains all of the characters at least once and some of the characters more than once.

Program PHONE

The fourth problem merged two ordered phone lists into one printed output list with no duplicates. Since there was input from two files, ONE and TWO, there are several cases to test in your output.

1. File ONE is empty and file TWO is not.
2. File TWO is empty and file ONE is not.
3. Both are empty.
4. Neither is empty.

In this program there are other data dependent conditions which should be tested.

1. File ONE has the lowest phone number.
2. File TWO has the lowest phone number.
3. The first number in both files is the same.
4. The last number in both files is the same.

Program SOLITAIRE

There were no inputs to this program. It simulated the playing of a card game and printed out the number of times the game is won in 1000 tries.

How can you tell if it works? You can't as it now stands. Some intermediate print-outs must be inserted during the testing phase to determine if the two main procedures, SHUFFLE and PLAYGAME, work correctly.

To see if Procedure SHUFFLE works we need to see the contents of DECK. This presents an unexpected problem. For readability of the code we used a user-defined data type SUIT. Now we need to print out the contents of DECK, which is of type SUIT, but user-defined types cannot be written out. What can we do? Rewrite the program? No. We cannot write out data type SUIT, but we can write out the ORD of a variable of type SUIT.

Therefore, for testing purposes, we insert the following statement right after the CASE statement in procedure SHUFFLE.

```
FOR CARDCTR := 1 TO 52 DO
    WRITELN (ORD(DECK[LCV]))
```

The algorithm PLAYGAME can be checked in several ways. A WRITELN statement could be inserted before each card is placed face up. However, this would produce 52 lines of output. A shortcut would be to print those remaining face up at the end of each game. Of course, to actually test the program, you would have to take the output listing of DECK and play the game by hand.

What happens if you don't win a game in, say, 10 test tries? Can you be sure that your algorithm would correctly recognize a winning situation? To be sure, you must write a special procedure SHUFFLE which simply sets the values of DECK in a winning configuration. The program could be run with this special SHUFFLE once to test this branch of the program if it had not been tested by chance.

Testing and Debugging Hints

1. If your program seems to execute but there is no output, check your data file.

   Most programs are written assuming that there will be some data in the input file. If an EOF is encountered immediately, there will be no data. What happens in that case? If the data is to go into an array with a counter keeping track of the length of the array, that length will be zero. Most likely all subsequent processing will be skipped. A way to test for this is with

   ```
   IF  EOF(file)
       THEN write error message
       ELSE continue processing
   ```

2. Plan your testing in advance.

   While you are doing your top-down design, make notes to yourself about where you might want to put in debug WRITE statements for testing purposes.

3. Be sure your index is initialized and incremented correctly.

   See what happens in the following simple reading loop when the incrementation is incorrect.

   ```
   VAR LIST : ARRAY[1..10] OF INTEGER;
       .
       .
       .
       LCV := 0;
   ```

```
WHILE NOT EOF DO
    BEGIN
        READLN (LIST[LCV]);
        LCV := LCV + 1
    END
```

The first time this loop is executed, a subscript-out-of-range error will occur. If you correct that problem by initializing LCV to 1, your count is off by 1. That is, LCV points not to the last one stored but to that location plus 1. How can we fix this? Initialize the LCV to zero and increment LCV before you do the read. Now it comes out right.

4. If you run out of memory space, check your array parameters.

Using an array variable as a VAR parameter uses the array structure already in memory. Using an array variable as a value parameter creates another copy of the array structure, thus using more memory (possibly too much).

5. Make sure your arrays are large enough for your processing.

Trying to read and store more data than your array can hold causes a subscript range error. Stop reading when the limit of your array is reached and print out an appropriate message.

Declare the largest array you might need, and use a variable to keep track of the length of the sub-array you actually use.

Summary ───────────────────────

Chapter 10 has been designed to make you feel more comfortable with the use of one-dimensional arrays. Five sample problems have been examined which use one-dimensional arrays in different ways. Although these problems have been couched in concrete terms for teaching purposes, the basic techniques will come up again and again in your programming career.

Much of the art of programming is being able to abstract from the description of a specific problem and recognize that you have previously seen something similar. These problems should give you a set of techniques to use in future problems.

The concept of a one-dimensional array will be extended in Chapter 11 to a table with rows and columns. Chapter 12 will introduce an additional data structure called a record. If you thoroughly understand one-dimensional arrays, these extensions will not only seem easy to use, but eminently logical.

Exercises ───────────────────────

1. Write a Pascal function INDEX which searches an INTEGER array LIST for an INTEGER value VALU. The place in the array where VALU is found is re-

turned. There are LENGTH values in LIST. If VALU is not in the array, set INDEX to 0.

2. Write a procedure MERGE which merges two ordered files, ONE and TWO, into an ordered array COMB. Duplicates are removed. COMB is the only array you are to use. The data in ONE and TWO are to be processed as they are read. ONE and TWO are input parameters and COMB and LENGTH (number of elements in COMB) are output parameters.

3. Design an appropriate data structure for the following problems.

   a. A record store sells classical records (A), jazz records (B), rock records (C), and others (D). Sales receipts are kept in the following format.

   > CODE (1 character, either A, B, C, or D)
   > AMT (amount of sale)

   The owner of the store wants to total the amount of sales for each record category.

   b. A payroll master file is made up of the following data.

   > ID (5 digit number)
   > RATE (hourly salary)
   > DEP (number of dependents)

   A transaction file is made up each month of the following data.

   > ID (5 digit number)
   > HOURS (number of hours worked)

   The payroll file is ordered. The transaction file is not.

4. Describe algorithms using the data structures in Problems 3a and 3b. (Your answer should be like the discussion sections. You are not being asked for a top-down design.)

5. Change Program COUNTALL so that it produces the same output as Program CHARCOUNT. Both programs appeared in Chapter 10.

Pre-Test

1. Write a Pascal function FOUND which searches a REAL array LIST for a REAL value greater than the value VALUE. If such a value is found, the function returns TRUE. Otherwise it returns FALSE. LIST is of type ARY. The number of elements in LIST should be a parameter.

2. Write a procedure PAR which takes as input two parallel arrays A and B of length N. This procedure should return as output the product of those elements of B where the corresponding elements of A are negative.

3. Write a Pascal program MERGE which merges two ordered files, UNO and DOS, onto an output file named TRES. Duplicates should be removed. You are not to use arrays.

Multi-Dimensional Arrays

Goals

To be able to define multi-dimensional array types.

To be able to declare multi-dimensional array variables.

To be able to access the elements of a multi-dimensional array.

To be able to write procedures to do the following types of organized accessing with a two-dimensional array:
- *access each cell by row*
- *access each cell by column*
- *access each cell randomly*
- *access each cell in a specified row*
- *access each cell in a specified column*
- *access each cell in the two diagonals*

To be able to choose between the following data structures for a particular problem:
- *two-dimensional array vs. parallel arrays*
- *arrays vs. simple variables*

DATA STRUCTURES

Let's list the basic elements of programming:

1. Problem solving and algorithm design (top-down design methodology)
2. Statement structures (sequence, selection, loop, procedure)
3. Data structures
4. A programming language (Pascal).

We have demonstrated that there is much more to programming than merely knowing the syntax and semantics of a programming language. In addition to a design methodology and ways to structure statements, the way data is structured is an important part of programming.

The only data structure we have discussed so far is the one-dimensional array. Being able to reference a group of data objects by one name simplifies the design of many algorithms. There are other built-in data structures in Pascal, as well as those we can build ourselves. Data structure plays an important role in the design process. The data structure you choose directly affects your design: how you structure your data affects the algorithms you use to process that data. We will discuss the role of data structures in the design process later in this chapter.

We stated that all data structures are ultimately composed of some simple scalar data type. However, our definition of arrays allows for any component (base) type for the elements of the array.

ARRAY

A structured data type composed of a fixed number of components of the same type with each component directly accessed by the index.

So the type definition

```
TYPE WORD = ARRAY[1..10] OF CHAR;
     LIST = ARRAY[1..100] OF WORD;
```

creates a pattern for a valid data structure. A variable of type LIST is an array whose elements are each a one-dimensional array of type CHAR. This structure is called a two-dimensional array. Notice that the contents of each cell in the structure are of a simple scalar type, CHAR. Figure 11-1 is what a variable of type LIST looks like.

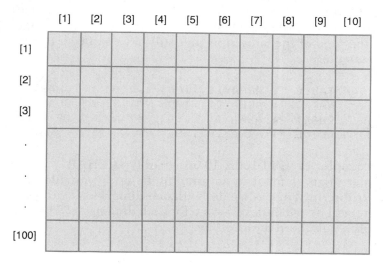

Figure 11-1.

TWO-DIMENSIONAL ARRAYS

In mathematics a vector is a one-dimensional array; a matrix a two-dimensional array. In everyday English, a two-dimensional array is a table with rows and columns. The contents of any element in a two-dimensional array is composed of a scalar type. The subscripts of the array can be of any scalar type (except REAL).

In our example of type LIST, we could have also defined it by

```
TYPE LIST = ARRAY[1..100] OF ARRAY[1..10] OF CHAR;
```

and declared a variable of type LIST by

```
VAR TABLE : LIST;
```

We could also define the type of the variable in the variable declaration by

```
VAR TABLE : ARRAY[1..100] OF ARRAY[1..10] OF CHAR;
```

but then we wouldn't have a type LIST to use for other variable declarations or for use in a formal parameter list.

There is also an abbreviated form that we can use. For example,

```
TYPE LIST = ARRAY[1..100,1..10] OF CHAR;
VAR TABLE : LIST;
```

or

```
VAR TABLE : ARRAY[1..100,1..10] OF CHAR;
```

produce the same data structure as our previous array variable TABLE. We say that TABLE is a two-dimensional array with 100 rows and 10 columns (and $100 \times 10 = 1000$ cells). We can change the limits of the range or change the type of the subscripts and still have a 100×10 array.

For example,

```
VAR TABLE  : ARRAY[1..100, 1..10] OF CHAR;
    MATRIX : ARRAY[1..100, -4..5] OF CHAR;
    CHART  : ARRAY[1..100, 'A'..'J'] OF CHAR;
    GUIDE  : ARRAY[0..99,  -10..-1] OF CHAR;
```

are all examples of valid 100 x 10 arrays of type CHAR.

We refer to an element in an array by its array variable name and its indexes (subscripts) just as we did with one-dimensional arrays, but in this case there will be two indexes—one for each dimension. The first element of TABLE would be referenced by

```
TABLE[1][1]
```

first dimension ⌐   ⌐ second dimension

or the usual abbreviation

```
TABLE[1,1]
```

As with one-dimensional arrays, the subscripts can be any expression, not just constants. For example,

```
TABLE[2,J]
TABLE[I,J]
TABLE[I+1,5]
```

are all valid references to elements of TABLE, assuming that I and J are of type INTEGER and their values are in the declared index ranges.

The index type can be different for each dimension. Just be careful that the value of an expression referencing a dimension is of the index type for that dimension.

Let's look at an example using a two-dimensional array. If we are given these declarations:

```
VAR FREQ : ARRAY[1..3,1..5] OF INTEGER;
    ROW, COL : INTEGER;
```

then this program fragment

```
FOR ROW := 1 TO 3 DO
    FOR COL := 1 TO 5 DO
        FREQ[ROW,COL] := COL;
```

would initialize the value of each cell to the number of the column the cell is in.

FREQ

COL	[1]	[2]	[3]	[4]	[5]

ROW

	[1]	[2]	[3]	[4]	[5]
[1]	1	2	3	4	5
[2]	1	2	3	4	5
[3]	1	2	3	4	5

Figure 11-2.

Notice that one row of the table was filled in at a time. That is, ROW stayed at 1, while COL varied from 1 to 5. Then ROW became 2 and stayed there until COL had again varied from 1 to 5. In a nested loop situation we talk about the innermost counter running faster, i.e., COL takes on all of its values before ROW is incremented.

We wanted to initialize every element of the array, so FOR loops were appropriate. However, during processing of this array, we may not want to access every element, or we may want to terminate the process if some condition changes. If so, a WHILE loop would be more appropriate than a FOR loop (i.e., nested WHILE loops or a WHILE loop within a FOR loop).

Two-dimensional arrays are useful for describing two-dimensional objects such as chessboards, maps, timetables, etc. No matter what a two-dimensional array represents in your program (i.e., the semantics of the values), when processing the array or table there are only five things that you might want to do.

1. Access or look at each cell in a systematic way, i.e.,
   (a) By rows
   (b) By columns

2. Access a cell randomly.
3. Process a row.
4. Process a column.
5. Process one or both diagonals.

Let's look at the Pascal code to do each of these tasks in the form of a procedure.

1. ACCESS each element or cell (where ROWLIMIT is the number of rows, COLLIMIT is the number of columns, TABLE is the name of the array and ARY is the array type).
   (a) By rows. (See Figure 11-3a.) (PRINTRESULT and GETDATA in Program ABSENT in the next section process each element by row.)

```
PROCEDURE ACCESSBYROW(ROWLIMIT,COLLIMIT:INTEGER;
                           VAR TABLE:ARY);
VAR ROW,COL : INTEGER;
BEGIN
   FOR ROW := 1 TO ROWLIMIT DO
       FOR COL := 1 TO COLLIMIT DO
           BEGIN
               (* process TABLE[ROW,COL] *)
               .
               .
           END
END;
```

   (b) By columns. (See Figure 11-3b.) (FINDAVERAGE in Program AB-SENT processes each element by column.)

```
PROCEDURE ACCESSBYCOL(ROWLIMIT,COLLIMIT:INTEGER;
                           VAR TABLE:ARY);
VAR ROW,COL : INTEGER;
BEGIN
   FOR COL := 1 TO COLLIMIT DO
       FOR ROW := 1 TO ROWLIMIT DO
           BEGIN
               (* process TABLE[ROW,COL] *)
               .
               .
           END
END;
```

These two procedures process the entire array (or the limits passed by ROWLIMIT and COLLIMIT) by rows or by columns. If we want to stop processing if some condition changes, we would use WHILE loops instead of FOR loops.

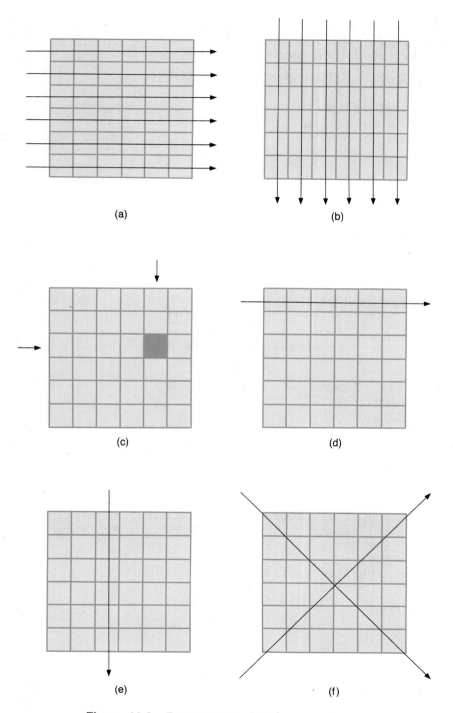

Figure 11-3. Processing Two-Dimensional Arrays

The difference between (a) and (b) is that the loops are reversed. The outer loop determines the major order of access (row or column) and the inner loop controls the access to individual elements.

2. ACCESS a cell randomly (See Figure 11-3c.)

```
PROCEDURE ACCESSRAN(ROW,COL : INTEGER; VAR TABLE : ARY);
BEGIN
    (* process TABLE[ROW,COL] *)

      •
      •
END;
```

This procedure simply processes a given cell of an array.

3. PROCESS a row (See Figure 11-3d.)

```
        PROCEDURE PROCESSROW(ROW,COLLIMIT : INTEGER;
                             VAR TABLE : ARY);
        VAR COL : INTEGER;
        BEGIN
          FOR COL := 1 TO COLLIMIT DO
               BEGIN
                   (* process TABLE[ROW,COL] *)

                     •
                     •
               END
        END;
```

This procedure processes a given row of an array. Notice that the column is varied from 1 to the COLLIMIT. Processing could be terminated by some condition by using a WHILE loop.

4. PROCESS a column (See Figure 11-3e.)

```
        PROCEDURE PROCESSCOL(COL,ROWLIMIT : INTEGER;
                             VAR TABLE : ARY);
        VAR ROW : INTEGER;
        BEGIN
          FOR ROW := 1 TO ROWLIMIT DO
               BEGIN
                   (* process TABLE[ROW,COL] *)

                     •
                     •
               END
        END;
```

This procedure processes a given column of an array. Notice that the row is varied from 1 to the ROWLIMIT. Again, processing could be terminated by some condition by using a WHILE loop.

5. PROCESS diagonals (See Figure 11-3f.)

```
PROCEDURE PROCESSDIAG(LIMIT : INTEGER; VAR TABLE : ARY);
VAR DIAG : INTEGER;
BEGIN
   FOR DIAG := 1 TO LIMIT DO
        BEGIN
            (* process TABLE[DIAG,DIAG] the diagonal from top-left to bottom-right *)
            ∎
            (* process TABLE[LIMIT-DIAG+1,DIAG] the diagonal from bottom-left to
            top-right *)
            ∎
        END
END;
```

This procedure processes both diagonals of an array. One or the other process can be removed if not desired. We assumed that the array was square for this procedure. To go from bottom left to upper right, we need to start the first index at the limit and decrement each iteration, while the second index starts at 1 and is incremented each iteration. The FOR loop takes care of the second index. We could introduce a new index variable for the first index but $(LIMIT-DIAG+1)$ calculates to the right value at each iteration.

The preceding procedures were set up assuming the indexes to be of type INTEGER and to range from 1 to some INTEGER limit. They can be generalized to any type of index (i.e., indexes of type CHAR or an enumerated type) by also passing the lower limits for row and column and changing the type declarations for ROW, COL, COLLIMIT, and ROWLIMIT. The processes in the body of each procedure can be whatever processing is desired. Trivial processes may not call for separate procedures and could be part of other blocks of code.

Notice that row and column limits were passed as parameters. This allows partial processing of the array (sub-array processing) when some of the elements aren't being used or when not all the elements have been initialized.

Here are two examples using the procedures just described. Let's assume these declarations in the main program:

```
CONST RDIM = 10;
      CDIM = 10;
TYPE RRANGE = 1..RDIM;
     CRANGE = 1..CDIM;
     MAP = ARRAY[RRANGE,CRANGE] OF BOOLEAN;
VAR CHART : MAP;
    SUM : INTEGER;
```

To find the sum of the number of TRUE elements of the fifth row we could make the call

```
            PROCESSROW(5, CDIM, CHART, SUM)
```

to this general summing procedure:

```
PROCEDURE PROCESSROW(ROW, COLLIMIT : INTEGER;
                    VAR TABLE : MAP; VAR SUM : INTEGER);
VAR COL : INTEGER;
BEGIN
  SUM := 0;
  FOR COL := 1 TO COLLIMIT DO
      IF TABLE[ROW,COL]
         THEN SUM := SUM + 1
END;
```

To initialize the bottom-left to top-right diagonal cells to the value FALSE, we could make the call

```
            PROCESSDIAG(10, CHART)
```

to this procedure:

```
PROCEDURE PROCESSDIAG(LIMIT : INTEGER; VAR TABLE : MAP);
VAR DIAG : INTEGER;
BEGIN
  FOR DIAG := 1 TO LIMIT DO
      TABLE[LIMIT - DIAG + 1, DIAG] := FALSE
END;
```

Notice that all of our examples use ROW and COL as subscript identifiers. When working with arrays, it is helpful to choose subscript identifiers which have meaning to you. Form the habit of using them. If you have a math background, you might want to follow the subscript convention of using I for the row designator and J for the column designator.

A word of caution is in order. ROW and COL, or I and J, as row and column designators have meaning to you but not to the compiler. The identifier in the first subscript position is the designator for the first dimension and the identifier in the second subscript position is the designator for the second dimension. If you said

```
            TABLE[COL, ROW]
```

COL would refer to the first dimension and ROW would refer to the second dimension.

■ SAMPLE PROBLEM

Problem: Management would like to see the daily absenteeism patterns of each department in the company for a normal week. The weekly absentee figures are kept on file. Each data line contains the daily figures for departments A through F. Print out a table showing each department's daily absenteeism and the percentage difference (+ or −) from the department's weekly average.

Discussion: Each data line contains the daily data for every department, not the weekly data for a single department. We need to save every department's daily data in order to figure the weekly average. This would involve 30 variables: 5 workdays (Monday-Friday) for 6 departments (A-F). A two-dimensional array would be easier than 30 separate variables.

As we read the data:

	A	B	C	D	E	F	
data line ⟶	2	1	1	3	4	1	Monday
data line ⟶	1	0	1	3	0	0	Tuesday
data line ⟶	0	0	0	2	0	0	Wednesday
data line ⟶	1	0	1	1	2	0	Thursday
data line ⟶	2	0	0	2	1	2	Friday

we can fill an array having the same structure. Notice how the form of the data affected our choice of data structure.

We can sum each column (department) to find the department averages. After comparing the daily department absentee figures to the department average, we can print out a table with the daily percentage difference from each department's average. This is how the output might appear:

	A	+−%	B	+−%	C	+−%	D	+−%	E	+−%	F	+−%
MONDAY	2	67	1	400	1	67	3	36	4	186	1	67
TUESDAY	1	−17	0	−100	1	67	3	36	0	−100	0	−100
WEDNESDAY	0	−100	0	−100	0	−100	2	−9	0	−100	0	−100
THURSDAY	1	−17	0	−100	1	67	1	−55	2	43	0	−100
FRIDAY	2	67	0	−100	0	−100	2	−9	1	−29	2	233

Input: 5 lines (Monday-Friday) of absentee data (integer) for 6 departments (A-F)

Output: Table of the week showing daily department absenteeism and percentage difference from weekly department average

Data Structures: Two-dimensional array for daily department absentee figures where the rows are weekdays and the columns are department numbers
One-dimensional array for average weekly department absenteeism

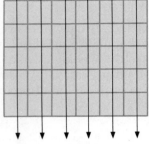

Absentee data
[A] [B] [C] [D] [E] [F]

Department averages
[A] [B] [C] [D] [E] [F]

[MONDAY]
[TUESDAY]
[WEDNESDAY]
[THURSDAY]
[FRIDAY]

MAIN   **Level 0**

```
GETDATA
FINDAVERAGE
PRINTRESULT
```

PRINTRESULT finds the percentage difference and prints the table.

GETDATA   **Level 1**

```
FOR days MONDAY through FRIDAY DO
    FOR departments A through F DO
        READ(TABLE[DAY,DEPT])
```

input by row

FINDAVERAGE

```
FOR departments A through F DO
    Initialize SUM to zero
    FOR days MONDAY through FRIDAY DO
        SUM = SUM + TABLE[DAY,DEPT]
    AVE[DEPT] = SUM / 5
```

process by columns

weekly average for each dept.

PRINTRESULT

```
Print column header
FOR days MONDAY through FRIDAY DO
      print day label
      FOR departments A through F DO
            print TABLE[DAY,DEPT]
            percentdiff = ROUND((TABLE[DAY,DEPT] −
                        AVE[DEPT])/AVE[DEPT])
            print percentdiff
```

Design Tree Diagram:

```
PROGRAM ABSENT(INPUT, OUTPUT);                  (* This program produces
                                                   an absentee table *)
TYPE DAYTYPE = (MONDAY, TUESDAY, WEDNESDAY, THURSDAY,
                 FRIDAY);
     DEPTYPE = (A, B, C, D, E, F);
     ARYTYPE = ARRAY[DAYTYPE, DEPTYPE] OF INTEGER;
     LISTYPE = ARRAY[DEPTYPE] OF REAL;
VAR  TABLE : ARYTYPE;                           (* Table of absentee data *)
     AVE : LISTYPE;                             (* List of dept. averages *)

(**********************************************************)

PROCEDURE PRINTRESULT(DATA : ARYTYPE; VAR AVE :LISTYPE);
VAR DAY : DAYTYPE;
    DEPT : DEPTYPE;
    PERCENTDIFF : INTEGER;
BEGIN   (*PRINTRESULT*)
   WRITELN(' ':12, ' A +-% B +-% C +-% D +-% E +-% F +-%');
   WRITELN(' ':11,'------------------------------------');
   FOR DAY := MONDAY TO FRIDAY DO
        BEGIN
          CASE DAY OF
             MONDAY      : WRITE('MONDAY     ');
             TUESDAY     : WRITE('TUESDAY    ');
             WEDNESDAY   : WRITE('WEDNESDAY  ');
```

```
                THURSDAY      : WRITE('THURSDAY  !');
                FRIDAY        : WRITE('FRIDAY     !')
            END;  (* CASE *)
            FOR DEPT := A TO F DO
                BEGIN
                   WRITE(DATA[DAY,DEPT]:3);
                   PERCENTDIFF := ROUND((DATA[DAY, DEPT] -
                             AVE[DEPT]) * 100 / AVE[DEPT]);
                   WRITE(PERCENTDIFF:5)
                END;
            WRITELN
        END
END;   (*PRINTRESULT*)

(************************************************************)

PROCEDURE FINDAVERAGE(DATA : ARYTYPE; VAR AVE : LISTYPE);
VAR DAY : DAYTYPE;
    DEPT : DEPTYPE;
    SUM : REAL;
BEGIN  (*FINDAVERAGE*)
  FOR DEPT := A TO F DO
      BEGIN
         SUM := 0;
         FOR DAY := MONDAY TO FRIDAY DO
             SUM := SUM + DATA[DAY,DEPT];
         AVE[DEPT] := SUM / 5
      END
END;   (*FINDAVERAGE*)

(************************************************************)

PROCEDURE GETDATA(VAR DATA : ARYTYPE);
VAR DAY : DAYTYPE;
    DEPT : DEPTYPE;
BEGIN  (*GETDATA*)
  FOR DAY := MONDAY TO FRIDAY DO
      BEGIN
         FOR DEPT := A TO F DO
             READ(DATA[DAY,DEPT]);
         READLN
      END
END;   (*GETDATA*)

(************************************************************)

BEGIN    (* ABSENT *)
  GETDATA(TABLE);
  FINDAVERAGE(TABLE, AVE);
  PRINTRESULT(TABLE, AVE)
END.     (* ABSENT *)
```

Our program closely parallels our top-down design. Array types were declared in the TYPE section to be used in formal parameter lists.

■

MULTI-DIMENSIONAL ARRAYS

Pascal places no limit on the dimensions of an array, so arrays with more than two dimensions are allowed. The number of dimensions of an array is the same as the number of indexes needed to reference a particular cell. A three-dimensional array is an array of an array of an array:

```
VAR SALES : ARRAY[ITEMS] OF ARRAY[STORES] OF
            ARRAY[MONTHS] OF INTEGER;
```

or in abbreviated form

```
VAR SALES : ARRAY[ITEMS, STORES, MONTHS] OF INTEGER;
```

where ITEMS, STORES, and MONTHS have been defined as subranges. Figure 11-4 shows what SALES look like. The total number of elements is the product of the number of elements in each dimension. That means that a 100 × 100 × 100 array would have one million elements! This exceeds the limit of most computers.

MULTI-DIMENSIONAL ARRAY

An array of one or more arrays (as opposed to a one-dimensional array whose components are of a scalar type).

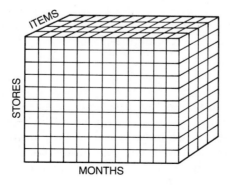

MONTHS

Figure 11-4.

One way to systematically access each location in a multi-dimensional array is as follows: let the right-most subscript be referenced by the inner-most loop control variable, let the next-to-the-right-most subscript be referenced by the next-to-the-innermost loop control variable, etc. This will help you keep your array processing straight so you don't miss any cells. Let's look at an example of this using a three-dimensional array. If we are given these declarations:

```
VAR STOCK : ARRAY[1..3,1..5,1..5]OF INTEGER;
    K,L,M : INTEGER;
```

then this program fragment

```
FOR K := 1 TO 3 DO
    FOR L := 1 TO 5 DO
        FOR M := 1 TO 5 DO
            STOCK[K,L,M] := 0;
```

would initialize all the cells to zero. (See Figure 11-5.)

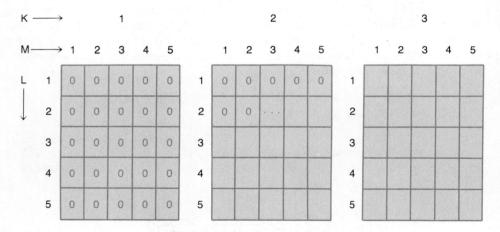

Figure 11-5.

Within the nested FOR loops the M subscript varies most rapidly, followed by the L subscript and then the K subscript. As in the case of one- and two-dimensional arrays, we must tell the compiler in the declarations section how many locations are to be reserved for a multi-dimensional array.

When we don't know how many data items we may have to put in an array, or we want to keep our programs general and easily expandable, we can declare an array to be larger than our anticipated need. If we do this, we must keep track of that part of the array we are using, by means of counters or limit values for each dimension. (This is the same sub-array processing we discussed in Chapter 10.)

Let's do an example. Assume these declarations:

```
TYPE ITEMS = 1..4;
     STORES = 1..10;
     MONTHS = 1..12;
VAR  SALES : ARRAY[ITEMS, STORES, MONTHS] OF INTEGER;
     ITEMCT, STORCT, MONTHCT : INTEGER;
     ITEM, STORE, MONTH, AMT : INTEGER;
```

If we currently have 8 stores (we're building 2 more) and it's only June (month 6), then we won't have any sales information for part of the array. Using the counters ITEMCT, STORCT and MONTHCT, we can keep track of the part of the array actually being used. The following program fragment will sum and print the total number of each item sold year-to-date by the chain of stores.

```
FOR ITEM := 1 TO ITEMCT DO
    BEGIN
      AMT := 0;
      FOR STORE := 1 TO STORCT DO
          FOR MONTH := 1 TO MONTHCT DO
              AMT := AMT + SALES[ITEM,STORE,MONTH];
      WRITELN('ITEM# ',ITEM:3,'  SALES TO DATE = ',AMT:6)
    END
```

Notice that we held each ITEM constant in the outer FOR loop while we summed that item's sales by MONTH and STORE. Accessing each cell this way conforms to our suggestion of referencing the right-most subscript by the innermost loop. This is logical in this case because of what each dimension means and how we want to process the data. However, our previous suggestion was only a general guideline. If we want to find the total number of each item sold monthly for the chain of stores we could use the following program fragment.

```
FOR ITEM := 1 TO ITEMCT DO
    BEGIN
      WRITELN('ITEM# ',ITEM:3);
      FOR MONTH := 1 TO MONTHCT DO
          BEGIN
            AMT := 0;
            FOR STORE := 1 TO STORCT DO
                AMT := AMT + SALES[ITEM,STORE,MONTH];
            WRITELN('MONTH ',MONTH:2,' SALES - ',AMT:5)
          END;
      WRITELN
    END
```

Slight changes in the algorithm would be needed to find the:

1. total number of each item sold monthly by each store,
2. total number of each item sold year-to-date by each store,
3. etc.

Of course, the format of the output may also dictate changes in the algorithm.

The algorithms we choose to solve a problem determine the kinds of control structures we use to code them. We have mentioned that in some cases WHILE loops are preferable to FOR loops in processing arrays. This is true when there are several terminating conditions for a loop. For example, in reading data into an array, you must watch for the end-of-file as well as guard against overfilling the array. The FOR loop is only a count-controlled loop and doesn't permit additional terminating conditions. In the following example, the WHILE loop controls the reading loop to prevent reading past the end-of-file or trying to overfill the array.

```
PROGRAM READPRESSURES(INPUT, OUTPUT);   (* Program to read 5 pressures
                                        per data line and find column averages *)
VAR READINGS : ARRAY[1..60, 1..5] OF REAL;
    CT, COL, ROW : INTEGER;
    SUM : REAL;
BEGIN
  CT := 0;
  WHILE NOT EOF AND (CT < 60) DO              (* while more pressures *)
    BEGIN
      CT := CT + 1;
      FOR COL := 1 TO 5 DO             (*read 5 pressures from each line*)
          READ(READINGS[CT,COL]);
      READLN
    END;
  IF NOT EOF                          (* check if array full and more data *)
    THEN WRITELN('ARRAY FULL, MORE DATA IN FILE.');
  FOR COL := 1 TO 5 DO                          (*find column averages*)
      BEGIN
        SUM := 0;
        FOR ROW := 1 TO CT DO
            SUM := SUM + READINGS[ROW,COL];
        WRITELN('COLUMN ', COL:1, ' AVERAGE = ',
                (SUM/CT):8:2)
      END
END.
```

Some typical output from this program could look like this:

```
COLUMN 1 AVERAGE =   650.00
COLUMN 2 AVERAGE =   623.18
COLUMN 3 AVERAGE =  1006.12
```

```
COLUMN 4 AVERAGE  =      32.10
COLUMN 5 AVERAGE  =     649.56
```

In the program, the variable CT keeps track of how full the array is (allows sub-array processing). Values are read into each row of the array (process by rows). After the values are read in, the average of each column of the array (process by columns) is found and printed out. Figure 11-6 shows what the READINGS array looks like.

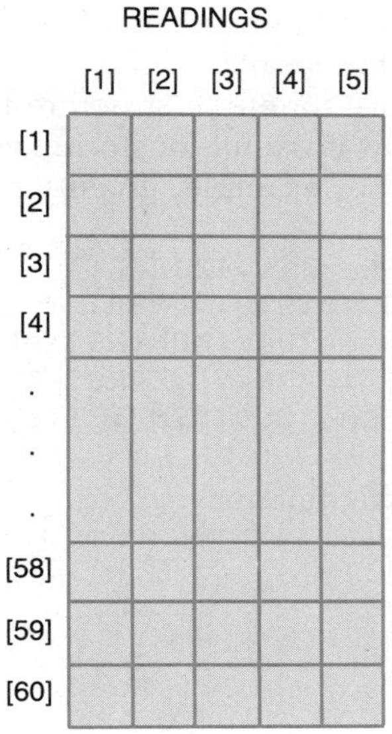

Figure 11-6.

Quite often, you will search an array for certain values. For example, you may want to know if any element of an array is negative. It is not necessary to go through the entire array once you have found a negative value. Given these declarations:

```
VAR LIST : ARRAY[1..10,1..5] OF INTEGER;
    NEG : BOOLEAN;
    ROW, COL : INTEGER;
```

the following program fragment would stop searching the array once a negative value was found.

```
NEG := FALSE;
ROW := 1;
WHILE NOT NEG AND (ROW <= 10) DO
  BEGIN
```

```
            COL := 1;
            WHILE NOT NEG AND (COL <= 5) DO
                IF LIST[ROW,COL] < 0
                    THEN NEG := TRUE
                    ELSE COL := COL + 1;
                ROW := ROW + 1
            END;
```

If we had used nested FOR loops, we would have searched through the entire array even if the very first element were negative. The inefficiency in using FOR loops might not hurt us for a 5×10 array, but what if there were 10,000 elements in the array?

Arrays (or any variables—simple or structured) of the same type can be assigned to each other. This is useful for storing values in a component of a multi-dimensional array. For example, given these declarations:

```
        TYPE MONTHS = 1..12;
             YEARS = 1950..1990;
             ITEM = ARRAY[MONTHS] OF INTEGER;
        VAR  TABLE : ARRAY[YEARS] OF ITEM;
             NEWITEM, OLDITEM : ITEM;
```

the following are valid assignments:

```
.
.
NEWITEM := OLDITEM;                    (* a one-dimensional array assignment *)
.
.
TABLE[1976] := NEWITEM;        (* first dimension (row) of two-dimensional array
                                          assigned value of a one-dimensional array *)
OLDITEM := TABLE[1956]              (* one-dimensional array assigned value of
                                          a row of a two-dimensional array *)
```

Notice how an element of TABLE was assigned the values in NEWITEM. The array variables in this example are shown in Figure 11-7.

Be careful, though, when *comparing* arrays. Comparison of arrays must be done cell by cell. For example, the following code would find if TABLE[1975] is equal to OLDITEM:

```
            EQUAL := TRUE;
            I := 1;
            WHILE EQUAL AND (I <= 12) DO
                IF TABLE[1975,I] = OLDITEM[I]
                    THEN I := I + 1
                    ELSE EQUAL := FALSE
```

but the following code:

```
IF TABLE[1975] = OLDITEM
   THEN EQUAL := TRUE
```

is *not* a valid comparison.

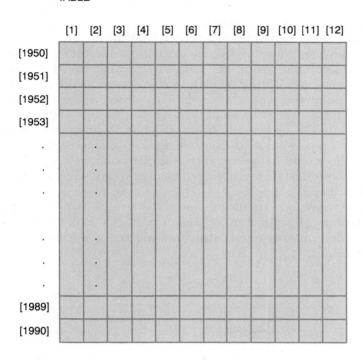

TABLE

NEWITEM

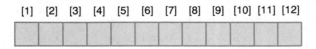

OLDITEM

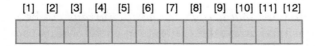

Figure 11-7.

DATA STRUCTURES AND THE DESIGN PROCESS

When writing a design, the choice of data structures is just as important as the choice of algorithms. Deciding on a data structure requires knowledge of the algorithms to be applied to the data. In like manner, the choice of algorithms requires knowledge of the way in which data will be structured. The development of program design and the choice of data structures occur in parallel and cannot be separated.

During analysis of the problem, you must specify the input and required output. Programs operate on data, and the form of the input data is needed to know how to transform the data into the output. The actual data objects will require certain operations performed on them.

As you develop your design, you assume that lower level modules can perform these operations on the data. As a result, your MAIN module reflects your general solution by calling these lower level modules.

At some point you must choose the data structures (which may only be simple variables). Your choice of data structure limits your choices of the algorithms used to operate on the data. Overall program efficiency may suffer from a poor choice of data structure. You may realize that another data structure would be better. If so, you can backtrack (go up the design tree) to previous design decisions and change your choice of data structures and/or algorithms.

Using an array for structuring your data is useful when storing or processing groups of similar or related data. Let's look at some possible choices in determining a data structure and see if we can come up with some guidelines.

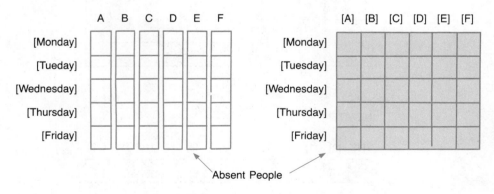

Figure 11-8.

1. *Two-dimensional arrays vs. parallel arrays:* To be able to use a two-dimensional array, the contents of each location must be of the same type. In Program ABSENT, each location in the array TABLE contained an INTEGER value which represented the number of people

who were absent. There were six departments named A,B,C,D,E and F. Six parallel one-dimensional arrays could have been used to represent the same data. But since each cell represented the same thing, absent people, it made sense to use a two-dimensional array. (See Figure 11-8.)

Let's look at another example. Exercise problem 3.b. in Chapter 10 described a situation in which you had a payroll master file made up of three pieces of data per person:

ID	(5 digit number)
RATE	(hourly salary)
DEP	(number of dependents)

The solution suggested using three parallel one-dimensional arrays. If RATE were kept in cents so that all three related items would be integer, would a two-dimensional array be a better representation? No. It would be legal but would not make much sense. One column would represent an identification number; one column would represent an hourly rate; and one column would represent the number of dependents. Row processing would have no meaning. If what you will want to do is strictly column processing, then parallel arrays are a better data structure. (See Figure 11-9.)

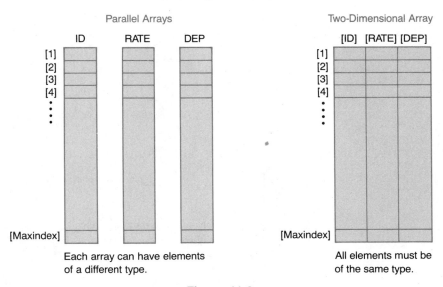

Figure 11-9.

2. *Array vs. simple variables:* The question to ask yourself when you are deciding whether to use an array or not is: "Can I process as I read, or must all the data be read in before I can process it?" For example, to find the average of a set of test grades, each test grade can be added into the sum as it is read. All you need are simple variables—no data

structures are needed. What if you want to compare each grade to the average? Since the average is not calculated until all the grades have been read, in this case each individual grade must be kept in memory. Therefore, the test grades should be stored in an array. (See Figure 11-10.)

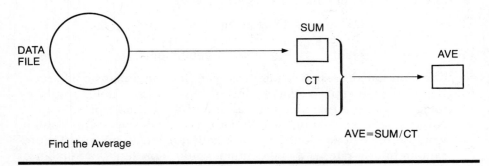

Find the Average

Find the Average and Compare to Each Grade

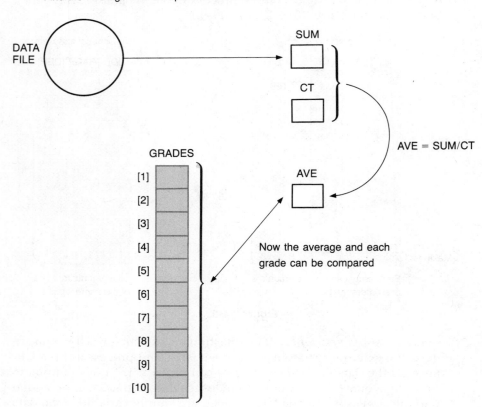

Figure 11-10.

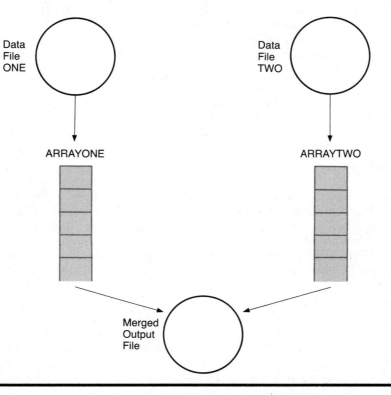

Data Structures Unnecessary for Merge

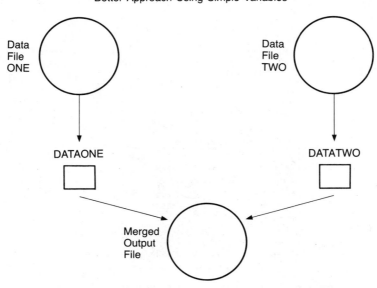

Better Approach Using Simple Variables

Figure 11-11.

In Chapter 10 we developed a program which merged two one-dimensional arrays. We did this to give you more experience working with arrays while we introduced the concept of merging. We did, however, point out that the choice of two arrays for the data structure was inefficient because two simple variables could have been used. (We merged two lists of phone numbers. By comparing only one number at a time from each file and storing the smaller number in a third file, we could have avoided the need for two arrays to hold the two lists of phone numbers in memory.) Using an array when one is not necessary is expensive in two ways: more storage is used, and accessing an element in an array takes more time than accessing a simple variable. (See Figure 11-11.)

These suggestions presuppose that you know where to begin. What if you look at a problem and don't even know what your choices for structuring data are? Go back and carefully examine the problem statement. Do you understand what is being asked? Could you do what is being asked for by hand? If so, what sort of forms would you use? Would you set up a table on a sheet of paper with rows and columns? Would you set up a column and make hash marks? More than likely the correct data structure will resemble the forms you would create to do the job by hand.

If you could not do the job by hand, your problem is more fundamental than the choice of a data structure. You need a clarification of the problem. Try writing down everything you know about the problem. Then write down what your output must be. Now try writing down what you must have as input to produce that output. Refer, if necessary, to the problem-solving heuristics in Chapter 2.

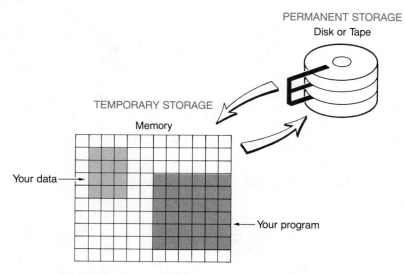

Figure 11-12. Temporary and Permanent Storage.

Whatever data structures (or simple variables) you choose to solve a problem, keep in mind that these variables are temporarily stored in memory. Program output can be saved permanently in external files (stored on disk or tape or printed on the printer). (See Figure 11-12.)

Go back to Chapter 3 now and reread the few pages on top-down design. Integrate the reading with your new knowledge of data structures and your programming experience.

In APPENDIX I we have expanded our top-down design methodology to include the specification of data structures. During the design process it is desirable to defer details to as low a level as possible. However, it is important to specify the data structures early enough to aid in design decisions and guide algorithm development. Our design outline now looks like this:

INPUT:
OUTPUT:
DATA STRUCTURES:
ASSUMPTIONS (IF ANY):
MAIN MODULE
REMAINING MODULES BY LEVELS

You know that several iterations through the design process are usually necessary. As you travel down the design tree you make a series of design decisions. If a decision proves unwise or incorrect, it is easy to backtrack

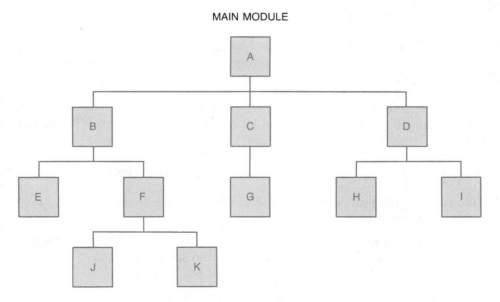

Figure 11-13.

and try something else. It may even be necessary to go back to your choice of data structures if they prove unwieldy or impossible to implement. This doesn't mean you will have to discard unaffected modules. For example, in the design tree in Figure 11-13, at E you may see that you need to change B. This may or may not affect F (or J or K) and probably won't affect the other modules. Even the discovery at J that A needs to be changed may not affect C or D or other modules, but only require a reorganization of the design tree.

■ SAMPLE PROBLEM

The pastime of trying to catch a greased pig (usually in a mud-filled pigpen) can be seen at rodeos and fairs. Trying to catch a slippery pig that doesn't want to be caught results in more than one muddy face. It would be a lot cleaner (but not as much fun) to simulate this activity on the computer.

OINK!

Problem: Design an interactive screen-oriented game called "The Greased Pig Contest" with the following rules:

1. The contestant is called 'C'.
2. The greased pig is called 'P'.
3. Obstacles (such as the slop trough) will be denoted by a '*'.
4. The number of moves for 'C' is limited to 20.
5. The pigpen is an 8 × 16 playing board.
6. Moves off the edge of the pigpen will continue in the same direction but from the opposite edge.
7. Both 'C' and 'P' move after 'C' has entered his move. (The program makes the move for 'P' according to the values from a random number generator.)
8. 'C' and 'P' stop for obstacles.
9. The screen is updated after each move.
10. The game ends when 'P' and 'C' are in the same square ('C' wins) or 'C' runs out of moves ('C' loses).

Figure 11-14 shows what a typical screen could look like.

Discussion: Since this is to be an interactive screen-oriented program, several assumptions have to be made:

1. Both the INPUT and OUTPUT files can be assigned to the terminal.
2. The terminal has a 24 line × 80 column screen.
3. A random number generator is available.

Writing a screen-oriented game program requires more attention to output (the graphics that appear on the screen). Figure 11-14 shows a

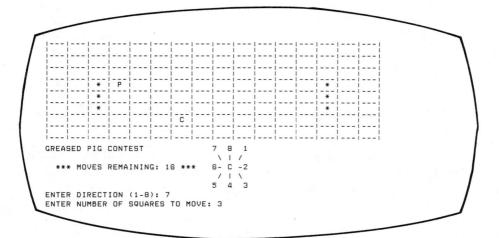

Figure 11-14.

typical screen layout that utilizes all 24 lines of a terminal screen. The pigpen display was represented by a two-dimensional array containing the players—'C' for the contestant, 'P' for the pig—and stars representing the slop troughs. The question, though, is what the pigpen should look like in memory.

After quite a bit of analysis of this problem, we decided to let the pigpen array look exactly like the screen representation (but minus the pig and the contestant). Another choice would be an 8×16 array (or whatever size is desired) to store the obstacle and player positions and to generate the actual display when needed, but this seemed inefficient.

If the pigpen is actually 8×16 squares, then the display array (as shown) ends up using 17×65 cells to store spaces, the contents of each square and square boundary walls. Each character in the display requires a cell in the display array. To make sure the pig and the contestant are always in the center of a square in the display requires appropriate scaling factors. The scaling factors needed for the display array chosen are:

Display row position = 2 * row position of square
Display column position = 4 * column position of square − 1

(Remember, for a pigpen containing 8 × 16 squares the display array contains 17 × 65 characters.) Let's look at a small part of the display array to see how the scaling factors work. Looking at the top left-hand corner of the display

```
|---|---|--
|   |   |
|---|---|--
|   | C |
|---|---|--
|   |   |
```

we see that the first square of the pigpen is represented by characters stored in 15 cells of the display array: 6 vertical bars, 6 horizontal bars and 3 enclosed spaces (blanks).

```
|---|
|   |
|---|
```

In the above example we show the contestant, 'C', in the square occupying the second row and second column of the pigpen. By using the scaling factors:

$$\text{Display row} = 2 * 2 \qquad (4)$$
$$\text{Display column} = 4 * 2 - 1 \qquad (7)$$

we compute that 'C' occupies the [4,7] position in the display array. If you count the character positions, you will see that this is the correct position in the display array for the example above. We will need to use these scaling factors whenever 'C' or 'P' makes a move. For example, we just showed that a pigpen position of [2,2] for a player is a display position of [4,7]. If we move the player one square to the right (pigpen position [2,3]), the new display position would be [4,11]. By the way, the display and the scaling factors were not at all intuitive. They required some trial and error before arriving at a satisfactory solution.

Displaying the rules on the screen is straightforward and can be left to a separate procedure.

The number of variables to be initialized calls for a separate procedure. Initializing the display array can be done (after a little thought) by using appropriate multiples to generate the walls and spaces of each square of the pigpen. The positions of the obstructions (slop-troughs) and the starting positions of the players (contestant and pig) can be set up as global constants. This allows these positions to be changed easily (if desired) in the CONST section of the program. (Of course, the players starting positions and the positions of the obstructions could be randomly generated for each game.)

If the pigpen array is treated as a template, we can pass it and the players' positions as value parameters to a procedure that handles the screen display. This procedure could insert the players in the array (using the scaling factors) and display it on the screen. We chose to do this so we would never have to erase the players from the global array (they are never in there) in order to move them around. (Changes in a value parameter don't affect the actual parameter.)

We also used the scaling factors to see if a player (contestant or pig) is trying to move into a square with an obstruction. We created a procedure to return the position, held in a temporary variable, of either player after moving one square in a specified direction. (Of course, this procedure has to take care of moves off the edge of the pigpen.) If the temporary variable represents a free position, then the player is assigned this new position. Moves continue one square at a time until a player moves the proper distance or hits an obstruction. After the move, the screen is rewritten.

The contestant can be prompted on the screen for the direction and number of squares to be moved, but the program needs to generate the pig's moves. A random number generator, similar to the one used in Program SOLITAIRE in Chapter 10, is used to generate the pig's moves.*

Input: Direction of move (1..8)
 Number of squares to move

Output: Game screen showing:
 pigpen
 number of moves left
 request for move data or display of win/loss status

Data Structures: Two-dimensional array to display pigpen (DISPLAY)
 2 one-dimensional arrays to hold contestant (C) and pig (P) positions

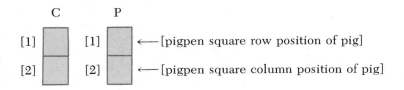

C   P

[1] ⬜   [1] ⬜ ⟵—[pigpen square row position of pig]

[2] ⬜   [2] ⬜ ⟵—[pigpen square column position of pig]

---

* Again we assume that our random number generator is a function that returns a value between 0.00 and 1.00. Many applications, such as games and other simulations, require a random number generator. These functions are generally tailored to the characteristics of the particular machine being used. Random numbers generated by an algorithm are actually *pseudo* random—a seemingly random series of numbers that will actually start repeating itself at some point. Some systems do not provide a random function, so it will be necessary for you to write your own. There are many texts available that treat the topic of computer random number generators in detail.

MAIN

RULES
INITIALIZE
WHILE game not over DO
    SHOWSCREEN
    CONTESTANTMOVE
    PIGMOVE
    check for winner
FINISH game

RULES

display rules on screen

INITIALIZE

initialize pigpen display array
initialize variables

SHOWSCREEN

insert player positions in pigpen display array
display pigpen array and moves remaining

SHOWSCREEN is passed the display array and player positions as value parameters.

CONTESTANTMOVE

REPEAT
    prompt for DIRECTION
    READ DIRECTION
UNTIL DIRECTION is valid (between 1 and 8)
prompt for DISTANCE to move
READ DISTANCE
MAKEMOVE

Accepts only a valid DIRECTION.

When reading integer values interactively, our particular system will not accept invalid characters. With most systems the program will have to check for invalid data.

PIGMOVE

DISTANCE = TRUNC(random function * 100) mod WIDTH
DIRECTION = TRUNC(random function * 100) MOD 8 + 1
MAKEMOVE

FINISH

> IF winner
>   THEN display message that pig is caught
>   ELSE display message that pig is loose and out of moves

MAKEMOVE   **Level 2**

> WHILE still possible to move DO
>   MOVEASQUARE returning temporary position
>   decrement the number of squares left to move
>   IF player is obstructed
>   THEN OBSTRUCTION is TRUE
>   ELSE player's position = temporary position

MOVEASQUARE   **Level 3**

> Find temporary row and column position   Returns temporary
>   according to direction of one-square   position to MAKEMOVE.
>   move

The tree diagram for the final design looks like this:

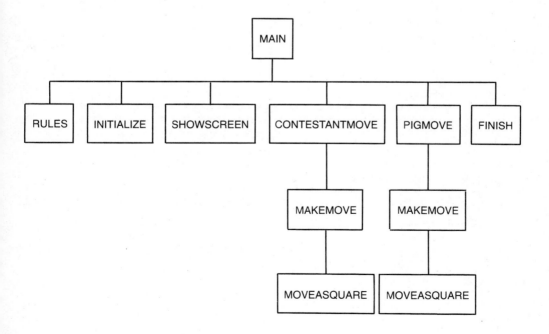

```
PROGRAM GREASEDPIG(INPUT, OUTPUT);        (*This program is an interactive
              game simulation of a greased pig contest. See the problem for the game rules*)
CONST  MAXMOVES = 20;                          (*maximum number of moves*)
       HEIGHT = 8;                             (*number of rows in pigpen*)
       WIDTH = 16;                             (*number of columns in pigpen*)
       ROWC = 5;                               (*starting row - contestant*)
       COLC = 2;                               (*starting col - contestant*)
       ROWP = 5;                               (*starting row - pig*)
       COLP = 4;                               (*starting col - pig*)
       OBSTROW1 = 4;                           (*first row - obstruction*)
       OBSTROW2 = 5;                           (*second row - obstruction*)
       OBSTROW3 = 6;                           (*third row - obstruction*)
       OBSTCOL1 = 3;                           (*first col - obstruction*)
       OBSTCOL2 = 14;                          (*second col - obstruction*)
TYPE PLAYER = ARRAY[1..2] OF INTEGER;     (*row and column positions*)
     MATRIX = ARRAY[1..24,1..80] OF CHAR; (*maximum screen size*)
VAR C, P : PLAYER;                             (*arrays for contestant and pig positions*)
    WINNER : BOOLEAN;                          (*winner flag*)
    DISPLAY : MATRIX;                          (*display array to represent pigpen*)
    MOVECT : INTEGER;                          (*number of moves left to play*)
(***********************************************************)
PROCEDURE FINISH(WINNER : BOOLEAN);
BEGIN (*FINISH*)
  IF WINNER
    THEN
      BEGIN
        WRITELN('CONGRATULATIONS!!');
        WRITELN('YOU HAVE CAUGHT THE GREASED PIG.')
      END
    ELSE
      BEGIN
        WRITELN('OINK! OINK!');
        WRITELN('THE PIG IS STILL LOOSE AND YOU HAVE RUN',
                ' OUT OF MOVES.')
      END
END;  (*FINISH*)
(***********************************************************)
PROCEDURE SHOWSCREEN(DISPLAY : MATRIX; C, P : PLAYER;
                          MOVECT : INTEGER);   (* Insert players in
                               display array and write array to the screen *)
VAR I, J : INTEGER;
BEGIN (*SHOWSCREEN*)
  DISPLAY[2 * P[1], 4 * P[2] - 1] := 'P'; (* insert pig in display *)
  DISPLAY[2 * C[1], 4 * C[2] - 1] := 'C';     (* insert contestant *)
  FOR I := 1 TO 2 * HEIGHT + 1 DO        (* Height of display array using *)
    BEGIN                                       (* the scaling factors. *)
      FOR J := 1 TO 4 * WIDTH + 1 DO      (* width of display array *)
          WRITE(DISPLAY[I, J]);
      WRITELN
    END;
```

```
        WRITELN('GREASED PIG CONTEST              7  8  1');
        WRITELN('                                  \  |  /  ');
        WRITELN('  *** MOVES REMAINING:  ', MOVECT:2,
                                 '  ***     6 - C - 2');
        WRITELN('                                  /  |  \  ');
        WRITELN('                                 5  4  3')
      END;  (*SHOWSCREEN*)
      (*************************************************************)
      PROCEDURE MAKEMOVE(VAR PIECE : PLAYER; DISTANCE,
                         DIRECTION : INTEGER);  (* Move a player a square
            at a time while the move is not obstructed and there are squares left in the move *)
      VAR TEMP : PLAYER;                             (* temporary player *)
          OBSTRUCTION : BOOLEAN ;
          (*************************************************************)
          PROCEDURE MOVEASQUARE(VAR TEMP : PLAYER; DIRECTION :
                               INTEGER);
          BEGIN (*MOVEASQUARE*)
            CASE DIRECTION OF                    (* get new row position *)
              1,7,8 : IF TEMP[1] = 1
                        THEN TEMP[1] := HEIGHT
                        ELSE TEMP[1] := TEMP[1] - 1;
              3,4,5 : IF TEMP[1] = HEIGHT
                        THEN TEMP[1] := 1
                        ELSE TEMP[1] := TEMP[1] + 1;
              2,6   : ;
            END; (*CASE*)
            CASE DIRECTION OF                   (* get new column position *)
              5,6,7 : IF TEMP[2] = 1
                        THEN TEMP[2] := WIDTH
                        ELSE TEMP[2] := TEMP[2] - 1;
              1,2,3 : IF TEMP[2] = WIDTH
                        THEN TEMP[2] := 1
                        ELSE TEMP[2] := TEMP[2] + 1;
              4,8   : ;
            END  (*CASE*)
          END; (*MOVEASQUARE*)
          (*************************************************************)
      BEGIN (*MAKEMOVE*)
        OBSTRUCTION := FALSE;
        TEMP := PIECE;               (* Assigns player's position to temporary player *)
        WHILE (DISTANCE > 0) AND NOT OBSTRUCTION DO
          BEGIN
            MOVEASQUARE(TEMP, DIRECTION); (* Move temp. player one square *)
            DISTANCE := DISTANCE - 1;  (* Decrement distance by one square *)
            IF DISPLAY[2 * TEMP[1], 4 * TEMP[2] - 1] = '*'
               THEN OBSTRUCTION := TRUE
               ELSE PIECE := TEMP          (* If no obstruction, move the player -
                                            contestant or pig - one square *)
          END
      END; (*MAKEMOVE*)
```

```
(*************************************************************)
PROCEDURE CONTESTANTMOVE(VAR C : PLAYER);          (* Get contestant's
                 choices for direction and distance, and make the contestant's move *)
VAR DIRECTION, DISTANCE : INTEGER;
BEGIN
                                                          (* get move *)
  REPEAT
    WRITE('ENTER DIRECTION (1-8): ');
    READLN(DIRECTION);
  UNTIL (DIRECTION >= 1) AND (DIRECTION <= 8);
  WRITE('ENTER NUMBER OF SQUARES TO MOVE: ');
  READLN(DISTANCE);
  MAKEMOVE(C, DISTANCE, DIRECTION)
END;
(*************************************************************)
PROCEDURE PIGMOVE(VAR P : PLAYER);     (* Use random number generator
                 to get the pig's direction and distance, and make the pig's move *)
VAR DIRECTION, DISTANCE : INTEGER;
BEGIN
  DISTANCE := TRUNC(RANDOM(0) * 100) MOD WIDTH;
                   (* Generates random distance for pig from 0 to 15 squares *)
  DIRECTION := TRUNC(RANDOM(0) * 100) MOD 8 + 1;
                       (* Generates random direction for pig from 1 to 8 *)
  MAKEMOVE(P, DISTANCE, DIRECTION)
END
(*************************************************************)
PROCEDURE INITIALIZE(VAR WINNER : BOOLEAN; VAR MOVECT :
                     INTEGER; VAR DISPLAY : MATRIX);
              (* Initialize variables: move counter, win flag, player starting positions,
                 obstruction positions, walls and blanks in pigpen display array *)
VAR ROW, COL : INTEGER;
    CH : CHAR;
BEGIN (*INITIALIZE*)
  WINNER := FALSE;
  MOVECT := MAXMOVES;         (* sets move counter to max number of moves *)
  C[1] := ROWC;                             (* initialize contestant's *)
  C[2] := COLC;                             (* starting position *)
  P[1] := ROWP;                             (* initialize pig's starting *)
  P[2] := COLP;                             (* position *)
  FOR ROW := 1 TO 2 * HEIGHT + 1 DO         (* initialize display array *)
      BEGIN                                 (* using scaling factors *)
        IF ROW MOD 2 = 1
            THEN CH := '-'                   (* set horizontal walls *)
            ELSE CH := ' ';                  (* set pigpen square blanks *)
        FOR COL := 1 TO 4 * WIDTH + 1 DO
            IF COL MOD 4 = 1
                THEN DISPLAY[ROW,COL] : = '|'(* set vertical walls *)
                ELSE DISPLAY[ROW,COL] := CH; (* set horiz. wall or *)
      END;                                                (*blank *)
```

```
      DISPLAY[2 * OBSTROW1, 4 * OBSTCOL1 - 1]  :=  '*';      (* enter *)
      DISPLAY[2 * OBSTROW2, 4 * OBSTCOL1 - 1]  :=  '*'; (* obstruct. *)
      DISPLAY[2 * OBSTROW3, 4 * OBSTCOL1 - 1]  :=  '*';       (* into *)
      DISPLAY[2 * OBSTROW1, 4 * OBSTCOL2 - 1]  :=  '*';        (* the *)
      DISPLAY[2 * OBSTROW2, 4 * OBSTCOL2 - 1]  :=  '*';    (* display *)
      DISPLAY[2 * OBSTROW3, 4 * OBSTCOL2 - 1]  :=  '*';      (* array *)
   END;  (*INITIALIZE*)
(***************************************************************)
PROCEDURE RULES;        (* Display rules of the game on the screen for contestant *)
BEGIN  (*RULES*)
   WRITELN;
   WRITELN;
   WRITELN('WELCOME TO "THE GREASED PIG CONTEST".');
   WRITELN;
   WRITELN('THE RULES ARE SIMPLE:');
   WRITELN;
   WRITELN('       - YOU ARE THE CONTESTANT - "C".');
   WRITELN('       - YOU ARE AFTER THE PIG  - "P".');
   WRITELN('       - YOU HAVE ', MAXMOVES:1, ' MOVES TO',
            ' CATCH THE PIG.');
   WRITELN('       - AFTER EACH MOVE YOU MUST GIVE THE',
            ' DIRECTION AND');
   WRITELN('         DISTANCE YOU WISH TO MOVE.');
   WRITELN('       - IF YOU OR THE PIG GO OFF THE EDGE',
            ' OF THE PIGPEN,');
   WRITELN('         YOU CONTINUE FROM THE OPPOSITE SIDE.');
   WRITELN('       - BOTH YOU AND THE PIG MOVE',
            ' SIMULTANEOUSLY.');
   WRITELN('       - BOTH YOU AND THE PIG MUST STOP',
            ' FOR SLOP TROUGHS');
   WRITELN('         (MARKED BY ASTERISKS).');
   WRITELN('       - YOU WIN WHEN YOU OCCUPY THE SAME',
            ' SQUARE AS THE PIG.');
   WRITELN;
   WRITELN('PRESS <RETURN> WHEN YOU ARE READY TO START.');
   READLN                 (* satisfied by the <eoln> generated by <RETURN> key *)
END;  (*RULES*)
(***************************************************************)
BEGIN  (*MAIN*)
   RULES;
   INITIALIZE(WINNER, MOVECT, DISPLAY);
   WHILE NOT WINNER AND (MOVECT > 0) DO
      BEGIN
         SHOWSCREEN(DISPLAY, C, P, MOVECT);
         CONTESTANTMOVE(C);
         PIGMOVE(P);
         IF (C[1] = P[1]) AND (C[2] = P[2])        (* check if both in
                                                       same square *)
```

```
      THEN WINNER := TRUE;
        MOVECT := MOVECT - 1        (* decrement the moves left by one *)
    END;
  FINISH(WINNER)
END.  (*MAIN*)
```

Procedure MOVEASQUARE deserves further discussion. MOVEASQUARE is nested in MAKEMOVE because it has no meaning outside of its relation to MAKEMOVE. It could have been coded in several ways, but all that matters is that it moves a player one square in the direction specified in the call from Procedure MAKEMOVE. A player can only move in one of eight directions (Figure 11-15).

Procedure MOVEASQUARE must also take care of moves off the edge of the pigpen (Figure 11-16). Two CASE statements are used in Procedure MOVEASQUARE—one to find the new row position and one to find the new column position of the player, depending on the current position and direction to be moved.

Let's analyze Procedure MOVEASQUARE a little more. In the first CASE statement (finding a new row position), if a player is in the first row and the move is in direction 1, 7 or 8, the player's row position is wrapped around to the other side of the array (the last row). Similarly, if the player is in the last row and the move is in direction 3, 4 or 5, the player's row position is wrapped around to the other side of the array (the first row). When the move is not off the edge of the pigpen, the row position is simply incremented or decremented by one as required. Notice that since directions 2 and 6 don't change the row position, no action is taken. The second CASE statement for finding a new column position works in a similar manner.

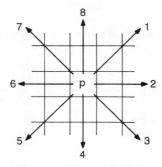

Figure 11-15.

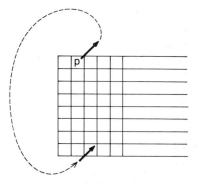

Figure 11-16.

As you learn more of the features of Pascal, you may want to add them to this game program in order to make it more efficient and/or more interesting to play.

■

TESTING AND DEBUGGING

The same errors are likely to occur with multi-dimensional arrays that occur with one-dimensional arrays. Subscript range errors are most common. Trying to access undefined (uninitialized) cells may cause an undefined value error.

Nested loop structures are more complex and can lead to subtle errors in logic that don't generate run-time errors. The syntax may be valid, but what you intended to happen is not exactly what you coded.

Testing and Debugging Hints

1. Initialize all cells of an array if there is any chance that you will attempt to access the entire array. If you will use only part of an array, keep track (with counters, pointers, etc.) of what you are using. This will prevent run-time errors that may arise when trying to use undefined values.
2. Use subrange types for index variables and be careful in parameter passing to avoid array index range errors.
3. Follow some systematic order in processing array subscripts in nested loops.
4. Define data types globally to prevent type mismatches when passing arrays as parameters.

5. Use the proper number of subscripts with array names when referencing a cell in an array.
6. ROW and COL are good index identifiers, but they have no meaning in Pascal. Remember, the first subscript is the row and the second is the column.

Summary

Since the components of an array can be of any type, we can have arrays of arrays (multi-dimensional arrays). This lets us structure our data in a convenient form. A two-dimensional array can be thought of as an array of one-dimensional arrays, a three-dimensional array as an array of two-dimensional arrays. Multi-dimensional arrays are data structures reflecting more than one data relationship.

Nested FOR loops are handy in processing multi-dimensional arrays. WHILE loops should be used when terminating conditions involve more than a simple counter variable.

Design and choice of data structure occur in parallel. Choosing appropriate data structures requires careful analysis of the problem and knowledge of the algorithms available. So far, our choice is between simple variables and arrays or between one-dimensional arrays and multi-dimensional arrays. Our decision depends upon the order of processing, algorithm efficiency, ease of implementation, memory size, etc. The correct data structures will often resemble the forms you would create to do the job by hand.

When a design decision results in an inefficient algorithm or in implementation problems, we must backtrack (go up the design tree) and change that design decision. (It is much easier to alter our design than to change a half-finished program.)

Exercises

1. An array is a collection of identical type elements referenced by a single name and a subscript to indicate a particular element. A multi-dimensional array is not a different data type, it is simply an array whose elements are themselves arrays.   T   F

2. Given the following declarations
```
PROGRAM VOTECOUNT(INPUT,OUTPUT);
CONST CANLIMIT = 4;
      PRELIMIT = 47;
TYPE CRANGE = 1..CANLIMIT;
     PRANGE = 1..PRELIMIT;
     VOTETALLY = ARRAY[CRANGE,PRANGE] OF INTEGER;
```

```
VAR   PRIMARY,ELECTION : VOTETALLY;
      PRETOTAL,TOTAL : INTEGER;
      PRECINCT : PRANGE;
      CANDIDATE : CRANGE;
```

answer the following as True or False.

a. The following statements woud find the winner of the election.

```
TOTAL := 0;
FOR CANDIDATE := 1 TO CANLIMIT DO
    FOR PRECINCT := 1 TO PRELIMIT DO
        TOTAL := TOTAL + ELECTION[CANDIDATE,PRECINCT];
IF CANDIDATE > TOTAL
    THEN WRITELN('THE WINNER IS CANDIDATE ',CANDIDATE:1);
```

T   F

b. The following statements would sum the number of votes cast for all candidates in the 3rd precinct.

```
PRECINCT := 3;
PRETOTAL := 0;
FOR CANDIDATE := 1 TO CANLIMIT DO
    PRETOTAL := PRETOTAL +
                ELECTION[PRECINCT,CANDIDATE];
```

T   F

c. The following statements would sum the votes for candidate 1 across all precincts.

```
CANDIDATE := 1;
TOTAL := 0;
FOR PRECINCT := 1 TO PRELIMIT DO
    TOTAL := TOTAL + ELECTION[CANDIDATE,PRECINCT];
```

T   F

3. Write a program segment that will initialize the elements of an array TABLE to zero given the following declarations.

```
TYPE RANGE1 = 0..60;
     RANGE2 = 1..36;
VAR  TABLE : ARRAY[RANGE1,RANGE2] OF INTEGER;
     A : RANGE1;
     B : RANGE2;
```

4. Write a procedure that initializes the diagonals of an NxN array to the character stored in input parameter CH. The array and character variable are to be passed as parameters. Assume this global declaration:

```
TYPE LIST = ARRAY[1..N,1..N] OF CHAR;
```

5. Write a procedure that finds the maximum value in an MxN integer array. Pass the array as a parameter. Assume a global array type TABLE.

Pre-Test

1. The elements of an array can themselves be arrays, and the elements of those arrays can be arrays, thus allowing 2, 3 or n-dimensional array structures.   T   F

2. A logging operation keeps records of 37 loggers' monthly production for purposes of analysis using the following array structure.

```
CONST   NUMLOGGERS = 37;
TYPE    MONTHS = 1..12;
VAR     CUTDATA : ARRAY[1..NUMLOGGERS,MONTHS] OF INTEGER;
        MONTHLYHIGH,MONTHLYTOTAL,
        YEARLYTOTAL,HIGH : INTEGER;
        MONTH,BESTMONTH : MONTHS;
        LOGGER,BESTLOGGER : 1..NUMLOGGERS;
```

Answer the following as either True or False.

a. The following statement would assign the January log total for logger number 7 to MONTHLYTOTAL.

```
        MONTHLYTOTAL := CUTDATA[7,1]        T     F
```

b. The following statements would compute the yearly total for logger number 11.

```
    YEARLYTOTAL := 0;
    FOR MONTH := 1 TO 12 DO
        YEARLYTOTAL := YEARLYTOTAL + CUTDATA[MONTH,11];
                                                     T     F
```

c. The following statements would find the BESTLOGGER (most logs cut) in March.

```
        MONTHLYHIGH := 0;
        FOR LOGGER := 1 TO NUMLOGGERS DO
            IF CUTDATA[LOGGER,3] > MONTHLYHIGH
                THEN
                    BEGIN
                        BESTLOGGER := LOGGER;
                        MONTHLYHIGH := CUTDATA[LOGGER,3]
                    END;
                                                     T     F
```

d. The following statements would find the logger with the highest monthly production and his best month.

```
        HIGH := 0;
        FOR MONTH := 1 TO 12 DO
            FOR LOGGER := 1 TO NUMLOGGERS DO
                IF CUTDATA[LOGGER,MONTH] > HIGH
                    THEN
                        BEGIN
                            HIGH := CUTDATA[LOGGER,MONTH];
                            BESTLOGGER := LOGGER;
```

```
          BESTMONTH := MONTH
     END;
```

T F

3. Write a procedure that will initialize the elements of one specific row of an array to the value 1. The row to be set to 1 is passed as a parameter. Assume the following declarations in the main program.

```
CONST  COLLIM = 50;
       ROWLIM = 40;
TYPE   ROWRANGE = 0..ROWLIM;
       COLRANGE = 0..COLLIM;
       ARY = ARRAY[ROWRANGE,COLRANGE] OF INTEGER;
VAR    TABLE : ARY;
       COL,ROW : INTEGER;
```

Do not reference global variables directly in your procedure.

4. Write a function that will return TRUE if all the elements of an array passed as a parameter are positive, otherwise FALSE. Use the same declarations in the main program as in question 3.

Records 12

Goals

To be able to define a record data type.

To be able to declare a record variable.

To be able to access, compare and assign values to the individual components of a record variable.

To be able to define data types which include hierarchical records and arrays of records.

To be able to access, compare and assign values to the individual components of record variables of the above data types.

To be able to choose the appropriate data structure, given a specific problem.

To be able to sort an array of records.

RECORDS

In Chapter 9 we mentioned the built-in data structures in Pascal: arrays, records, sets and files. In this chapter we discuss the record data type. (The record is not available in some programming languages which is another reason for Pascal's appeal.)

Of these four data structures, we have, so far, examined only arrays in detail. Records are similar to arrays in that they can both represent a group of elements with a common name. However, while the elements of an array (single or multi-dimensional) must all be of the same type, the elements of a record may be of different types.

Arrays are useful for storing and accessing data items of the same type by using a common name and varying a subscript. We have seen that parallel arrays can be used for relating items that describe the same object.

```
TYPE LIST = ARRAY[1..100] OF INTEGER;
VAR FREQ : LIST;
    ID : LIST;
```

We can even handle items of different data types this way.

```
VAR CHARLIST : ARRAY[1..100] OF CHAR;
    FREQ : ARRAY[1..100] OF INTEGER;
    RATIO : ARRAY[1..100] OF REAL;
```

In each case the selection of data items describing the same object is done by using the same subscript in each array.

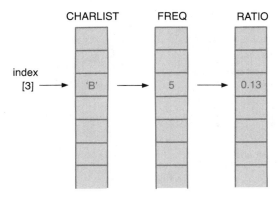

Figure 12-1. Parallel Arrays.

Since the elements of an array must be of the same type, we couldn't use a multi-dimensional array here (each item is of a different type). We had to use (and keep track of) three separate data structures: CHARLIST, FREQ and RATIO. (See Figure 12-1.)

If we want to use a single data structure in which the elements can be of different types, we can use the RECORD.

RECORD

A structured data type with a fixed number of components (not necessarily of the same type) that are accessed by name, *not subscript.*

```
TYPE PERSON = RECORD
                  field identifier : type;
                      .
                      .
                  field identifier : type
              END ;
```

FIELD IDENTIFIER

The name of a component in a record.

To represent our opening example using records instead of parallel arrays, we would define a record with three parts (fields): CH (character), FREQ (frequency), and RATIO. This record would represent the items with the same subscript in the three arrays. We would then define an array of these, thus representing the three arrays as one data structure: an array of records. (See Figure 12-2.)

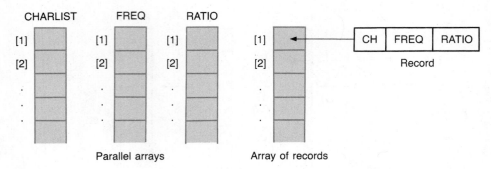

Figure 12-2.

But we have jumped ahead of ourselves. We will now discuss how to define a record type, declare variables of that type, and access items within the record variable. Let's use a record to describe students with the following information: name, sex, social security number, marital status, and classification.

```
TYPE PERSON = RECORD
                NAME : ARRAY[1..30] OF CHAR;
                SEX : (MALE, FEMALE);
                SSNO : ARRAY[1..11] OF CHAR;
                MS : (SINGLE, MARRIED);
                CLASS : 1..6
              END; (*RECORD*)
VAR STUDENT : PERSON;
```

NAME, SEX, SSNO, MS and CLASS are the field identifiers within the record type PERSON. These field identifiers will be used to access the different components of the variable STUDENT declared to be of type PERSON. Let's look at this record definition in detail.

NAME is an array of CHAR with room for 30 characters. The assumption in this definition is that no name will be larger than 30 characters. If it is, those characters beyond 30 cannot be represented.

SEX is a user-defined data type with two values: MALE and FEMALE. SSNO is an 11-element character array. A social security number could be kept as an integer (without hyphens); but the choice here is to carry the digits and hyphens as characters.

MS (marital status) is a user defined data type with the values MARRIED and SINGLE. Finally, CLASS is a subrange type where a 1 represents a freshman, 2 a sophomore, etc.

Because we are discussing records, not choice of data item representation, we have shown how these items are represented by looking at the type definition. Actually the process goes the other way: you decide how you wish the data items to be represented and then write the type definitions.

Figure 12-3 would be a picture representation of the record variable STUDENT, of type PERSON. Assuming that the values shown are in STUDENT, how do we access them?

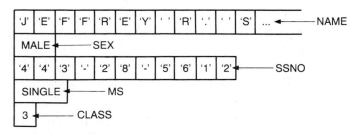

Figure 12-3.

`STUDENT.NAME`	accesses the character array which holds the name
`STUDENT.SEX`	accesses the sex
`STUDENT.SSNO`	accesses the character array which holds the social security number
`STUDENT.MS`	accesses the marital status
`STUDENT.CLASS`	accesses the classification

The expression used to access a field in a record is called the *field selector*.

FIELD SELECTOR

The expression used to access components of a record variable, formed by using the record variable name and the field identifier separated by a period.

In the case of the student NAME field, which is an array, you would have to further specify the index to access individual characters. For example, the following loop would print the name.

```
FOR I := 1 TO 30 DO
    WRITE(STUDENT.NAME[I])
```

In grouping the items (fields) describing an object, a record may be a more logical description of the data and may be conceptually easier to handle than other data structures. When the record variable name and the field identifiers reflect the meaning of the data, programs become easier to read and write. Even in the case where all the components are of the same type, a record may be the best choice of data structures.

Let's develop an example using the record data structure. A parts wholesaler wants to computerize his operation. Until now he has kept his inventory on handwritten 8×10 cards. A typical inventory card contains the following data:

$$
\begin{aligned}
&\text{part number} &&: \text{1A3321} \\
&\text{description} &&: \text{cotter pin} \\
&\text{cost} &&: 0.012 \\
&\text{quantity on hand: 2100}
\end{aligned}
$$

When writing the inventory control program, a record would be a natural choice for describing a part. Each item on the inventory card could be a field of the record. The record definition would look like this:

```
TYPE PARTTYPE = RECORD
                 PARTNUM : ARRAY[1..6] OF CHAR;
                 DESCR : ARRAY[1..20] OF CHAR;
                 COST : REAL;
                 QTY : INTEGER
               END;   (*RECORD*)
VAR PART : PARTTYPE;       (* declares a record variable of type PARTTYPE *)
```

Figure 12-4 shows how we might visualize the record variable PART.

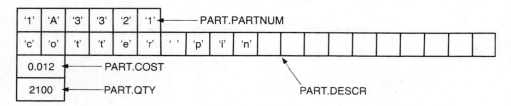

Figure 12-4.

The following assignment statements show how values could be assigned to fields of PART.

```
PART.COST := 2.34;
PART.QTY := 36
```

Let's review the syntax of the record definition. The reserved words RECORD and END bracket the field declarations.

```
TYPE RECTYPE = RECORD
                 FIELD1 : FIELDTYPE1;
                 FIELD2 : FIELDTYPE2;
                   .
                   .
                 FIELDN : FIELDTYPEN
               END;   (*RECORD*)
```

Notice that the field identifiers are followed by a colon and a type *just like the declaration of any variable*. The field selectors of a record variable are actually treated and used as any other declared variable would be. Field selectors can be used in expressions.

```
PART.QTY := PART.QTY + 24;
IF PART.COST <= 5.00
    THEN WRITELN('COST = ', PART.COST:4:2)
```

If the parts wholesaler supplies inventory data that looks like this:

```
2B3310Ring, Piston          2.95 15
```

then the following program segment would store the data in the appropriate record fields.

```
FOR I := 1 TO 6 DO
    READ(PART.PARTNUM[I]);
FOR I := 1 TO 20 DO
    READ(PART.DESCR[I]);
READLN(PART.COST, PART.QTY)
```

The field selector *is the variable name* for each field. It must be complete: the record variable name followed by a period followed by the field identifier.

HIERARCHICAL RECORDS

Just as the components of an array can be of any type, so can the components of a record. We have seen cases where the type of a field identifier is an array. A component of a record can also be another record. Records whose components are themselves records are called hierarchical records.

Let's look at an example where such a structure is appropriate. The owner of a small machine shop has asked us to write a Pascal program to keep information about the machines in her shop. She wants to keep static descriptive information such as the identification number, a verbal description of the machine, the purchase date, and the cost. Statistical information must also be kept such as the number of downdays, the fail rate and the date of last service.

What is a reasonable representation for keeping all of this information? This information can be divided into two groups: one which changes and one which does not. In addition there are two dates to be kept: date of purchase and date of last service. These observations suggest a record describing a date, a record describing the statistical data and an overall record containing the other two as components. The following type definition reflects this structure.

```
TYPE DATE = RECORD
                MONTH : 1..12;
                DAY : 1..31;
                YEAR : 1800..2050
            END;  (*RECORD*)
     STATS = RECORD
                FAILRATE : REAL;
                LASTSERVICED : DATE;
                DOWNDAYS : INTEGER
            END;  (*RECORD*)
     MACHINEREC = RECORD
                    ID : INTEGER;
                    DESCR : ARRAY[1..20] OF CHAR;
                    MAINTHISTORY : STATS;
                    PURCHDATE : DATE;
                    COST, DEPRVALUE : REAL
                END;  (*RECORD*)
VAR MACHINE : MACHINEREC;
```

Notice that two of the components (fields) of the record MACHINEREC
are themselves records. PURCHDATE is of record type DATE and
MAINTHISTORY is of record type STATS. Notice also that one of the components of record type STATS is a record type. LASTSERVICED is of record type DATE.

If record variable MACHINE is being used to describe a hydraulic
press, it might look like Figure 12-5.

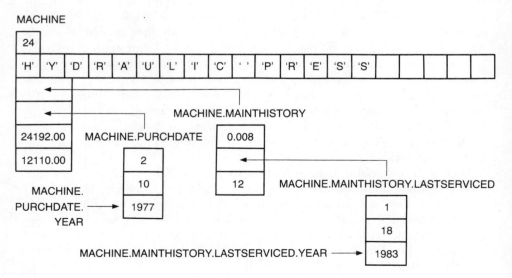

Figure 12-5.

Here are some examples of how the components of MACHINE could be manipulated. Assuming that MACHINE already contains valid values, the following statements would print out certain parts of the variable MACHINE.

```
WRITELN('MACHINE # ', MACHINE.ID:1);
WRITELN;
WRITELN('PURCHASE DATE - ', MACHINE.PURCHDATE.MONTH:1,
        '/', MACHINE.PURCHDATE.DAY:1, '/',
        MACHINE.PURCHDATE.YEAR:1);
WRITELN('TOTAL DOWNDAYS SINCE PURCHASE - ',
        MACHINE.MAINTHISTORY.DOWNDAYS:1);
WRITELN('LAST SERVICED DURING ',
        MACHINE.MAINTHISTORY.LASTSERVICED.MONTH:1, '/',
        MACHINE.MAINTHISTORY.LASTSERVICED.YEAR:1);
```

The output from these statements might look like this.

```
MACHINE # 24

PURCHASE DATE - 2/10/1977
TOTAL DOWNDAYS SINCE PURCHASE - 12
LAST SERVICED DURING 1/1983
```

Notice that a field width specification of one was used for all integers. This ensures that the numbers will be printed just where you want them. The alphabetic strings, describing what the values are that are being printed, all have an ending blank. Since Pascal will expand the field width to ensure that all the digits of a number are printed, using a field width of one guarantees that there will be just one blank between the label and the number.

If we want to check for excessive downtime, we can use the following statement.

```
        IF MACHINE.MAINTHISTORY.FAILRATE > 0.10
            THEN WRITELN('EXCESSIVE DOWNTIME')
```

If another date variable representing the current date is declared

```
            VAR CURDATE : DATE;
```

and the MACHINE has just been serviced, we can change the last service date with the following statements.

```
MACHINE.MAINTHISTORY.LASTSERVICED.MONTH := CURDATE.MONTH;
MACHINE.MAINTHISTORY.LASTSERVICED.DAY := CURDATE.DAY;
MACHINE.MAINTHISTORY.LASTSERVICED.YEAR := CURDATE.YEAR
```

Since Pascal allows assignment of one data structure to another of the same type, a simpler way of setting the date would be

```
        MACHINE.MAINTHISTORY.LASTSERVICED := CURDATE
```

ARRAYS OF RECORDS

Although single records can be useful, many applications require a collection of records. For example, a business will need a list of parts records, and a school will need a list of student records. Arrays are ideal for this. We simply define an array whose components are records!

Here is an example of a class roster represented by an array of student records:

```
TYPE STUDENT = RECORD
                   NAME : ARRAY[1..20] OF CHAR;
                   CLASS : 1..6;              (* student classification *)
                   GDPT : REAL                (* grade point average *)
               END;  (*RECORD*)
     LIST = ARRAY[1..500] OF STUDENT;

VAR ROLL : LIST;
```

This can be visualized as shown in Figure 12-6.

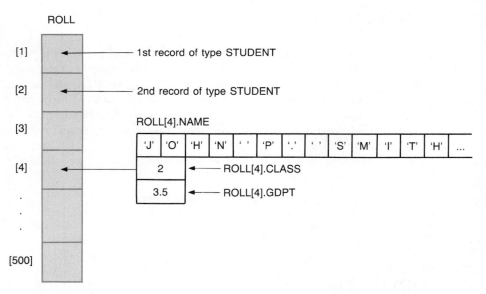

Figure 12-6.

An element of ROLL is selected, as usual, by a subscript. ROLL[4] is the fourth element of ROLL. However, each element of ROLL is a record of type STUDENT. In order to access the grade point average of the fourth student in the ROLL, we use the following expression.

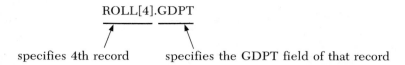

ROLL[4].GDPT

specifies 4th record   specifies the GDPT field of that record

If we want to access the first character of the fourth student's name, we use the following expression.

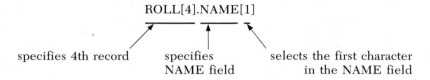

ROLL[4].NAME[1]

specifies 4th record   specifies   selects the first character
                        NAME field   in the NAME field

In our earlier example of a machine record description, we declared a record variable MACHINE. It is most likely, though, that we will need an inventory list of all the machines in the machine shop or business. We can expand our VAR section to declare an array of machine records.

```
VAR MACHINE : MACHINEREC;          (* one machine *)
    INVENTORY : ARRAY[1..150] OF MACHINEREC;   (* an array of
                                                  machines*)
```

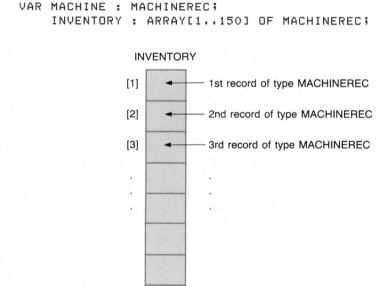

Figure 12-7.

Figure 12-7 shows this array of records. We can now assign MACHINE to any component of the INVENTORY list. The assignment

```
INVENTORY[5] := MACHINE
```

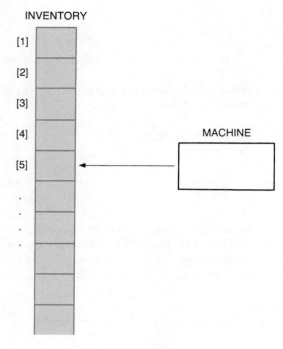

Figure 12-8.

is valid because the elements of INVENTORY are of the same type as MACHINE. (See Figure 12-8.)

Since most of us have little experience with the problem of keeping records on heavy machinery, let's switch to a problem in a more familiar area. Let's write a procedure to update mailing labels for magazine subscriptions. The procedure will take a list of subscribers, the number of subscribers and the current date. The procedure will remove subscribers whose subscriptions have expired and print the current list.

The components of the subscriber list array are records containing mailing label information. The following declarations are in the main program.

```
TYPE DATE = RECORD
             MO : 1..12;                              (* month *)
             YR : 0..99                  (* last two digits of the year *)
           END;  (*RECORD*)
     SUBREC = RECORD
               NAME : ARRAY[1..20] OF CHAR;
               ADDR1 : ARRAY[1..15] OF CHAR;
               ADDR2 : ARRAY[1..20] OF CHAR;
               EXPDATE : DATE
             END;  (*RECORD*)
     LIST = ARRAY[1..500] OF SUBREC;
```

The following procedure removes old subscribers from the magazine subscription list and prints out the new current list.

```
PROCEDURE UPDATE(VAR SUBLIST : LIST; VAR LENGTH :
                 INTEGER; CURDATE : DATE);
VAR I, J : INTEGER;
BEGIN
  I := 1;
  WHILE I <= LENGTH DO                          (* while more subscribers *)
    IF (SUBLIST[I].EXPDATE.YR > CURDATE.YR ) OR     (* check if *)
       ((SUBLIST[I].EXPDATE.YR = CURDATE.YR) AND      (*subscr.*)
       (SUBLIST[I].EXPDATE.MO >= CURDATE.MO))       (* is current *)
       THEN I := I + 1          (* increment index to check next subscriber *)
       ELSE
          BEGIN
             FOR J := I TO LENGTH-1 DO          (* remove subscriber*)
                 SUBLIST[J] := SUBLIST[J+1];          (* from list *)
             LENGTH := LENGTH - 1               (* shorten list *)
          END;
  FOR I := 1 TO LENGTH DO                       (* print subscriber list *)
       BEGIN
          FOR J := 1 TO 20 DO
              WRITE(SUBLIST[I].NAME[J]);   (* name of i-th subscriber *)
          WRITELN;
          FOR J := 1 TO 15 DO
              WRITE(SUBLIST[I].ADDR1[J]); (*address of i-th subscriber*)
          WRITELN;
          FOR J := 1 TO 20 DO
              WRITE(SUBLIST[I].ADDR2[J]);
          WRITELN;
          WRITELN('EXP - ', SUBLIST[I].EXPDATE.MO:1, '/',
                  SUBLIST[I].EXPDATE.YR:1);
          WRITELN
       END
END;
```

The procedure is passed the subscription list as a variable parameter, so any changes are made to the actual list itself. Note that the declaration of the variable parameter (formal parameter) for the subscription list uses the LIST type defined in the global TYPE section. The current date is passed as a value parameter for determining if a subscription is current or not.

Procedure UPDATE does a linear scan through the list of records examining the EXPDATE field of each record. Expiration dates older than the current month and year result in that record being removed from the list.

Some typical output from this procedure might look like this. (Again note the use of one as the field width specification for the month and year.)

```
        .
        .
        .
SMITH, JOHN
926 OAK AVENUE
FARMINGDALE, NY 07221
EXP - 3/91

SMITH, ROBERT L.
1832 WALNUT HIL
DALLAS, TX 75220
EXP - 12/83

SMYTHINGTON, ELIZABE
463-C HIGHPOINT
DOOLITTLE, MO 10035
EXP - 8/84
        .
        .
```

Some of the data appears truncated because names were assumed to be 20 characters or less. You may have received mail with computer generated mailing labels that had your name or address either abbreviated or truncated.

The type definitions we have used in some of our examples in this chapter have been hierarchical. We use this same hierarchical approach with modules in our top-down designs. Defining data types one level at a time reduces complexity.

The following is another example of a hierarchical approach to structuring data. A property management company stores data on its clients and their property in an array of client records. Each record contains the client's name, address, year-to-date billings and a list of the client's property. The property list contains records describing each property, its address, the number of units and the year-to-date income, expenses and taxes for the property.

```
TYPE STRING = ARRAY[1..30] OF CHAR;
     PROPERTY = RECORD
                    DESCR, ADDR : STRING;
                    NUMUNITS : INTEGER;
                    INCOME, EXPENSES, TAXES : REAL
                END;  (*RECORD*)
     PROPLIST = ARRAY[1..30] OF PROPERTY;
     CLIENT = RECORD
                    NAME, ADDR : STRING;
                    BILLINGS : REAL;
                    HOLDINGS : PROPLIST
                END;  (*RECORD*)
     LIST = ARRAY[1..100] OF CLIENT;
```

```
VAR CLIENTS : LIST;
    ACLIENT : CLIENT;
    APROPERTY : PROPERTY;
    I, COUNT : INTEGER;
    STR : STRING
```

Figure 12-9 is a pictorial illustration of these declarations.

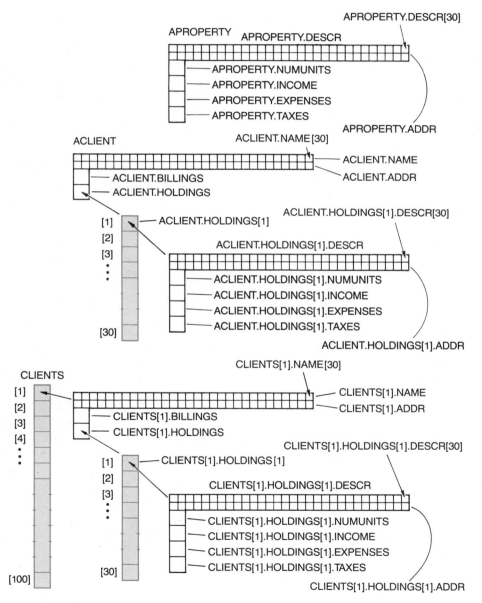

Figure 12-9.

Given these declarations, the following statements would be valid in the body of the program:

```
CLIENTS[4].HOLDINGS[1].DESCR := STR;

CLIENTS[51].NAME := STR;

IF CLIENTS[I].BILLINGS > 100.0
        THEN WRITELN('CLIENT ', I:1);

ACLIENT := CLIENTS[62];

ACLIENT.NAME[2] := STRING[2];

CLIENTS[I].HOLDINGS[2] := APROPERTY
```

and the following statements would be invalid:

```
IF CLIENT.BILLINGS := 0.0              (* client is not a variable name *)
    THEN COUNT := COUNT + 1;

CLIENTS[20].NAME := ACLIENT;              (* not equivalent types - *)
                                          (* missing field identifier *)

CLIENTS[4].HOLDINGS[2] := STR;            (* not equivalent types *)

APROPERTY.TAXES := ACLIENT.HOLDINGS.TAXES
                                  (* missing subscript for HOLDINGS *)
```

The following chart describes what is being accessed at each level of the CLIENTS list:

CLIENTS[I]	a record of type CLIENT
CLIENTS[I].NAME	a character array of type STRING
CLIENTS[I].ADDR	a character array of type STRING
CLIENTS[I].BILLINGS	a real
CLIENTS[I].HOLDINGS	an array of records of type PROPERTY
CLIENTS[I].NAME[J]	a character
CLIENTS[I].ADDR[J]	a character
CLIENTS[I].HOLDINGS[J]	a record of type PROPERTY
CLIENTS[I].HOLDINGS[J].DESCR	a character array of type STRING
CLIENTS[I].HOLDINGS[J].ADDR	a character array of type STRING
CLIENTS[I].HOLDINGS[J].NUMUNITS	an integer
CLIENTS[I].HOLDINGS[J].INCOME	a real
CLIENTS[I].HOLDINGS[J].EXPENSES	a real
CLIENTS[I].HOLDINGS[J].TAXES	a real
CLIENTS[I].HOLDINGS[J].DESCR[K]	a character
CLIENTS[I].HOLDINGS[J].ADDR[K]	a character

MORE ON CHOOSING DATA STRUCTURES

In Chapter 11 we discussed how we might go about choosing a data structure from among simple variables, one-dimensional arrays, parallel arrays and two-dimensional arrays. A close examination of the steps we would take if solving the problem by hand often reveals a reasonable choice for a data structure (for example, an array for a written list of numbers).

Program design and the choice of data structures occur in parallel. However, just as we push details in our top-down design to as low a level as possible, we should defer the choice of a data structure until we are ready to develop modules to operate on it. Some details don't become clear until part of the design is developed.

Now we have added the Pascal record to our set of choices. For many problems where we could use parallel arrays or even multi-dimensional arrays, the record or an array of records may be more appropriate. We no longer have the restriction that all elements in the structure must be of the same type. Let's again use exercise problem 3b in Chapter 10 as an example. A payroll master file made up of three pieces of data per person

ID	(5 digit number)
RATE	(hourly salary)
DEP	(number of dependents)

led us to suggest using three one-dimensional arrays in parallel. However, it makes more sense to use an array whose cells are each a record describing a person. (See Figure 12-10.)

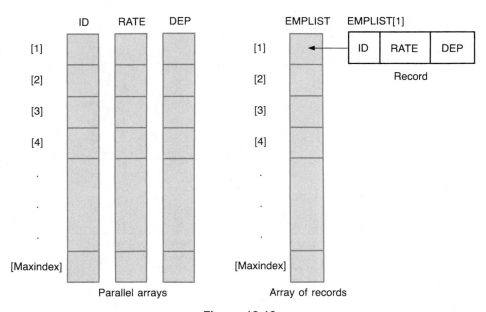

Figure 12-10.

Records are often a good logical description of our data, with the record names and field identifiers reflecting the meaning of the variables and the relationships among them. Records are easy to handle conceptually because we usually think in terms of related data items (not necessarily of the same types) which are attributes describing a single object. Programs are easier to read and write if the structure of the program variables accurately reflects the logical relationships among the items in the real world.

Our data structures and program designs should be as simple and straightforward as possible. When simple variables will do, why complicate your program with a structured data type? Although records may be a logical description of the data, they (or some other data structure) may not really be needed in a particular program. Scrutinize your choice of data structures and algorithms to make sure that you are not adding unnecessary complexity to your programs.

SORTING

It is frequently useful for the values in a data structure to be ordered. For example, we might have an array of stock numbers that we would like to put in either ascending or descending order. Or we might have an array of words that we want in alphabetical order.

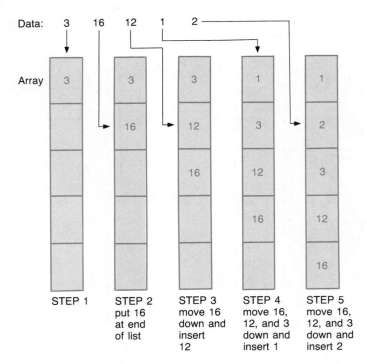

Figure 12-11. Insertion Sort

Arranging values in order is known as sorting. In Chapter 9 we discussed the ordering inherent in any ordinal type. Because of this ordering we can compare and sort, in ascending or descending order, any ordinal type. Various sorting algorithms are available to do this. One of the simplest sorting techniques is the insertion sort. As data is read in, it is inserted in its correct place in the data structure.

For example, let's insert integer values in a list (array) sorted in ascending order. This is accomplished by searching for the first value in the list that is greater than the one we want to insert. We make room for the new value by shifting all the values from the greater one and above *down* one place, thereby increasing by one the number of defined items in the list. (In the beginning, when the list is empty, we don't need to search it; simply store the first value as the first item in the list.) Figure 12-11 shows an example of inputting and sorting five numbers in ascending order.

The following program segment represents this insertion sort.

```
VAR LIST : ARRAY[1..MAXLENGTH] OF INTEGER;
    NUM, LENGTH, PTR, I : INTEGER;
    FOUND : BOOLEAN;
    .
    .

BEGIN
  .
  .
  LENGTH := 0;
  READ(NUM);
  WHILE NOT EOF AND (LENGTH<MAXLENGTH) DO   (* while more values *)
    BEGIN                                   (* and the list is not full *)
      PTR := 1;
      FOUND := FALSE;
      WHILE NOT FOUND AND (PTR <= LENGTH) DO      (* search list *)
        IF NUM < LIST[PTR]
          THEN FOUND := TRUE
          ELSE PTR := PTR + 1;
      FOR I := LENGTH DOWNTO PTR DO               (* shift upper values *)
        LIST[I+1] := LIST[I];
      LIST[PTR] := NUM;                           (* insert value *)
      LENGTH := LENGTH + 1;                        (* increment length *)
      READ(NUM)                                   (* read a new value *)
    END;
```

Notice that this algorithm works even for an empty list. The first time through the body of the outer WHILE loop the value of PTR is greater than the LENGTH, so neither the inner WHILE loop used for searching the list nor the FOR loop used to shift values in the list is executed. After the first value is inserted, the inner WHILE loop will be used to search the list.

We have discussed searching and sorting arrays composed of scalar types. Our discussion also applies to arrays of record types as long as an appropriate field is used as the "key". In other words, a field selector is the variable used for comparisons during the search and sort. In the above example, LIST might have been an array of records.

```
TYPE RECTYPE = RECORD
               DESC : ARRAY[1..10] OF CHAR;
               VALU : INTEGER
               END; (*RECORD*)
     VAR LIST : ARRAY[1..MAXLENGTH] OF RECTYPE;
```

Instead of a comparison to LIST[PTR], the field selector LIST[PTR].VALU could have been used (VALU being the field used as the key).

Let's look at some problems where sorting an array of records is necessary.

■ SAMPLE PROBLEM

Problem: The airport manager wants a list of arriving and departing flights sorted by flight number. The data for each flight is in the form

<flight number>	(integer)
<airline>	(character string)
<arrival time>	(integer)
<arriving from>	(character string)
<departure time>	(integer)
<going to>	(character string)

with each flight's data occupying one data line. The list is on a file. It needs to be sorted, printed out and put back in the file in sorted form. There are less than 500 flights.

Discussion: Using an array of records for the data structure is strongly suggested by the form of the data. We can use the insertion sort we have just discussed: read the data for each flight and insert it into its correct place in the list (array of records) according to the field we are using (in this case the flight number).

Input: Sets of flight data:

flight number	(FLTNUM)
airline	(CARRIER)
arrival time	(INTIME)
arriving from	(ORIG)
departure time	(OUTIME)
going to	(DEST)

Output: Printed list of flights sorted by flight #
Sorted list back in original file

Data Structures: Array of flight records

MAIN   Level 0

```
WHILE more flights DO
    GETFLIGHTDATA
    INSERT
PRINTLIST
SAVEDATA
```

GETFLIGHTDATA   Level 1

```
Input flight data into a flight record
```

INSERT

```
WHILE NOT FOUND AND more list DO
    IF new flight# < list flight#
        THEN FOUND = TRUE
        ELSE check next list item
Shift upper part of list
Insert new item in list
Increment list length
```

This is the insertion sort we discussed in the previous section.

PRINTLIST

```
WHILE more list DO
    Generate a new page and write
        a heading prior to every 50
        lines of flight data written
    Write a line of flight data
```

Pascal has a standard procedure called PAGE. See APPENDIX B.

SAVEDATA

```
WHILE more list DO
    Write a line of flight data to FLTS file
```

Design Tree Diagram:

```
                          ┌─────────┐
                          │  MAIN   │
                          └─────────┘
        ┌──────────────┬───────┴───────┬──────────────┐
┌───────────────┐ ┌─────────┐  ┌─────────────┐ ┌──────────┐
│ GETFLIGHTDATA │ │ INSERT  │  │  PRINTLIST  │ │ SAVEDATA │
└───────────────┘ └─────────┘  └─────────────┘ └──────────┘
```

```
PROGRAM FLIGHTLIST(FLTS,OUTPUT);          (* This program sorts and prints
                                           a list of flights by flight number *)
TYPE STRING = ARRAY[1..10] OF CHAR;
     TIME = 0..2400;                               (* 24-hour clock *)
     FLTREC = RECORD
                  FLTNUM : 0..9999;               (* flight number *)
                  CARRIER : STRING;               (* airline name *)
                  INTIME : TIME;                  (* arrival time *)
                  ORIG : STRING;                  (* arriving from *)
                  OUTIME : TIME;                  (* departure time *)
                  DEST : STRING                   (* destination *)
              END;  (* RECORD *)
     FLTLIST = ARRAY[1..500] OF FLTREC;
VAR LIST : FLTLIST;
    FLT : FLTREC;
    FLTS : TEXT;
    LENGTH : INTEGER;
(**************************************************************)
PROCEDURE GETFLIGHTDATA(VAR FLTS:TEXT; VAR FLT : FLTREC);
VAR I : 1..10;
BEGIN (*GETFLIGHTDATA*)
   READ(FLTS, FLT.FLTNUM);                  (* read in flight number *)
   FOR I := 1 TO 10 DO
       READ(FLTS, FLT.CARRIER[I]);          (* read in name of airline *
   READ(FLTS, FLT.INTIME);                  (* read in arrival time *)
   FOR I := 1 TO 10 DO
       READ(FLTS, FLT.ORIG[I]);       (* read in where flight came from *)
   READ(FLTS, FLT.OUTIME);                  (* read in departure time *)
   FOR I := 1 TO 10 DO
```

```
        READ(FLTS, FLT.DEST[I]);              (* read in destination *)
    READLN(FLTS)
END;  (*GETFLIGHTDATA*)
(*************************************************************)
PROCEDURE INSERT(VAR LIST : FLTLIST; FLT : FLTREC;
                VAR LENGTH : INTEGER);
VAR PTR, I : INTEGER;
    FOUND : BOOLEAN;
BEGIN (*INSERT*)
  PTR := 1;
  FOUND := FALSE;
  WHILE NOT FOUND AND (PTR <= LENGTH) DO         (* search list *)
    IF FLT.FLTNUM < LIST[PTR].FLTNUM
       THEN FOUND := TRUE
       ELSE PTR := PTR + 1;
  FOR I := LENGTH DOWNTO PTR DO               (* shift upper values *)
      LIST[I+1] := LIST[I];
  LIST[PTR] := FLT;                           (* insert value *)
  LENGTH := LENGTH + 1                 (* increment length of list *)
END;  (*INSERT*)
(*************************************************************)
PROCEDURE PRINTLIST(VAR LIST : FLTLIST; LENGTH : INTEGER);
VAR I, J : INTEGER;
BEGIN (*PRINTLIST*)
  FOR I := 1 TO LENGTH DO
      BEGIN
        IF (I MOD 50) = 1              (* for every 50 lines generate *)
           THEN                        (* a new page and print heading *)
             BEGIN
               PAGE(OUTPUT);
               WRITELN('FLT# CARRIER     ARRIVES FROM',
                  '      DEPARTS TO');
               WRITELN
             END;
        WRITE(LIST[I].FLTNUM:3,'  ');
        FOR J := 1 TO 10 DO
            WRITE(LIST[I].CARRIER[J]);
        WRITE(' ', LIST[I].INTIME:4,'  ');
        FOR J := 1 TO 10 DO
            WRITE(LIST[I].ORIG[J]);
        WRITE(' ', LIST[I].OUTIME:4,'  ');
        FOR J := 1 TO 10 DO
            WRITE(LIST[I].DEST[J]);
        WRITELN
      END
END;  (*PRINTLIST*)
(*************************************************************)
PROCEDURE SAVEDATA(VAR FLTS : TEXT; VAR LIST : FLTLIST;
                   LENGTH : INTEGER);
VAR I, J : INTEGER;
```

```
BEGIN
  FOR I := 1 TO LENGTH DO
      BEGIN
        WRITE(FLTS, LIST[I].FLTNUM);
        FOR J := 1 TO 10 DO
            WRITE(FLTS, LIST[I].CARRIER[J]);
        WRITE(FLTS, LIST[I].INTIME);
        FOR J := 1 TO 10 DO
            WRITE(FLTS, LIST[I].ORIG[J]);
        WRITE(FLTS, LIST[I].OUTIME);
        FOR J := 1 TO 10 DO
            WRITE(FLTS, LIST[I].DEST[J]);
        WRITELN(FLTS)
      END
END; (*SAVEDATA*)
(*********************************************************)
BEGIN (*MAIN*)
  RESET(FLTS);
  LENGTH := 0;
  WHILE NOT EOF(FLTS) DO
    BEGIN
      GETFLIGHTDATA(FLTS, FLT);
      INSERT(LIST, FLT, LENGTH);
    END;
  PRINTLIST(LIST, LENGTH);
  REWRITE(FLTS);
  SAVEDATA(FLTS, LIST, LENGTH)
END. (*MAIN*)
```

The main program is almost identical to our top-down design. Notice that RESET was used to open file FLTS for reading. When we were ready to write the sorted data back onto file FLTS, we had to use REWRITE to make it an output file.

If the input data from file FLTS looked like this:

```
326 DELTA       1210 ATLANTA    1300 DALLAS
213 AMERICAN    1105 NEW YORK   1215 CHICAGO
348 DELTA       0800 CHICAGO    0830 DALLAS
901 SOUTHWEST   1930 HOUSTON    2110 DALLAS
123 EASTERN     2100 ATLANTA    2220 MIAMI
```

then the output from procedure PRINTLIST would look like this:

```
FLT# CARRIER    ARRIVES FROM    DEPARTS TO

123  EASTERN    2100 ATLANTA    2220 MIAMI
213  AMERICAN   1105 NEW YORK   1215 CHICAGO
326  DELTA      1210 ATLANTA    1300 DALLAS
348  DELTA       800 CHICAGO     830 DALLAS
901  SOUTHWEST  1930 HOUSTON    2110 DALLAS
```

The output from procedure SAVEDATA would be in this same order by flight number, but would be written to file FLTS. Notice that the times are given on a 24-hour clock.

∎

∎ SAMPLE PROBLEM

Problem: In the previous problem the airport manager wanted a list of arriving and departing flights sorted by flight number. File FLTS contained data on each flight in the form

<flight number>
<airline>
<arrival time>
<arriving from>
<departure time>
<going to>

and program FLIGHTLIST sorted the flights by flight number, put the sorted data back in file FLTS, and printed out the sorted list.

Now the airport manager wants program FLIGHTLIST modified to include a printed list of the flights sorted by arrival time.

Discussion: We can add a procedure to Program FLIGHTLIST that re-sorts the list of flights by arrival time. Fortunately the 24-hour clock is used to represent time, so we don't have to worry about sorting AM and PM separately. For the purposes of this problem we will assume that no flights originate at this airport (i.e., there is an arrival time for every flight).

Sorting an unsorted array is a common problem. In this case we have an array sorted by flight number, but it is actually unsorted if the arrival time is used as the key.

Our insertion sort algorithm was developed to insert data (as it was read) into its correct place in an array. Can we use the same algorithm for data already in an array? Yes, with a slight modification. But since sorting is such an important topic and there are so many sorting algorithms to choose from, let's look at an entirely different one.

First, let's consider how we would do it by hand. If you were given a sheet of paper with a column of twenty numbers on it, and you were asked to write the numbers in order, you would probably do the following:

1. Look for the smallest number.
2. Write it on the paper in a second column.
3. Cross off the number in the original column.
4. Repeat the process, always looking for the smallest remaining in the original list, until all the numbers have been crossed off.

This algorithm could be directly implemented in Pascal, but it would require two arrays: the original one and a second one into which you move the elements in order. If your list of numbers is very large, you might not have enough memory. A slight variation of this by-hand algorithm, however, allows us to sort the elements in place. That is, not to use a second array. Instead of moving an element to a second array and crossing it off the original list, we will put it in its proper place in the original array by swapping places with the element in that place.

If our array is called LIST and contains N values, we can state the algorithm as follows.

FOR LCV := 1 TO N DO

Find minimum of LIST[LCV]..LIST[N]
Swap with LIST[LCV]

This sort is an exchange (or interchange) sort known as straight selection.

In using this sort to solve this problem, we will search for the flight with the earliest arrival time and exchange that flight record with the first record in the list. Then we will search for the next earliest arrival time and exchange that flight record with the second record in the list, and continue in the same fashion with the rest of the list. The sort is accomplished by exchanging pairs of array elements until the array is sorted.(Of course, exchanging two variables—two elements in the array—requires a temporary variable

```
TEMP  := LIST[A];
LIST[A]  := LIST[B];
LIST[B]  := TEMP;
```

so no values are lost.)

Figure 12-12 shows how this sort works. We show only the arrival times for simplicity and have limited the list to six flights.

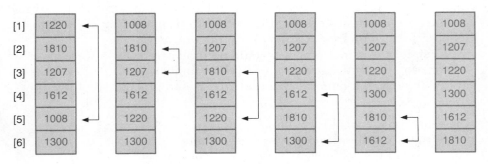

Figure 12-12. Straight Selection Exchange Sort.

Input: Sets of flight data

Output: Printed list of flights sorted by flight #
Sorted list back in original file
Printed list of flights sorted by arrival time

Data Structures: Array of flight records

We will use Program FLIGHTLIST and add an exchange sort procedure to re-sort the list and print it out. The MAIN module now looks like this:

MAIN

```
WHILE more flights DO
    GETFLIGHTDATA
    INSERT
PRINTLIST
SAVEDATA
SORT
PRINTLIST
```

SORT

```
FOR I = 1 TO LENGTH −1 DO
    Find the record with the earliest
    arrival time in the rest of the
    list and exchange the Ith record
    with it.
```

We use LENGTH −1 because once you get to the last item the list is already sorted.

The rest of the modules are the same as for the previous program.

Design Tree Diagram:

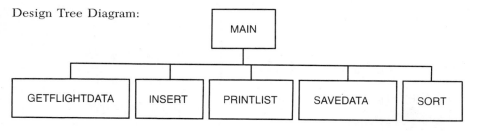

In addition to the example input

```
326 DELTA        1210 ATLANTA     1300 DALLAS
213 AMERICAN     1105 NEW YORK    1215 CHICAGO
348 DELTA         800 CHICAGO      830 DALLAS
901 SOUTHWEST    1930 HOUSTON     2110 DALLAS
123 EASTERN      2100 ATLANTA     2220 MIAMI
```

and output:

```
FLT# CARRIER     ARRIVES FROM     DEPARTS TO

123  EASTERN     2100 ATLANTA     2220 MIAMI
213  AMERICAN    1105 NEW YORK    1215 CHICAGO
326  DELTA       1210 ATLANTA     1300 DALLAS
348  DELTA        800 CHICAGO      830 DALLAS
901  SOUTHWEST   1930 HOUSTON     2110 DALLAS
```

we showed for program FLIGHTLIST, the calls to Procedure SORT and Procedure PRINTLIST would generate this additional output:

```
FLT# CARRIER     ARRIVES FROM     DEPARTS TO
348  DELTA        800 CHICAGO      830 DALLAS
213  AMERICAN    1105 NEW YORK    1215 CHICAGO
326  DELTA       1210 ATLANTA     1300 DALLAS
901  SOUTHWEST   1930 HOUSTON     2110 DALLAS
123  EASTERN     2100 ATLANTA     2220 MIAMI
```

sorted by arrival time.

```
PROGRAM FLIGHTLIST(FLTS,OUTPUT);

TYPE ...

VAR ...

PROCEDURE GETFLIGHTDATA ...

PROCEDURE INSERT ...

PROCEDURE PRINTLIST ...

PROCEDURE SAVEDATA...
```

Declarations from the previous listing of program FLIGHTLIST.

```
(*************************************************************)
PROCEDURE SORT(VAR LIST : FLTLIST; LENGTH : INTEGER);
                              (*sort in ascending order by arrival time*)
VAR TEMP : FLTREC;
    EARLIEST, I, J : INTEGER;
```

```
BEGIN (*SORT*)
  FOR I := 1 TO LENGTH - 1 DO
      BEGIN
          EARLIEST := I;                          (*save Ith position*)
          TEMP := LIST[I];                        (*save Ith value*)
          FOR J := I + 1 TO LENGTH DO        (*search rest of list for*)
              IF LIST[J].INTIME < TEMP.INTIME   (*a smaller value*)
                  THEN
                      BEGIN
                          EARLIEST := J;              (*save position*)
                          TEMP := LIST[J]             (*save value*)
                      END;
          LIST[EARLIEST] := LIST[I];              (* exchange *)
          LIST[I] := TEMP                          (* places *)
      END
END;  (*SORT*)
(****************************************************************)
BEGIN (*MAIN*)
  RESET(FLTS);
  LENGTH := 0;
  WHILE NOT EOF(FLTS) DO
    BEGIN
      GETFLIGHTDATA(FLT, FLTS);
      INSERT(LIST, FLT, LENGTH);
    END;
  PRINTLIST(LIST, LENGTH);                         (* print list *)
  REWRITE(FLTS);
  SAVEDATA(FLTS, LIST, LENGTH);
  SORT(LIST, LENGTH);
  PRINTLIST(LIST, LENGTH)                          (* print new list *)
END.  (*MAIN*)
```

The main program now has the call to SORT added.

■

WITH STATEMENT

When working with record variables, we may repeatedly access one or more fields of a record variable in a small section of code. As we have seen, field selectors can get rather long and cumbersome. The WITH statement allows us to abbreviate the notation by specifying the record name once and then using just the field identifiers to select the record components.
  The form of the WITH statement is:

WITH record variable DO
statement

Look at the section of code on the left which reads in the flight number and carrier name from Program FLIGHTLIST. This is rewritten on the right with a WITH statement.

```
READ(FLTS, FLT.FLTNUM);           WITH FLT DO
FOR I := 1 TO 10 DO                 BEGIN
  READ(FLTS,FLT.CARRIER[I]);          READ(FLTS, FLTNUM);
                                      FOR I := 1 TO 10 DO
                                        READ(FLTS, CARRIER[I])
                                    END
```

Within the scope of the WITH statement, field identifiers are treated as variable identifiers. That is, within the scope of the WITH statement the record component can be selected by the field identifier alone—*not* by the full field selector.

WITH statements can be nested. For example, the statement

WITH record variable1 DO
WITH record variable2 DO
statement

is allowed. This can be abbreviated to:

WITH record variable1, record variable2 DO
statement

Subrecords of records can also be referenced using the WITH statement. Assuming the MACHINE record declaration we looked at earlier in this chapter, the statement

```
IF MACHINE.MAINTHISTORY.FAILRATE > 0.08
   THEN WRITELN('FAILURE RATE FOR MACHINE ', MACHINE.ID:1,
                ' - ', MACHINE.MAINTHISTORY.FAILRATE:5:2)
```

can also be written as

```
WITH MACHINE.MAINTHISTORY DO
   IF FAILRATE > 0.08
      THEN WRITELN('FAILURE RATE FOR MACHINE ',
                  MACHINE.ID:1, ' - ', FAILRATE:5:2)
```

MACHINE.MAINTHISTORY is not only a field selector but also a record variable (a subrecord of MACHINE).

When using arrays of records, the record variable is an array element selected by a subscript. Using the ROLL array of student records declared earlier in this chapter, the loop

```
        FOR I := 1 TO LENGTH DO
            BEGIN
```

```
SUM := SUM + ROLL[I].GDPT;
   .
   .
```

can be written as

```
FOR I := 1 TO LENGTH DO
   WITH ROLL[I] DO
      BEGIN
         SUM := SUM + GDPT;
         .
         .
```

However, putting the loop within the WITH statement

```
WITH ROLL[I] DO
   FOR I := 1 TO LENGTH DO
      BEGIN
         SUM := SUM + GDPT;
         .
         .
```

is *not* allowed. Within the body of the WITH statement the subscript of the record variable may not be changed.

Identifiers in a Pascal program must be unique in order to avoid ambiguities. However, identifiers may be used again and again as field identifiers of different records (because there are no ambiguities in this case). For example, the declarations:

```
TYPE STRING = ARRAY[1..20] OF CHAR;
     PERSON = RECORD
                 NAME : STRING;
                 AGE, SOCSECNO : INTEGER;
                 SEX : (MALE, FEMALE)
              END;  (*RECORD*)
       CITY = RECORD
                 NAME, STATE : STRING;
                 POP : INTEGER
              END;  (*RECORD*)
VAR NAME : STRING;
    MEMBER : PERSON;
    ROSTER : ARRAY[1..100] OF PERSON;
    CITYLIST : ARRAY[1..1000] OF CITY;
    .
    .
```

are valid even though the identifier NAME is used in three places. No ambiguities arise because the variables NAME, MEMBER.NAME, ROSTER[I].NAME and CITYLIST[J].NAME are all unique. Repeating identifiers in different record field lists is not recommended, however, because of the possible confusion in reading and writing the program.

Ambiguities can also arise when using the WITH statement. For example, using the above declarations, to what does the identifier NAME in this statement refer? (Abbreviated form of WITH is shown on the right.)

```
WITH ROSTER[I] DO              WITH ROSTER[I], MEMBER DO
    WITH MEMBER DO                 BEGIN
        BEGIN
            .                            .
            .                            .
            FOR K := 1 TO 20 DO      FOR K := 1 TO 20 DO
              READ(NAME[K]);            READ(NAME[K]);
            .                            .
            .                            .
        END                          END
```

Since NAME is a field identifier of the specified record variables in the WITH statement, it does *not* apply to the variable NAME. That's the first ambiguity. The second ambiguity arises in that NAME is a field of *both* ROSTER[I] and MEMBER. The compiler applies the scope rules and decides that NAME is a field of MEMBER, the innermost of the nested scopes. This may or may not be how you intended the code to be translated.

The WITH statement can help the compiler optimize code. It can also save some writing and possibly make the program more readable. However, it should be used with discretion, as its use can sometimes lead to confusing and even ambiguous programs.

TESTING AND DEBUGGING

With larger programs and/or more complex data structures, the chance for errors in our programs increases. Whatever we can do to improve the readability and understandability of our programs will help to prevent bugs, or at least to speed the debugging process. The top-down design methodology is one way of handling complexity and organizing our thinking.

Another way is to get into the habit of using the TYPE declaration section. For example, the type of a record variable can be defined in the VAR section.

```
VAR PART : RECORD
             ID : INTEGER;
             COLOR : (RED, GREEN, YELLOW, BLUE);
             QTY : INTEGER;
             COST : REAL
           END;  (*RECORD*)
```

However, using the TYPE section gives us more flexibility:

```
TYPE COLORTYPE = (RED, GREEN, YELLOW, BLUE);
     PARTREC = RECORD
                 ID : INTEGER;
                 COLOR: COLORTYPE;
                 QTY : INTEGER;
                 COST : REAL
               END;  (*RECORD*)

VAR PART : PARTREC;
```

Now we can use the types COLORTYPE and PARTREC for any other variable declarations we need, as well as in the formal parameter lists of procedures and functions. Using this hierarchical approach in our type definitions (similar to the hierarchy of our design modules) makes it easier to create and use data structures.

Although there may be several possible data structures we could use in a problem, our actual choice can significantly simplify our design (and thus reduce the chances for bugs in our program). The use of records often leads to a more logical description of our data. Because a record may be conceptually easier to handle than another data structure, debugging (if necessary) will be easier.

We must specify the field selector when referencing a component of a record. However, we can refer to the entire record as a unit when passing parameters or assigning one record variable to another of the same type.

Running out of memory space is one run-time error that may occur. If this happens and you can't increase your memory space, you may have to decrease the size of your data structures (for example, reducing a 2,000 element array to a 500 element array). If you can't do this, you may have to change your approach to the problem, changing both the data structures and the algorithms.

Of course, the problem of running out of memory space might be caused by something as simple as passing a large data structure as a value parameter rather than as a variable parameter. Passing the data structure as a value parameter causes another copy of the data structure to be created. There may not be enough memory space for the copy. If you won't be making unwanted changes to elements in a large data structure, pass it as a variable parameter.

Running out of memory space can also be caused by recursion (a procedure or function calling itself), whether the recursion is intentional or not. This happens because each call to the procedure or function requires more memory space for actual parameters, local variables and other overhead.

Testing and Debugging Hints

1. Be sure to specify the full field selector when referencing a component of a record variable. The only exception is when using a WITH statement where the record variable is already specified.
2. When using arrays in records or arrays of records, be sure to include the subscript with the array name when accessing individual components.
3. Process each field of a record separately, except when assigning one record variable to another (of the same type) or passing the record as a parameter.
4. Beware of possible confusion or ambiguity when using the WITH statement.
5. Avoid using the same field identifiers in different record types, even though this is allowed.
6. If the record variable in a WITH statement is a record from an array of records, do not change the subscript of the specified record variable within the WITH statement.

Summary

The record is a useful data structure for grouping data of different types relating to a single object. The record may be a more logical description of the data than another data structure. In fact, the form of the data may indicate a record as the best choice. Records play an important role in business data processing.

We can use a record variable to refer to the record as a whole, or we can use a field selector to access any individual field (component) of the record. Records of the same type may be assigned directly to each other; however, comparison of records must be done field by field. Reading and writing records is also done field by field.*

Since the components of arrays and records can be of any type, structured types can be built, such as records with array components and arrays of records.

The development of Program FLIGHTLIST is a good example of what happens in the real world. Modifications were made to the program over time. Maintaining (modifying and debugging) a company's software may be the main function of a programmer. Maintenance can account for more time than the original development of a program. Adherence to good programming practices such as top-down design and structured modular programming, as well as a careful choice of data structures, can significantly reduce maintenance time and costs. For example, notice how easily Program FLIGHTLIST was modified.

---

* Unless files of records are used. This is discussed in Chapter 13.

The WITH statement can be used to abbreviate the field selector. However, the possible savings in program writing time, ease of reading and code optimization may be more than offset by resulting confusion and/or ambiguity. The WITH statement should be used with caution.

Exercises

1. Write a record declaration containing the following information about a text book.
   —Title (string of characters)
   —Number of authors
   —Author name(s) (string of characters)
   —Publisher (string of characters)
   —Year of publication

2. a. Write a record declaration containing the following information about a student.
   —Name (string of characters)
   —Social security number (string of characters)
   —Classification (freshman, sophomore, junior, senior)
   —Grade point average
   —Sex (M, F)

   b. Declare a record variable of the type in part a, and write a program segment which prints the information in each field.

   c. Declare ROLL to be an array variable of 3,000 records of the type in part a.

3. Write a procedure to initialize the fields of a record variable of the type in problem 1. Character string fields should be blanks, numeric fields should be zero.

4. Write a program segment to read in a set of part numbers and associated unit costs. Keep the data sorted by part number as you read it in. Use an array of records with two fields, NUM and PRICE, to represent each pair of input values. Assume one pair of input values per line of data.

5. Write a hierarchical Pascal record description for the following. Each record and user-defined ordinal type should have a separate type definition.
   A student with:
   —Name (up to 30 characters)
   —Student ID number
   —Credit hours to date
   —Number of courses taken
   —Course grades (a list of up to 50 elements containing the course ID and the lettergrade)
   —Date first enrolled (month and year)
   —Classification (FRESH,SOPH,JR,SR,GRAD)
   —Grade point average

6. Given the following declarations:

```
TYPE CODE = ARRAY[1..25] OF CHAR;
     REF = RECORD
```

```
                          TOKEN : ARRAY[1..2000] OF CODE;
                          SYMBOL : ARRAY[1..20] OF CODE
                    END;  (*RECORD*)
            MAP = RECORD
                          MAPCODE : CODE;
                          STYLE : (FORMAL, BRIEF);
                          CHART : REF
                    END;  (*RECORD*)
       VAR GUIDE : ARRAY[1..200] OF MAP;
           AMAP : MAP;
           AREF : REF;
           I, COUNT : INTEGER;
           ACODE : CODE;
```

Answer the following as True for valid or False for invalid statements in the main program. (Assume valid variables have defined values.)

a. IF MAP.STYLE = BRIEF
          THEN COUNT := COUNT + 1   T   F

b. GUIDE[1].CHART.TOKEN[2] := AMAP   T   F

c. GUIDE[6].CHART := AREF   T   F

d. AMAP.MAPCODE[1] := AREF.TOKEN[1]   T   F

e. GUIDE[100].CHART.TOKEN[1,2] := ACODE[2]   T   F

f. GUIDE[20].TOKEN[1] := ACODE   T   F

g. IF GUIDE[20].STYLE = FORMAL
          THEN GUIDE[20].CHART.TOKEN[1,1] := 'A' T   F

h. AMAP := GUIDE[5]   T   F

i. AMAP.CHART := AREF   T   F

7. Using the declarations in exercise 6, write statements to do the following:

   a. Assign the value in the CHART field of AMAP to AREF.

   b. Assign AMAP to the fourth element of GUIDE.

   c. Assign ACODE to the MAPCODE field of the tenth element of GUIDE.

   d. Compare the first characters in ACODE and in the MAPCODE field of the second element of GUIDE. If they are equal, then output the MAPCODE field and the STYLE field of the second element of GUIDE.

   e. Compare AMAP.CHART and AREF for equality. Show which elements (if any) are not equal by outputting the subscripts indicating the appropriate TOKEN fields and/or SYMBOL fields. For example, if the second TOKEN field of both records is not equal, you would output a

2

and so on for the remaining non-equal elements.

Pre-Test

1. a. Declare a record type called APT for an apartment locator service. The following information should be included.

LANDLORD—up to 20 characters
ADDRESS   —up to 20 characters

BEDROOMS—integer
PRICE   —real

b. Declare AVAILABLE to be an array variable of up to 200 records of type APT.
c. Write a procedure to read values into the fields of a variable of type APT. (The
    record variable is passed as a parameter.) The data is read in the same order as
    the items in the record.

2. Given the following declarations,

```
TYPE NAME = ARRAY[1..25] OF CHAR;
     BOX  = RECORD  LENGTH,WIDTH,HEIGHT:INTEGER;
                    CUBE:BOOLEAN
            END;
     MAP  = RECORD  STREET:ARRAY[1..2000] OF NAME;
                    PARK:ARRAY[1..20] OF NAME
            END;
     CITY = RECORD  CITYNAME:NAME;
                    POP:INTEGER;
                    LOC:(NE,NW,SE,SW,NC,SC);
                    LIST:MAP
            END;
VAR  CITYLIST:ARRAY[1..200] OF CITY;
     CARTON:BOX;
     PACKING:ARRAY[1..80] OF BOX;
     ACITY:CITY;
     AMAP:MAP;
     I,COUNT:INTEGER;
     HANDLE:NAME;
```

answer the following as True for valid or False for invalid statements in the main
program. (Assume valid variables have defined values and each statement is
independent of the actions of the others.)

a. ACITY:=CITYLIST[5]   T F
b. CARTON :=COUNT   T F
c. CITYLIST[6].LIST:=AMAP   T F
d. PACKING.WIDTH:=I   T F
e. ACITY.CITYNAME[1]:=AMAP.STREET[1]   T F
f. CITYLIST[100].LIST.STREET[1,2]:=HANDLE[2]   T F
g. IF PACKING[3].CUBE
        THEN COUNT:=COUNT + 1   T F
h. IF CITYLIST[20].LOC = SW
        THEN CITYLIST[20].LIST.STREET[1,1]:='D'   T F
i. ACITY.POP:=I   T F
j. IF CUBE
        THEN COUNT:=I   T F
k. I:=CITY.POP   T F
l. ACITY.LIST:=AMAP   T F
m. IF CITY.LOC = NW
        THEN COUNT:=COUNT + 1   T F
n. CITYLIST[1].LIST.STREET[2]:=HANDLE   T F
o. PACKING[100].LENGTH:=I   T F
p. CITYLIST[20].STREET[1]:=HANDLE   T F

Additional Data Structures 13

Goals

To be able to declare and manipulate multiple input and output files in a Pascal program.

To be able to use EOLN to process text files.

To be able to declare variables of type PACKED ARRAY.

To be able to access, compare and assign values to packed array variables.

To be able to create and input files with structured components.

To be able to access and manipulate file buffer variables.

To be able to use the procedures GET and PUT to perform a specific task.

To be able to define a set data type.

To be able to declare a set variable.

*To be able to determine the results of the set operations (+, *, −, IN) on specific sets.*

In this chapter we will finish our discussion of the built-in data structures in Pascal. We have discussed arrays and records. Files, which were introduced in Chapter 6, will now be covered in much greater detail. Although, so far, we have worked only with text files, Pascal allows the components of a file to be of any type (not just characters as in text files).

The set, like the record, is a data structure not available in many programming languages. We will discuss its usefulness and how to work with it.

We will also introduce an option available in Pascal which allows Pascal to optimize the use of memory. This option, called packing, can be applied both to records and to arrays. It is useful when working with character data.

TEXT FILES

Programs communicate with the outside world and with each other through files. Results that a human should see are written to a file which goes to a printer or a terminal. Data that needs to be saved to be used again must be written to a file to be saved on a peripheral storage device. Data cannot stay in memory after program execution, because memory space is needed by other programs; also, the contents of memory may be lost if the computer is turned off.

As we saw in Chapter 1, a variety of peripheral devices can be attached to a computer. (See Figure 13-1.) Input data might come from a terminal, a

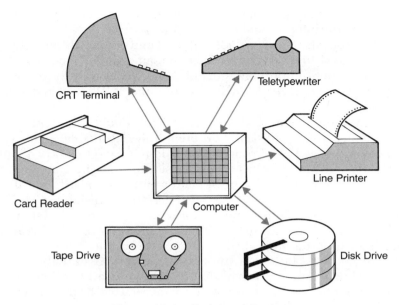

Figure 13-1. Peripheral Devices.

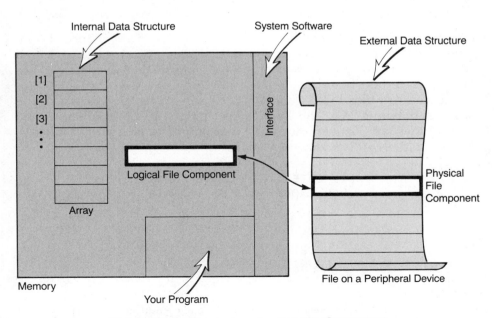

Figure 13-2. Physical vs. Logical File Component.

card reader, a tape drive, a disk drive, or a teletypewriter. Output might go to a terminal, a printer, a tape drive, or a disk drive.

All of these physical devices look different and operate differently. However, Pascal makes them all appear to be the same kind of logical device. In other words, input, output and storage devices may vary physically, but there is no distinction made in the READ and WRITE statements in a program.

Data on different peripheral devices is represented differently. For example, data on a disk is physically different from data displayed on a terminal. However, we as Pascal programmers do not have to worry about this difference. When our programs access these files, the file components are changed from their physical representation into a standard logical representation. (See Figure 13-2.) Who or what does this translation? The Pascal run-time support system, in conjunction with the operating system of the particular machine you are using, translates from the physical file to the logical file or from the logical file to the physical file.

Files are not fixed in length since they are stored external to memory. The file is similar to the array in that it represents a list of components; however, only one component of a file is accessible to the program at a time.

FILE

A data structure consisting of a sequence of components all of the same type.

Pascal files are sequential files in that they consist of a sequence of components which must be accessed in a fixed order. Since files are stored externally, each component is much slower to access than a component of a data structure in memory.

The standard files INPUT and OUTPUT are predeclared for use as file variables of type TEXT. The variable declarations are done automatically, and the files are "opened" for input and output automatically.* That is, the declarations and statements:

```
TYPE TEXT = FILE OF CHAR;
VAR INPUT, OUTPUT : TEXT;
        •
        •
        •
RESET(INPUT);
REWRITE(OUTPUT)
```

---

* The file is initialized so the reading or writing "pointer" is positioned at the beginning of the file.

are assumed by the compiler. All other file variables *must* be declared, and the procedures RESET and REWRITE must be used to prepare them for input or output. The file INPUT may be defined on your system as the terminal or the card reader. (A deck of cards is a file.) The file OUTPUT may be defined on your system as the terminal or the printer.

The standard procedures RESET and REWRITE specify if a file is to be used for input or output.

RESET(F)   —   Open a file, F, and prepare to read from the beginning. If the file is empty or doesn't exist then EOF(F) is TRUE.

REWRITE(F)   —   Open a file, F, and prepare to write at the beginning. The old contents of the file (if any) are lost.

We have seen that a file can be used for both input and output at different points in a program. File FLTS in Program FLIGHTLIST in Chapter 12 was both an input and an output file. Information on airline flights was read from file FLTS, updated, and rewritten back into file FLTS.

We use files for input and output to the program by listing them in the program heading as program parameters. For example,

```
PROGRAM EXAMPLE(FILE1, FILE2, OUTPUT, FILE3);
```

FILE1, FILE2, OUTPUT and FILE3 are called external files because they are created or printed outside of the program or are saved between runs of the program.

A file can also be used strictly as a data structure internal to the program. For example, a procedure or program may need more memory space for temporary data storage than is available. A file variable can be declared as a local file variable of the procedure or program. First REWRITE is used to prepare the file for output, and then, when you need to read the data back in, RESET is used to prepare the file for reading. Files internal to the program are not listed in the program heading and are destroyed when the program terminates.

Files may be passed as parameters to procedures. They must be passed as variable parameters rather than as value parameters, because a copy of the file can't be stored in memory—files are external to memory, and we have access to only one file component at a time.* Being able to pass a file variable as a parameter allows us to use the same procedure with different files. For example, a procedure which reads values and returns the sum of those values might have a heading as follows:

```
PROCEDURE SUMVALUES(VAR DATAFILE : TEXT; VAR SUM : INTEGER);
```

---

* Assignment of one file to another is not allowed for the same reason.

In the body of the procedure, a READ statement would specify the file name (formal parameter):

```
READ(DATAFILE, VALU)
```

which would be the file variable (actual parameter) used in the procedure call. The calls:

```
SUMVALUES(FILE1, SUM1);
SUMVALUES(INPUT, SUM2);
SUMVALUES(DATA, SUM3)
```

would return the sum of the values read from each of the files FILE1, INPUT and DATA, respectively.

Text files are composed of characters, but they are also divided into lines through the use of the <eoln> character. The standard procedures READLN and WRITELN and the function EOLN are strictly for use with text files. READLN and WRITELN recognize and generate this file structure. EOLN is TRUE at the end of a line when the last character is read and the next character is the <eoln> character. Reading one more character at the end of a line returns a blank because the end-of-line marker (<eoln> character) is unreadable. If this extra blank affects your processing, then use a READLN whenever EOLN becomes TRUE. This moves the file position past the line marker to the beginning of the next line (or possibly the end-of-file if that was the last line).

Here is a representation of a text file containing two lines of characters.

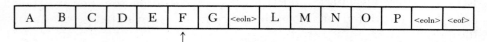

The reading pointer " ↑ " indicates that the character 'F' was read last. The next character read would be 'G', at which point EOLN becomes TRUE. Doing a READLN at this point would leave the pointer ready to read the 'L'.

The functions EOLN and EOF are assumed to be for the file INPUT unless a different file is specified, as in EOF(DATAFILE).

The following segment of code reads and processes characters and indicates the end of each line:

```
WHILE NOT EOF DO
   BEGIN
      WHILE NOT EOLN DO
         BEGIN
            READ(CH);
            process(CH)
         END;
      WRITELN('THAT WAS A LINE');
      READLN                        (* moves reading pointer past <eoln> *)
   END
```

To copy FILE1 to FILE2 exactly, you could use this segment of code:

```
WHILE NOT EOF(FILE1) DO
  BEGIN
    WHILE NOT EOLN(FILE1) DO
      BEGIN
        READ(FILE1,CH);
        WRITE(FILE2,CH)
      END;
    READLN(FILE1);
    WRITELN(FILE2)                    (* writes <eoln> character *)
  END
```

Notice that priming reads are not used in either of the above examples. The purpose of a priming read is to detect the end-of-file and protect against processing after a real or integer read when no more values are in the file (but EOF wasn't TRUE after the last read). A priming read isn't necessary when doing character reads because either EOLN or EOF is TRUE after the last character is read. Walk through the following code, which uses a priming read, and satisfy yourself that the last character in a line never gets printed.

```
READ(CH);
WHILE NOT EOLN DO
  BEGIN
    WRITE(CH);
    READ(CH)
  END
```

Input from text files is done character by character. When we do an integer or real read, the procedure READ looks at every character to see where the number begins and ends on the line, and then it converts the characters of the number to a numeric value.

Numeric reads ignore blanks to find the start of a numeric value and continue until the first non-numeric character. In character reads, the next character is read no matter what it is. Here are some examples of mixed numeric and character reads. These are the variable declarations:

```
VAR CH1, CH2 : CHAR;
    A : REAL;
    I, J : INTEGER;
```

This is the data line:

```
123 X 42.5 -16 QR28K-16ZP<eoln>
```

These are the statements in the body of the program with the values of the variables shown on the right after each read. (We did this already in Chapter 3. If you have never had the error message 'TRIED TO READ PAST

EOF' you can skip this example.)

Statement	Variable values after the READ		
READ(CH1, I, CH2);	CH1: '1'	I: 23	CH2: ' '
READ(CH1, CH2, A);	CH1: 'X'	CH2: ' '	A: 42.5
READ(I, CH1, CH2);	I: −16	CH1: ' '	CH2: 'Q'
READ(CH2, J, CH1);	CH2: 'R'	J: 28	CH1: 'K'
READ(CH1, I)	CH1: '−'	I: 16	

Reading data character by character allows more control over data validation. If you are doing integer reads and there is an invalid character in the file, you will get a run-time error. You can avoid this by doing character reads and doing your own integer conversions. Invalid characters can be detected and reported, and processing can continue if desired. This technique can be used if we have a variable number of values on different lines of data, and our compiler balks at encountering <eof> while trying to read a numeric value.

Let's write a procedure READINT to read and convert unsigned integer values from a text file. This procedure is similar to the READ procedure in Pascal, but reads and returns only one integer value (VALU) at a time. Also, where the Pascal READ procedure will stop at the first non-numeric character while reading a number, procedure READINT considers any non-numeric characters, besides a blank, an error. A Boolean flag READERROR is set to TRUE if a character other than a blank or a numeric digit is read, or if EOF becomes TRUE.

```
PROCEDURE READINT(VAR DATAFILE : TEXT; VAR VALU : INTEGER;
                  VAR READERROR : BOOLEAN);
VAR CH : CHAR;
BEGIN
  VALU := 0;
  READERROR := FALSE;
  IF EOF(DATAFILE)
     THEN READERROR := TRUE
     ELSE REPEAT                              (*read past leading blanks*)
             READ(DATAFILE, CH)
          UNTIL (CH <> ' ') OR EOF(DATAFILE);
  IF EOF(DATAFILE)
     THEN READERROR := TRUE
     ELSE WHILE CH IN ['0'..'9'] DO       (*read and convert integer*)
             BEGIN
                VALU := VALU*10 + ORD(CH) - ORD('0');
                READ(DATAFILE,CH)
             END;
  IF CH <> ' '
     THEN READERROR := TRUE                (*invalid character in data*)
END;
```

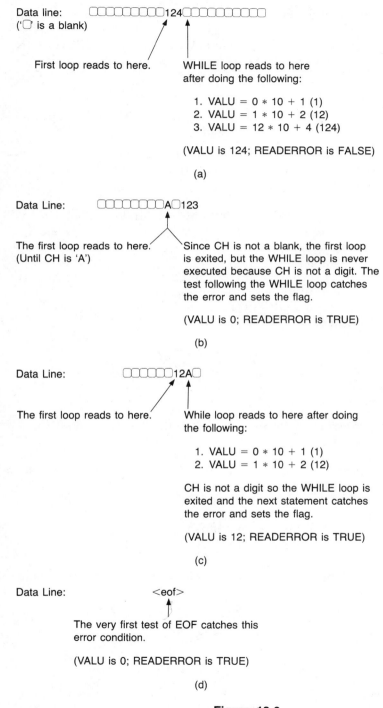

Data line: ⬚⬚⬚⬚⬚⬚⬚⬚124⬚⬚⬚⬚⬚⬚⬚⬚
('⬚ is a blank)

First loop reads to here.

WHILE loop reads to here
after doing the following:

1. VALU = 0 * 10 + 1 (1)
2. VALU = 1 * 10 + 2 (12)
3. VALU = 12 * 10 + 4 (124)

(VALU is 124; READERROR is FALSE)

(a)

Data Line: ⬚⬚⬚⬚⬚⬚⬚⬚A⬚123

The first loop reads to here.
(Until CH is 'A')

Since CH is not a blank, the first loop
is exited, but the WHILE loop is never
executed because CH is not a digit. The
test following the WHILE loop catches
the error and sets the flag.

(VALU is 0; READERROR is TRUE)

(b)

Data Line: ⬚⬚⬚⬚⬚⬚12A⬚

The first loop reads to here.

While loop reads to here after doing
the following:

1. VALU = 0 * 10 + 1 (1)
2. VALU = 1 * 10 + 2 (12)

CH is not a digit so the WHILE loop is
exited and the next statement catches
the error and sets the flag.

(VALU is 12; READERROR is TRUE)

(c)

Data Line: <eof>

The very first test of EOF catches this
error condition.

(VALU is 0; READERROR is TRUE)

(d)

Figure 13-3.

Note that we make use of the fact that reading a line marker (<eoln> character) returns a blank.

This program uses the Pascal set notation and the reserved word IN (used to test set membership). The expression

                    CH IN ['0'..'9']

is equivalent to

            ('0' <= CH) AND (CH <= '9')

We will have more to say about sets later in this chapter.

Figure 13-3 contains diagrams describing the execution of procedure READINT with four different lines of data. (Each example is independent.)

In Chapter 5 we told you that you would be able to do character reads and convert them to numeric data values. Procedure READINT is one approach.

Pascal allows the components of a file to be of any data type. For example, we can have files of records, arrays, or integers. So far, we have only used files that are divided into lines and whose components are characters (i.e., type TEXT). INPUT and OUTPUT are predeclared text files. We will discuss non-text files later in this chapter.

PACKED ARRAYS

Pascal allows a packing option for records and arrays. This is accomplished by prefixing the type definition with the symbol PACKED.

```
TYPE DATE = PACKED RECORD
                MONTH : 1..12;
                DAY : 1..31;
                YEAR : 1800..2050
            END;  (*RECORD*)
     NAME = PACKED ARRAY[1..20] OF CHAR;
```

Packing a data structure makes more efficient use of memory storage space because several items of data may be "packed" into a single memory location.*

---

* This is actually implementation-dependent. For example, in many microcomputers a memory location (known as a memory word) is only large enough to contain the code for one character, so packing a character array doesn't save any memory space. On larger computers with memory words large enough to contain 4 or more characters, packing saves a lot of memory space.

> **PACKED ARRAY**
>
> An array which occupies as little memory space as possible by packing as many array components as possible into each memory word.

You may need to use the packed option when working with large data structures. However, there is a space/speed tradeoff. The packing and unpacking operations necessary to access and store items in a packed structure may require additional execution time. It's up to you to determine your space and time requirements.

A packed array of characters is termed a string or string variable.

> **STRING**
>
> A collection of characters that is interpreted as a single data item; a packed character array.

One of the advantages of packing a character array is that we can print the string variable directly rather than character by character. The statement:

```
WRITE(NAME)
```

prints the packed array NAME. However, we cannot read into the array in this manner. When reading characters from a file, arrays (packed or unpacked) must be filled cell by cell.

Since a string variable is an array, its length is fixed by its type definition. You cannot store more characters in a string than its length allows. If the value to be stored is shorter than the length of the string, it may be necessary to use padding blanks (assigning the "blank" character to the unused array cells). For example, given the declarations

```
TYPE STRING = PACKED ARRAY[1..10] OF CHAR;
VAR WORD1, WORD2 : STRING;
```

the following are invalid assignments.

```
WORD1 := 'BIG'                   (less than 10 characters)
WORD2 := 'INFINITESIMAL'         (more than 10 characters)
```

These, however, are valid.

```
WORD1 := 'TREMENDOUS'
WORD2 := 'SMALL     '
WORD1 := 'BIG       '
```

As with unpacked arrays, string variables of the same type can be assigned to one another:

```
WORD1 := WORD2
```

Unlike other structured types, relational operators can be used with strings of equal length. Strings are ordered according to the ordering of the character set. The characters of each string are compared one by one from left to right. The first unequal pair determine the order. For example,

```
WORD1 <> WORD2
WORD2 <= 'TREMENDOUS'
WORD1 = 'TREMENDOUS'
'SMALL     ' > WORD2
```

are all valid expressions. The Boolean value of these expressions depends on the lexicographic ordering of the character set. Words will usually be ordered as in the dictionary.* Remember that unpacked arrays cannot be compared in this manner; they must be compared cell by cell.

Packing character arrays gives us the best of both worlds. We can treat them as a simple variable or access each element separately. For example, if we wanted to set a string of length 10 to all blanks, we could do it in either of two ways:

```
CONST BLANKS = '          '    or    FOR I := 1 TO 10 DO
    .                                    WORD1[I] := ' ';
    .
    .
    WORD1 := BLANKS;
```

The following program (which just reads in characters and writes them out again) gives some examples of declaring and using strings.

```
PROGRAM EXAMPLE(INPUT, OUTPUT);
CONST A = 'HOWDY, PARDNER';              (* string constant *)
VAR B : PACKED ARRAY[1..10] OF CHAR;     (* string variable *)
    I : INTEGER;
    CH : CHAR;
BEGIN
    WRITELN(A);                          (* string constant *)
    FOR I := 1 TO 10 DO
        BEGIN
            READ(CH);
            B[I] := CH
        END;
```

---

* In some character sets, blank has greater value than the letters. This can change the lexicographic ordering of packed arrays, so it may be desirable to use some character other than blank as a filler.

```
WRITELN(' THE TEXT IS: ');                    (* literal string *)
WRITELN(B);                                    (* string variable *)
END;
```

NOTE: Unlike standard arrays, packed
arrays can be printed directly
by using the array variable
name without subscripts.

Given this input data:

□□SO□LONG!□□□

the output from the program would be

```
HOWDY, PARDNER
 THE TEXT IS:
  SO LONG!
```

Notice in the FOR loop that the statement

```
READ(B[I])
```

was not used. If B were an unpacked array, this statement would be perfectly valid. However, standard Pascal does not allow a component of a
packed structure to be passed as a variable parameter, so a character variable was used in the read and the value assigned to the appropriate cell of
the array. (Some implementations do allow reading directly into the cell of
a packed array. You might try yours to see if it does.)

Sometimes we want the advantages of packing an array, but not the disadvantages. (Advantages: comparing and writing strings directly; disadvantages: increased access time and limitations on parameter passing of components.) If, in Program EXAMPLE, a second array variable were declared
like this:

```
VAR C : ARRAY[1..10] OF CHAR;
```

then the following code would serve to read the values into the unpacked
array C and copy the values into the packed array B.

```
FOR I := 1 TO 10 DO
   READ(C[I]);
FOR I := 1 TO 10 DO
   B[I] := C[I]
```

Actually, Pascal provides two standard procedures—PACK and UN-
PACK—so that packing and unpacking can be done in a single operation.

PACK(U, I, P)   Copies the elements beginning at subscript position I of
                 array U into packed array P beginning at the first subscript
                 position of P.

UNPACK(P, U, I) Copies the elements beginning at the first subscript position of packed array P into unpacked array U beginning at subscript position I.

The above code could now be reduced to:

```
FOR I := 1 TO 10 DO
   READ(C[I]);
PACK(C, 1, B)
```

In Chapter 12, many of the examples of record variables contained character array fields. These fields also can be made string variables.

```
TYPE PERSON = RECORD
              NAME : PACKED ARRAY[1..20] OF CHAR;
              SEX : (M, F);
              AGE : INTEGER
           END; (*RECORD*)
```

Let's look at some programs that use strings and records containing strings.

■ SAMPLE PROBLEM

Problem: Our publisher has asked us to produce an index for this text. The first step in this process is to decide which words should go into the index; the second is to produce a list of the pages where each word occurs.

Instead of trying to choose the words out of our heads (thin air), we decided to let the computer produce a list of all the words used in this manuscript and their frequency of occurrence. We could then go over that list and choose which words to put in the index.

Discussion: Since we need to create a list of words and their frequency of occurrence, the first thing we must do is to define a "word". Once we do that we can develop an algorithm to create a list of them.

Looking back over the paragraph above, what is a tentative definition of word in this context? How about "something between two blanks"? Or better yet, a "character string between two blanks." That definition works for most of the words. However, all words before '.' and ',' would have the '.' and ',' attached. Also, words with quotes would cause a problem.

Does the following definition take care of the problems?

Word :   a string of characters between markers where markers
are blanks and all punctuation marks.

Yes, this should work if the <eoln> character is read as a blank (which it is).

An algorithm would be: find the beginning of a word and collect letters into an array until an end of word marker is found.

After we have a word, we need to check to see if it is one we have had before. If it is, we increment the frequency count and continue looking for the next word. If it is a new one, we need to put it in our list of words. (Does this sound familiar? It should. Look at Program DESIGNCT in Chapter 10.) We now make the design decision to store the word in a packed array to make the search routine easier.

Since an ordered list would be much simpler to work with in developing our index, why not just use the insertion sort (discussed in Chapter 12) every time we get a new word? That insertion sort used a linear search to find a position in a list. Now we can use a faster method called a binary search.

A binary search is based on the principle of divide and conquer. In this problem, it involves dividing the list in half (divide by 2—that's why it's called "binary" search) and determining if the word is in the upper or lower half. This is done successively until the word is found (or at least the place where it goes if it's not in the list).

This method is analogous to the way we look up words in a dictionary: we compare the word we're looking for with a word on the page that is open. If the word we're looking for comes alphabetically before the words on the page, we continue our search with the left-hand section of the dictionary. Otherwise, we continue with the right-hand section. We do this successively until we find our word. If it is not there, then we realize we have misspelled it or our dictionary isn't complete.

The algorithm for a binary search is as follows, where the list of values is called TABLE and the value you are looking for is called VALU. (See Figure 13-4.)

1. Compare VALU to TABLE[MIDDLE].
    If VALU = TABLE[MIDDLE], then you have found it.
    If VALU < TABLE[MIDDLE], then VALU is in the first half of TABLE if it is in the table at all.
    If VALU > TABLE[MIDDLE], then VALU is in the second half of TABLE if it is in the table at all.
2. Redefine TABLE to be that half of TABLE which VALU will be in (if it is there at all) and repeat the process in 1.
3. Stop when you have found VALU or know it isn't there. (You know that VALU isn't there when there is nowhere else to look and you still have not found it.)

This algorithm makes intuitive sense. With each comparison, at best you find the value for which you are searching; at worst you eliminate one half of the TABLE from consideration.

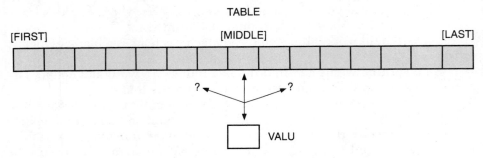

Figure 13-4. Binary Search.

In Chapter 10 we discussed working within a sub-array of an array. An implementation of a binary search is that type of problem. We need to keep track of the index of the first possible place to look (FIRST) and the last possible place to look (LAST).

Now this algorithm can be expressed in terms of VALU and TABLE and through the indexes FIRST, MIDDLE and LAST.

```
WHILE (LAST >= FIRST) AND NOT FOUND DO
   BEGIN
    MIDDLE := (FIRST + LAST) DIV 2;
    IF VALU < TABLE[MIDDLE]
       THEN LAST := MIDDLE - 1
       ELSE IF VALU > TABLE[MIDDLE]
              THEN FIRST := MIDDLE + 1
              ELSE FOUND := TRUE
   END
```

VALU	FIRST	LAST	MIDDLE	TABLE[MIDDLE]	Terminating condition of loop
24	1	11	6	103	
	1	5	3	72	
	1	2	1	12	
	2	2	2	64	
	2	1			LAST < FIRST is TRUE (value not found)
106	1	11	6	103	
	7	11	9	200	
	7	8	7	106	FOUND is TRUE (value found)
406	1	11	6	103	
	7	11	9	200	
	10	11	10	300	
	11	11	11	400	
	12	11			LAST < FIRST is TRUE (value not found)

We have done a code walk-through for several input values. The re-sults of searching for the values of 24, 106, or 406 are shown, assuming that array TABLE contains the values shown in Figure 13-5.

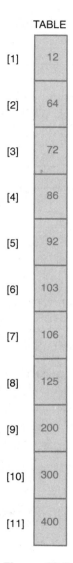

TABLE

[1]	12
[2]	64
[3]	72
[4]	86
[5]	92
[6]	103
[7]	106
[8]	125
[9]	200
[10]	300
[11]	400

Figure 13-5.

Sorry for the detour, but a binary search is an important algorithm and you may want to use it often. Now let's return to our problem and use a binary search in a specific context.

Input: Text file

Output: Ordered list of words and their frequency of occurrence

Data Structures: A packed array (WORD) to hold a word
An array (TABLE) of records containing a word and its frequency of occurrence

MAIN   Level 0

```
GETWORD(WORD)
WHILE more words and table not full DO
     INSERT(WORD, TABLE, LENGTH)
     GETWORD(WORD)
IF table full
    THEN error message
    ELSE PRINTLIST(TABLE, LENGTH)
```

GETWORD   Level 1

```
READ character
WHILE NOT EOF AND NOT (character = letter) DO        Skip over blanks
     READ character                                  and non-letters.
IF NOT EOF
   THEN WHILE NOT EOF AND (character = letter) DO     Read characters
           IF CT <= WORDSIZE                          until a separator
             THEN WORD[CT] = character                is found up to
                 increment CT                         max of 20 letters.
           READ character
        FOR CT TO WORDSIZE DO                         Fill rest of the
           insert blank in WORD                       word with blanks.
```

INSERT

```
WHILE (LAST >= FIRST) AND NOT FOUND
     search for WORD
IF FOUND
    THEN increment FREQ
    ELSE
        insert WORD
        increment LENGTH
```

PRINTLIST

```
FOR 1 TO LENGTH DO
   print TABLE element
```

Design Tree Diagram:

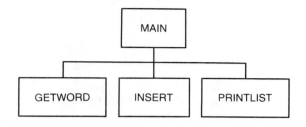

```
PROGRAM CONCORDANCE (INPUT, OUTPUT);        (* This program generates a
                                            concordance of the unique words in a text *)
CONST TABLESIZE = 1000;
      WORDSIZE = 20;
TYPE STRING = PACKED ARRAY[1..WORDSIZE] OF CHAR;
     ENTRY = RECORD
                  WORD : STRING;
                  FREQ : INTEGER
             END; (*RECORD*)
     LIST = ARRAY[1..TABLESIZE] OF ENTRY;
VAR WORD : STRING;
    TABLE : LIST;
    LENGTH : INTEGER;
(*********************************************************)
PROCEDURE GETWORD (VAR WORD : STRING);
VAR CH : CHAR;
    CT : INTEGER;
BEGIN (*GETWORD*)
  READ (CH);
  WHILE NOT EOF AND NOT (CH IN ['A'..'Z']) DO      (* look for a *)
    READ (CH);                                     (* letter *)
  IF NOT EOF
    THEN
      BEGIN
        CT := 1;
        WHILE NOT EOF AND (CH IN ['A'..'Z']) DO        (* get a *)
          BEGIN                                        (* word *)
            IF CT <= WORDSIZE
              THEN
                BEGIN
                  WORD[CT] := CH;
                  CT := CT + 1
                END;
            READ (CH)
          END;
        FOR CT := CT TO WORDSIZE DO          (* pad with blanks *)
            WORD[CT] := ' '
      END
END; (*GETWORD*)
(*********************************************************)
```

```
PROCEDURE INSERT (WORD : STRING; VAR TABLE : LIST;
                  VAR LENGTH: INTEGER);
VAR I, FIRST, MIDDLE, LAST : INTEGER;
    FOUND : BOOLEAN;
BEGIN (*INSERT*)
   FIRST := 1;
   LAST := LENGTH;
   FOUND := FALSE;
   WHILE (LAST >= FIRST) AND NOT FOUND DO          (* Binary search *)
      BEGIN
        MIDDLE := (FIRST + LAST) DIV 2;
        IF WORD < TABLE[MIDDLE].WORD
           THEN LAST := MIDDLE - 1
           ELSE IF WORD > TABLE[MIDDLE].WORD
                   THEN FIRST := MIDDLE + 1
                   ELSE FOUND := TRUE
      END;
   IF FOUND
      THEN TABLE[MIDDLE].FREQ := TABLE[MIDDLE].FREQ + 1
      ELSE                                      (* WORD not in TABLE *)
         BEGIN
            FOR I := LENGTH DOWNTO FIRST DO       (* shift part *)
               TABLE[I + 1] := TABLE[I];          (* of TABLE *)
            LENGTH := LENGTH + 1;         (* increment TABLE length *)
            TABLE[FIRST].WORD := WORD;            (* insert WORD *)
            TABLE[FIRST].FREQ := 1
         END
END; (*INSERT*)
(******************************************************************)
PROCEDURE PRINTLIST (TABLE : LIST; LENGTH : INTEGER);
VAR I : INTEGER;
BEGIN (*PRINTLIST*)
   WRITELN('WORD                      FREQ');
   FOR I := 1 TO LENGTH DO
      WRITELN (TABLE[I].WORD, TABLE[I].FREQ:10)
END; (*PRINTLIST*)
(******************************************************************)
BEGIN (*CONCORDANCE*)
   GETWORD (WORD);
   LENGTH := 0;
   WHILE NOT EOF AND (LENGTH < TABLESIZE) DO
      BEGIN
         INSERT (WORD, TABLE, LENGTH);
         GETWORD (WORD)
      END;
   IF LENGTH = TABLESIZE
      THEN WRITELN ('TABLE FULL')
      ELSE PRINTLIST (TABLE, LENGTH)
END. (*CONCORDANCE*)
```

Note that the data is in file INPUT but could just as easily be in a different data file.

■

■ **SAMPLE PROBLEM**

Problem: Write a simple interactive program that allows a user to review and update line items in a file. Each line contains descriptive data on different products produced by a company. The program should enable the user to be able to do the following tasks.

- delete a line
- insert a new line
- replace a line
- show the next line
- quit the review

No line is longer than 75 characters. The line items are in file ITEMS.

Discussion: We can use a packed array to hold each line as we read it in from the ITEMS file or the terminal. In fact, the same procedure can be used to read a data line from both the ITEMS file and the terminal (user). We simply change the file variable used in the actual parameter list in the call to the procedure.

The procedure to read a command should contain a loop to check for a valid command or prompt the user to re-enter a command.

Processing a command suggests a CASE statement. Since each command is a single character, this meets the requirement that case labels be constants of an ordinal type. Each command as it is read in can be matched with a case label list to determine what action should be taken (save a string, get a new string, quit, etc.).

When the interactive session is over, the updated temporary file can be copied back to the original ITEMS file, using the copy routine discussed earlier in this chapter.

Input: Data lines from file ITEMS
Data lines from the terminal
Commands from the terminal ('D'—delete string,
'I' —insert string,
'R' —replace string,
'N'—next string,
'Q'—quit)

Output: Messages to the terminal
Data lines to a temporary file
Updated copy back in ITEMS file

Data Structures: Packed array to hold data line

MAIN Level 0

```
WHILE more items AND NOT QUIT DO
    GETSTRING
    WRITE string on screen
    GETCOMMAND
    PROCESSCOMMAND
IF no more items
    THEN message
    ELSE TRANSFER the rest of the items file
                    to the temporary file
TRANSFER the temporary file to the items file
```

GETSTRING Level 1

```
WHILE NOT EOLN DO
    READ into string
```

GETCOMMAND

```
REPEAT
    WRITE prompt
    READ command
UNTIL valid command
```

PROCESSCOMMAND

```
CASE command OF
    delete—don't save old string
    insert—save old string, GETSTRING, save new string
    replace—GETSTRING, save new string
    next—save old string
    quit—save old string, QUIT = TRUE
```

TRANSFER Same code to do file-to-file copy shown earlier in this chapter.

Design Tree Diagram:

```
                          ┌──────────────┐
                          │     MAIN     │
                          └──────────────┘
        ┌──────────────┬──────────┴──────────┬──────────────┐
┌───────────────┐ ┌──────────────┐ ┌──────────────────┐ ┌──────────────┐
│   GETSTRING   │ │  GETCOMMAND  │ │  PROCESSCOMMAND  │ │   TRANSFER   │
└───────────────┘ └──────────────┘ └──────────────────┘ └──────────────┘
                                            │
                                    ┌──────────────┐
                                    │   GETSTRING  │
                                    └──────────────┘
```

```
PROGRAM UPDATE(INPUT, OUTPUT, ITEMS);          (* Interactive program to
                                      review and update a file of line items *)
TYPE STRING = PACKED ARRAY[1..75] OF CHAR;
VAR ITEMS, TEMP : TEXT;
    QUIT : BOOLEAN;
    CH : CHAR;
    S : STRING;
(*************************************************************)
PROCEDURE GETSTRING(VAR F : TEXT; VAR S : STRING);
VAR I : INTEGER;
    CH : CHAR;
BEGIN (*GETSTRING*)
  FOR I := 1 TO 75 DO                           (* initialize to blanks *)
      S[I] := ' ';
  I := 0;
  WHILE NOT EOLN(F) AND (I <= 75) DO            (* get string *)
    BEGIN
      I := I + 1;
      READ(F, CH);
      S[I] := CH
    END;
  READLN(F)
END;  (*GETSTRING*)
(*************************************************************)
PROCEDURE GETCOMMAND(VAR CH : CHAR);
BEGIN (*GETCOMMAND*)
  REPEAT
    WRITELN('COMMANDS:  <D>ELETE  <I>NSERT  <R>EPLACE',
            '  <N>EXT  <Q>UIT');
    WRITE('ENTER COMMAND: ');
    READLN(CH);
  UNTIL CH IN ['D', 'I', 'R', 'N', 'Q']
END;  (*GETCOMMAND*)
(*************************************************************)
```

```
PROCEDURE PROCESSCOMMAND(CH : CHAR; VAR QUIT : BOOLEAN;
                        VAR S : STRING);
BEGIN (*PROCESSCOMMAND*)
   CASE CH OF
      'D' : ;                                        (* DELETE *)
      'I' :BEGIN                                      (* INSERT *)
            WRITELN(TEMP, S);                    (* save old string *)
            WRITE('ENTER ITEM TO BE INSERTED: ');
            GETSTRING(INPUT, S);
            WRITELN(TEMP, S)                     (* save new string *)
         END;
      'R' :BEGIN                                     (* REPLACE *)
            WRITE('ENTER REPLACEMENT ITEM: ');
            GETSTRING(INPUT, S);
            WRITELN(TEMP, S)                     (* save new string *)
         END;
      'N' :WRITELN(TEMP, S);       (* NEXT *)    (* save old string *)
      'Q' :BEGIN                                      (* QUIT *)
            WRITELN(TEMP, S);                    (* save old string *)
            QUIT := TRUE
         END
   END  (*CASE*)
END; (*PROCESSCOMMAND*)
(************************************************************)
PROCEDURE TRANSFER(VAR F1, F2 : TEXT);
VAR CH : CHAR;
BEGIN (*TRANSFER*)
  WHILE NOT EOF(F1) DO
    BEGIN
      WHILE NOT EOLN(F1) DO
        BEGIN
          READ(F1, CH);
          WRITE(F2, CH)
        END;
      READLN(F1);
      WRITELN(F2)
    END
END;  (*TRANSFER*)
(************************************************************)
BEGIN (*MAIN*)
  RESET(ITEMS);
  REWRITE(TEMP);
  QUIT := FALSE;
  WHILE NOT EOF(ITEMS) AND NOT QUIT DO
    BEGIN
      GETSTRING(ITEMS, S);              (* get a string from file ITEMS *)
      WRITELN('ITEM:  ', S);            (* write the string on the screen *)
      GETCOMMAND(CH)
      PROCESSCOMMAND(CH, QUIT, S)
    END;
```

```
IF EOF(ITEMS)
    THEN WRITELN('NO MORE ITEMS')
    ELSE TRANSFER(ITEMS, TEMP);          (* transfer rest of file *)
REWRITE(ITEMS);
RESET(TEMP);
TRANSFER(TEMP, ITEMS)                     (* copy back to original file *)
END.  (*MAIN*)
```

Figure 13-6 shows what part of a screen from an interactive session with this program might look like.

```
ITEM:    A2304 - anti-static cloth, dusting
COMMANDS: <D>ELETE  <I>NSERT  <R>EPLACE  <N>EXT  <Q>UIT
ENTER COMMAND: N
ITEM:    A2309 - anti-static spray
COMMANDS: <D>ELETE  <I>NSERT  <R>EPLACE  <N>EXT  <Q>UIT
ENTER COMMAND: N
ITEM:    A2408 - anti-static solution
COMMANDS: <D>ELETE  <I>NSERT  <R>EPLACE  <N>EXT  <Q>UIT
ENTER COMMAND: D
ITEM   A2500 - alternator, 10 amp
COMMANDS: <D>ELETE  <I>NSERT  <R>EPLACE  <N>EXT  <Q>UIT
ENTER COMMAND: R
ENTER REPLACEMENT ITEM: A2500 - alternator, 15 amp
  .
  .
  .
```

Figure 13-6.

FILES

In the beginning of this chapter we described the sequential file as a data structure consisting of a sequence of components and having no fixed length. Since sequential files are the only files in standard Pascal, they are known simply as files.*

* Some implementations of Pascal also support random (direct) access files.

> **FILE**
>
> A data structure consisting of a sequence of components all of the same type.

The definition of a file does not limit the type of the file components. We can have files of any type, simple or structured.* Only INPUT and OUTPUT are predeclared as file variables (of type TEXT). All other file variables must be declared in the program. The following declarations are all valid.

```
TYPE STRING = PACKED ARRAY[1..40] OF CHAR;
     PART = RECORD
               DESCR : STRING;
               ID : INTEGER;
               COST : REAL
            END; (*RECORD*)
     NAME = ARRAY[1..20] OF CHAR;

VAR INFILE, OUTFILE : TEXT;
    MAIL : FILE OF NAME;
    WORDS : FILE OF STRING;
    INVTRY : FILE OF PART;
    LETTER : NAME;
    WORD : STRING;
    APART : PART;
```

Notice that INFILE is a text file, MAIL is a file of arrays, WORDS is a file of strings, and INVTRY is a file of records. Also declared are variables of the component types in order to manipulate a component of each file.

FILE BUFFERS

We have access to only one component of a file at any one time. Whenever we declare a file variable, we automatically create another variable known as the file buffer variable. The buffer variable is denoted by the file name followed by an up-arrow (↑). For example, the buffer variable for file INFILE is written as

$$INFILE \uparrow$$

---

* A file of files is not generally allowed. There may also be restrictions on the use of files as elements of other structured types.

This buffer variable is the "window" through which we can either inspect (read) or append (write) file components. The logical file component shown in Figure 13-2 is actually the file buffer variable.

Whenever we do a READ or WRITE operation, we are actually manipulating the file buffer variable. In Figure 13-7a, the character 'F' was read last. The buffer variable INFILE ↑ contains the next component to be read; in this case the character 'G'. The statement

READ(INFILE, CH)

actually assigns the value in INFILE ↑ to CH, and INFILE ↑ gets the next component in the file. (See Figure 13-7b.) INFILE ↑ would now contain a blank because it is accessing the <eoln> marker and the <eoln> character is stored as a blank. EOLN is currently TRUE. The statement

READLN(INFILE)

would move the "window" to the component past the <eoln> marker, and EOLN would be FALSE. (See Figure 13-7c.)

File INFILE

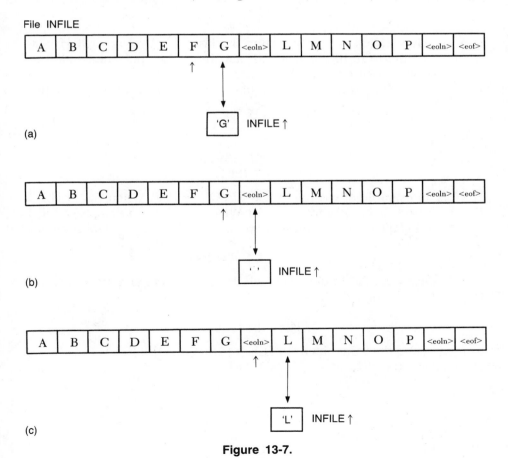

(a)

(b)

(c)

Figure 13-7.

Pascal provides the standard procedures GET and PUT to manipulate the buffer variable directly.

GET(F)   Advances the current position of file F to the next component and assigns the value of the component to the buffer variable F ↑.

PUT(F)   Appends the value of the buffer variable F ↑ to the file F.

In fact, these two procedures are the primitive operators out of which the procedures READ and WRITE are built. The statement

```
READ(INFILE, CH)
```

is equivalent* to

```
CH := INFILE↑;
GET(INFILE)
```

Look at the preceding pictures and examples of reading from file INFILE until you understand the operation of the READ procedure in terms of the buffer variable and GET. If a

```
READ(INFILE, CH)
```

is done when INFILE ↑ is accessing the last <eoln> marker, CH is assigned a blank, EOF becomes TRUE and INFILE ↑ becomes undefined (no next component exists).

That explains file input. What about outputting to a file? The statement

```
WRITE(OUTFILE, CH)
```

is equivalent to

```
OUTFILE↑ := CH;
PUT(OUTFILE)
```

Here is an example of writing to text file OUTFILE. When OUTFILE is first prepared for output by using REWRITE, the file is empty, EOF is TRUE and OUTFILE ↑ is undefined. (See Figure 13-8a.) The statement

```
OUTFILE↑ := CH
```

assigns a value to the buffer (assume CH contains the character 'C'). (See Figure 13-8b.) Then the statement

```
PUT(OUTFILE)
```

would append the value in OUTFILE ↑ to the file OUTFILE. (See Figure 13-8c.) After the PUT operation, OUTFILE ↑ is again undefined. Notice

---

* Note that this equivalence holds only if the variable CH is of the type CHAR.

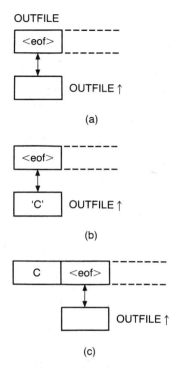

OUTFILE

(a)

(b)

(c)

Figure 13-8.

that EOF is always TRUE for an output file. The foregoing example is identical to what would have happened if the statement

```
WRITE(OUTFILE, CH)
```

had been used instead.

Before introducing GET and PUT and the file buffer, we had to declare a separate variable of the same type as the file component to use in our READ and WRITE statements. We can dispense with this extra variable now and use the file buffer directly with GET and PUT. In the following example, the routine on the left (shown earlier) which copies a file can be rewritten as shown on the right with GET and PUT.

```
     (* uses READ & WRITE *)                    (* uses GET & PUT *)

WHILE NOT EOF(FILE1) DO              WHILE NOT EOF(FILE1) DO
   BEGIN                               BEGIN
      WHILE NOT EOLN(FILE1) DO            WHILE NOT EOLN(FILE1) DO
         BEGIN                              BEGIN
            READ(FILE1,CH);                    FILE2↑ := FILE1↑;
            WRITE(FILE2,CH)                    PUT(FILE2);
         END;                                  GET(FILE1)
```

```
    READLN(FILE1);                      END;
    WRITELN(FILE2)                      GET(FILE1);
END;                                    WRITELN(FILE2)
                                    END;
```

We still need the WRITELN to generate the <eoln> marker when dealing with text files. However, the <eoln> marker does not exist for non-text files, so, if FILE1 and FILE2 are non-text files, the above code reduces to:

```
WHILE NOT EOF(FILE1) DO
    BEGIN
        FILE2↑ := FILE1↑;
        PUT(FILE2);
        GET(FILE1)
    END
```

The procedures READ and WRITE are not defined in standard Pascal for non-text files, though some implementations do support this. So, for non-text files, we must use GET and PUT and the file buffer variable. For example, if INVTRY is a file of parts records, INVTRY ↑ represents a record in INVTRY, and

```
GET(INVTRY)
```

would assign the next record in INVTRY to INVTRY ↑. We can access components (fields) of INVTRY ↑ in the usual way with a field selector.

```
IF INVTRY↑.ID > 999
    THEN...
```

The following program is another version of the common file merge problem. But this time we use GET, PUT and non-text files. The files INVTRY and NEWITEMS need to be merged back into INVTRY, so a temporary internal file TEMP is needed to hold the merged data prior to rewriting it to INVTRY.

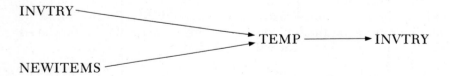

Since TEMP is an internal file it does not exist after program termination. The sorting key is the ID field.

```
PROGRAM MERGE(INVTRY, NEWITEMS);          (* Program to merge INVTRY
                                          and NEWITEMS files onto INVTRY *)
TYPE STRING = PACKED ARRAY[1..40] OF CHAR;
    PART = RECORD
```

```
                    DESCR : STRING;
                    ID : INTEGER;
                    COST : REAL
                 END; (* RECORD *)
        VAR INVTRY, NEWITEMS, TEMP : FILE OF PART;
        BEGIN   (* MERGE *)
           RESET(INVTRY);
           RESET(NEWITEMS);
           REWRITE(TEMP);
           WHILE NOT EOF(INVTRY) AND NOT EOF(NEWITEMS) DO
               BEGIN
                  IF  INVTRY↑.ID < NEWITEMS↑.ID
                      THEN
                          BEGIN
                              TEMP↑ := INVTRY↑;
                              GET(INVTRY)
                          END
                      ELSE
                          BEGIN
                              TEMP↑ := NEWITEMS↑;
                              GET(NEWITEMS)
                          END;
                  PUT(TEMP)
               END;
           WHILE NOT EOF(INVTRY) DO            (* if file NEWITEMS finished first *)
               BEGIN                           (* write rest of file INVRTY *)
                  TEMP↑ := INVTRY↑;
                  PUT(TEMP);
                  GET(INVTRY)
               END;
           WHILE NOT EOF(NEWITEMS) DO          (* if file INVTRY finished first *)
               BEGIN                           (* write rest of file NEWITEMS *)
                  TEMP↑ := NEWITEMS↑;
                  PUT(TEMP);
                  GET(NEWITEMS)
               END;
           REWRITE(INVTRY);
           RESET(TEMP);
           WHILE NOT EOF(TEMP) DO                             (* copy file *)
               BEGIN
                  INVTRY↑ := TEMP↑;
                  PUT(INVTRY);
                  GET(TEMP)
               END
        END.  (* MERGE *)
```

The following program is a modification of the original Program FLIGHT-LIST in Chapter 12. This time, instead of being a text file, file FLTS is a file of records containing packed arrays. The procedures GET and PUT (rather than READ and WRITE) are now used to access file FLTS.

■ SAMPLE PROBLEM

Problem: The airport manager wants a list of arriving and departing flights sorted by flight number. The data for each flight is in the form

\<flight number\>	integer field
\<airline\>	10 character string
\<arrival time\>	integer field
\<arriving from\>	10 character string
\<departure time\>	integer field
\<going to\>	10 character string

with each flight's data contained in a record. The string fields are packed. The list of flight records is in file FLTS. The list needs to be sorted, printed out and put back to the file in sorted form. There are less than 500 flights.

Discussion: This problem statement is virtually identical to the problem statement for the original Program FLIGHTLIST in Chapter 12. The only difference is that file FLTS is not a text file but rather a file of records.

The original top-down design is still valid, and you might want to look at it again. The only changes we need to make are in the program itself. In the declaration section STRING needs to be a packed array of CHAR and FLTS needs to be a file of FLTREC.

Accessing the components (records) in file FLTS must now be done with GET and PUT rather than READ and WRITE. This shortens procedures GETFLIGHTDATA and SAVEDATA considerably, because we can read or write an entire record directly rather than having to do it field by field. Note, however, that writing to OUTPUT must still be done field by field because OUTPUT is a TEXT file.

Using packed arrays for some of the record fields shortens procedure PRINTLIST because we can print packed arrays directly.

Compare the following Program FLIGHTLIST with the original in Chapter 12 and study the changes made.

```
PROGRAM FLIGHTLIST(FLTS,OUTPUT);          (* This program sorts and prints
                                           a list of flights by flight number *)
TYPE STRING = PACKED ARRAY[1..10] OF CHAR;
     TIME = 0..2400;                       (* 24 hr clock *)
     FLTREC = RECORD
                 FLTNUM : 0..9999;          (* flight number *)
                 CARRIER : STRING;          (* airline name *)
                 INTIME : TIME;             (* arrival time *)
                 ORIG : STRING;             (* arrival from *)
                 OUTIME : TIME;             (* departure time *)
                 DEST : STRING              (* destination *)
```

```
               END;   (* RECORD *)
      FLTLIST = ARRAY[1..500] OF FLTREC;
      FLTYPE = FILE OF FLTREC;
VAR LIST : FLTLIST;
    FLT : FLTREC;
    FLTS : FLTYPE;
    LENGTH : INTEGER;
(*********************************************************)
PROCEDURE GETFLIGHTDATA(VAR FLTS : FLTYPE;
                        VAR FLT : FLTREC);
BEGIN (*GETFLIGHTDATA*)
   FLT := FLTS↑;
   GET(FLTS)
END;   (*GETFLIGHTDATA*)
(*********************************************************)
PROCEDURE INSERT(VAR LIST : FLTLIST; FLT : FLTREC;
                 VAR LENGTH : INTEGER);
VAR PTR, I : INTEGER;
    FOUND : BOOLEAN;
BEGIN (*INSERT*)
  PTR := 1;
  FOUND := FALSE;
  WHILE NOT FOUND AND (PTR <= LENGTH) DO          (* search list *)
    IF FLT.FLTNUM < LIST[PTR].FLTNUM
       THEN FOUND := TRUE
       ELSE PTR := PTR + 1;
    FOR I := LENGTH DOWNTO PTR DO                 (* shift upper values *)
       LIST[I+1] := LIST[I];
    LIST[PTR] := FLT;                             (* insert value *)
    LENGTH := LENGTH + 1                          (* increment length of list *)
END;   (*INSERT*)
(*********************************************************)
PROCEDURE PRINTLIST(VAR LIST : FLTLIST; LENGTH : INTEGER);
VAR I : INTEGER;
BEGIN (*PRINTLIST*)
  FOR I := 1 TO LENGTH DO
      BEGIN
        IF (I MOD 50) = 1                         (* for every 50 lines generate *)
           THEN                                   (* a new page and print heading *)
             BEGIN
               PAGE(OUTPUT);
               WRITELN('FLT# CARRIER    ARRIVES FROM',
                     '     DEPARTS TO');
               WRITELN
             END;
         WITH LIST[I] DO
            WRITELN(FLTNUM:3, '   ', CARRIER,' ', INTIME:4 ,
                  ' ',ORIG, '  ', OUTIME:4,' ', DEST)
      END
END;   (*PRINTLIST*)
(*********************************************************)
```

```
PROCEDURE SAVEDATA(VAR FLTS : FLTYPE; VAR LIST : FLTLIST;
                   LENGTH : INTEGER);
VAR I : INTEGER;
BEGIN
   FOR I := 1 TO LENGTH DO
       BEGIN
           FLTS↑ := LIST[I];
           PUT(FLTS)
       END
END; (*SAVEDATA*)
(******************************************************)
BEGIN (*MAIN*)
  RESET(FLTS);
  LENGTH := 0;
  WHILE NOT EOF(FLTS) DO
    BEGIN
      GETFLIGHTDATA(FLTS, FLT);
      INSERT(LIST, FLT, LENGTH);
    END;
  PRINTLIST(LIST, LENGTH);
  REWRITE(FLTS);
  SAVEDATA(FLTS, LIST, LENGTH)
END. (*MAIN*)
```

For this program we were given a file of records (FLTS). Where did this file come from?

When FLTS was a text file, it could have been created by an editor or word processor or entered via a card reader from punched cards. But to have a file of records or any other structured file, the file must be created by a Pascal program. What a non-text file looks like is strictly implementation dependent and will vary from system to system and compiler to compiler.

The implication in this case is that a Pascal program created file FLTS either by creating the file originally or by reading the data from a TEXT file in character form and writing it out in record form to file FLTS. Program FLIGHTLIST could have been used in a modified form to do this.

SETS

Sets are a structured data type unique to Pascal among the more commonly used programming languages. In mathematics, a set is a collection, group or class of objects. Pascal sets are just the same, with the restriction that the objects of a set must be of the same type. In mathematics a set may be of any size; however, in Pascal there is an implementation-dependent limit on the size of a set.

SET

A structured data type composed of a collection of distinct elements (members) chosen from the values of the base type.

```
TYPE LETTERSET =  SET OF 'A'..'Z';
VAR VOWELS, CONSONANTS : LETTERSET;
```

To declare a set type you use the following syntax:

SET OF base type

The type LETTERSET in the example above describes a set type where the base type is the letters of the alphabet. The statement

```
VAR VOWELS, CONSONANTS : LETTERSET;
```

actually creates two set variables of this type. VOWELS and CONSO-NANTS are undefined (like all variables) until you initialize them in your program. Be careful; each is a structure which can contain none, one, or a combination of alphabetic characters. They do not start out with the letters in them.

To put elements into a set, you must use an assignment statement.

```
VOWELS := ['A', 'E', 'I', 'O', 'U']
```

puts the elements 'A', 'E', 'I', 'O', 'U' into the set variable VOWELS. Notice that []'s are used here, not ()'s.

We cannot access the individual elements of a set, but we can ask if a particular element is a member of a set variable. We can also do the standard set operations: union, intersection and difference.

Before describing these operations, however, let's define some terms.

SUBSET

The set A is a subset of the set B if each element of A is an element of B.

EMPTY SET

The set with no members at all.

UNIVERSAL SET

The set consisting of all values of the base type.

+ (Union): the union of two set variables is a set made up of those elements which are in either or both.

* (Intersection): the intersection of two set variables is a set made up of those elements occurring in both set variables.

− (Difference): the difference between two set variables is a set made up of those elements in the first set variable but not in the second.

The following examples illustrate the three set operations. LET1 and LET2 are of type LETTERSET defined previously.

Statement	Results
LET1 := ['A', 'B', 'C'];	['A', 'B', 'C']
LET2 := LET1 + ['X', 'Y', 'Z'];	['A', 'B', 'C', 'X', 'Y', 'Z']
LET1 := LET1 − LET2;	[]
LET1 := LET1 + ['X', 'W'];	['X', 'W']
LET1 := LET1 + ['X', 'Z'];	['X', 'W', 'Z']
LET2 := LET1 * LET2	['X', 'Z']

Let's look at these operations using a picture called a Venn diagram. VOWELS can be shown as a subset of its universal set as in Figure 13-9.

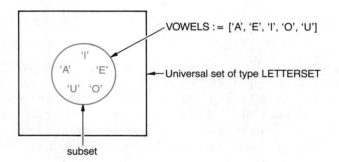

VOWELS := ['A', 'E', 'I', 'O', 'U']

Universal set of type LETTERSET

subset

Figure 13-9.

If we assign elements to LET1 and LET2

```
LET1 := ['A', 'B', 'C', 'D'];
LET2 := ['C', 'D', 'E', 'F', 'G']
```

we can picture them as in Figure 13-10.

The union of LET1 and LET2 would be all the unique elements belonging to either or both sets (shaded area in Figure 13-11a). The intersection of LET1 and LET2 would be only those elements belonging to both sets (shaded area in Figure 13-11b). The difference between sets depends on the order of the operands. Remember, the difference between two sets is all elements of one that are not also elements of the other. (See Figures 13-11c and 13-11d.)

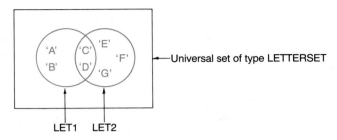

Figure 13-10.

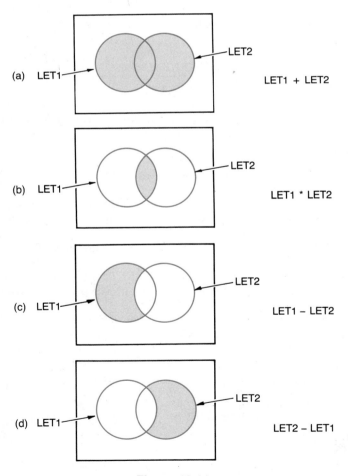

Figure 13-11.

If we want to add one element to a set, we use the union operator:

```
VOWELS := VOWELS + ['Y']
```

To delete an element from a set, we use the difference operator:

```
VOWELS := VOWELS - ['Y']
```

Adding an element that is already in a set has no effect, just as deleting an element that is not in a set has no effect.

If we wanted to initialize VOWELS and CONSONANTS to the vowels and consonants respectively, we would use these statements:

```
VOWELS := ['A', 'E', 'I', 'O', 'U'];
CONSONANTS := ['A',,'Z'];
CONSONANTS := CONSONANTS - VOWELS
```

This is a lot easier than listing every letter we want in CONSONANTS.

The relational operators (=, <>, >=, <=, <, >) can all be applied to sets. In addition, there is a test for set membership.

Expression	Returns TRUE if
SET1 = SET2	SET1 and SET2 are identical
SET1 <> SET2	there is at least one element in SET1 not in SET2 or there is at least one element in SET2 not in SET1
SET1 <= SET2	all the elements in SET1 are in SET2
SET1 < SET2	all the elements in SET1 are in SET2 and there is at least one element in SET2 not in SET1
SET1 >= SET2	all the elements in SET2 are in SET1
SET1 > SET2	all the elements in SET2 are in SET1 and there is at least one element in SET1 not in SET2
element IN SET1	element is a member of SET1

Since IN is a new operator, let's look at it a little more closely.

```
IF CH IN ['A', 'E', 'I', 'O', 'U']
    THEN statement
```

is equivalent to:

```
IF (CH='A') OR (CH='E') OR (CH='I') OR (CH='O') OR (CH='U')
    THEN statement
```

We could also have used

```
IF CH IN VOWELS
    THEN statement
```

if VOWELS had been initialized to ['A', 'E', 'I', 'O', 'U']. Testing for set membership is a much faster operation than evaluating a long expression in an IF statement, and it certainly is easier to read.

Ordering has no meaning in sets. The assignment

```
VOWELS := ['A', 'E', 'I', 'O', 'U']
```

is the same as

```
VOWELS := ['E', 'O', 'A', 'U', 'I']
```

so it doesn't matter how we list values within the set brackets.

We've used subranges to assign values to sets. As usual, the second value must be greater than the first. For example,

```
LET1 := ['C'..'A']
```

actually makes LET1 the empty set. This is what we wanted:

```
LET1 := ['A'..'C']
```

Since ordering has no meaning, we could have

```
LET1 := ['P'..'T', 'A'..'C', 'Z', 'K'..'M']
```

although it makes better sense to list the values in a more readable order.

Just like variables of other types, we need to initialize the value of a set variable before we manipulate it. If we want a set to be empty before adding elements to it, then the assignment to the empty set

```
LET1 := []
```

should be used.

In Chapter 8 we noted that the result of executing a CASE statement, where the case selector does not match any of the constants in the case label list, is undefined. The SET data structure can be used to determine if the case selector is in the set of labels; and, if it is not, you can decide what to do about it.

One of the examples used in Chapter 8 was

```
CASE GRADE OF
    'A', 'B' : WRITE('GOOD WORK');
        'C' : WRITE('AVERAGE WORK');
    'D', 'F' : WRITE('POOR WORK')
END  (*CASE*)
```

If GRADE does not contain an 'A', 'B', 'C', 'D' or 'F'', you might get a run-time error, or the statement might be skipped, depending on your compiler. You can prevent this from happening by checking to be sure GRADE is one of the case labels (by using the test for set membership).

```
IF GRADE IN ['A', 'B', 'C', 'D', 'F']
    THEN CASE GRADE OF
            'A', 'B' : WRITE('GOOD WORK');
               'C' : WRITE('AVERAGE WORK');
            'D', 'F' : WRITE('POOR WORK')
        END   (*CASE*)
    ELSE WRITELN('ERROR IN VALUE FOR GRADE')
```

The general pattern for this test would be as follows:

IF case selector IN [case label list]
  THEN CASE statement
  ELSE whatever you wish to do under this condition

■ **SAMPLE PROGRAM**

Problem: Make a list of all the letters which appear in a piece of text.

Discussion: We will read in the text, character by character, adding each to the set of characters we are collecting. If we have seen that character before, adding it to the set does nothing, because adding an element which is already there makes no changes in the set.

When we are ready to print, we will use a FOR loop from 'A' to 'Z' asking if that letter is a member of the set. If it is, we print it.

Input: A file of text (DATA)

Output: A list of the alphabetic characters appearing in DATA

Data Structures: CHSET—a SET of CHAR in which the characters we see are accumulated

MAIN PROGRAM   Level 0

```
WHILE more characters DO
    READ CH
    CHSET is CHSET + CH
FOR LET = 'A' TO 'Z' DO
    IF LET IN CHSET
        print LET
```

This can be coded directly. No further refinement is necessary.

```
PROGRAM CT(DATA,OUTPUT);
TYPE LETTERS = SET OF CHAR;
VAR CHSET : LETTERS;                          (* set of characters *)
    LET, CH : CHAR;
    DATA : TEXT;
BEGIN
   RESET(DATA);
   CHSET := [];                               (* initialize CHSET to empty set *)
   READ(DATA, CH);
   WHILE NOT EOF(DATA) DO
      BEGIN
         CHSET := CHSET + [CH];
         READ(DATA, CH)
      END;
   FOR LET := 'A' TO 'Z' DO
      IF LET IN CHSET                          (* print the members of the set *)
         THEN WRITELN(LET)
END.
```

In this example, the component type of LETTERS was CHAR. On some machines this would be 64 different characters; on other machines it would be 256 different characters. For more efficient programs, compilers limit the number of elements allowed in the base type of a set. This is not a Pascal limitation, but rather a limitation of various compilers. Check yours to find out what the limits are.

■

TESTING AND DEBUGGING

Input validation is important in programs used in a production environment. We have discussed some approaches to validation of input by using specialized procedures to read and convert characters to integer data values. Errors in the data can be reported, but processing can continue. Interactive programs and batch programs will handle error conditions differently.

If our data structures use too much memory, we can conserve memory space at the expense of efficiency by using the "packed" attribute. On some computers the space savings is by a factor of four or more. Using packed data structures on microcomputers doesn't save any space because a memory word and a character are usually the same size.

Testing and Debugging Hints

1. Declare all file variables, other than INPUT and OUTPUT, and use RESET and REWRITE on these files. Specify the file variable when using READ(LN), WRITE(LN), EOF and EOLN.
2. Files passed as parameters to a procedure must be variable parameters.
3. Remember that a character read when EOLN is TRUE returns a blank.
4. Protect against index range errors when using packed arrays (as with all arrays).
5. When passing strings as parameters, make sure that the formal and actual parameters are of the same type.
6. Don't attempt to store more characters than there are cells in a packed array. Conversely, padding with blanks may be necessary.
7. Don't read directly into an element of a packed array. Passing components of a packed structure as a variable parameter is not allowed.
8. Don't use the value in an input file buffer when EOF is TRUE for that file; the file buffer variable is undefined when EOF is TRUE.
9. Initialize set variables before using them.
10. Don't attempt to print sets directly.
    Test elements for set membership and print each element that is a member.
11. Always use brackets to denote sets.
    The statement

    ```
    LET1 := LET1 + 'A'
    ```

    is not valid. Both operands must be sets (and of the same type). Using brackets around the 'A' makes it a set, so

    ```
    LET1 := LET1 + ['A']
    ```

    is a valid statement.
12. Remember that the standard operators $(+, -, *)$ have different meanings when used with set variables.

Summary ━━━━━━━━━━━━━━━━━━━━━━━━━━━

The sets of input and output data used by programs are known as files. Pascal programs can use multiple input and output files. EOLN is a standard function used in processing text files. EOF is a standard function used in processing any type of file.

Files are not limited in length and are important for storage of data both before and after program execution. Because of their greater storage capacity, files can be used internally in a program where an array would be too big for the available memory space.

A string is a packed array. It is a convenient way to store and manipulate data from text files. It is also a more efficient way of using memory, although at the expense of execution speed.

Packed arrays are manipulated in the same way as unpacked arrays. Both can be assigned to array variables of the same type. Packed arrays of type CHAR have some advantages. They can be assigned string constants of the proper length, compared to string constants or other packed arrays of the same type, and written directly to an output file by using the array variable name only (no need for subscripts).

Sets are a structured data type unique to Pascal among the more commonly used programming languages. A set type is declared which says what the elements of the set can be (component type). Set variables are then defined to be of that set type. Union, intersection and difference—standard set operations—are provided. The standard relational operators are defined between sets. One additional operator, IN, is defined between an element of the base type and a set variable.

Exercises _____

1. Write a function which returns the length of a string passed as a parameter. Padded blanks are not counted. Use this type definition:

   ```
   TYPE STRING = PACKED ARRAY[1..20] OF CHAR;
   ```

2. Write a procedure which reads from a text file (passed as a parameter) a data line and returns the line in reverse order in a packed array. Add padded blanks if necessary. Use this type definition:

   ```
   TYPE LINE = PACKED ARRAY[1..80] OF CHAR;
   ```

3. Write a procedure that reads from a text file and returns a symbol composed of five characters. Each symbol is enclosed in asterisks ('*'). Verify the beginning and ending asterisks for each symbol. Use this type definition:

   ```
   TYPE SYMBOL = PACKED ARRAY[1..5] OF CHAR;
   ```

4. Write a program segment which reads 20 words from DATAFILE (a text file) and writes them back on DATAFILE in ordered form. Use this type definition:

   ```
   TYPE WORD = PACKED ARRAY[1..20] OF CHAR;
   ```

5. Write a Boolean function that returns TRUE if the contents of two packed arrays passed as parameters are equal; otherwise, it returns FALSE. Assume this type declaration in the main program.

   ```
   TYPE WORD = PACKED ARRAY[1..10] OF CHAR;
   ```

6. Given the following declarations,

```
TYPE STRING20 = PACKED ARRAY[1..20] OF CHAR;
     STRING10 = PACKED ARRAY[1..10] OF CHAR;
     MAN = RECORD
               NME : STRING20;
               ADDR : STRING20;
               CLASS : 1..6;
               SEX : (M, F)
           END;
VAR STR : STRING20;
    I : 1..20;
    J : 1..10;
    WORD : STRING10;
    PERSON : MAN;
```

write a program segment to print the values in variable PERSON. Assume PERSON contains valid values.

7. Use the declarations in exercise 6 to answer the following statements as True for valid and False for invalid. Assume valid variables have defined values.

a. FOR I := 1 TO 10 DO
      PERSON.NME[I] := WORD[I]   T   F
b. WRITE(STR)   T   F
c. READ(WORD[J])   T   F
d. WRITE(STR[J])   T   F
e. IF WORD = 'LARGE'
      THEN I := J   T   F
f. READ(STR)   T   F
g. WORD := 'TIGHT'   T   F
h. STR := PERSON.NME   T   F
i. PERSON.NME := WORD   T   F
j. WORD[1] := STR[1]   T   F

8. Write a program segment which inputs values from a file of arrays and prints the average of each array. Process until the end of file. Assume these declarations and initializations:

```
TYPE LIST = ARRAY[1..10] OF INTEGER;
VAR ALIST : LIST;
    DATA : FILE OF LIST;
    I : 1..10;
    SUM : INTEGER;
    AVERAGE : REAL;
      .
    RESET(DATA);
    SUM:=0;
      .
      .
```

9. Rewrite the following using set notation:
  a. (0 < I) AND (I < 25)
  b. (CH = 'A') OR (CH = 'J') OR (CH = 'K')
  c. (X = 1) OR (X > 50) AND (X <= 100)

10. a. Given the enumerated type:

```
TYPE MONTHS = (JANUARY,FEBRUARY,MARCH,APRIL,MAY,
              JUNE,JULY,AUGUST,SEPTEMBER,
              OCTOBER,NOVEMBER,DECEMBER);
```

  Declare a type MONTHSET which is a set of months.

  b. Given:

```
VAR   SUMMERMONTHS, WINTERMONTHS, NEWSET,
      SCHOOLMONTHS, JMONTHS : MONTHSET;
```

  Assign the months June, July, and August to SUMMERMONTHS.
  c. Assign the months December, January, and February to WINTER-MONTHS.
  d. Assign the months September through May to SCHOOLMONTHS.
  e. Assign the months that begin with the letter 'J' to JMONTHS.
  f. Show the contents of NEWSET after the following operations.

```
NEWSET := SUMMERMONTHS + WINTERMONTHS       _____
NEWSET := SUMMERMONTHS * JMONTHS            _____
NEWSET := SUMMERMONTHS * WINTERMONTHS       _____
NEWSET := SCHOOLMONTHS - JMONTHS            _____
NEWSET := WINTERMONTHS - SUMMERMONTHS       _____
```

  g. Give the value of each Boolean expression below:

```
SUMMERMONTHS * WINTERMONTHS = []           _____
SUMMERMONTHS <> SCHOOLMONTHS               _____
WINTERMONTHS >= SCHOOLMONTHS               _____
WINTERMONTHS - JMONTHS <= SCHOOLMONTHS     _____
```

Pre-Test

1. Write a program segment which counts the number of characters in the first line of a data file. Use INPUT as the file, CH as the character variable, COUNT as an integer variable. Assume there is more than one line of data in INPUT.

2. Declare a string variable called NAME consisting of 25 characters.

3. Write a program segment which reads an entire file (INPUT) and prints each line that starts with a '*'. (Don't print the '*')

4. Write a procedure which accepts any text file as a parameter, reads a line of text and returns the line in a packed array. Assume no line is longer than 80 characters. Pad the array with blanks if the line is shorter than 80 characters. Assume these declarations in the main program.

```
TYPE LINE = PACKED ARRAY[1..80] OF CHAR;
```

5. Write a Boolean function that returns TRUE if a packed array contains the word 'INDIGENOUS', otherwise returns FALSE. Assume these declarations in the main program.

```
TYPE WORD = PACKED ARRAY[1..10] OF CHAR;
```

6. Given the following declarations,

```
TYPE NAME = PACKED ARRAY[1..20] OF CHAR;
     WORD = PACKED ARRAY[1..10] OF CHAR;
     PERSON = RECORD
                 NME:NAME;
                 ADDR:NAME;
                 AGE:1..200;
                 SEX:(M,F)
              END;
VAR  HANDLE:NAME;
     TOKEN:WORD;
     STUDENT:PERSON;
     I:1..20;
     J:1..10;
```

answer the following statements as True for valid and False for invalid. (Assume valid variables have defined values and each statement is independent of the actions of the others.)

a. READ(HANDLE)   T   F
b. WRITE(HANDLE)   T   F
c. READ(TOKEN[J])   T   F
d. WRITE(HANDLE[J])   T   F
e. IF TOKEN = 'BIG'
       THEN I:=J   T   F
f. TOKEN := 'VERY LARGE'   T   F
g. HANDLE := STUDENT.NME   T   F
h. STUDENT.NME := TOKEN   T   F
i. TOKEN[1] := HANDLE[1]   T   F
j. FOR I:=1 TO 10 DO
       STUDENT.NME[I]:=TOKEN[I]   T   F

7. a. Define a set type that can contain any of the alphabetic characters (uppercase only).
   b. Declare three set variables (SETA, SETB, SETC) of the type in part a.
   c. Assign 'A'..'N' to SETA.
   d. Assign 'K'..'Z' to SETB.
   e. Show the contents of SETC after the following operations.

```
SETC := SETA + SETB                      _____
SETC := SETA - SETB                      _____
SETC := SETA * SETB                      _____
SETC := SETB - SETA                      _____
```

   f. Evaluate the following expressions.

```
SETA <> SETB                             _____
SETA <= SETB                             _____
SETA * SETB > SETA                       _____
SETA + SETB >= SETA                      _____
```

Pointers and Linked Lists 14

Goals

To be able to declare pointer variables.

To be able to manipulate pointer variables.

To be able to create dynamic variables.

To be able to distinguish between a pointer variable and the dynamic variable to which it points.

To be able to create dynamic data structures such as linked lists.

To be able to access the elements in a linked list.

To be able to insert elements into and delete elements from a linked list.

DYNAMIC DATA STRUCTURES

In the declaration of an array variable, the index range specification is a type and thus cannot be a variable. In other words, the compiler must know how many locations to assign to the array. Arrays (and all the data structures stored in memory) are static variables; their size is fixed at compile-time.

A static variable is around as long as the part of the program (block) in which it is declared is executing. This means that those variables declared in the VAR section of the main program are always there (during execution). Those variables declared in the VAR sections of procedures and functions are around from the time they are called until control is passed back to the invoking routine.

Pascal also has a mechanism for creating dynamic variables. This means that you can define a type at compile-time, but not actually create any variables of that type until run-time.

These dynamic variables can be created or destroyed at any time during execution of the program. They can be defined as being of any simple or structured type.

We reference a dynamic variable not by name but through a pointer. A pointer is a variable which contains the address (location) in memory of the dynamic variable it references. Every new dynamic variable created has an associated pointer to reference (select) it.

Let's look at the ways in which a dynamic variable can be useful.

In previous chapters we used static variables such as arrays and records to structure our data. These work very well for many applications, but they do have some disadvantages. We saw that a record could contain components of different data types and is often a logical way to describe our data. However, we usually need a collection (or list) of these records, so we use an array of records. We can keep a list of data objects in a file or, when working with the list in memory, in an array. We can think of a list as a one-dimensional array, no matter how complex the structuring of the array components (multi-dimensional array, nested records, etc.). (See Figure 14-1.)

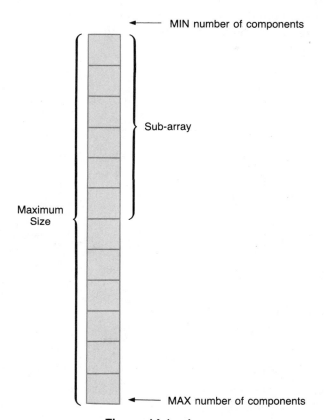

Figure 14-1. Array.

The usual approach is to declare an array large enough to hold the maximum amount of data we could logically expect. Since we usually have less data than the maximum, the length of the sub-array in which we do have values is kept, so only that part of the array with values in it is accessed. This sub-array can vary in length during execution from zero components (MIN) to the maximum (MAX) in the array.

What if we don't know how many components we need? We can always guess about the length and provide code to report the error condition of trying to overfill the array. What if we want the list of components kept in sorted form? We have algorithms to sort arrays. How about inserting or deleting a component? Inserting or deleting array components involves shifting part of the array by one component in one direction or the other. If the list (array) is very large, insertion or deletion of components can take a significant amount of time.

We can use dynamic variables to overcome these problems of a static variable such as the array. We can create new components for our list only as they are needed, by using dynamic variables as components. By having each component contain the link or pointer to the next component in the list, we can create a dynamic data structure that can expand or contract as the program executes. (See Figure 14-2.)

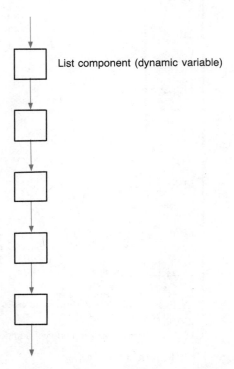

List component (dynamic variable)

Figure 14-2. Dynamic Data Structure

We don't have to know in advance how long the list will be. The only limitation now is the amount of available memory space. We can easily change the order of the components just by changing the pointer values. (See Figure 14-3a.) Insertion and deletion of components are easier and faster; simply change one or two pointer values. (See Figures 14-3b and 14-3c.)

We can use dynamic variables and pointers to create lists and more complex data structures that can expand and contract during program execution. These dynamic data structures are extremely flexible, allowing easy insertion and deletion of components. We discuss some of these dynamic data structures later in this chapter, but first we need to look at the pointer mechanism in more detail.

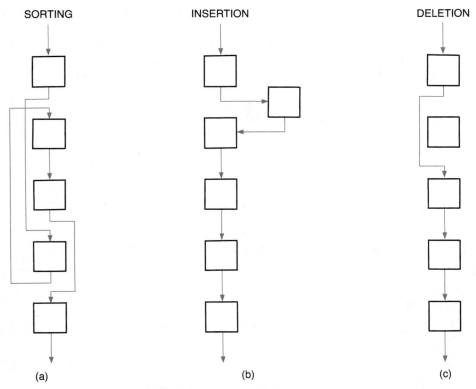

Figure 14-3. Manipulating a Dynamic Data Structure.

POINTERS

Dynamic variables are referenced not by name but through a pointer. The pointer type is a pre-defined data type in Pascal.

POINTER

A simple data type, consisting of an unbounded set of values, which addresses or otherwise indicates the location of a variable of a given type.

```
TYPE RANGE = 1..25;
     COLOR = (RED, GREEN, BLUE);

VAR PTR1 : ↑RANGE;
    PTR2 : ↑COLOR;
    PTR3 : ↑BOOLEAN;
```

The word "pointer" is not a reserved word in Pascal; "pointer" is not used in defining a pointer variable.

In the boxed example, PTR1, PTR2 and PTR3 are pointer variables as denoted by the ↑ in their type definitions. The first declaration is read: "PTR1 is a pointer to a variable of type RANGE". PTR1 can point to an integer variable whose value is in the subrange 1 to 25. The declaration causes the compiler to name a memory location PTR1, the contents of which will be a memory address. However, as usual, the value of PTR1 is not yet defined.

PTR1

```
┌─────┐
│  ?  │
└─────┘
```

Even though PTR1 exists, the variable it is pointing to (dynamic or referenced variable) does not.

REFERENCED VARIABLE

A variable accessed not by name but through a pointer variable; a dynamic variable.

To create a referenced variable, the standard procedure NEW is used.

NEW(P)—Creates a variable of the type referenced by pointer P, and stores a pointer to the new variable in P.

The statements

```
NEW(PTR1);
NEW(PTR2);
NEW(PTR3)
```

would leave the address in PTR1, PTR2 and PTR3 of each of the newly created referenced variables.

How do we access the newly created variables? The pointer variable followed by ↑ gives us the variable pointed to. For the referenced variables we just created, these are valid assignments:

```
PTR1↑ := 18;
PTR2↑ := RED;
PTR3↑ := TRUE
```

Figure 14-4 shows the results of these assignments.

The value of a pointer is an integer on most machines, as memory locations have addresses ranging from zero to the size of that memory. However, a pointer type is not an integer type. Remember, Pascal is a strongly-

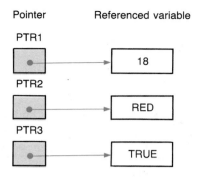

Figure 14-4. Pointer and Its Referenced Variable.

typed language. We could not assign an integer value to a pointer. We can't even assign PTR1, PTR2 and PTR3 to each other, since they do not point to variables of the same type. (We can assign pointers of the same type to each other.) There is no provision for printing a pointer value. Figure 14-5 pictures a pointer and the variable it is referencing.

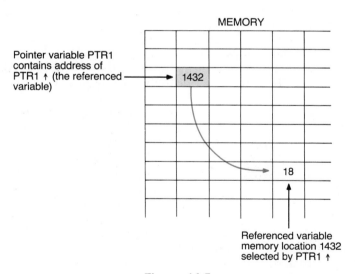

Figure 14-5.

Pointers are important for creating dynamic data structures. Since we must have some way of linking each component to the next one in the structure, each component must contain a link or pointer that points to the next component in the structure. The record is ideal as a component of a dynamic data structure. It can contain fields of different types with the pointer being one of them. For example:

```
TYPE PTRTYPE = ↑PERSON;              (* a pointer to a person record *)
      PERSON = RECORD
                  NAME : PACKED ARRAY[1..20] OF CHAR;
                  NEXT : PTRTYPE     (* a pointer to the next list element *)
              END; (*RECORD*)
VAR PTR : PTRTYPE;
```

When defining a dynamic variable you describe what the variable can look like in the TYPE section. In the VAR section you declare a variable to be a *pointer* to a variable of that type. When you need one of the referenced variables , you use the procedure NEW which has as its argument a pointer declared in the VAR section. This procedure creates the variable, but, instead of returning the created variable itself, it returns a pointer to it. You use that pointer to access the variable itself.

Notice that the definition of PTRTYPE includes the identifier PERSON which is not yet defined. A type identifier must be used in the definition of a pointer type. This type identifier is an exception to the general rule that identifiers must be declared before they are used. This allows us to define a pointer to an object (referenced variable) before defining the object itself.

Before the body of the program, no variables of type PERSON exist. To get a variable of type PERSON, the procedure

```
NEW(PTR)
```

is invoked during run-time. On return from NEW, a record variable of type PERSON has been created. Information on where it is located is left in pointer variable PTR. Note that the fields of this new variable are undefined.

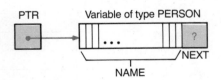

This is called dynamic storage allocation because the variables of type PERSON are created as we need them in the program.

Repeated use of NEW allows us to generate additional variables of this type. Between these calls to NEW, we link the variable we have just gotten to the previous one to form a dynamic data structure. (See Figure 14-6.)

Pointers always reference un-named variables. Pointers themselves may be named or un-named. That is, we may create a chain of un-named pointers dynamically with each one pointing to the one that follows it. Such a chain, however, must have at least one named pointer variable pointing to it or we will have no way at all of accessing it. It's a bit like those party games where people have to follow a chain of clues, each clue telling

MEMORY

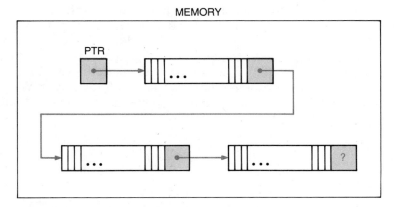

Figure 14-6. Creating a Dynamic Data Structure

where the next will be found and so on until a prize is found. If the location of the first clue weren't given, there would be no way to start along the chain. If the given location were for a clue in the middle of the chain, there would be no way to find the preceding clues.

When a dynamic variable such as PTR↑ is no longer needed, DIS-POSE(PTR) will return it so that memory space(s) can be assigned later if needed. This is called returning it to available space.

DISPOSE(P)—Destroys the variable referenced by pointer P. That is, the locations occupied by the variable are returned to be assigned to some other variable.

Any operation that is legal on a named variable of a certain type is legal on a dynamic variable of that type. However only assignment and a test for equality are legal operations on pointer variables. For example, given these declarations

```
TYPE RANGE = 1..25;
VAR PTRA, PTRB : ↑RANGE;
```

we can do the following:

```
NEW(PTRA);                                      (* create a dynamic variable*)
NEW(PTRB);                                       (* create a dynamic variable *)
READ(PTRA↑, PTRB↑);              (* read values into these dynamic variables *)
WRITELN('THE SUM OF ',PTRA↑:1,' AND ',          (* print out the sum of *)
           PTRB↑:1,' IS ',PTRA↑+PTRB↑:1)     (*these dynamic variables*)
```

Notice that PTRA↑ + PTRB↑ is legal because we are adding the contents of the two variables of type RANGE pointed to by PTRA and PTRB. PTRA + PTRB would not be legal because you cannot add pointer variables. We can only assign pointers of the same type or compare them for equality or inequality. In other words, we can make two pointers reference the same variable, or we can test whether or not two pointers point to the same variable. In Figure 14-7a we are comparing the addresses contained in the pointer variables, not the contents of these memory addresses. After the assignment in Figure 14-7b, we have no way to get to the variable containing the value of 15 unless some other pointer is referencing it. We cannot even dispose of it for reuse. If we do this too much, we can eventually run out of memory space.

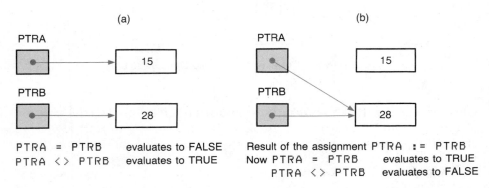

Figure 14-7.

We will use the assignment and the tests for equality/inequality of pointers in creating and using dynamic data structures.

LINKED LISTS

One of the data structures we can build using dynamic variables and pointers is known as a linked list. In fact, this is the linked structure we described in the first part of this chapter.

Since we can only access dynamic variables by a pointer (↑), do we have to have as many pointer variables as there are dynamic variables (components) in the list? What's the advantage of this? None, if that is how we used them. However, what we do is to make a chain of these variables. We keep track of the first one in the list and then store within each one a pointer to the next one. That is, each dynamic variable will be a record with one field containing a pointer to the next.

The following segment of code creates a list of 5 variables of type SOMERECORD, all linked together. (See Figure 14-8.)

```
TYPE POINTER = ↑SOMERECORD;
      SOMERECORD = RECORD
                  (* Other fields *)
```

```
                    NEXT : POINTER
              END;   (* RECORD *)
VAR   LIST,                    (* The pointer to the first component in the list *)
      PTR1,                    (* The pointer to the last component in the list *)
      PTR2 : POINTER;             (* The pointer to the newest component *)
      LCV : INTEGER;
BEGIN
  NEW(LIST);
  PTR1 := LIST;                    (* LIST is the external pointer *)
  FOR LCV := 1 TO 4 DO
    BEGIN
      NEW(PTR2);
      PTR1↑.NEXT := PTR2;
      PTR1 := PTR2
    END;
  PTR1↑.NEXT := NIL
```

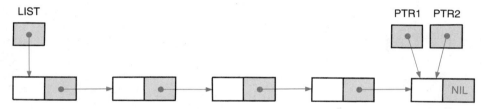

Figure 14-8. Linked List.

How does this code create a list? Why do we need three pointers? Let's do a logical code walk-through and see just how this algorithm works.

`NEW(LIST);`
A variable of type SOMERECORD is created. The pointer is left in LIST. LIST will remain unchanged as the pointer to the first one. LIST is called the external pointer to the list.

`PTR1 := LIST;`
Our algorithm gets a new variable and stores its pointer in the NEXT field of the last component in the list. Therefore, we need to keep track of the last component so we can assign to its pointer field the newly created variable.

`FOR LCV := 1 TO 4 DO`
A count controlled loop is used to add the last 4 components to the list.

`BEGIN`
`  NEW(PTR2);`
Another variable of type SOMERECORD is created with PTR2 pointing to it.

`PTR1↑.NEXT := PTR2;`	The pointer to the newly created variable is stored in the NEXT field of the last component in the list.
`PTR1 := PTR2`	PTR1 is again pointing to the last component in the list.
`END;`	
`PTR1↑.NEXT := NIL`	The NEXT field of the last component in the list is assigned the special termination value NIL.

The sequence of diagrams in Figure 14-9 shows how a component is added to the list (i.e., what happens in the body of the FOR loop).

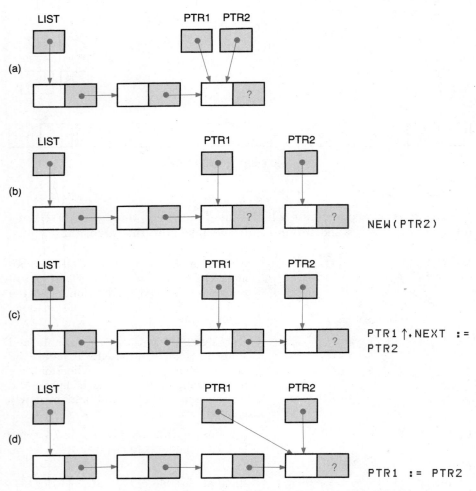

Figure 14-9. Adding a Component to a Linked List.

Notice that we assigned the NIL value to the last pointer in the list. NIL is a reserved word that can be assigned to any pointer variable. It means that the pointer points to nothing. Its importance lies in the fact that we can compare the link field of each component in the list to NIL to see when we have reached the end of the list. This technique is used when searching (traversing) the list.

As another example, let's set up the structure to build a list of playing cards.

```
TYPE POINTER = ↑CARD;
     CARD = RECORD
               SUIT : (C, D, H, S);
               NUM : 1..13;
               LINK : POINTER
            END; (* RECORD *)
VAR CURRENT, FIRST, PTR : POINTER;
    .
    .
    .
```

A record type CARD has been defined with three fields: SUIT, NUM and LINK. Three pointer variables, CURRENT, FIRST and PTR, have been defined. Why are there no variables of type CARD? We are creating a *dynamic* data structure composed of dynamic variables. Declarations in the VAR section are *static*. We will get a new variable of type CARD every time we call NEW with a variable of type POINTER as an argument. We keep track of these CARD type variables by linking them together, using the LINK field of the variables of type CARD.

Let's look at the code, a piece at a time, that creates the list of playing cards.

```
BEGIN
   NEW(FIRST);
   FIRST↑.SUIT := C;
   FIRST↑.NUM := 1;
   CURRENT := FIRST;
```

At this point, we have created a record variable of type CARD and stored a C in the suit field and a 1 in the value field. This represents the ace of clubs.

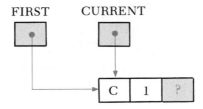

Now we want to get another CARD type variable, put a C in the suit field and a 2 in the value field and hook it up to the first component in the list. We do this by putting a pointer to the new component in the link field of the one before.

```
NEW(PTR);
PTR↑.SUIT := C;
PTR↑.NUM := 2;
FIRST↑.LINK := PTR;          (* link first and second *)
```

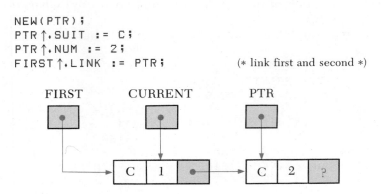

The following code will complete creating the entire deck.

```
CURRENT := PTR;
FOR I := 3 TO 52 DO
  BEGIN
    NEW(PTR);
    IF CURRENT↑.NUM = 13
      THEN  (* CHANGE SUIT *)
        BEGIN
          PTR↑.SUIT := SUCC(CURRENT↑.SUIT);
          PTR↑.NUM := 1
        END
      ELSE  (* INCREMENT NUMBER *)
        BEGIN
          PTR↑.SUIT := CURRENT↑.SUIT;
          PTR↑.NUM := CURRENT↑.NUM + 1
        END;
    CURRENT↑.LINK := PTR;
    CURRENT := PTR
  END;
```

Finally, we use the predefined pointer constant NIL, which means that the pointer variable points to nothing. Note that this is not the same thing as undefined. This value is used to end the list, so that

```
CURRENT↑.LINK := NIL
```

should follow the FOR loop.

Remember that PTR↑ refers to the variable being pointed to by PTR. This is the only way we can access a CARD type variable (dynamic variable).

Now that we have looked at two examples of creating a linked list, let's look at algorithms used to process linked lists. For example, we might need to insert a component into a linked list, delete from a linked list or print a linked list.

The following sections on linked lists will all use these declarations:

```
TYPE POINTER =  ↑NODE;
     NODE = RECORD
                 INFO : INTEGER;
                 NEXT : POINTER
            END;  (* RECORD *)
VAR LIST : POINTER;               (* pointer to the first element *)
```

Printing the elements of a linked list is the easiest, so let's begin there.

Printing a Linked List

To print (or access in sequential order) the elements in a linked list, we begin by printing the values of the first element, then the second, then the third and so on until we reach the end. This looks like a loop of some sort where the expression is "while not end of list". What we will have to do is to use a pointer as a loop control variable. To increment it each time, we will set it to the NEXT field of the current record. The end of loop condition will be when the pointer is equal to NIL.

```
PROCEDURE PRINT(LIST : POINTER);      (* LIST is the external pointer *)
VAR P : POINTER;                      (* loop control variable *)
BEGIN
   P := LIST;                         (* initialize P to first element *)
   WHILE P <> NIL DO
     BEGIN
        WRITE(P↑.INFO);
        P := P↑.NEXT                   (* advance P *)
     END
END;
```

This procedure will work even for an empty list (LIST = NIL). If the linked list contains these values

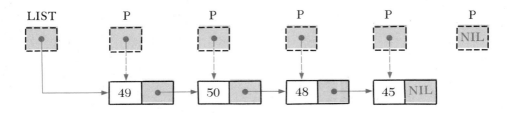

then the procedure would produce this output:

```
49      50      48      45
```

The different values that the local variable (pointer) P has during execution are shown in dotted lines in the diagram.

Inserting into a Linked List

A procedure for inserting into a linked list must have two parameters: a linked list and the element to be inserted. "Into" a linked list is ambiguous. It could mean inserting an element as the first element in the list, or inserting an element into its proper place in accordance with some ordering (alphabetic or numeric). Let's examine these two situations separately.

To insert an element as the first one in a linked list requires only two steps: create the new element and make it the first. (See Figure 14-10.)

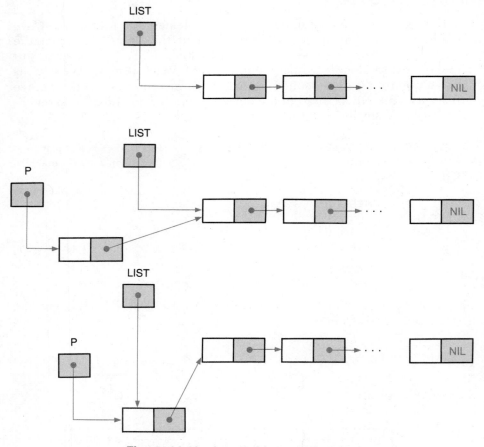

Figure 14-10. Inserting into a Linked List

```
PROCEDURE PUSH(VAR LIST : POINTER; ELEMENT :INTEGER);
                        (* Procedure to insert an element at the head of a list. *)
VAR P : POINTER;                                      (* temporary pointer *)
BEGIN
   NEW(P);                                          (* create new element *)
   P↑.INFO := ELEMENT;       (* assign value of ELEMENT to the new element *)
   P↑.NEXT := LIST;                   (* link to previous first element *)
   LIST := P                (* external pointer points to the new element *)
END;
```

Note that before calling PUSH the first time, LIST will have to have been set to NIL.

To insert an element into its proper place involves the additional step of finding its proper place. We will have to loop through all of the nodes (elements of the list) until we find one whose INFO field is greater than the value we wish to insert. (This assumes maintaining a list sorted in increasing order.) The following fragment will do this search.

```
PTR := LIST;
WHILE (PTR↑.INFO < ELEMENT) DO
    PTR := PTR↑.NEXT
```

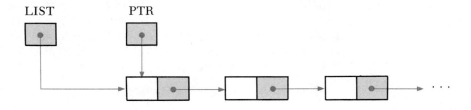

If the node referenced by PTR is the one whose value is greater than the one to be inserted, then the new element should be inserted before that node. This causes a problem; we need to know the previous node in the list so we can change its pointer field to point to the new element. We will have to keep track of two pointers as we go through the list: the pointer to the current node and the pointer to the previous node. The following fragment will do this.

```
PTR := LIST;
WHILE (PTR↑.INFO < ELEMENT) DO
   BEGIN
      BACK := PTR;
      PTR := PTR↑.NEXT
   END
```

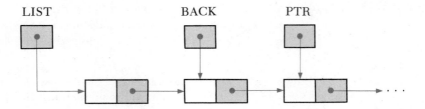

This takes care of the case where the element goes in the middle of the list. What happens about the two end cases, when the new element should be the first or the last? If the new element is the first, we can use the same algorithm which we have just written. If it is the last we will have trouble, because the test

$$PTR \uparrow . INFO < ELEMENT$$

causes an error at the end of the list. Trying to access PTR ↑ when PTR is NIL will give a run-time error.

Our loop will have to have two conditions. Our first thought would be to use

$$(PTR <> NIL) \ AND \ (PTR \uparrow . INFO < ELEMENT)$$

but this won't work. Most Pascal compilers will evaluate both sides of the expression even if the first evaluates to FALSE. That is, PTR being NIL will not stop PTR ↑ .INFO from being evaluated. We will have to use our old friend the Boolean variable FOUND. We will initialize it to FALSE and change it to TRUE when we find the place to insert the element.

$$(PTR <> NIL) \ AND \ NOT \ FOUND$$

This takes care of the three cases: the insertion at the front, the middle and the end. The following procedure represents our general insertion algorithm.

```
PROCEDURE INSERT(VAR LIST : POINTER; ELEMENT : INTEGER);
        (* Procedure to insert an element in a list while maintaining the sorted order. *)
VAR FOUND : BOOLEAN;
    P, PTR, BACK : POINTER;                        (* local pointers *)
BEGIN
  NEW(P);
  P↑.INFO := ELEMENT;                              (* get a new node *)
  BACK := NIL;                         (* initialize back and current pointers *)
  PTR := LIST;
  FOUND := FALSE;
  WHILE (PTR <> NIL) AND NOT FOUND DO
    IF PTR↑.INFO > ELEMENT
        THEN FOUND := TRUE
        ELSE
          BEGIN
```

```
            BACK := PTR;
            PTR := PTR↑.NEXT
        END;
    P↑.NEXT := PTR;
    IF BACK = NIL              (* if BACK is NIL, the element must be the first *)
        THEN LIST := P                                      (* insert as first *)
        ELSE BACK↑.NEXT := P
END;
```

Note two things about this procedure. The first is that the parameter LIST had to be a VAR parameter for the case where the new element was inserted as the first element. The second thing to notice is that it will work for INFO fields of any scalar type by changing the type of ELEMENT.

Let's go through this code for each of the three cases.

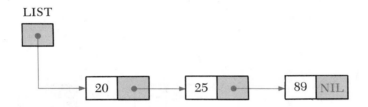

Let's insert the number 15 into the list. We get a new node (P↑) and put 15 into the INFO field. Our back pointer (BACK) is set to NIL, our loop pointer PTR is set to point to the first element, and FOUND is initialized to FALSE.

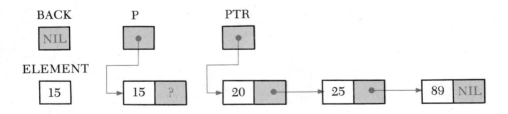

PTR is not NIL, and FOUND is FALSE, so the WHILE loop is executed. PTR↑.INFO is greater than ELEMENT (20 > 15), so FOUND is set to TRUE. The WHILE loop is not executed again. P↑.NEXT is set to PTR. BACK is NIL (indicating that the new element will be the first) so LIST is set to P.

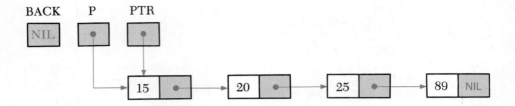

Now let's insert the number 17 into the new list. Our initialization is the same as above, except that P ↑ .INFO now contains 17. The expression in the IF statement in the WHILE loop is FALSE (15 < 17), so BACK is set to PTR and PTR is advanced to PTR ↑ .NEXT. The WHILE loop is executed again and now the expression in the IF statement is TRUE so FOUND is set to TRUE. The situation now looks like this:

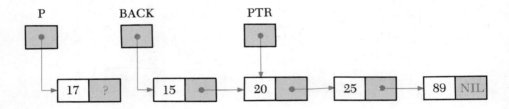

The WHILE loop is not executed since FOUND is now TRUE. P ↑ .NEXT is set to PTR. BACK is not NIL so BACK ↑ .NEXT becomes P.

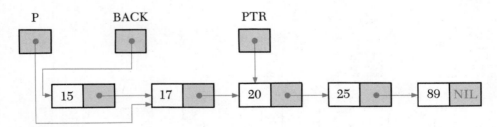

The third case is where the element needs to be inserted at the end of the list. Let's insert the number 100. Rather than going through all the iterations of the WHILE loop, let's pick up where the following diagram represents the situation.

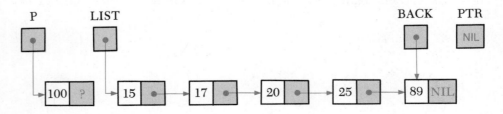

The WHILE loop is not executed because PTR is NIL. P↑.NEXT becomes PTR (NIL in this case) and BACK↑.NEXT becomes P. The entire list looks like this at the end of the three insertions:

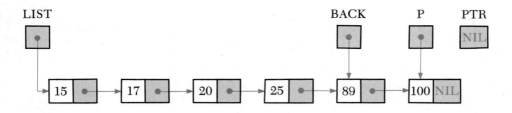

Deleting from a Linked List

To delete a node from a linked list, we must know which node is to be deleted. This can be specified as the i-th node or by looking for a node with a certain INFO field to delete. We will look at two deletions: deleting the first node and deleting a node with a specified INFO field.

Removing the first node is the mirror image of inserting an element as the first node. The value of the INFO field of the first node removed from the list will be sent back as an output parameter. (See Figure 14-11.)

```
PROCEDURE POP(VAR LIST : POINTER; VAR ELEMENT : INTEGER);
                              (* Procedure to remove the first element in a list. *)
VAR P : POINTER;
BEGIN
    P := LIST;                        (* save LIST to return to available space *)
    ELEMENT := LIST↑.INFO;
    LIST := LIST↑.NEXT;
    DISPOSE(P)                        (* send P↑ back to be used again *)
END;
```

To delete a node whose INFO field is a certain value is very similar to the INSERT procedure. The difference is that we are looking for a match here, not an INFO field greater than our element. (See Figure 14-12.)

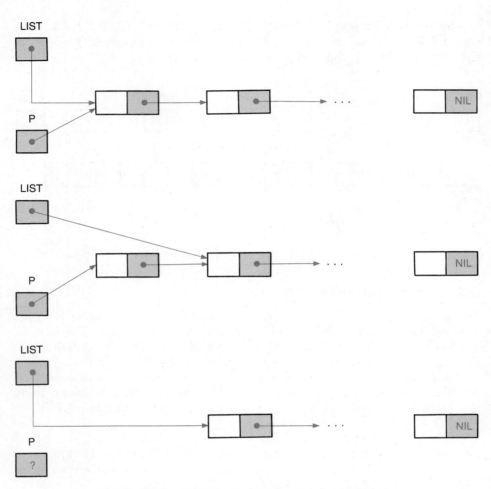

Figure 14-11. Deleting the First Node of a Linked List

```
PROCEDURE DELETE(VAR LIST : POINTER; ELEMENT : INTEGER);
VAR P, PTR : POINTER;
BEGIN
  IF ELEMENT = LIST↑.INFO
    THEN LIST := LIST↑.NEXT              (* first element is deleted *)
    ELSE
      BEGIN
        PTR:= LIST;
        WHILE PTR↑.NEXT↑.INFO <>ELEMENT DO
          PTR:= PTR↑.NEXT;
        P := PTR↑.NEXT;
        PTR↑.NEXT := PTR↑.NEXT↑.NEXT;
        DISPOSE(P)                       (* returning P↑ to available space *)
      END
END;
```

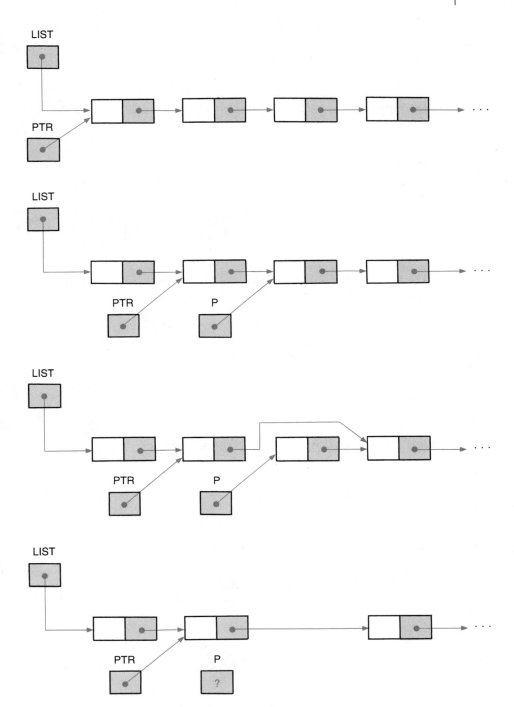

Figure 14-12. Deleting from a Linked List

Note that this procedure avoided having to keep a back pointer by using PTR↑.NEXT↑.INFO and PTR↑.NEXT↑.NEXT. This works even if P↑.NEXT↑.NEXT is NIL. However, if no match is found, there will be a run-time error when P↑.NEXT is NIL.

Pointer expressions can be very complex. Let's now examine some pointer expressions.

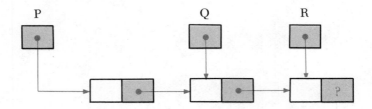

P, Q, and R point to nodes in a list. To access the fields of the nodes, you use P↑, Q↑ and R↑. Convince yourself that the following equivalences are true.

```
P↑.NEXT = Q
P↑.NEXT↑ = Q↑
P↑.NEXT↑.NEXT = R
P↑.NEXT↑.NEXT↑ = R↑
Q↑.NEXT = R
Q↑.NEXT↑ = R↑
```

Remember the semantics of the assignment statement:

```
P := Q       assigns the value of pointer Q to pointer P.
P↑ := Q↑     assigns the value of the variable referenced by Q to the
             variable referenced by P.
```

For these variables

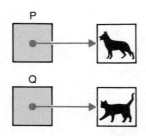

the assignment

$$P↑ := Q↑$$

yields

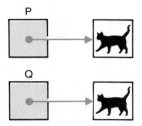

Now both P and Q each point to a different variable containing a CAT. However, the assignment

$$P \; := \; Q$$

would have yielded

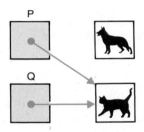

The variable containing a DOG is still there but P doesn't point to it anymore. In fact, unless the poor old DOG can be accessed some other way—another pointer points to it—it is lost forever. It is sitting there in memory, but there is no way to reach it, to use it, or to send the space back to be used again.

■ SAMPLE PROBLEM

Problem: A FORTUNE 500 company is having a stockholders meeting. When people arrive for the meeting, their names are entered at a console. You are to write a program to keep a list of these attendees. At the end of the meeting the list of attendees will be printed in alphabetic order.

Discussion: The total number of stockholders is 50,000; however, no more than 500 stockholders have ever attended any meeting. If you use an array to store their names, the index type must be 1..50000 because they might all come! If you use dynamic storage, you will need only as much storage space as there are people.

Input: Last name ',' first name (a carriage return will end the first name) (FNAME and LNAME—each a string of 10 characters)

Output: First name followed by last name, in alphabetical order.

Data Structures: Linked list of records containing names (LIST).

MAIN   **Level 0**

```
WHILE more people DO
    GETNAME
    INSERT in LIST
SORT LIST
PRINT LIST
```

GETNAME   **Level 1**

```
GETLAST
GETFIRST
```
The first and last names will be kept separately

INSERT IN LIST We already have two insert routines. Which shall we use? The one called PUSH inserts an element as the first in the list. The one called INSERT inserts an element in its proper place. PUSH is much faster, but INSERT would create the list in order. Either way is acceptable. Let's use the INSERT routine here, so that we would not have to sort the list before printing it. The algorithm will be the same; only a few details will need to be changed since the element to be inserted is different.

SORT LIST This is no longer needed.

PRINT LIST We can use Procedure PRINT from earlier in the chapter, but with the WRITE statement changed.

GETLAST   **Level 2**

',' ends lastname

```
WHILE more letters DO
    READ character
    LNAME[I] is character
```

GETFIRST

> WHILE more letters DO
>   READ character
>   FNAME[I] is character

Carriage return <eoln> ends name

GETLAST and GETFIRST are actually the same routine, so we can combine them into GETNAME. Only the end of the name marker is different (a ',' in one place and an <eoln> in the other). They are just like the GETWORD routine in Chapter 13, but simpler. There is no <eof> to worry about since an <eoln> ends the name.

Now the only problem is to recognize the last person. Since this is an interactive program, the prompt 'ENTER NAME' will be given after each name is processed. Why don't we have the word 'NONE' in place of a name to signal that the last person has signed in? The sentinel can be treated exactly like a name. When the last name is 'NONE', then the list is printed.

Design Tree Diagram:

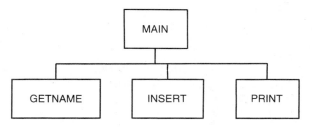

```
PROGRAM STOCKHOLDERS(INPUT,OUTPUT);          (* Program to sort and
                                             print names of attending stockholders *)
CONST BLANKS = '          ';
TYPE  STRING10 = PACKED ARRAY[1..10] OF CHAR;
      POINTER = ↑PERSON;
      PERSON = RECORD
                 FNAME,
                 LNAME : STRING10;
                 NEXT : POINTER
               END; (*RECORD*)
VAR   LIST : POINTER;
      TEMPNAME : PERSON;
(*************************************************************)
PROCEDURE GETNAME(VAR NAME : STRING10);
VAR   CH : CHAR;
      I : INTEGER;
BEGIN  (* GETNAME *)
   NAME := BLANKS;                            (* set name to blanks *)
```

```
READ(CH);
I := 1;
WHILE NOT EOLN AND (CH <> ',') DO
    BEGIN
        IF I <= 10                          (* protect the array against names *)
            THEN NAME[I] := CH;             (* longer than 10 characters *)
        READ(CH);
        I := I + 1
    END;
IF EOLN AND (I <= 10)
    THEN
        BEGIN
            NAME[I] := CH;                  (* include last character of first name *)
            READLN
        END
END;  (* GETNAME *)
(********************************************************)
PROCEDURE INSERT(VAR LIST : POINTER; ELEMENT : PERSON);
VAR    FOUND : BOOLEAN;
       P, BACK, PTR : POINTER;              (* local pointers *)
BEGIN  (* INSERT *)
    NEW(P);
    P↑ := ELEMENT;
    BACK := NIL;
    PTR := LIST;
    FOUND := FALSE;
    WHILE (PTR <> NIL) AND NOT FOUND DO
        IF PTR↑.LNAME > ELEMENT.LNAME
            THEN FOUND := TRUE
            ELSE
                BEGIN
                    BACK := PTR;
                    PTR := PTR↑.NEXT;
                END;
    P↑.NEXT := PTR;
    IF BACK = NIL               (* if BACK is NIL, the element must be the first *)
        THEN LIST := P                          (* insert as first *)
        ELSE BACK↑.NEXT := P
END;  (* INSERT *)
(********************************************************)
PROCEDURE PRINT(LIST : POINTER);      (* LIST is the external pointer *)
VAR P : POINTER;                          (* loop control variable *)
BEGIN (* PRINT *)
    P := LIST;                            (* initialize P to first element *)
    WHILE P <> NIL DO
        BEGIN
            WRITELN(P↑.FNAME, ' ', P↑.LNAME);
            P := P↑.NEXT                      (* advance P *)
        END
END; (*PRINT*)
(********************************************************)
```

```
BEGIN   (* MAIN *)
   LIST := NIL;                              (* initialize LIST *)
   WRITELN('PLEASE ENTER NAME');
   GETNAME(TEMPNAME.LNAME);
   WHILE TEMPNAME.LNAME <> 'NONE      ' DO
      BEGIN
         GETNAME(TEMPNAME.FNAME);
         INSERT(LIST, TEMPNAME);
         WRITELN('PLEASE ENTER NAME');
         GETNAME(TEMPNAME.LNAME)
      END;
   PRINT(LIST)
END.   (* MAIN *)
```

■

OTHER DATA STRUCTURES

There are many other dynamic data structures besides linked lists which you can build yourself. Since this is not a data structures text, we will briefly describe several without actually using them in sample programs.

Stacks

Did you notice the funny procedure names PUSH and POP in the section on working with linked lists? The names come from terminology dealing with a stack.

A stack is defined as a dynamic data structure where accesses are made from only one end. You can insert an element as the first (PUSH) and you can remove the first element (POP).

This data structure models many things in real life. Accountants call it LIFO, which stands for last in first out. The plate holder in a cafeteria has this property. You can take only the top plate. When you do, the one below it rises to the top so the next person can take one.

Canned goods on your grocer's shelf exhibit this property. When you take the first can in a row, you are taking the last can put in that row.

The set of diagrams in Figure 14-13 show what happens when you push an element on a given stack and then pop the stack. For obvious reasons, the pointer to the top of the stack is often called TOP.

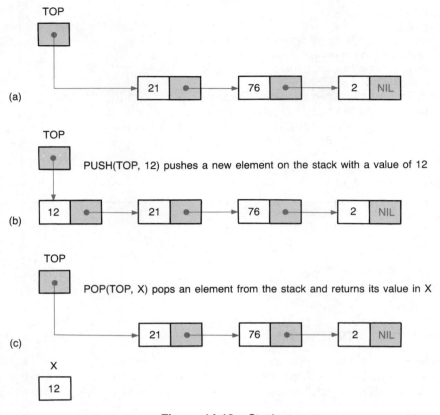

Figure 14-13. Stack.

Stacks are extremely useful in computing. If you wanted to print out a line of characters in reverse order you could do the following:

```
TOP := NIL;                          (* initializes a linked list (stack) *)
WHILE NOT EOLN DO                    (* whose external pointer is TOP *)
  BEGIN
    READ(CH);
    PUSH(TOP,CH)
  END;
WHILE TOP <> NIL DO
  BEGIN
    POP(TOP,CH);
    WRITE(CH)
  END
```

The last character read would be the first one printed and so on.

Queues

A queue (pronounced like the letter 'Q') is a dynamic data structure in which elements are entered at one end and removed from the other end. Accountants call this FIFO for first in first out. This sounds like a waiting line in a bank or supermarket. Indeed, queues are used to simulate this type of situation.

While the terminology used when referring to the insert and remove operations on stacks is standard (PUSH, POP), no such standardization exists with queues. The operation of inserting at the rear is called by many names in the literature: INSERT, ENTER, and ENQ are three common ones. Correspondingly the operation of removing from the front is variously called DELETE, REMOVE and DEQ. We choose to call our procedures ENQ and DEQ. Since we will be accessing both ends, we will need two external pointers: FRONT and REAR. (See Figure 14-14.)

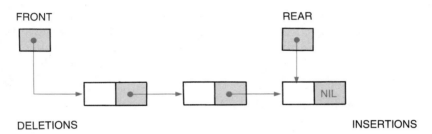

FRONT

REAR

DELETIONS

INSERTIONS

Figure 14-14. Queue.

To insert an element at the REAR we must take care of two cases: when the queue is empty and when it has at least one element. If the queue is empty (REAR = NIL) then we must set both REAR and FRONT to point to the element which is entering the queue. If there is at least one element in the queue already, we have to insert the new element after REAR ↑ and redefine REAR to point to the new element.

For the next two procedures we will use the following declarations.

```
TYPE NODEPTR = ↑NODETYPE;
     NODETYPE = RECORD
                    ELEMENT : INTEGER;
                    NEXT : NODEPTR
                END;  (* RECORD *)

VAR NODE : NODETYPE;
    FRONT, REAR : NODEPTR;
    NUM : INTEGER;
```

```
PROCEDURE ENQ(VAR FRONT, REAR : NODEPTR; NUM : INTEGER);
                        (* Procedure to insert an element at the rear of a queue *)
VAR PTR : NODEPTR;
BEGIN
   NEW(PTR);
   PTR↑.ELEMENT := NUM;
   PTR↑.NEXT := NIL;
   IF REAR = NIL
      THEN
         BEGIN
            REAR := PTR;
            FRONT := PTR
         END
      ELSE
         BEGIN
            REAR↑.NEXT := PTR;
            REAR := PTR
         END
END;
```

To remove an element from the front is actually just like popping a stack. In fact, we can just use procedure POP. The only additional thing to be done is to check to see if the queue is empty after removing the element. If it is, REAR must be set to NIL.

```
PROCEDURE DEQ(VAR FRONT, REAR : NODEPTR;
              VAR ELEMENT: INTEGER);
                     (* Procedure to remove an element from the front of a queue *)
BEGIN
   POP(FRONT, ELEMENT);
   IF FRONT = NIL
      THEN REAR := NIL
END;
```

There are other ways to implement stacks and queues, but since these structures will vary greatly in size during run-time, they are often implemented as linked lists as we have described here.

Binary Trees

The concept of a linked list can be extended to structures containing nodes with more than one pointer field. One of these structures is known as a tree. The diagram in Figure 14-15 is called a binary tree—each node has at most two offspring.

The tree is referenced by an external pointer to the special node called the *root*. The root has two pointers: one to its left child and one to its right child. Each child again has two pointers: one to its left child and one to its right child.

Binary search trees are trees that have the property that the information

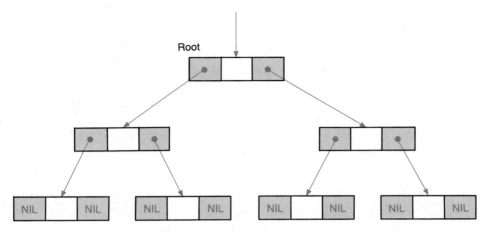

Figure 14-15. Binary Tree.

in any node is greater than the information in any node of its left child and any of its children, and less than the information in its right child and any of its children.

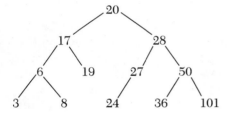

The above tree is an example of a binary search tree. The reason it is so useful is that if you are looking for a certain number, you can tell which half of the tree it is in by one comparison. You can then tell what half of that half it is in by one comparison. This continues until either you find it or you determine it is not there.

Let's try it with the number 50.

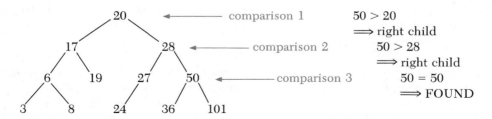

Now let's look for 18, a number that is not there.

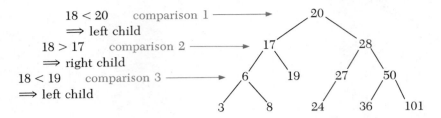

18 < 20   comparison 1 ───────→
⟹ left child
18 > 17   comparison 2 ───────→
⟹ right child
18 < 19   comparison 3 ───────→
⟹ left child

The left child of 19 is NIL so 18 isn't in the tree. Not only do we know it is not there, if we want to insert it, we are at the right place.

■ **SAMPLE PROBLEM**

Problem: In Chapter 13 we wrote a program to create a list of all the words which appeared in a text file. This list was to be used to help build the index for this book. The list was to be scanned (by us, as humans), and non-computer related words were to be removed. This revised list of words will form the input to this problem. The text must be scanned a second time for each occurrence of the selected words, and a list kept of each page on which the word appears.

Discussion: The job of building an index is usually done by using 3x5 cards. There is one card for each word, and when the word is found on a page, the page number is written on the card. Some cards have only one or two page numbers written on them, and some words are used so frequently that additional cards have to be clipped to the original one.

We will base our program on this by-hand algorithm. The only real problem will be to keep track of which page of the text we are working on. Text editing systems usually have a special character (or set of characters) which is interpreted by a printer as "eject to a new page." Looking for this character and incrementing the page count when it is found, would be one way to keep track of page numbers.

Another way would be to count the number of lines and increment the page count when a certain number of lines have been read. For example, this text has 46 lines per page. We will use this second scheme here, incrementing the page count each time we read 46 lines. Counting lines, however, will make our algorithm to get a word look slightly different from the one in the previous chapter.

A word boundary was defined in Program CONCORDANCE to be any nonalphabetic character. Since reading an <eoln> returns a blank, line boundaries were ignored. Now we must recognize line boundaries in order to count the number of lines. In designing this change there are several possibilities to consider.

A word can be ended by an <eoln>.
A word can be ended by a nonalphabetic character.

There can be blanks at the end of lines.
There can be complete blank lines.

We can make our algorithm simpler by remembering that EOLN looks at the file buffer variable. We can ask if the next character is the end of line character, increment our count if it is, yet not change our basic processing. The next iteration can read and process that <eoln> as we did before.

Because of this wide variation in the number of page numbers for each word, this is an ideal situation in which to use linked lists. We can have an array of records with two fields. One field will be the word to be included in the index, and the second field will be the external pointer to the linked list which will contain the pages on which the word appears.

Input: The list of words to be included in the index (in INPUT) (these words are one per line)
The text of the book (in BOOK)

Output: The list of words, with each word followed by the page numbers on which it appears.

Data Structures: An array of records (WORDLIST) with two fields (WORD and PAGELIST).

WORDLIST

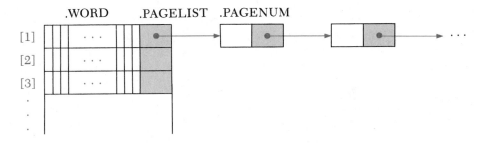

MAIN   Level 0

```
GETWORDLIST
WHILE more text DO                      EOF (BOOK) loop
    GETAWORD
    SEARCH WORDLIST for WORD            returning INDEX
    IF FOUND                           where found
        THEN PUSH PAGENUM on PAGELIST
WHILE more words DO                     count controlled
    PRINT WORD                         loop
    PRINT PAGELIST
```

GETWORDLIST   Level 1

> WORDCT = 0
> WHILE more words DO
>   increment WORDCT
>   CHARCT = 1
>   Repeat
>   Get a character
>   Put character in word in List
>   Increment CHARCT
>   Until EOLN
>   Initialize PAGELIST to NIL

EOF(INPUT) loop
GETWORDLIST returns the
number of words in the index.

GETAWORD

> Set WORD to all blanks
> REPEAT
>   IF EOLN
>   THEN increment LINECT
>   READ another character
> UNTIL character is alphabetic or EOF
> CT = 1
> IF NOT EOF
>   THEN
>   INCREMENT page count
>   REPEAT
>   IF CT is less than wordsize
>   THEN put character into WORD
>   increment CT
>   IF EOLN
>   THEN increment LINECT
>   READ another character
>   UNTIL character is nonalphabetic or EOF

Skip
nonalphabetic
character

SEARCH

> Same as binary search used in Chapter 13.
> INDEX of where found is returned. Show
> whether the word was FOUND or not. Index
> is undefined if FOUND is FALSE.

PUSH

> Same as developed earlier in this chapter

PRINT

Same as developed earlier in this chapter

Prints the PAGELIST of a word in WORDLIST.

INCREMENT   **Level 2**

```
IF LINECT > LINESPERPAGE
   THEN PAGE = PAGE+(LINECT DIV LINESPERPAGE)
        LINECT = LINECT MOD LINESPERPAGE
```

Design Tree Diagram:

```
PROGRAM INDEX(INPUT,OUTPUT,BOOK);              (* This program prints the
                          page numbers where selected words appear in a text file *)
CONST LINESPERPAGE = 46;
      TABLESIZE = 1000;
      WORDSIZE = 20;
      BLANKS = '                    ';
TYPE STRING = PACKED ARRAY[1..WORDSIZE] OF CHAR;
     PAGEPTR = ↑PAGENODE;
     INDEXTYPE = RECORD
                     WORD : STRING;
                     PAGELIST : PAGEPTR
                 END;  (*RECORD*)
     PAGENODE = RECORD
                    PAGENUM : INTEGER;
                    NEXT : PAGEPTR
                END;  (*RECORD*)
     INDEXLIST = ARRAY[1..TABLESIZE] OF INDEXTYPE;
VAR  WORDLIST : INDEXLIST;
     ONEWORD : STRING;
```

```
        LCV,
        NUMWORDS,
        PAGE,
        INDEX,
        LINECT : INTEGER;
      FOUND : BOOLEAN;
      BOOK : TEXT;
(************************************************************)
PROCEDURE INCREMENT(VAR PAGE, LINECT : INTEGER);
BEGIN    (*INCREMENT*)
  IF LINECT > LINESPERPAGE
      THEN
        BEGIN
          PAGE := PAGE + (LINECT DIV LINESPERPAGE);
          LINECT := LINECT MOD LINESPERPAGE
        END
END;      (*INCREMENT*)
(************************************************************)
PROCEDURE GETAWORD(VAR DATA : TEXT; VAR WORD : STRING;
                   VAR PAGE, LINECT : INTEGER);
VAR CH : CHAR;
    CT : INTEGER;
BEGIN    (*GETAWORD*)
  WORD := BLANKS ;                        (* set WORD to all blanks*)
  REPEAT
    IF EOLN(DATA)
      THEN LINECT := LINECT + 1;
    READ(DATA, CH)
  UNTIL (CH IN ['A'..'Z']) OR EOF(DATA);
  CT := 1;
  IF NOT EOF(DATA)
      THEN
        BEGIN
          INCREMENT(PAGE, LINECT);
          REPEAT
            IF CT <= WORDSIZE
                THEN
                  BEGIN
                    WORD[CT] := CH;
                    CT := CT + 1
                  END;
            IF EOLN(DATA)
                THEN LINECT := LINECT + 1;
            READ(DATA, CH)
          UNTIL NOT (CH IN ['A'..'Z']) OR EOF(DATA)
        END
END;      (*GETAWORD*)
(************************************************************)
PROCEDURE GETWORDLIST(VAR WORDLIST : INDEXLIST;
                      VAR WORDCT : INTEGER);
```

```
VAR CHARCT : INTEGER;
    CH : CHAR;
BEGIN   (*GETWORDLIST*)
  WORDCT := 0;
  WHILE NOT EOF DO
    BEGIN
      WORDCT := WORDCT + 1;
      WORDLIST[WORDCT].WORD := BLANKS;
      CHARCT := 1;
      REPEAT
        READ(CH);
        WORDLIST[WORDCT].WORD[CHARCT] := CH;
        CHARCT := CHARCT + 1;
      UNTIL EOLN;
      WORDLIST[WORDCT].PAGELIST := NIL;
      READLN
    END
END;   (*GETWORDLIST*)
(*******************************************************)
PROCEDURE SEARCH(ONEWORD : STRING; VAR FOUND : BOOLEAN;
                 VAR INDEX : INTEGER; NUMWORDS : INTEGER;
                 WORDLIST : INDEXLIST);
VAR  FIRST, MIDDLE, LAST : INTEGER;
BEGIN   (*SEARCH*)
  FIRST := 1;
  LAST := NUMWORDS;
  FOUND := FALSE;
  WHILE (LAST >= FIRST) AND NOT FOUND DO
    BEGIN
      MIDDLE := (FIRST + LAST) DIV 2;
      IF ONEWORD < WORDLIST[MIDDLE].WORD
          THEN LAST := MIDDLE - 1
          ELSE IF ONEWORD > WORDLIST[MIDDLE].WORD
                  THEN FIRST := MIDDLE + 1
                  ELSE
                    BEGIN
                      FOUND := TRUE;
                      INDEX := MIDDLE
                    END
    END
END;    (*SEARCH*)
(*******************************************************)
PROCEDURE PUSH(VAR LIST : PAGEPTR; ELEMENT : INTEGER);
VAR P : PAGEPTR;
BEGIN   (*PUSH*)
  NEW(P);
  P↑.PAGENUM := ELEMENT;
  P↑.NEXT := LIST;
  LIST := P
END;    (*PUSH*)
(*******************************************************)
```

```
PROCEDURE PRINT(LIST : PAGEPTR);
VAR P : PAGEPTR;
BEGIN   (*PRINT*)
  P := LIST;
  WHILE P <> NIL DO
    BEGIN
      WRITE(P↑.PAGENUM:4);
      P := P↑.NEXT
    END
END;    (*PRINT*)
(********************************************************)
BEGIN   (*MAIN*)
  RESET(BOOK);
  GETWORDLIST(WORDLIST, NUMWORDS);
  PAGE := 1;
  LINECT := 1;
  WHILE NOT EOF(BOOK) DO
    BEGIN
      GETAWORD(BOOK, ONEWORD, PAGE, LINECT);
      SEARCH(ONEWORD, FOUND, INDEX, NUMWORDS, WORDLIST);
      IF FOUND
          THEN PUSH(WORDLIST[INDEX].PAGELIST, PAGE)
    END;
  FOR LCV := 1 TO NUMWORDS DO
    BEGIN
      WRITE(WORDLIST[LCV].WORD);
      PRINT(WORDLIST[LCV].PAGELIST);
      WRITELN
    END
END.    (*MAIN*)
```

Program INDEX made use of four procedures developed elsewhere in the book. Procedures PUSH and PRINT could be used with no modifications. The binary search portion of Procedure INSERT was used directly as Procedure SEARCH. Procedure GETAWORD, although modified, was based on the algorithm developed in Program CONCORDANCE.

Would it have been possible to use Procedure GETAWORD to read in the original list of words? On the surface this seems a good solution. However, Procedure GETAWORD has been made fairly complicated by the necessity of counting lines and incrementing a page counter. The format for the list of words in the index is such that a much simpler algorithm can be used.

Our design tree is simple. In fact, the program is quite simple. We must confess, however, that the first version was not. In fact, the second one wasn't either. The program shown here is actually our third iteration through the design process.

CHOICE OF DATA STRUCTURE

At the beginning of this chapter we pointed out that deletions and insertions into a list are time consuming when using an array to represent the list. Insertions and deletions in a linked list representation are indeed simpler and faster. However, there are operations on lists which are simpler in an array representation.

Let's look at the operations you might want to apply to a list and examine the advantages and disadvantages of each representation.

1. Read items sequentially into a list.
2. Access all the items in the list in sequence.
3. Insert/delete the first item in a list.
4. Insert/delete the last item in a list.
5. Insert/delete the n-th item in a list.
6. Access the n-th item in a list.
7. Sort the items in a list.
8. Search the list for a specific item.

Reading sequentially into a list is a little faster using an array representation because procedure NEW doesn't have to be called for each item. Accessing the items in sequence takes approximately the same amount of time for both structures.

Inserting/deleting the first item in a list is much faster using a linked representation. Conversely, inserting/deleting the last item in a list can be done much more efficiently in an array representation because you have direct access to the last element and no shifting is required. In a linked representation, you have to search through the entire list to find the last element.

On the average, the time spent on inserting/deleting the n-th item from a list should be about equal. A linked representation would be better for small values of n, and an array representation would be better for values of n near the end of the list.

Accessing the n-th element is *much* faster using an array representation. You can access it directly by using n as the index into the array. In a linked representation, you would have to access the first n-1 items to reach the n-th item.

In sorting an existing linked list, you can remove the elements one by one and insert them in place into a second linked list. When you finish, you can set the external pointer of the original list to point to the first element of the new list. If you DISPOSE each node as you remove an item, you will not use any additional memory space for your sorted list. With a linked list you are, however, limited to this type of sorting algorithm. With an array representation, you can use much faster sorting algorithms.

Searching a list for a specific item is much faster in general in an array representation because you can use a binary search. If the items in the list to be searched are not ordered, the two representations would be about the same.

When trying to decide whether to use an array representation of a list or a linked representation, determine which of these operations will be applied most frequently. Use this analysis to determine which would be better in the context of your particular problem.

There is one additional point to consider. How accurately can you predict the maximum number of items in the list? Does the number of items in the list fluctuate widely? If you know the maximum and it remains fairly constant, an array representation is probably called for. Otherwise, it would be better to choose a linked representation in order to use memory more efficiently.

TESTING AND DEBUGGING

Pointer variables contain memory addresses. We can't print out these values; even if we could, they might not tell us what we need to know to debug a program. Programs using pointers are therefore sometimes more difficult to debug than programs without them.

It is hard to tell whether or not our pointer variables contain valid values. We can print out the values (debug WRITE statements) of the variable referenced by a pointer, which might help us in our debugging. This assumes, of course, that the pointer is pointing to something.

Programmers often make errors in referencing variables with pointers. Careful attention must be paid to complex pointer expressions. It is also important to distinguish between the pointer value itself and the thing the pointer is pointing to.

Testing and Debugging Hints

1. Be sure a pointer is not NIL before accessing its referenced variable.

   If PTR is a pointer which is either NIL or undefined, accessing PTR ↑ will give you a run-time error. Be careful with compound expressions in your WHILE loop. On most compilers, both sides of expressions with AND or OR are evaluated, regardless of the outcome of the first expression evaluated. That is why

   ```
   (PTR <> NIL) AND (VALU <> PTR↑.NUM)
   ```

   will cause an error when VALU is not found.

2. Remember that DISPOSE(P) leaves P undefined; trying to access P ↑ will cause a run-time error.

3. Return variables to available space when you are finished with them.

   When deleting an element from a linked list, use DISPOSE to return those memory cells for later use. In a large program, if you do not do this, you might run out of memory.

   If you have DISPOSEd of unneeded variables and you still run out of memory space, check to be sure you do not have an inadvertent recursive call or an infinite loop in which NEW is called. Another possibility is that you are passing a large data structure as a value parameter.

4. Pass a pointer as a parameter, not the object being pointed to.
5. Keep track of pointers. Changing pointer values prematurely may cause problems when you try to get back to the referenced variable.
6. Pointers must be of the same type in order to compare them or assign one to another.
7. Don't confuse a pointer with the variable it points to.

P := Q   copies the contents of Q into P.

P ↑ := Q ↑   copies the contents of the variable to which Q points into the variable to which P points.

P ↑ := Q } are illegal because one is a pointer and one is
P := Q ↑ } the variable being pointed to.

Summary

Pascal has a predefined data type called a pointer. You declare a pointer in the TYPE section by putting an ↑ before the type to which the pointer is to point. (A pointer type is always associated with a specific type to which it points.)

A dynamic variable is defined by the procedure NEW. Its argument is a pointer variable. NEW returns the pointer to the newly created variable. These variables have no names; their contents can be referenced by the pointer variable followed by ↑.

Linked lists are created by defining records with two (or more) fields, where one field is a pointer to records of its own type. The pointer to the first is saved in a place called the external pointer to the list, and the pointer to each succeeding one is placed in the pointer field of the one before. NIL is put in the pointer field of the last one to indicate the end of the list.

Many interesting data structures can be built using pointers. Stacks, queues and trees are three which you will use often in real life problems.

Exercises

Use these declarations in the following questions·

```
TYPE POINTER = ↑NODE;
     NODE = RECORD
               INFO : INTEGER;
               NEXT : POINTER
            END; (*RECORD*)
     VAR  P, Q, R : POINTER;
```

1. Show what the following commands do to the schematic diagram of a linked list.

a. P := P↑.NEXT

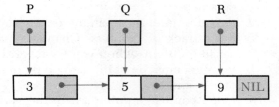

b. Q := P

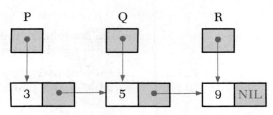

c. R := P↑.NEXT

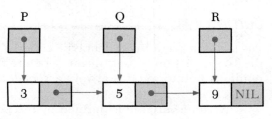

d. P↑.INFO := Q↑.INFO

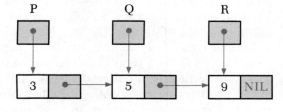

e. P↑.INFO :=
    Q↑.NEXT↑.INFO

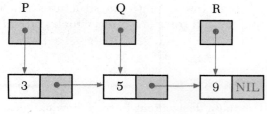

f. R↑.NEXT := P

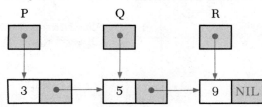

2. Write one statement (using the ↑ notation) to effect the change indicated by the dotted line.

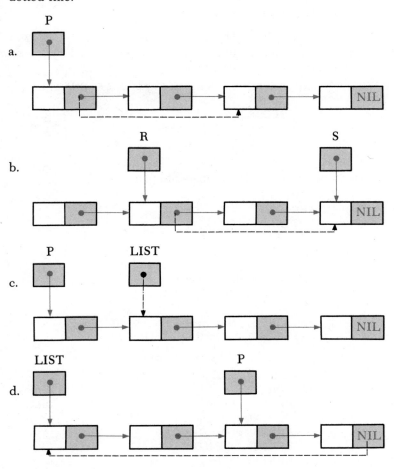

3. Show what is written by the following segments of code.

a. NEW(P);
   NEW(Q);
   P↑.INFO := 5;
   Q↑.INFO := 6;
   P := Q;
   P↑.INFO := 1;
   WRITELN(P↑.INFO, Q↑.INFO)

b. NEW(P);
   P↑.INFO := 3;
   NEW(Q);
   Q↑.INFO := 2;
   NEW(P);

```
P↑.INFO := Q↑.INFO;
Q↑.INFO := 0;
WRITELN(P↑.INFO, Q↑.INFO)
```

4. Answer this question as True or False.

   The following type declaration is illegal, since PTR = ↑NODE is a forward reference to an undefined type called NODE.

```
TYPE STRING = PACKED ARRAY[1..10] OF CHAR;
     PTR = ↑NODE;
     NODE = RECORD
                 NAME : STRING;
                 NEXT : PTR
            END;
```

5. Show what is written by the following segment of code.

```
NEW(P);
NEW(Q);
P↑.INFO := 0;
P↑.NEXT := Q;
Q↑.NEXT := NIL;
Q↑.INFO := 5;
P↑.NEXT↑.NEXT := P;
Q↑.INFO := Q↑.NEXT↑.INFO;
P := Q;
P↑.NEXT↑.INFO := 2;
WRITELN(P↑.INFO, Q↑.INFO)
```

6. Given these declarations for a linked list of company employees:

```
TYPE PTR = ↑EMPLOYEE;
     EMPLOYEE = RECORD
                    NAME : PACKED ARRAY[1..25] OF CHAR;
                    DEPTNO : 1..20;
                    EMPNO : 0..1000;
                    SALARY : INTEGER;
                    NEXT : PTR
                END;  (* RECORD *)
VAR    P, EMPLOYEES : PTR;
```

   a. Initialize EMPLOYEES, a pointer to a company list, with a special dummy first node (header node), which contains a zero employee number. Assume that the list will be ordered by employee number.
   b. Write a segment of code to read in data about an employee, and to store it in a node (to be inserted later into the linked list of employees). Assume that the data about each employee is located on a separate line of input in the format:

col.	1-25	27-28	30-33	35-40
	NAME	DEPTNO	EMPNO	SAL

   Feel free to use any additional variables you need.
   c. Write a procedure to insert a new employee node into the list you initialized in (a). The procedure will take EMPLOYEES (pointer to the list) and EMP (pointer to the new employee's node, filled with the data in (b)).

7. Debug the following. Assume these global declarations:

```
TYPE NODE = RECORD
                    INFO : INTEGER;
                    NEXT : ↑NODE
              END;
```

a.
```
FUNCTION EVEN (P : ↑NODE) : BOOLEAN;
BEGIN
    IF P↑.INFO MOD 2 = 0
        THEN EVEN := TRUE
        ELSE EVEN := FALSE
END;
```

b.
```
PROCEDURE SUCCESSOR (P : PTR);
BEGIN
    WHILE P <> NIL DO
        WRITELN(P↑.INFO, ' IS FOLLOWED BY ',
                P↑.NEXT↑.INFO)
END;
```

Pre-Test

Use these declarations in the following questions:

```
TYPE PTR = ↑NODE
     NODE = RECORD
                  INFO : CHAR;
                  LINK : PTR
              END;  (*RECORD*)
VAR S, T, P : PTR;
```

1. Show what the following commands do to the schematic diagram of a linked list.

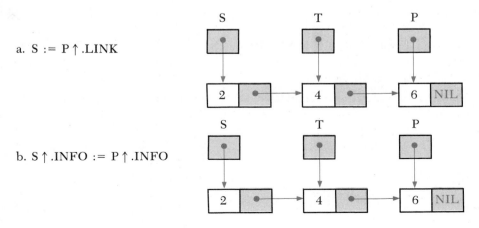

a. S := P↑.LINK

b. S↑.INFO := P↑.INFO

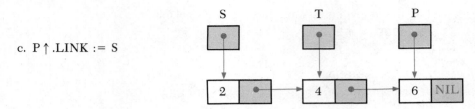

c. P↑.LINK := S

2. Write one statement (using ↑ notation) to effect the change indicated by the dotted line.

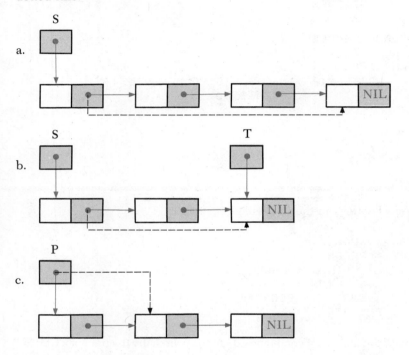

a.

b.

c.

3. Write an INTEGER function EVENSUM which will sum the INFO fields of all nodes whose INFO fields are even.

4. Write a procedure READNSTORE which will read in the INTEGER numbers in a file and store them in numerical order in a linked list pointed to by LIST. Use EOF to tell the end of the data.

5. Write an integer function ODDNODESUM which sums the INFO fields of the first node, the third node, the fifth node, etc.

Appendixes

APPENDIX A RESERVED WORDS

AND	END	MOD	REPEAT
ARRAY	FILE	NIL	SET
BEGIN	FOR	NOT	THEN
CASE	FORWARD	OF	TO
CONST	FUNCTION	OR	TYPE
DIV	GOTO	PACKED	UNTIL
DO	IF	PROCEDURE	VAR
DOWNTO	IN	PROGRAM	WHILE
ELSE	LABEL	RECORD	WITH

(EXTERN, FORTRAN, GLOBAL, LOCAL, OTHERWISE, VALUE and others may be reserved words in some implementations.)

APPENDIX B STANDARD IDENTIFIERS

Standard Constants

FALSE   TRUE   MAXINT

Standard Types

INTEGER   BOOLEAN   REAL   CHAR   TEXT

Standard Files

INPUT   OUTPUT

Standard Functions

	Parameter type	*Result type*	*Returns*
ABS(X)	INTEGER or REAL	Same as parameter	Absolute value of X
ARCTAN(X)	INTEGER or REAL	REAL	Arctangent of X in radians
CHR(X)	INTEGER	CHAR	Character whose ordinal number is X
COS(X)	INTEGER or REAL	REAL	Cosine of X (X is in radians)
EOF(F)	FILE	BOOLEAN	End-of-file test of F
EOLN(F)	FILE	BOOLEAN	End-of-line test of F
EXP(X)	REAL or INTEGER	REAL	e to the X power
LN(X)	REAL or INTEGER	REAL	Natural logarithm of X
ODD(X)	INTEGER	BOOLEAN	Odd test of X
ORD(X)	Ordinal (scalar except REAL)	INTEGER	Ordinal number of X
PRED(X)	Ordinal (scalar except REAL)	Same as parameter	Unique predecessor of X (except when X is the first value)
ROUND(X)	REAL	INTEGER	X rounded
SIN(X)	REAL or INTEGER	REAL	Sine of X (X is in radians)
SQR(X)	REAL or INTEGER	Same as parameter	Square of X
SQRT(X)	REAL or INTEGER	REAL	Square root of X
SUCC(X)	Ordinal (scalar except REAL)	Same as parameter	Unique successor of X (except when X is the last value)
TRUNC(X)	REAL	INTEGER	X truncated

Standard Procedures

	Description
DISPOSE(P)	Destroys the dynamic variable referenced by pointer P by returning it to the available space list.
GET(F)	Advances the current position of file F to the next component and assigns the value of the component to F ↑ .
NEW(P)	Creates a variable of the type referenced by pointer P, and stores a pointer to the new variable in P.
PACK(U, I, P)	Copies the elements beginning at subscript position I of array U into packed array P beginning at the first subscript position of P.
PAGE(F)	Advances the printer to the top of a new page before printing the next line of text file F.
PUT(F)	Appends the value of the buffer variable F ↑ to the file F.
READ(F,variable list)	Reads data values from text file F (if F is not specified, default is INPUT) and assigns these values to the variable(s) in the variable list in order until the list is satisfied.
READLN(F,variable list)	Same as READ except advances the file pointer past the end-of-line after satisfying its variable list.
RESET(F)	Resets file F to its beginning for reading.
REWRITE(F)	Resets file F to its beginning for writing; old contents of F are lost.
UNPACK(P, U, I)	Copies the elements beginning at the first subscript position of packed array P into array U beginning at subscript position I.
WRITE(F,parameter list)	Writes the data in the order specified in the parameter list to text file F (if F is not specified, default is OUTPUT).
WRITELN(F,parameter list)	Same as WRITE except generates an end-of-file after satisfying its parameter list.

(Some compilers provide additional types, files, functions and/or procedures. Check the manual for your specific implementation to see what is available.)

APPENDIX C PASCAL OPERATORS AND SYMBOLS

+		plus or set union
−		minus or set difference
*		times or set intersection
/		divide
DIV		integer divide
MOD		remainder from integer divide (modulus)
<		is less than
<=		is less than or equal to
=		is equal to
<>		is not equal to
>=		is greater than or equal to
>		is greater than
AND		Boolean conjunction
OR		Boolean inclusive disjunction
NOT		Boolean negation
IN		test set membership
:=		becomes
,		separates items in a list
;		separates statements
:		separates variable name and type; separates case label and statement; separates statement label and statement
'		delimits character and string literals
.		decimal point, record selector and program terminator
..		subrange specifier
↑	@	file and pointer variable indicator
(		starts parameter list or nested expression
)		ends parameter list or nested expression
[	(.	starts subscript list or set expression
(*	{	starts a comment
*)	}	ends a comment
]	.)	ends subscript list or set expression

APPENDIX D PRECEDENCE OF OPERATORS

NOTE: 1. Parentheses can be used to change the order of precedence.
2. When operators of equal precedence are used, they are executed in left to right order.

NOT	Highest precedence
* / DIV MOD AND	
+ − OR	
< <= = >= > <> IN	Lowest precedence

APPENDIX E SYNTAX DIAGRAMS

PROGRAM

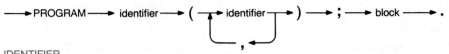

IDENTIFIER

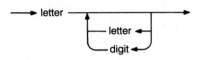

BLOCK

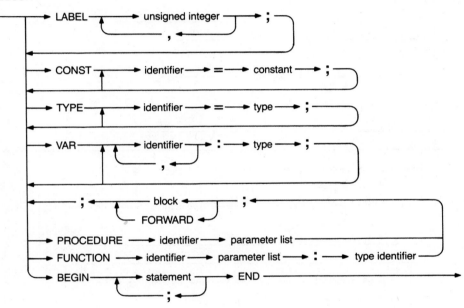

CONSTANT

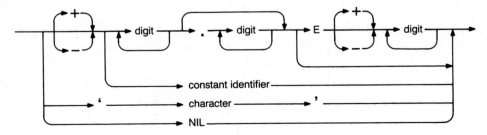

TYPE

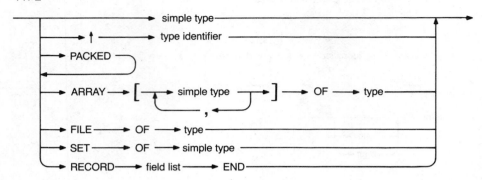

SIMPLE TYPE

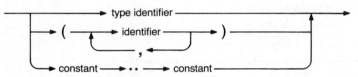

FIELD LIST

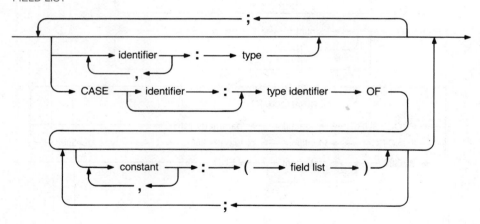

PARAMETER LIST

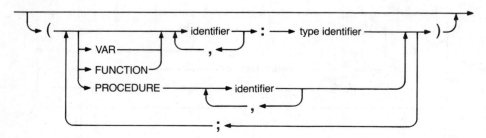

STATEMENT

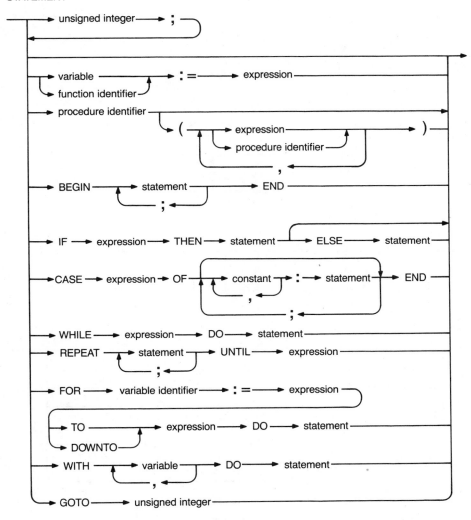

VARIABLE

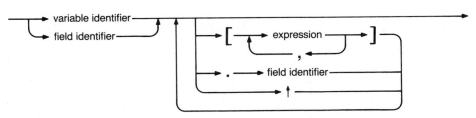

EXPRESSION

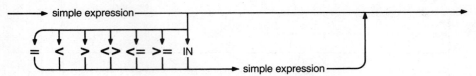

SIMPLE EXPRESSION

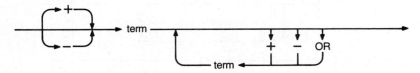

TERM

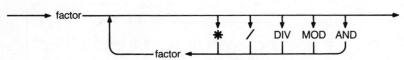

FACTOR

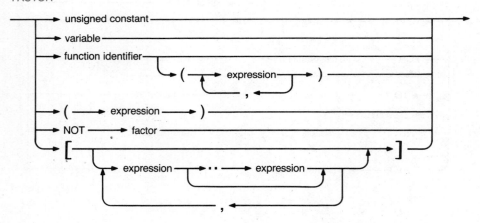

APPENDIX F STRUCTURE DIAGRAMS

The following diagrams illustrate the flow of control of each construct.
(Note: Statements can be compound statements.)

Sequence

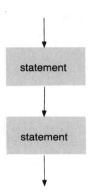

Selection

If-Then

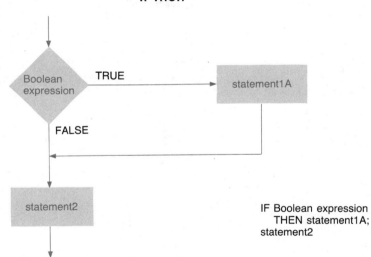

```
IF Boolean expression
   THEN statement1A;
statement2
```

If-Then-Else

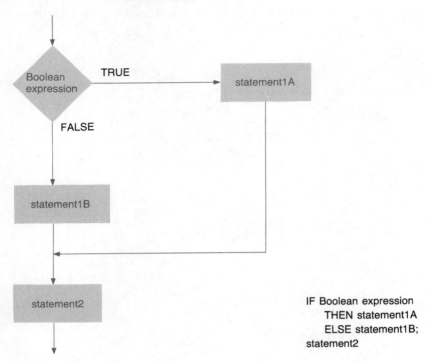

IF Boolean expression
    THEN statement1A
    ELSE statement1B;
statement2

Case

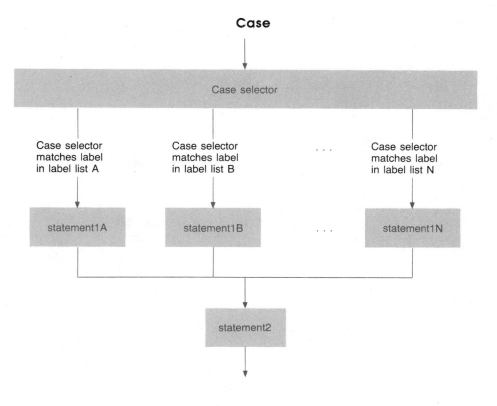

```
CASE case selector OF
    label list A : statement1A;
    label list B : statement1B;
    .
    .
    .
    label list N : statement1N
END
```

Where statement1N is the last in the series of actions.

Loop

While

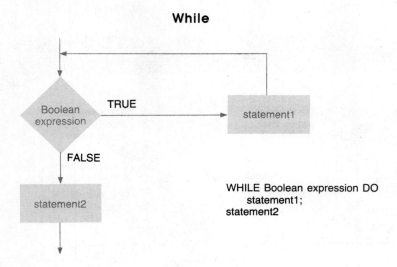

WHILE Boolean expression DO
    statement1;
statement2

Repeat-Until

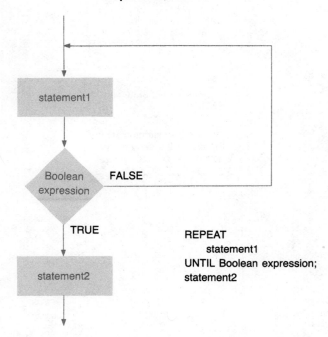

REPEAT
    statement1
UNTIL Boolean expression;
statement2

For

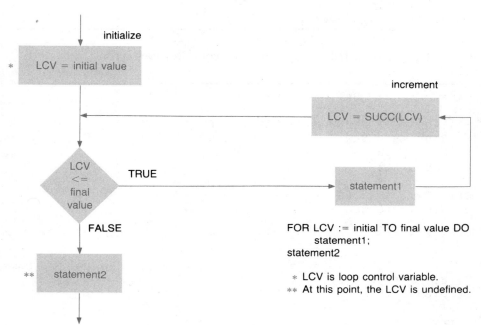

FOR LCV := initial TO final value DO
    statement1;
statement2

* LCV is loop control variable.
** At this point, the LCV is undefined.

APPENDIX G SAMPLE PROGRAM LISTINGS WITH ERROR MESSAGES

Program listing with compile-time errors.

```
Line,    Addr   S#1   P#1   ERRORS

   1-D      3 PROGRAM ERRORS(INPUT, OUTPUT);
   2-D      3 VAR I : INTEGER;
   3-D      4     J : 1..10;

S#1   P#1    ERRORS     lev1
   4.0       0 BEGIN                              Undeclared identifier
   5.1       9    A := 50
Error  1 **** #104                               Semi-colon missing
   6.1      11    FOR J := 1 TO 20 DO
Error  2 **** #6                                 Undeclared identifier
   7.2      28       BEGIN
   8.3      30          I := J + A;
Error  3 **** #104
   9.3      35          WRITELN(I)
  10.2      55       END
  11.0      55 END.

   3 Errors,   11 Lines
```

```
    6:   Illegal symbol (possibly missing ';' on line
         above)
  104:   Undeclared identifier
```

Corrected program listing with another compile-time error.

```
Line,    Addr   S#1   P#1   ERRORS

   1-D      3 PROGRAM ERRORS(INPUT, OUTPUT);
   2-D      3 VAR I : INTEGER;
   3-D      4     J : 1..10
   4-D      5     A : REAL;

S#1   P#1     ERRORS       lev1
   5,0        0 BEGIN
   6,1        9    A := 50;
   7,1       16    FOR J := 1 TO 20 DO
   8,2       33       BEGIN
   9,3       35          I := J + A;  ←───────Expression doesn't return
Error  1 **** #129                     an integer result
  10,3       45          WRITELN(I)
  11,2       65       END
  12,0       65 END,
```

1 Errors,   12 Lines

```
  129:   Type conflict of operands
```

Corrected program listing with run-time error.

```
Line,    Addr   S#1   P#1   ERRORS

   1-D      3 PROGRAM ERRORS(INPUT, OUTPUT);
   2-D      3 VAR I : INTEGER;
   3-D      4     J : 1..10;
   4-D      5     A : INTEGER;

S#1   P#1     ERRORS       lev1
   5,0        0 BEGIN
   6,1        9    A := 50;
   7,1       14    FOR J := 1 TO 20 DO
   8,2       31       BEGIN
   9,3       33          I := J + A;
  10,3       40          WRITELN(I)
  11,2       60       END
  12,0       60 END,
```

no Errors,   12 Lines,

Output from above program.

```
51
52
53
54
55
56
57
58
59
60                                    ─Run-time error

! Value range error
At   S#1  P#1   ERRORS        I#29      Line 10
Value= 11, Limit= 10
```

The variable J was assigned a value of 11 during execution, which is outside its range of permissible values.

APPENDIX H COMPILER ERROR MESSAGES

The following error codes are produced by the compiler to inform the user of a compiler error. The list defines the error code number and a description of the meaning of the error.

1:      Error in simple type
2:      Identifier expected
3:      'PROGRAM' expected
4:      ')' expected
5:      ':' expected
6:      Illegal symbol (possibly missing ';' on line above)
7:      Error in parameter list
8:      'OF' expected
9:      '(' expected

10:      Error in type
11:      '[' expected
12:      ']' expected
13:      'END' expected
14:      ';' expected (possibly on line above)
15:      Integer expected
16:      '=' expected
17:      'BEGIN' expected
18:      Error in declaration part
19:      Error in <field-list>

20:      ',' expected
21:      '*' expected

50:    Error in constant
51:    ':=' expected
52:    'THEN' expected
53:    'UNTIL' expected
54:    'DO' expected
55:    'TO' or 'DOWNTO' expected in FOR statement
56:    'IF' expected
57:    'FILE' expected
58:    Error in <factor> (bad expression)
59:    Error in variable

101:    Identifier declared twice
102:    Lower bound exceeds upper bound
103:    Identifier is not of the appropriate class
104:    Undeclared identifier
105:    Sign not allowed
106:    Number expected
107:    Incompatible subrange types
108:    File not allowed here
109:    Type must not be REAL

110:    <tagfield> type must be scalar or subrange
111:    Incompatible with <tagfield> type
112:    Index type must not be REAL
113:    Index type must be scalar or subrange
114:    Base type must not be REAL
115:    Base type must be scalar or a subrange
116:    Error in type of standard procedure parameter
117:    Unsatisfied forward reference
118:    Forward referenced type identifier in variable declaration
119:    Must not repeat parameter list for a FORWARD declared procedure

120:    Function result type must be scalar, subrange or pointer
121:    File value parameter not allowed
122:    Must not repeat result type for a FORWARD declared function
123:    Missing result type in function declaration
124:    F-format for reals only
125:    Error in type of standard function parameter
126:    Number of parameters does not agree with declaration
127:    Illegal parameter substitution
128:    Result type does not agree with declaration
129:    Type conflict of operands

130:    Expression is not of set type
131:    Tests on equality allowed only
132:    Strict inclusion not allowed
133:    File comparison not allowed

134: Illegal type of operand(s)
135: Type of operand must be Boolean
136: Set element type must be scalar or subrange
137: Set element types must be compatible
138: Type of variable is not array
139: Index type is not compatible with declaration

140: Type of variable is not record
141: Type of variable must be file or pointer
142: Illegal parameter substitution
143: Illegal type of loop control variable
144: Illegal type of expression
145: Type conflict
146: Assignment of files not allowed
147: Label type incompatible with selecting expression
148: Subrange bounds must be scalar
149: Index type must not be INTEGER

150: Assignment to standard function is not allowed
151: Assignment to formal function is not allowed
152: No such field in this record
153: Type error in READ
154: Actual parameter must be a variable
155: Control variable must be local and not a parameter
156: Multidefined case label
157: Too many cases in CASE statement
158: No such variant in this record
159: REAL or string tagfields not allowed
160: Previous declaration was not FORWARD
161: Previously declared as FORWARD
162: Parameter size must be constant
163: Missing variant in declaration
164: Substitution of standard procedure/function not allowed
165: Multidefined label
166: Multideclared label
167: Undeclared label
168: Undefined label
169: Base type of set exceeds implementation limit

170: Value parameter expected
171: Standard file was re-declared
172: Undeclared external file
173: FORTRAN procedure or function expected
174: Pascal procedure or function expected
175: Missing file INPUT in program heading
176: Missing file OUTPUT in program heading

201: Error in real constant—digit expected
202: String constant must not exceed source line
203: Integer constant exceeds range
204: Digit exceeds radix

250: Too many nested scopes of identifiers
251: Too many nested procedures and/or functions
252: Too many forward references of procedure entries
253: Procedure too long
254: Too many long constants in this procedure
255: Too many errors on this source line
256: Too many external references
257: Too many externals
258: Too many local files
259: Expression too complicated

300: Division by zero
301: No case provided for this value
302: Index expression out of bounds
303: Value to be assigned is out of bounds
304: Element expression out of range

398: Implementation restriction
399: Feature NOT implemented

APPENDIX I TOP-DOWN DESIGN METHOD

(1) ANALYZE THE PROBLEM
(2) WRITE THE MAIN MODULE
(3) WRITE THE REMAINING MODULES
(4) RESEQUENCE AND REVISE AS NECESSARY

1. ANALYZE THE PROBLEM
   Understand the problem. Understand what is given (INPUT) and what is required (OUTPUT). Specify INPUT and OUTPUT formats. Think. How would you do it by hand? State the data structures needed (if any). Develop an overall algorithm or general plan of attack. List assumptions (if any).

2. WRITE THE MAIN MODULE
   Use English or pseudo-code to restate the problem in the main module. Use module names to divide the problem into functional areas. If this module is too long (more than 10 to 15 statements) you are at too low a level of detail. Introduce any control structures (such as looping or selection) that are needed at this point. Resequence logically if needed. Postpone details to lower levels. The main module may change during further refinement.

Don't worry if you don't know how to solve an unwritten module at this point. Just pretend you have a "smart friend" who has the answer and postpone it until later refinements have been made. All you have to do in the main module is to give the names of lower level modules that provide certain functions. Use meaningful module names.

3. WRITE THE REMAINING MODULES

There is no fixed number of levels. Modules at one level can specify more modules at lower levels. Each module must be complete although it references unwritten modules. Do successive refinements through each module until each statement can be directly translated into a Pascal statement.

4. RESEQUENCE AND REVISE AS NECESSARY

Plan for change. Don't be afraid to start over. Several iterations through the design may be necessary. Backtrack to inappropriate design decisions. Try to maintain clarity. Express yourself simply and directly.

Top-Down Design Outline

INPUT DESCRIPTION:
OUTPUT DESCRIPTION:
DATA STRUCTURES:
ASSUMPTIONS (IF ANY):
MAIN MODULE
REMAINING MODULES BY LEVELS

The final product of your design is your program. Your program should reflect the structure of your top-down design. The main module should be the main program.

APPENDIX J PROGRAM DOCUMENTATION

1. Use meaningful identifier names in your programs.
2. The first lines of comment after the program heading should contain: (* Your name.
   The date.
   A brief description of the problem and what the program does.
   *)
3. Your top-down design can be a separate document, or you can insert it as comment lines immediately following the above:

```
(* INPUT: by form and type
   OUTPUT: by form and type
   DATA STRUCTURES: if any
   ASSUMPTIONS: if any
   MAIN MODULE
   REMAINING MODULES BY LEVELS
       .
       .
       .
*)
```

Every module must be expanded. Use English or pseudo-code. Pascal code is not necessary here since your program shows the code. Your program must reflect your top-down design.

4. Comment the main BEGIN-END pairs of programs, procedures and functions.

```
PROGRAM TUTTIFRUTTI(INPUT,OUTPUT);
    .

BEGIN (* TUTTIFRUTTI *)
    .
    .

END. (* TUTTIFRUTTI *)
```

5. Comment the END for CASE statements and RECORD definitions.

```
CASE X OF
    1   : statement;
    2,3 : statement;
    4   : statement
END (* CASE *)
```

6. Comment procedures and functions immediately before their headings with a brief description of their purpose.

7. Comment code where necessary for clarity. Don't tell how or why something is done, but what is being done. Pseudo-code from your top-down design is excellent for this.

APPENDIX K PROGRAM FORMATTING*

These suggestions will lead to more readable programs.

1. Each statement must begin on a separate line.
2. Each line shall be less than or equal to 72 characters.
3. At least one space must appear before and after ':=' and '='. At least one space must appear after ':'.
4. At least one blank line (or other recognizable dividing line) must appear before PROCEDURE and FUNCTION declarations.

---

* Reprinted with permission of Hayden Book Company from *Pascal With Style: Programming Proverbs*, by Henry F. Ledgard, Paul A. Nagin, and John F. Huares. Copyright © 1978.

5. PROGRAM, PROCEDURE, and FUNCTION headings must begin at the left margin. However, nested procedures and functions should be indented according to the level of nesting.
6. The keywords REPEAT, BEGIN and END must stand on a line by themselves.
7. The main BEGIN-END block for programs, procedures and functions shall be lined up with the corresponding heading.
8. Each statement within a BEGIN-END, REPEAT-UNTIL or CASE statement must be aligned. The bodies of CONST, TYPE and VAR declarations and BEGIN-END, FOR, REPEAT, WHILE, CASE and WITH statements must be indented from the corresponding header keywords. Be consistent with indenting.
9. An IF-THEN-ELSE statement must be displayed as:

```
        IF expression
            THEN statement
            ELSE statement
```

Of course <statement> can be a compound statement:

```
        IF expression
            THEN
                    BEGIN
                        statements
                    END
            ELSE
                    BEGIN
                        statements
                    END
```

An exception is allowed for multiple nesting (generalized case statement):

```
        IF expression THEN
            statement
        ELSE IF expression THEN
            statement

                .

                .

                .

        ELSE
            statement
```

APPENDIX L ADDITIONAL FEATURES OF PASCAL

Standard Pascal has some additional features not covered previously in the text. The syntax diagrams in APPENDIX E describe the Pascal language and show some of these additional features.

For the sake of completeness, these additional features are described in this appendix. They include the unconditional branch (GOTO statement), another structuring option for records (variant records), the use of functions and procedures as parameters, and a mechanism for forward referencing procedures and functions.

GOTO Statement

A GOTO statement, or unconditional branch, is provided in most common programming languages. Pascal is no exception, but, because all the control structures already exist, the GOTO should be rarely needed. In other languages an IF and a GOTO statement must be used to construct control structures. In Pascal the IF, CASE, WHILE, FOR and REPEAT control structures are more convenient and make programs more readable; they make the flow of control clearer.

The GOTO statement passes control directly from one point in a program to another. The GOTO must specify the label of a statement to which control is transferred. The label must be declared in the declaration section of the block. These are the rules concerning the GOTO statement:

1. All labels must be declared.
2. Label declarations precede all others in the block.
3. Labels are unsigned integers in the range 1 to 9999.
4. Each label may be declared only once, and it may be used to label only one statement.
5. A GOTO branch into a control structure or block (procedure or function) is not permitted. A GOTO branch out of a control structure or a block is permitted.

In the following example, the commented statements are the equivalent control structures for the code using the GOTO.

```
PROGRAM JUMP(INPUT,OUTPUT);
LABEL 10, 20, 30, 40;
CONST N = 2000;
VAR VALUE, SUM : INTEGER;
BEGIN (*JUMP*)
   SUM := 0;
10:IF EOF                    (*WHILE NOT EOF DO            *)
       THEN GOTO 20;         (*  BEGIN                     *)
   READLN(VALUE);            (*     READLN(VALUE);         *)
   SUM := SUM + VALUE;       (*     SUM := SUM + VALUE     *)
   GOTO 10;                  (*  END;                      *)
20:IF SUM <= N               (*IF SUM > N                  *)
       THEN GOTO 30;         (*                            *)
   WRITELN('MINORITY');      (*    THEN WRITELN('MINORITY')*)
   GOTO 40;                  (*                            *)
30:WRITELN('MAJORITY');      (*    ELSE WRITELN('MAJORITY')*)
40:
END. (*JUMP*)
```

Structured programming is characterized by the use of control structures with only one entry and one exit. Use of the GOTO leads to unstructured programming: multiple entry and exits from control structures. This makes programs harder to read, understand, modify and debug. Because of this the GOTO should be avoided. Use it only for exceptional circumstances and forward (not backward) jumps, such as exiting a procedure or program due to certain error conditions.

Overuse of the GOTO statement in Pascal is poor programming practice. Pascal contains all the control structures necessary to write a program without the GOTO.

Variant Records

Within a group of data objects described by a record type, there may be some variation in some of the attributes of those objects. Instead of declaring a record variable large enough to contain all these variations, you can use the variant record provided in Pascal. By listing the possible variant fields in the type definition, the variant to be used for a particular data object can be specified during execution. The compiler need allocate only enough space for the record variable to include the largest variant.

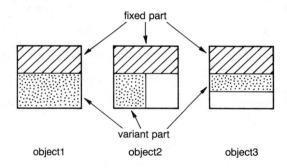

Records may contain a fixed and a variant part. If both are present, the fixed part must precede the variant part.

The following record definition contains a variant part.

```
TYPE ITEM = (ASSEMBLY, NUT, BOLT, WASHER);
     PART = RECORD
                ID : PACKED ARRAY[1..10] OF CHAR;
                QTY : INTEGER;
                TAG : ITEM;
                CASE ITEM OF
```

```
            ASSEMBLY : (DRAWINGID : PACKED ARRAY[1..6]
                                    OF CHAR;
                         CODE : 1..12;
                         CLASS : (A, B, C, D) );
         NUT, BOLT, WASHER : ()
         END; (*RECORD*)
```

This definition can be abbreviated to:

```
TYPE PART = RECORD
            ID : PACKED ARRAY[1..10] OF CHAR;
            QTY : INTEGER;
            CASE TAG : ITEM OF
              ASSEMBLY : (DRAWINGID : PACKED ARRAY[1..6]
                                      OF CHAR;
                           CODE : 1..12;
                           CLASS : (A, B, C, D) );
            NUT, BOLT, WASHER : ()
            END; (*RECORD*)
```

Several points can be made about defining and using variant records. We will use the above definition to illustrate.

1. A record definition may contain only one variant part, although field lists in the variant part may contain a variant part (nested variant).

2. All field identifiers within a record definition must be unique.

3. The tag field (TAG) is a separate field of a record (if present).

4. The tag field is used to indicate the variant used in a record variable.

5. The case clause in the variant part is not the same as a CASE statement.
   (a) There is no matching END for the CASE; the END of the record definition is used.
   (b) The case selector is a type (ITEM); the tag type, not the tag field.
   (c) Each variant is a field list labelled by a case label list. Each label is a constant of the tag type (ITEM).
   (d) The field lists are in parentheses.
   (e) The field lists define the fields and field types of that variant.

6. The tag type can be any ordinal type, but it must be a type identifier.

7. The tag field (TAG) can be absent, especially if the variant is indicated in the fixed part or somewhere else, but this is not good practice.

8. Several labels can be used for the same variant (NUT, BOLT, WASHER).

9. A field list can be empty, which is denoted by "()".

10. The variant to be used is assigned at run-time. The variant can be changed by assignments to other variant fields and the tag field. When a variant is used, data (if any) in a previous variant is lost.

11. The tag field does not appear in the field selectors for the variant fields.

12. It is an error to access a field that is not part of the current variant.

During execution, values can be assigned to the record variable as usual. Assuming the declaration

```
VAR APART, BPART : PART;
```

the following assignment statements are valid.

```
APART.ID := '18A32V1    ';
APART.QTY := 16;
APART.TAG := ASSEMBLY;
APART.DRAWINGID := '100C36';
APART.CODE := 8;
APART.CLASS := B
```

Different variables of the same record type will have different structures if assigned values to different variants. Assignments to BPART such as these:

```
BPART.ID := '1B15      ';
BPART.QTY := 200;
BPART.TAG := WASHER
```

give BPART a different structure than APART.

The case clause in the variant part of the record definition is often matched by a CASE statement in the body of the program. For example, the following program fragment could be used to print data about a record.

```
WRITELN('PART ID - ', APART.ID);
WRITELN('QTY - ', APART.QTY:1);
CASE TAG OF
   ASSEMBLY : WRITELN('ASSEMBLY : ', APART.DRAWINGID);
   NUT      : WRITELN('NUT');
   BOLT     : WRITELN('BOLT');
   WASHER   : WRITELN('WASHER')
END   (*CASE*)
```

Functions and Procedures as Parameters

Besides variable and value parameters, Pascal allows procedure and function parameters. That is, the actual parameter is a procedure or function identifier. The only restriction is that procedures and functions used as parameters may only have value parameters themselves.

This is a syntax diagram for a formal parameter list:

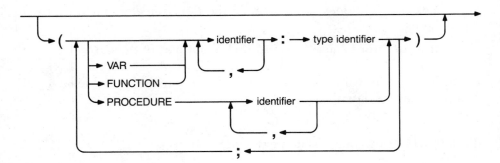

As an example, suppose we need a procedure that will find the minimum and maximum values of various functions within a specified range. The functions can be passed as a parameter to the procedure which can check the function's value at specified intervals.

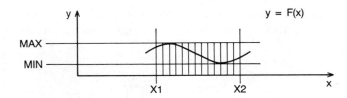

The procedure can evaluate the function F at each interval W and return the minimum and maximum values in MIN and MAX.

```
PROCEDURE MINMAX (FUNCTION F : REAL; X1, X2, W : REAL;
                  VAR MIN, MAX : REAL);
VAR VALU : REAL;              (* temporary variable to reduce the calls to F *)
BEGIN
  MIN := F(X1);
  MAX := MIN;
  X1 := X1 + W;
  WHILE X1 < X2 DO
    BEGIN
      VALU := F(X1);
```

```
      IF VALU < MIN
         THEN MIN := VALU;
      IF VALU > MAX
         THEN MAX := VALU;
      X1 := X1 + W
   END
END;
```

The procedure calls the function specified for F in the call to MINMAX. For example, the calls

```
         MINMAX (SIN, 0.5, 0.9, 0.01, MIN, MAX);
         MINMAX (RESPONSE, A, B, T, MIN, MAX);
         MINMAX (POLY, D1, D2, S, MIN, MAX)
```

are all valid calls to the procedure if RESPONSE and POLY are declared real functions, with one real formal parameter each (must be a value parameter). The other actual parameters must be real—all parameters must match in type.

The call to function F within MINMAX would substitute the function specified in the call to MINMAX. For example,

```
         VALU := F(X1)
```

within MINMAX would be evaluated as

```
         VALU := RESPONSE(X1)
```

if RESPONSE was specified in the call to MINMAX.

Forward Statement

Identifiers in Pascal must be defined before being used (the type identifier in the pointer type definition is an exception). We described recursion as a procedure or function calling itself. There are recursive situations where one procedure or function calls another which in turn calls the first.

```
  .
  .
(********************************************************)
PROCEDURE ONE (VAR A : ATYPE);
BEGIN
  .
  .
  TWO(X);
  .
  .
END;
```

```
(********************************************************)
PROCEDURE TWO (VAR B : BTYPE);
BEGIN
    .
    .
   ONE(Y);
    .
    .
END;
(********************************************************)
  .
  .
  .
```

In the above example, the call to procedure TWO in the body of procedure ONE is not allowed. The solution to this problem is to make a forward reference to procedure TWO by using the FORWARD statement.

```
  .
  .
(********************************************************)
PROCEDURE TWO (VAR B : BTYPE);
FORWARD;
(********************************************************)
PROCEDURE ONE (VAR A : ATYPE);
BEGIN
    .
    .
   TWO(X);
    .
    .
END;
(********************************************************)
PROCEDURE TWO;
BEGIN
    .
    .
   ONE(Y);
    .
    .
END;
(********************************************************)
  .
  .
  .
```

Notice that the parameter list (and the result type for a function) is written only in the forward reference; it is *not* repeated in the actual declaration of the procedure (or function). The compiler "remembers" the parameter declarations when it encounters the actual procedure.

APPENDIX M IMPLEMENTATIONS

(This appendix is not written for the beginning student; an understanding of Pascal is assumed.)

This book has presented standard Pascal as described in the *Pascal User Manual and Report*, by Jensen and Wirth. Although Pascal was originally designed as a teaching tool, its popularity as a commercial language has grown. Today, almost every major brand of computer, from microcomputers to mainframes, has at least one Pascal compiler written for it. Pascal implementations for use in commercial environments generally have extensions to the original language such as interactive I/O, random access to file components and additional character string processing and manipulation features.

Many of these extensions to Pascal are included in the draft ISO (International Standards Organization) standard for Pascal. Many current implementations of Pascal include some or all of the proposed ISO draft features.

Brief descriptions of two popular implementations of Pascal, including some of their extensions to standard Pascal, are given in this appendix. CDC Pascal 6000 is a mainframe implementation that is fairly close to standard Pascal. UCSD Pascal (developed at the University of California at San Diego) is representative of a number of microcomputer implementations.

CDC Pascal 6000

Pascal was originally implemented on a CDC 6600. This implementation is in widespread use, especially at universities. This implementation conforms closely to standard Pascal but includes some additional features which we will describe here.

We have brought up several times in the book that each implementation of Pascal will have restrictions imposed by the particular machine. CDC machines can have one of several character sets. You will need to check your implementation for this and other features such as the value of MAXINT or the precision of real numbers.

If no fieldwidth is specified in the WRITE statement, the following default values will be used.

integer	10 columns
real	22 columns
Boolean	10 columns
char	1 column

Only packed arrays less than 10 characters or a multiple of 10 characters may be compared. Sets are limited to 58 (or 59) components. Trailing blanks in lines of text files may be truncated (do not assume lines to be 80 characters), so use the EOLN function to check for line boundaries. The file list in the program heading must contain the file OUTPUT.

CDC Pascal 6000 contains some extensions to the language including segmented files, the provision to call external library routines (procedures and functions) and a string type called ALFA. Additional built-in procedures and functions are also provided.

Segmented files allow faster access to any part of a file. A segmented file is composed of segments. A file DATA can be declared as a segmented file

```
VAR DATA : SEGMENTED FILE OF component type;
```

and additional built-in procedures and functions used to manipulate it. RESET(DATA), REWRITE(DATA), EOLN(DATA) and PUT(DATA) work as usual. GET(DATA) must not be used if either EOS(DATA) or EOF(DATA) is TRUE. READ and WRITE can be used with segmented textfiles.

EOS(DATA) returns TRUE if file DATA is positioned at the end of a segment, otherwise FALSE. Returns TRUE whenever EOF(DATA) is TRUE.

PUTSEG(DATA) terminates a segment of file DATA. Used after data has been written to the file with a WRITE or PUT.

GETSEG(DATA) positions the file DATA at the beginning of the next segment. GET or READ may then be used to read the next component.

GETSEG(DATA, N) positions the file DATA at the beginning of the Nth segment from the current file position. $N > 0$ causes a forward count; $N < 0$ causes a backward count; $N = 0$ positions the file at the beginning of the current segment.

REWRITE(DATA, N) prepares the file DATA for writing at the beginning of the Nth segment from the current file position.

Pre-compiled library routines external to the program can be called from the program. The call to these external procedures (or functions) is in the form

```
PROCEDURE EXAMPLE (VAR PAR1 : INTEGER; PAR2 : REAL);
EXTERN;
```

or

```
PROCEDURE EXAMPLE2 (VAR PAR1 : INTEGER; PAR2 : REAL);
FORTRAN;
```

depending on whether a Pascal or FORTRAN library is being accessed.
ALFA is an additional predefined type

```
TYPE ALFA = PACKED ARRAY[1..10] OF CHAR;
```

that is a string variable of exactly 10 characters. It can be used like any packed array as described in this book.

The following are some of the additional built-in procedures:

DATE(string)	assigns the current date in the format "yy/mm/dd" to the string variable (of type ALPHA) specified.
TIME(string)	assigns the current time in the format "hh.mm.ss" to the string variable (of type ALPHA) specified.
MESSAGE(string)	writes the string specified into the dayfile. (Maximum string length of 40.)
LINELIMIT(file variable, limit)	causes the program to abort when the number of lines specified by the integer limit expression have been written to the file specified.
HALT	aborts the program and prints a post-mortem dump.

and functions:

CLOCK	returns the number of milliseconds of elapsed processor time since job initiation.
CARD(set)	returns the cardinality (number of members) of the set specified.
EXPO(number)	returns the contents of the exponent part of the real number specified.
UNDEFINED(number)	returns TRUE if the value of the number specified is indefinite or out-of-range.

This description of CDC Pascal 6000 is based upon the discussion of the implementation in the *Pascal User Manual and Report,* by Jensen and Wirth. Newer versions will vary, and you should refer to the manual for your local implementation. For example, some versions provide for interactive I/O. One approach lets INPUT be declared as the keyboard if a slash is placed in the program heading.

```
PROGRAM INTER (INPUT/, OUTPUT);
```

Another approach predefines TTY as the terminal device, so TTY can be the keyboard or the screen depending on whether RESET(TTY) or REWRITE(TTY) is used.

UCSD Pascal

UCSD Pascal includes its own operating system and utilities such as a filer, editor, linker and assembler. We only discuss its variations from, and extensions to, standard Pascal here. You should refer to the manual for information on using its operating system and system utilities. There are several versions of UCSD Pascal in existence, and some limits and capabilities will vary among versions.

This implementation has some differences from standard Pascal. Boolean variables cannot be printed by a WRITE statement. Procedures and functions cannot be used as parameters to procedures or functions. The DISPOSE procedure is not implemented, but memory can be recovered by using the additional procedures MARK and RELEASE. The procedures PACK and UNPACK are not provided since their operation is automatic when manipulating a packed variable in UCSD Pascal. Sets are limited to 4080 components (may be different in your version). Arrays or records of the same type can be compared for equality or inequality ('=' or '<> '). If none of the case labels in a CASE statement matches the value of the case selector, then no action is taken and execution continues with the next statement. The file list in the program heading is ignored (and is therefore unnecessary); filenames are specified in the procedures RESET and REWRITE.

Interactive I/O is provided by the additional file type INTERACTIVE. INPUT, OUTPUT and KEYBOARD are defined as being of type INTERACTIVE. INPUT is composed of characters typed at the terminal keyboard which are echoed on the terminal screen. KEYBOARD is the same as INPUT except there is no echo on the screen. OUTPUT is the screen. Input from interactive files is different from normal files. A

```
READ(F, CH)
```

from an INTERACTIVE file F is equivalent to

```
GET(F);
CH := F↑
```

which is the reverse of a normal file. When the INTERACTIVE file is opened, the file buffer is empty since a character has not been typed yet. EOLN and EOF for interactive files remain FALSE until the explicit end-of-line character (carriage-return) for EOLN or the end-of-file character for EOF is typed. Your code will probably need to be modified when reading from interactive files as opposed to normal text files.

Files internal to the program use RESET and REWRITE as usual. RESET is automatically performed on INPUT and KEYBOARD, as is REWRITE on OUTPUT. Other external files require a special form of RESET and REWRITE to associate the file variable with a specific file or device.

RESET(F, 'filename')   performs a reset of the file specified by 'filename' (can be a string variable or constant) and associates the file variable F with this file.

REWRITE(F, 'filename')   as above in RESET but opens the file for writing.

Random access to any record in a file of records is provided by the SEEK procedure. The syntax to this extension is in the form

SEEK(file variable, record number);

where the records are numbered sequentially from zero to the last record in the file. Performing a SEEK for a record number that is too large causes EOF(file variable) to be TRUE. After performing a SEEK for a particular record, it can be read using the GET procedure or overwritten using the PUT procedure. Two SEEKs in succession to the same file without an intervening GET or PUT should not be attempted.

A predefined type STRING is provided for easier string manipulation. Variables of type STRING are actually packed arrays of type CHAR but with a length attribute that can vary dynamically from zero to a maximum of 255. The default length of this type is 80,

```
TYPE STRING = PACKED ARRAY[1..80] OF CHAR;
```

but this limit can be set to any length up to 255.

```
VAR LINE : STRING;            (* default maximum length of 80 *)
    WORD : STRING[10];         (* maximum length of 10 *)
    PARA : STRING[255];        (* maximum length of 255 *)
```

The actual length of the string variable is determined by the data stored in it (blank fill is not required). Unequal length strings may be compared (the ordering is based upon the lexicographic ordering of the character set). Any size string value may be assigned to a string variable as long as it does not exceed the maximum length of the variable. String variables may be indexed (a particular character accessed) as in any array as long as the current dynamic length of the string is not exceeded (otherwise an index-out-of-range error is generated).

Direct string READs are allowed. However, only one string should be read at a time since the termination of an input string is indicated by <eoln>. If S1 and S2 are variables of type STRING and the statement

```
READLN(S1, S2)
```

is executed, the string S2 will be empty.

If a string variable is a parameter of a WRITE statement, only the actual string is printed (in a field width equal to the current dynamic length).

To manipulate strings more easily and increase their usefulness, UCSD Pascal provides several additional string functions:

LENGTH(string)	returns the integer value of the length of the string specified.
COPY(source string, index, size)	returns a string of the size specified taken from the source string beginning at the index position of the source string.
CONCAT(string list)	returns a string which is the concatenation of the strings specified. The string list is composed of any number of source strings separated by commas.
POS(pattern string, source string)	returns the beginning index position of the first occurrence in the source string of the pattern string. If no match is found, POS returns 0.

and procedures:

DELETE(destination string, index, size)	removes a substring of the size specified from the destination string beginning at the index specified.
INSERT(source string, destination string, index)	inserts the source string into the destination string beginning at the index specified of the destination string.

An individual character value may be assigned to a specific cell in a string by specifying the index. However, such an assignment does not affect the LENGTH of a string, so the length can become incorrect. To maintain the integrity of the LENGTH of a string, use a full string (non-indexed) assignment or a string procedure or function to change the value of a string.

Since a memory word length in microcomputers severely limits the value of MAXINT, another scalar type, LONG INTEGER, is provided. Long integers may be up to 36 digits. They are declared by using a length attribute in the type definition. For example, a long integer variable that could have a value of up to 15 digits in length could be declared by

```
VAR BIG : INTEGER[15];
```

Long integers are used just like integers; however, long integer results cannot be assigned to integer variables. A long integer value can be converted to an integer value by using the TRUNC procedure as long as the value is less than MAXINT.

UCSD supports the separate compilation of program modules. This is convenient for several reasons. Commonly used procedures can be kept in an external library of routines and called when needed. Also, program modifications can be made without requiring the entire program to be compiled again. This is particularly time-saving during program development when bugs can crop up frequently. These separate program modules are called UNITs.

There are three kinds of UNITs: intrinsic, regular and separate. Intrinsic units are stored in the system library. Regular units actually become part of the calling program's codefile. Separate units are like regular units, but only those portions actually used by the calling program are placed in the calling program's codefile.

All UNITs are composed of a heading, an INTERFACE part, an IMPLEMENTATION part, and initialization code. The heading specifies the type of unit (intrinsic, regular or separate). The INTERFACE includes all of the declarations and definitions available to the calling program. The IMPLEMENTATION part contains the code for procedures and functions declared in the INTERFACE part and any other declarations and definitions needed (these are not accessible to the calling program). The initialization code is used to initialize the unit and is not accessible to the calling program. The following is an example of a regular UNIT.

```
UNIT JUSTANEXAMPLE;                                    (* unit heading *)
(***********************************************************)
INTERFACE                          (* global declarations and definitions *)
    CONST PI = 3.14;
    TYPE BLOB = (SOFT, HARD, SQUISHY);
    VAR FRAMUS : STRING[15];
    PROCEDURE DOWHATCHA(NUM : INTEGER);
    FUNCTION DEVIOUS(LOWDOWN : REAL) : BOOLEAN;
(***********************************************************)
IMPLEMENTATION                     (* local declarations and definitions *)
    CONST ONLYHERE = 22;
    TYPE LIGHT = 1..6;
    VAR CTR : INTEGER;
        NAME : STRING[20];
        FLAG : BOOLEAN;
    (***********************************************************)
    PROCEDURE DOWHATCHA;
    BEGIN
      (* procedure body *)
    END;
    (***********************************************************)
    FUNCTION DEVIOUS;
    BEGIN
      (* function body *)
    END;
(***********************************************************)
BEGIN                                      (* unit initialization code *)
    (* initialization code *)
END.
```

UNITs used in a calling program must be declared immediately after the program heading. For example, the calling program indicates that it USES the above UNIT JUSTANEXAMPLE as follows.

```
PROGRAM CALLER;
USES JUSTANEXAMPLE;
CONST ...
   .
   .
```

Large programs may easily fill available memory, especially on a micro-computer. To allow programs to be larger than available memory, UCSD Pascal provides for a memory overlay technique through SEGMENT procedures and functions. This means that not all of the program has to be in memory at the same time, only the part being executed.

To declare a procedure or function as a program segment requires only that the additional reserved word SEGMENT precede the procedure or function declaration.

```
PROGRAM SEGMENTED;
(* declarations *)
(*******************************************************)
SEGMENT PROCEDURE ONE;
BEGIN (* ONE *)
   (* procedure body *)
END;  (* ONE *)
(*******************************************************)
SEGMENT FUNCTION TWO;
BEGIN (* TWO *)
   (* function body *)
END;  (* TWO *)
(*******************************************************)
PROCEDURE THREE;
BEGIN (* THREE *)
   (* procedure body *)
END;  (* THREE *)
(*******************************************************)
BEGIN (* SEGMENTED *)
   (* main program *)
END.  (* SEGMENTED *)
```

SEGMENT procedures and functions must precede any other executable blocks of code (procedures, functions or main program) in the program. The number of segments allowed depends on the version of UCSD Pascal you are using (anywhere from seven to 255). Each UNIT as well as the main program count as a segment.

The GOTO statement is more restricted in UCSD Pascal than in standard Pascal: only a branch to a label that is local to the same block containing the GOTO is allowed. The EXIT statement is provided to permit a clean exit from a procedure, function or program. It is useful for exiting a block (particularly a complicated or deeply nested block) when an error is encountered. EXIT requires a parameter to indicate the procedure, function or program to be exited.

EXIT (identifier)

The EXIT statement must be within the scope of its parameter. As with the GOTO, the EXIT should be used sparingly and with care to avoid poor program structure.

The following are some of the additional built-in procedures:

MARK(heappointer)	assigns to the heappointer the current top-of-heap. The heappointer is a user-defined pointer of type ↑INTEGER used to keep the location of the heap in memory.
RELEASE(heappointer)	assigns to the top-of-heap pointer the value of the heappointer.
MOVELEFT(source, destination, length)	moves from the source string to the destination string, starting from the left, the number of characters specified by length.
MOVERIGHT(source, destination, length)	moves from the source string to the destination string, starting from the right, the number of characters specified by length.
FILLCHAR(destination, length, character)	fills the destination string with the character specified to the length specified.
GOTOXY(x-coordinate, y-coordinate)	positions the cursor on the terminal screen at the coordinates specified. The top-left corner of the screen is position (0,0).

and functions:

SIZEOF(type or variable identifier)	returns the size in bytes of the entity specified by the identifier.
MEMAVAIL	returns the number of words of memory available (the memory words between the top-of-stack and top-of-heap).
SCAN(length, partial expression, array)	returns the number of characters scanned of the array. Termination of the scan is caused by matching the specified length or satisfying the expression. The partial expression may be either '<>' or '=' followed by a character value.
LOG(number)	returns the log base 10 of the number.
PWROFTEN(exponent)	returns the value of 10 to the exponent power.

Microcomputers are becoming very popular and widespread. UCSD Pascal is but one of several implementations available. Three other popular implementations for microcomputers are Pascal/M, Pascal/MT+, and Pascal/Z. UCSD Pascal includes its own operating system; the other three are designed to run under the CP/M operating system. UCSD Pascal and Pascal/M are very similar in their extensions to standard Pascal, and they both produce a P-code (intermediate pseudo-machine code) file as the result of compilation. To execute the P-code file requires an interpreter which is provided. Advantages of the P-code (interpreted) approach are faster compile time and greater ease of transporting the compiler from one machine to another (only the interpreter has to be rewritten for a different machine). In fact, implementations of UCSD Pascal exist for many machines, including both microcomputers and minicomputers. The other two implementations, Pascal/MT+ and Pascal/Z, produce machine code as the result of compilation. Compilation into machine code is slower than P-code compilation, but the resulting object code executes faster. One reasonable approach to software development would be to use a P-code compiler for development and a machine code compiler for the final production version. Pascal/MT+ is probably the closest implementation to the draft ISO standard.*

APPENDIX N CHARACTER SETS

The following charts show the ordering of the most common character sets: ASCII (American Standard Code for Information Interchange), EBCDIC (Extended Binary Coded Decimal Interchange Code) and CDC Scientific. Only printable characters are shown. The ordinal number for each character is shown in decimal. The blank character is denoted by a "□".

Left Digit(s) \ Right Digit	ASCII									
	0	1	2	3	4	5	6	7	8	9
3			□	!	"	#	$	%	&	'
4	(	)	*	+	,	–	.	/	0	1
5	2	3	4	5	6	7	8	9	:	;
6	<	=	>	?	@	A	B	C	D	E
7	F	G	H	I	J	K	L	M	N	O
8	P	Q	R	S	T	U	V	W	X	Y
9	Z	[	\	]	∧	–	`	a	b	c
10	d	e	f	g	h	i	j	k	l	m
11	n	o	p	q	r	s	t	u	v	w
12	x	y	z	{	I	}	~			

Codes 00–31 and 127 are nonprintable control characters.

*CDC is a trademark of Control Data Corporation. UCSD Pascal is a trademark of the Regents of the University of California. Pascal/M is a trademark of Sorcim. Pascal/MT+ and CP/M are trademarks of Digital Research. Pascal/Z is a trademark of Ithaca Intersystems.

Left Digit(s)	Right Digit → EBCDIC									
	0	1	2	3	4	5	6	7	8	9
6					□					
7					¢	.	<	(	+	|
8	&									
9	!	$	*	)	;	¬	–	/		
10							^	,	%	—
11	>	?								
12			:	#	@	'	=	"		a
13	b	c	d	e	f	g	h	i		
14						j	k	l	m	n
15	o	p	q	r						
16			s	t	u	v	w	x	y	z
17								\	{	}
18	[	]								
19				A	B	C	D	E	F	G
20	H	I								J
21	K	L	M	N	O	P	Q	R		
22							S	T	U	V
23	W	X	Y	Z						
24	0	1	2	3	4	5	6	7	8	9

Codes 00-63 and 250-255 are nonprintable control characters.

Left Digit(s)	Right Digit → CDC									
	0	1	2	3	4	5	6	7	8	9
0	:	A	B	C	D	E	F	G	H	I
1	J	K	L	M	N	O	P	Q	R	S
2	T	U	V	W	X	Y	Z	0	1	2
3	3	4	5	6	7	8	9	+	–	*
4	/	(	)	$	=	□	,	.	≡	[
5	]	%	≠	↦	V	∧	↑	↓	<	>
6	≤	≥	¬	;						

Glossary

ACM   Association for Computing Machinery, a professional society of computer scientists, programmers, and others interested in computers and data processing.

actual parameter   A variable or expression contained in a procedure or function call and passed to that procedure or function.

actual parameter list   The list of actual parameters contained in a procedure or function call.

address   A label (name, number or symbol) designating a location in memory.

algorithm   A step-by-step procedure for solving a problem in a finite amount of time.

allocate   To set aside space in memory. See dynamic and static allocation.

alphanumeric   A general term for human-readable alphabetic letters, numeric digits, and special characters that are machine processable.

ANSI   American National Standards Institute, an organization that promotes voluntary standards in the United States.

argument   See parameter.

arithmetic logic unit (ALU)   The computer component that performs arithmetic operations (addition, subtraction, multiplication, division) and logical operations (comparison of two values).

arithmetic operator   A symbol used in a numeric expression whose operation results in a numeric value.

array   A structured data type composed of a fixed number of components of the same type, with each component directly accessed by the index.

ASCII   American Standard Code for Information Interchange, a widely used encoding scheme for a character set composed of printable and control characters.

assembler A program that translates an assembly language program into machine code.

assembly language A language, similar to machine code, that uses mnemonics to represent operations and identifiers to represent addresses.

assignment operator The Pascal symbol ":=" used in an assignment statement.

assignment statement A statement that uses the assignment operator to assign a value to a variable or function.

base The number of digits used in a number system (e.g., decimal uses 10, binary uses 2).

base type The set of allowable values that a variable may take.

batch processing A technique for executing programs and data without intermediate user interaction with the computer.

binary operator An operator requiring two operands. See arithmetic operator, logical operator, relational operator.

binary tree A tree data structure in which each node has at most two offspring. See tree.

bit A BInary digiT (1 or 0) often used to represent information in a computer. Several bits make up a byte. See byte, word.

block A program unit consisting of an optional declarations part and a compound statement; program and procedure/function declarations consist of a heading and a block. Pascal is known as a block-structured language.

Boolean operator See logical operator.

branch See selection.

buffer An intermediate data storage area usually used to balance the different operating speeds of computer components (e.g., slow I/O and the faster CPU).

buffer variable See file buffer variable.

bug An error in a program that prevents compilation or execution or causes incorrect results.

byte A sequence of bits (often 8) used to encode a character within a computer. See word.

call A transfer of control from one portion of a program to a named subroutine (procedure or function).

cancellation error A loss in accuracy during addition or subtraction of numbers of widely differing sizes, due to limits of precision. See representational error.

cardinality The number of values contained in an ordinal type.

case statement A selection control structure that provides for multi-way selection of different courses of action; a generalization of the IF statement equivalent to nested IF-THEN-ELSE statements.

cathode ray tube (CRT) screen An electronic tube with a screen upon which visual information may be displayed (used in computer video terminals and television sets).

central processing unit (CPU) The "brain" of a computer, which interprets and executes instructions; the combination of the control unit and the arithmetic logic unit.

character set The set of machine-representable characters encoded according to a specific coding system. See collating sequence.

character string A string of alphanumeric characters. See string.

code All or part of a program. To write all or part of a program in a programming language. See programming language.

coding Writing code. See computer programming.

collating sequence The ordering of a computer's character set.

comment A note in a program intended for human understanding but ignored by the compiler.

comparison operator See relational operator.

compile To translate a program in a high-level language into machine language, using a compiler.

compile-time The phase of program translation (as opposed to the phase of program execution known as run-time).

compiler A program that translates a high-level language program (source code) into machine code (object code).

compiler options Selectable options chosen through command lines or program comment lines directing the compiler to perform compilation in certain ways.

component A logical part or element of a data structure.

component type See base type.

compound statement A group of statements between the Pascal reserved words BEGIN and END that are treated as a single statement.

computer A programmable electronic device that can store, retrieve, and process data.

computer program A sequence of instructions outlining the steps to be performed by a computer.

computer programming The process of planning a sequence of instructions for a computer to perform.

condition A Boolean expression used to determine the action of a selection or looping control structure.

conditional See selection.

constant A location in memory, referenced by a program constant name (identifier), where a data value is stored (this value cannot be changed).

control structure A construct that determines the flow of control in part of a program, and usually represented by a statement, with the basic types being the sequence, selection, and loop.

control unit The computer component that controls the actions of the other components in order to execute instructions (your program) in sequence.

data structure A composition of scalar types characterized by a particular structuring method.

data type See type.

declaration section The part(s) of a Pascal program where identifiers to be used in a procedure or program are specified.

default value An assumed value used by a system or compiler when no specific choice is given by the program or the user.

direct access See random access.

disk A secondary mass storage medium providing a large amount of permanent storage; a rotating magnetic disk used to store and retrieve magnetically encoded data through a read/write head that is in close proximity to the surface of the disk.

documentation Written descriptions, specifications, design, code and comments (internal and external to a program) which make a program readable, understandable, and more easily modified; also, a user's manual for a program. See self-documenting code.

dynamic allocation Creation of storage space in memory for a variable during run-time (as opposed to static allocation during compile-time). See referenced variable.

dynamic data structure A data structure that may expand and contract during run-time.

dynamic storage See dynamic allocation.

dynamic variable See referenced variable.

editor An interactive program that allows the user to create and alter text files such as data, programs, manuscripts, etc.

empty set The set with no members at all.

empty statement An allowable Pascal syntax, implying no action, that is created when two statement separators (such as a semi-colon and END) are used consecutively. Sometimes needed when no action is required after a case label list.

end-of-file (eof) marker The mechanism for indicating the end of a file.

end-of-line (eoln) marker The mechanism for indicating the end of a line. (Pascal returns a blank when this marker is read.)

enumerated type See user-defined type.

execute To carry out the instruction(s) in a statement or program; to run a program.

execution-time See run-time.

exponential notation See scientific notation.

expression A sequence of identifiers and/or constants, separated by compatible operators, that is evaluated at run-time.

external file A permanently stored file separate from the executing program.

field identifier The name of a component in a record.

field selector The expression used to access components of a Pascal record variable, consisting of the record variable name and the field identifier separated by a period.

fieldwidth specification In Pascal, a colon and integer value following a parameter in a WRITE statement, specifying the number of columns in which that parameter will be printed and right-justified.

file A data structure consisting of a sequence of components that are all of the same type; a collection of related data, usually stored on disk or tape, and referenced by a single name.

file buffer See file buffer variable.

file buffer variable A variable of the same type as the components of the file with which it is associated, and used as a "window" through which we can read or write file components. The logical file component.

floating point representation Also known as floating point notation. See scientific notation.

flow of control The order in which statements are executed in a program. See control structure.

for statement A looping control structure similar to a WHILE loop but with predefined initial and final values for the loop control variable, as well as automatic incrementing (or decrementing) of the loop control variable.

formal parameter A variable, declared and used in a procedure or function declaration, that is replaced by an actual parameter when the procedure or function is called.

formal parameter list The list of formal parameters contained in a procedure or function heading.

free format An allowable formatting of program statements characterized by no rules governing the indentation or number of syntax elements that may appear on a line of code.

function A subroutine that returns a value when called. See subroutine, parameter.

global identifier An identifier declared in the outermost block (main program); an identifier that is not local to a block but whose scope includes that block.

hardware The physical components of a computer.

high-level language A programming language that is closer to natural language than assembly language, and whose statements each translate into more than one machine language instruction.

identifiers Names that are associated with processes and objects and used to refer to those processes and objects. Pascal identifiers are made up of letters and numbers but must begin with a letter.

implementation The representation of a programming language on a particular computer system; a specific compiler and associated run-time support subroutines.

index An ordinal value identifying a particular component of a data structure such as an array.

infinite loop A loop whose terminating condition would never be reached; the loop would (theoretically) execute indefinitely and the program would never terminate.

initialize To assign an initial value to a variable.

input Any external data used by a program, from whatever source, such as a keyboard or disk file.

input/output (I/O) Media and devices used to achieve human/machine communication.

interactive processing Use of an interactive program; user interaction with a program usually by prompts, data entry, and commands made through a terminal.

interactive programming Use of an interactive system to create and compile programs through the use of an editor, compiler, debugger, and other tools.

interactive system Direct communication between the user and the computer; a terminal/computer connection allowing direct entry of programs and data and providing immediate feedback to the user.

interface A shared boundary where independent systems meet and act on or communicate with each other.

interpreter A program that translates each statement of a (usually) high-level language source program into a sequence of machine code instructions which are executed before the next statement of the source program is translated.

invoke See call.

ISO International Organization for Standardization, an organization that promotes voluntary standards.

label A name used in a computer program to identify an instruction, statement, data value, record, or file; an integer in the range 1 to 9999 declared in a Pascal label declaration and used to mark a particular statement, usually as the destination of an unconditional jump (GOTO).

literal A symbol that defines itself; a constant value such as a literal string or number.

listing See source listing.

local identifier An identifier declared in the block where it is used. See name precedence.

logical operator A symbol used in a Boolean expression whose operation results in a Boolean value of TRUE or FALSE.

loop A control structure that allows a statement(s) to be executed more than once (until a termination condition is reached).

loop control variable A variable (usually ordinal) used to control the number of times the body of a loop is executed.

machine code See machine language.

machine language The language used directly by the computer and composed of binary coded instructions.

main storage Also main memory. See memory.

memory The ordered sequence of storage cells (locations, words, places) in a computer that are accessed by address and used to temporarily hold the instructions and variables of an executing program. See secondary storage.

memory unit The internal data storage of a computer. See memory.

module An independent unit that is part of a whole; a logical part of a design or program, such as a procedure.

multi-dimensional array An array of one or more arrays.

name precedence The priority of a local identifier over a more global identifier, where the identifiers have the same name. See scope.

nested logic A control structure contained within another control structure.

NIL A constant in Pascal that can be assigned to a pointer variable, indicating that the pointer points to nothing.

object code The machine code producd by a compiler or assembler from a source program. Also called object program.

operating system The set of programs that manage computer resources.

operator A symbol that indicates an operation to be performed.

operator precedence See precedence rules.

ordinal type A set of distinct values that are ordered such that each value (except the first) has a unique predecessor and each value (except the last) has a unique successor; any scalar type except REAL.

output Data produced by a program and sent to an external file or device.

overflow A condition where the results of a calculation are too large to represent on a given machine. See precision.

packed array An array which occupies as little memory space as possible by having as many array components as possible packed into each memory word.

packed option A Pascal feature allowing more efficient storage of records and arrays.

parameter An expression passed in a procedure or function call. See actual parameter, formal parameter.

parameter list See actual parameter list, formal parameter list.

peripheral device An input, output, or auxiliary storage device of a computer.

pointer A simple data type, consisting of an unbounded set of values, which addresses or otherwise indicates the location of a variable of a given type.

powerset See universal set.

precedence rules The order in which operations are performed in an expression.

precision The maximum number of significant digits.

procedure A subroutine that is executed when called. See subroutine, parameter.

procedure call See call.

programming language A set of rules, symbols, and special words used to construct a program.

programming The planning, scheduling, or performing of a task or an event. See computer programming.

pseudo-code A mixture of English and Pascal-like control structures used to specify a design.

queue A data structure in which elements are entered at one end and removed from the other; a "first in, first out" (FIFO) structure.

random access The process of retrieving or storing elements in a data structure where the time required for such access is independent of the order of the elements.

range The smallest and largest allowable values.

range-checking The automatic detection of an out-of-range value being assigned to a variable.

real number One of the numbers that has a whole and a fractional part and no imaginary part.

record A structured data type with a fixed number of components (not necessarily of the same type) that are accessed by name (not subscript).

recursion The ability of a procedure or function to call itself.

referenced variable A variable accessed not by name but through a pointer variable; a dynamic variable; a variable created by the procedure NEW in Pascal.

relational operator A symbol that forms an expression with two values of compatible types, and whose operation of comparing these values results in a Boolean value of TRUE or FALSE.

repeat statement A looping control structure similar to a WHILE loop, except that there will always be at least one execution of the loop since the loop condition is tested after the body of the loop.

representational error An arithmetic error that occurs when the precision of the result of an arithmetic operation is greater than the precision of a given machine.

reserved word An identifier that has a specific meaning in a programming language and may not be used for any other purpose in a program.

root node The external pointer to a tree data structure; the top or base node of a tree.

round off To truncate (or make zero) one or more least significant digits of a number, and to increase the remaining least significant digit by one if the truncated value is more than half of the number base. Pascal provides a function to round off a real value to the nearest integer.

run-time The phase of program execution during which program instructions are performed.

scalar data type A set of distinct values (constants) that are ordered.

scientific notation A method of representing a number as an expression consisting of a number between 1 and 10 multiplied by the appropriate power of 10. Also called floating point notation.

scope The range or area within a program in which an identifier is known.

secondary storage Backup storage for the main storage (memory) of a computer, usually permanent in nature (such as tape or disk).

selection A control structure that selects one of possibly several options or paths in the flow of control, based upon the value of some expression.

self-documenting code A program containing meaningful identifier names, as well as the judicious use of clarifying comments.

semantics The set of rules which give the meaning of a statement.

sentinel A special data value used to mark the end of a data file.

sequential access The process of retrieving or storing elements in a fixed order in a data structure where the time required for such access is dependent on the order of the elements.

set A structured data type composed of a collection of distinct elements (members) chosen from the values of the base type.

side effects A change, within a procedure or function, to a variable that is external to, but not passed to, the procedure or function.

significant digits Those digits that begin with the first non-zero digit on the left and end with the last non-zero digit on the right (or a zero digit that is exact).

simple type A scalar type; a type that is not structured; any of the Pascal types INTEGER, REAL, BOOLEAN, CHAR or any user-defined (ordinal) type.

software Computer programs; the set of all programs available to a computer.

source code Also called source program; a program in its original form, in the language in which it was written, prior to any compilation or translation.

source listing A printout of a source program processed by a compiler and showing compiler messages, including any syntax errors in the program.

stack A data structure in which elements are entered and removed from only one end; a "last in, first out" (LIFO) structure.

statement An instruction in a programming language.

statement separator A symbol used to tell the compiler where one instruction ends and another begins in a program, such as the semi-colon in Pascal.

static allocation Creation of storage space in memory for a variable at compile-time (cannot be changed at run-time).

static data structure A data structure fixed in size at compile-time. See static allocation.

step-wise refinement A design method in which an algorithm is specified at an abstract level and additional levels of detail are added in successive iterations throughout the design process. See top-down design.

storage See memory.

string A collection of characters interpreted as a single data item; a packed character array.

structured design A design methodology incorporating a high degree of modularity, and employing generic control structures having only one entry and one exit. See top-down design.

structured programming The use of structured design and the coding of a program that parallels the structure of the design. See top-down programming.

structured type A type composed of more than one element, which at its lowest level is a simple type; any of the Pascal types ARRAY, RECORD, SET, and FILE.

subprogram See subroutine.

subrange type A data type composed of a specified range of any standard or user-defined ordinal type.

subroutine A collection of statements in a program, but not part of the main program, that is treated as a named entity, performs a specific task, and is capable of being called (invoked) from more than one point in the program; a function or procedure in Pascal.

subscript See index.

subscripted variable See array.

subset The set A is a subset of the set B if each element of A is an element of B.

syntax The formal rules governing the construction of valid statements in a language.

syntax diagram A pictorial definition of the syntax rules of a programming language.

system software The set of programs that improves the efficiency and convenience of using a computer, such as the operating system, editor and compiler.

tape A secondary mass storage medium providing a large amount of permanent storage; a thin plastic strip having a magnetic surface used to store and retrieve magnetically encoded data through a read/write head that is in close proximity to the surface of the tape.

text file A file of characters that is also divided into lines.

time sharing A method of operation in which a computer is shared by several users simultaneously.

top-down design A design methodology that works from an abstract functional description of a problem (top) to a detailed solution (bottom); a hierarchical approach to problem solving that divides a problem into functional sub-problems represented by modules, which are easier to solve and which may themselves be further broken down into modules. The design consisting of a hierarchy of separate modules (solutions), with lower level modules containing greater detail than higher level modules. See structured design.

top-down programming Programming that incorporates top-down design, and, through the use of procedures, functions, and control structures, maintains in the program the modularity and structure of the design.

top-down testing A technique for testing the modules (procedures and functions) of a program, as they are written, by calling them with actual parameters and providing stub (dummy) modules for those modules not yet written but referenced in the program.

trace To follow the logical flow of a program and determine the value of variables after each instruction. Also known as code walk-through and playing computer.

translator A program that translates from one programming language to another (usually machine code). See assembler, compiler, interpreter.

tree A data structure composed of a root node having offspring that are also nodes that can have offspring, and so on.

tree diagram A hierarchical chart showing the relationships of modules in a top-down design.

truncation The decrease in precision of a number by the loss or removal of one or more least significant digits.

type A formal description of the set of values that a variable of a given type may take or to which a datum of that type must belong.

type definition A definition of a data type in Pascal in the type declaration of a block, with the type identifier on the left of the equal sign ("=") and the definition on the right.

unary operator An operator requiring only one operand such as the logical operator NOT.

underflow A condition that occurs when the results of a calculation are too small to represent in a given machine.

universal set The set consisting of all values of the base type.

user-defined (enumerated) type The ordered set of distinct values (constants) defined as a data type in a program. See ordinal type.

value parameter A formal parameter that is a local variable of a procedure or function, but whose value is initialized to the value of an actual parameter in a call to the procedure or function.

variable A location in memory, referenced by a program variable name (identifier), where a data value can be stored (this value can be changed during program execution).

variable declaration The creation of a variable in Pascal in the variable declaration section of a block with the variable identifier on the left of the colon (":") and the type definition or identifier on the right.

variable parameter A formal parameter that is replaced by an actual parameter in a call to a procedure or function.

window See file buffer variable.

word A group of bits, one or more bytes in length, treated as a unit or location in memory, and capable of being addressed.

word size The number of bits comprising a word or location in memory.

Exercise Answers

CHAPTER 2

1. (a) invalid (b) valid (c) valid (d) invalid (e) valid
   (f) invalid (g) valid (h) invalid

2. (a) invalid (b) invalid (c) valid (d) invalid (e) valid
   (f) invalid (g) valid (h) valid

3. `CONST INCHESPERFOOT = 12;`

4. `VAR RATE, WEIGHT : REAL;`

5. 5

6. ```
   VAR BIRTHYR : INTEGER;
       GDPT : REAL;
       MARK : BOOLEAN;
       CODE : CHAR;
       ID : INTEGER;
   ```

7. ```
   WRITELN('***DANGER***');
   WRITELN('OVERVOLTAGE CONDITION')
   ```

8. TRUE

9. (a) `A := B + C;` or `C := A + B;`
   (b) `Y := CONTENTS;`
   (c) `X := B;`
   (d) `PROGRAM ONE(INPUT,OUTPUT);`
   (e) `CONST X = 18;`

10. TRUE

11. `WRITELN('AMOUNT = ', AMOUNT)`

12. COST IS
        300
    PRICE IS   30COST IS   300
    GRADE A COSTS   300

CHAPTER 3

1. TRUE

2. (a) 13.33 REAL
   (b) 2   INTEGER
   (c) 5   INTEGER
   (d) 13.75 REAL
   (e) −4 INTEGER
   (f) 1.0 REAL
   (g) Can't be evaluated—MOD operator is for integer operands only.

3. (a) 3   (b) 4   (c) 37   (d) 22   (e) 23   (f) 100

4. (a) READLN(SOCSEC, DEPTNO);
       READLN(DEDUCTCODE, REGHRS, OTHRS)
   (b) READ(STUDENTID, BLANK, CLASSCODE, BLANK, GRADE1,
           BLANK, GRADE2, BLANK, GRADE3, BLANK, GRADE4)
   (*BLANK is of type CHAR*)

5. TEMP   U
   VAR   R
   BEGIN   R
   CONST   R
   CONSTANT   U
   SIGNAL   U
   FLAG   U
   PROGRAM   R

6. A =   5 B =   2
   SUM =   7
           2
          -3

7. (A) 24   (B) 72   (C) 46   (D) 18

8.   X   Y   Z
     ─   ─   ─

     ─   ─   ─
     25   20   2
     47   20   2
      1   20   2
      1   20   10
      1   11   10
    −27   11   10
    −27   11   10
    −27   11   10

9. **Input:** invoice number, quantity ordered, unit price (INTEGERS)
   Output: input data and total price
   Assumptions: assume data is correct

   MAIN

   ```
   getdata
   gettotal
   printdata
   printtotal
   ```

   GETDATA

   ```
   READLN(INVNUM, QTY, UNITPRICE)
   ```

   GETTOTAL

   ```
   TOTAL = QTY * UNITPRICE
   ```

   PRINTDATA

   ```
   WRITELN('INVOICE NUMBER', INVNUM)
   WRITELN('QUANTITY ORDERED ', QTY,
           'UNIT PRICE ', UNITPRICE)
   ```

   PRINTTOTAL

   ```
   WRITELN('TOTAL PRICE = ', TOTAL)
   ```

   ```
   PROGRAM TOTALPRICE(INPUT,OUTPUT);
   VAR INVNUM, QTY, UNITPRICE, TOTAL : INTEGER;
   BEGIN
       READLN(INVNUM, QTY, UNITPRICE);
       TOTAL := QTY * UNITPRICE;
       WRITELN('INVOICE NUMBER ', INVNUM);
       WRITELN('QUANTITY ORDERED ', QTY, 'UNIT PRICE ',
               UNITPRICE);
       WRITELN('TOTAL PRICE =  ', TOTAL)
   END.
   ```

10. FALSE

CHAPTER 4

1. Not legal. (MINIMUMAGE <= AGE) AND (AGE < MAXIMUMAGE)

2. AVAILABLE := NUMBERORDERED <=
                   NUMBERONHAND - NUMBERRESERVED

3. VAR ELIGIBLE : BOOLEAN;
   •
   •
   •
   ELIGIBLE := TRUE;

4. (a) TRUE   (b) TRUE   (c) TRUE   (d) FALSE

5. CANDIDATE := (SATSCORE>=1100) AND (GPA>=2.5) AND
                  (AGE>15)

6. LEFTPAGE := (PAGENUMBER MOD 2) = 0   (*there are other ways*)

7. IF AGE > 64
      THEN WRITE('SOCIAL SECURITY')
      ELSE IF AGE < 18
              THEN WRITE('EXEMPT')
              ELSE WRITE('TAXABLE')

8. IF A > B
      THEN IF A > C
              THEN LARGEST := A
              ELSE LARGEST := C
      ELSE IF B > C
              THEN LARGEST := B
              ELSE LARGEST := C

   or

   IF A > B
      THEN LARGEST := A
      ELSE LARGEST := B;
   IF C > LARGEST
      THEN LARGEST := C

   or

   IF (A > B) AND (A > C)
      THEN LARGEST := A
      ELSE IF (B > A) AND (B > C)
              THEN LARGEST := B
              ELSE LARGEST := C

9. (a) ELIGIBLE TO SERVE
   (b) Nothing. The ELSE in the fourth line is part of the closest IF
       statement.

10. **Input:** birthday, birthmonth, birthyear (integers)
            current day, month, year (integers)

Output: birthdate
current age
Assumptions: data is correct

MAIN

```
getdata
findage
printbirthdate
printage
```

GETDATA

```
READ birthdate
READ current date
```

FINDAGE

```
IF (currentmonth > birthmonth) OR
    ((currentmonth = birthmonth) AND
    (currentday >= birthday))
    THEN AGE = currentyear − birthyear
    ELSE AGE = currentyear − birthyear − 1
```

PRINTBIRTHDATE

```
WRITELN('BIRTHDATE IS ', birthmonth, '/',
          birthday, '/', birthyear)
```

PRINTAGE

```
WRITELN('AGE IN YEARS = ', AGE)
```

```
PROGRAM COMPUTEAGE(INPUT,OUTPUT);
VAR BDAY, BMONTH, BYEAR,
    CURDAY, CURMONTH, CURYEAR, AGE : INTEGER;
BEGIN
    READ(BDAY, BMONTH, BYEAR);
    READ(CURDAY, CURMONTH, CURYEAR);
    IF (CURMONTH > BMONTH) OR
        ((CURMONTH = BMONTH) AND (CURDAY >= BDAY))
```

```
        THEN AGE := CURYEAR - BYEAR
        ELSE AGE := CURYEAR - BYEAR - 1;
    WRITELN('BIRTHDATE IS ', BMONTH:1, '/', BDAY:1,
            '/', BYEAR:2);
    WRITELN('AGE IN YEARS = ', AGE:1)
END.
```

Note: Your program and design may not look exactly like this. Also notice the fieldwidth specifications for the dates in the WRITELN statements. This gets rid of extra blanks so you would see '10/2/1960' output for an input of '02 10 1960'. The ':2' after BYEAR takes care of input years of either 2 or 4 digits. Chapter 5 discusses the fieldwidth specification in more detail.

11.
```
PROGRAM EXERCISE(INPUT,OUTPUT);
CONST A = 10;
      B = 5;
      C = 6;
VAR D, E, F : INTEGER;
BEGIN
    READ(D, E, F);
    IF (D > A)
        THEN D := A + D
        ELSE D := A;
    E := D + F;
    WRITE(' THIS PROGRAM DOES NOT MAKE ANY SENSE ',
          E, F, D)
END.
```

CHAPTER 5

1.
```
PROGRAM COUNT(INPUT,OUTPUT);
VAR INT, POSINT, NEGINT : INTEGER;
BEGIN
    POSINT := 0;
    NEGINT := 0;
    READ(INT);
    WHILE NOT EOF DO
        BEGIN
            IF INT < 0
                THEN NEGINT := NEGINT + 1
                ELSE IF INT > 0
                        THEN POSINT := POSINT + 1;
            READ(INT)
        END;
    WRITELN('NEGATIVE INTEGERS ', NEGINT,
            ' POSITIVE INTEGERS ', POSINT);
END.
```

2.
```
I := 16;
SUM := 0;
```

```
      WHILE I <= 26 DO
         BEGIN
            SUM := SUM + I;
            I := I + 2
         END
3.  I := 1;
    WHILE I <= 6 DO
       BEGIN
          J := 1;
          SUM := 0;
          WHILE J <= 5 DO
             BEGIN
                READ(DATA);
                SUM := SUM + DATA;
                J := J + 1
             END;
          WRITELN('CARD', I, ' SUM = ', SUM);
          READLN;
          I := I + 1
       END
```

Note: If the counters I and J were initialized to 0, the tests would be '<' instead of '<='.

```
4.  NEG := FALSE;
    COUNT := 1;
    WHILE (COUNT <= 10) AND NOT NEG DO
        BEGIN
           READ(DATA);
           IF DATA < 0
              THEN NEG := TRUE
              ELSE COUNT := COUNT + 1
        END
```

5. **Input:** N—number of integers followed by N integers
   Output: average
   Assumptions: data is correct

MAIN

```
getn
getdata (and find sum)
findaverage
printaverage
```

GETN

```
READ(N)
```

GETDATA

```
WHILE more data DO
      READ(INT)
      SUM = SUM + INT
```

FINDAVERAGE

```
AVE = SUM/N
```

PRINTAVERAGE

```
WRITELN 'AVERAGE = ' AVE
```

```
PROGRAM AVERAGE(INPUT,OUTPUT);
VAR N, I, SUM, INT : INTEGER;
    AVE : REAL;
BEGIN
    SUM := 0;
    I := 1;
    READ(N);
    WHILE I <= N DO
       BEGIN
          READ(INT);
          SUM := SUM + INT;
          I := I + 1
       END;
    AVE := SUM/N;
    WRITELN('AVERAGE = ', AVE)
END.
```

6.
```
OVERFLOW := FALSE;
WHILE NOT OVERFLOW DO
    BEGIN
       READ(LEVEL);
       IF LEVEL > 200.0
          THEN OVERFLOW := TRUE
    END
```

7.
```
PROGRAM TEMPSTAT(INPUT, OUTPUT);
VAR TEMP, HIGH, LOW, SUM, HOUR, AVERAGE : INTEGER;
BEGIN (*TEMP*)
  READ(TEMP);
  WRITELN(TEMP);
  HIGH := TEMP;
  LOW := TEMP;
```

```
       SUM := TEMP;
       HOUR := 1;
       WHILE HOUR < 24 DO
         BEGIN
           READ(TEMP);
           WRITELN(TEMP);
           SUM := SUM + TEMP;
           IF TEMP < LOW
               THEN LOW := TEMP
               ELSE IF TEMP > HIGH
                       THEN HIGH := TEMP;
           HOUR := HOUR + 1
         END;
       AVERAGE := SUM DIV 24;
       WRITELN('AVERAGE TEMPERATURE IS ', AVERAGE:4);
       WRITELN('HIGH TEMPERATURE IS ', HIGH:7);
       WRITELN('LOW TEMPERATURE IS ', LOW:8)
   END.  (*TEMP*)
```

8.
```
   READ(FIRST);
   WHILE NOT EOF DO
     BEGIN
       READ(SECOND);
       IF FIRST < SECOND
           THEN WRITELN(FIRST, SECOND)
           ELSE WRITELN(SECOND, FIRST);
       READ(FIRST)
     END
```

9. (a)
```
   WRITELN('SALES':13);
     WRITELN('WEEK1    WEEK2    WEEK3')
```
   (b)
```
   WRITELN(WEEK1:5, WEEK2:8, WEEK3:8)
```

CHAPTER 6

1. **Input:** integers
   Output: number of negative integers
                number of positive integers
   Assumptions: data is correct

   MAIN

   ```
   initialize
   processdata(NEGINT, POSINT)
   printvalues(NEGINT, POSINT)
   ```

INITIALIZE

```
initialize variables
```

PROCESSDATA

```
READ(INT)
WHILE NOT EOF DO
    IF INT < 0
        THEN NEGINT = NEGINT + 1
        ELSE IF INT > 0
                THEN POSINT = POSINT + 1
    READ(INT)
```

PRINTVALUES

```
WRITE(NEGINT, POSINT)
```

```
PROGRAM COUNT(INPUT,OUTPUT);
VAR NEGINT, POSINT : INTEGER;


(*****************************************************)

PROCEDURE PROCESSDATA(VAR NEGINT, POSINT : INTEGER);
VAR INT : INTEGER;
BEGIN (*PROCESSDATA*)
  READ(INT);
  WHILE NOT EOF DO
     BEGIN
        IF INT < 0
           THEN NEGINT := NEGINT + 1
           ELSE IF INT > 0
                   THEN POSINT := POSINT + 1;
        READ(INT)
     END
END; (*PROCESSDATA*)


(*****************************************************)

PROCEDURE PRINTVALUES(VAR NEGINT, POSINT : INTEGER);
BEGIN (*PRINTVALUES*)
   WRITELN('NEGATIVE INTEGERS ', NEGINT,
           ' POSITIVE INTEGERS ', POSINT)
END; (*PRINTVALUES*)
```

```
( ******************************************************** )
BEGIN  (*COUNT*)
    POSINT := 0;
    NEGINT := 0;
    PROCESSDATA(NEGINT, POSINT);
    PRINTVALUES(NEGINT, POSINT)
END.  (*COUNT*)
```

2. (a)
```
    PROCEDURE ADD(VAR N, M, ANSWER : INTEGER);
    VAR I : INTEGER;
    BEGIN
        ANSWER := 0;
        I := N;
        WHILE I <= M DO
            BEGIN
                ANSWER := ANSWER + I;
                I := I + 2
            END
    END;
```

(*Assumes N and M are even*)

(b)
```
    ADD(N, M, ANSWER)
```

(*Assumes N = 16 and M = 26*)
(*We can't use a constant for a variable parameter in the call to ADD, but we could for a value parameter as we shall see in Chapter 7*)

3. (a)
```
    PROCEDURE SUMS(VAR SUM : INTEGER;
                  VAR ALLPOSITIVE : BOOLEAN);
    VAR CT, DATA : INTEGER;
    BEGIN
        CT := 1;
        SUM := 0;
        ALLPOSITIVE := TRUE;
        WHILE ALLPOSITIVE AND (CT <= 10) DO
            BEGIN
                READ(DATA);
                IF DATA >= 0
                    THEN SUM := SUM + DATA
                    ELSE ALLPOSITIVE := FALSE;
                CT := CT + 1
            END
    END;
```

(*Assumes no premature EOF in data*)

(b)
```
    SUMS(SUM, ALLPOSITIVE)
```

4. See chapter text and glossary

5.   2   4   6   12

CHAPTER 7

1. TRUE

2. TRUE

3. TRUE

4. TRUE (Only if the identifier is not redeclared in an inner block.)

5. TRUE (Only if the referenced variable does not exist locally will the reference go to the closest outer block containing such a variable.)

6. (a) TRUE   (b) TRUE   (c) TRUE   (d) FALSE

7. (a) FALSE   (b) FALSE   (c) FALSE   (d) TRUE   (e) FALSE
   (f) TRUE   (g) FALSE   (h) TRUE   (i) TRUE   (j) TRUE

8. See text of Chapters 6 and 7 and glossary.

9. | A | 10 |
    | B | 7 |

    | X | 10 |
    | Y | 7 |
    | B | u |

    | A | 10 |
    | B | 17 |

10. | A | 5 |
    | B | 4 |

    | X | 5 |
    | Y | 4 |
    | B | u |

    | A | 9 |
    | B | 4 |

11. | A | 7 |
    | B | 10 |

    | X | 7 |
    | Y | 10 |
    | B | 10 |

    | A | 7 |
    | B | 7 |

12. PROGRAM SCOPERULES

```
┌──────────────────────────────────────────────────┐
│ VAR A, B : INTEGER                                 │
│                                                    │
│ PROCEDURE BLOCK1                                   │
│  ┌───────────────────────────────────────────┐    │
│  │ VAR A1, B1                                  │    │
│  │                                             │    │
│  │ PROCEDURE BLOCK2                            │    │
│  │  ┌──────────────────────────────────┐      │    │
│  │  │ VAR A, A2, B2 : INTEGER           │      │    │
│  │  └──────────────────────────────────┘      │    │
│  └───────────────────────────────────────────┘    │
│                                                    │
│ PROCEDURE BLOCK3                                   │
│  ┌───────────────────────────────────┐            │
│  │ VAR A3, B3 : INTEGER               │            │
│  └───────────────────────────────────┘            │
│                                                    │
└──────────────────────────────────────────────────┘
```

CHAPTER 8

1. ```
FUNCTION P5(DATA : REAL) : REAL;
BEGIN
   P5 := DATA * DATA * DATA * DATA * DATA
END;
```

2. ```
FUNCTION MIN(A, B, C : INTEGER) : INTEGER;
BEGIN
   IF (A<B) AND (A<C)
      THEN MIN := A
      ELSE IF (B<A) AND (B<C)
              THEN MIN := B
              ELSE MIN := C
END;
```

3. TRUE

4. FALSE

5. FALSE

6. ```
PROGRAM COUNT(INPUT, OUTPUT);
VAR INT, POSINT, NEGINT : INTEGER;
BEGIN
   POSINT := 0;
   NEGINT := 0;
   REPEAT
     READ(INT);
     IF NOT EOF
        THEN IF INT < 0
                THEN NEGINT := NEGINT + 1
                ELSE IF INT > 0
                        THEN POSINT := POSINT + 1
   UNTIL EOF;
   WRITELN('NEGATIVE COUNT = ', NEGINT,
           ' POSITIVE COUNT = ', POSINT)
END.
```

   ```
   I := 0;
   REPEAT
     I := I + 1;
     READ(DATA)
   UNTIL (DATA < 0) OR (I = 10)
   ```

7. ```
CASE GRADE OF
     'A' : SUM := SUM + 4;
     'B' : SUM := SUM + 3;
     'C' : SUM := SUM + 2;
     'D' : SUM := SUM + 1;
     'F' : WRITELN('STUDENT IS ON PROBATION')
END (*CASE*)
```

8. ```
CASE ERROR OF
      1 : WRITELN('INVALID INPUT');
      2 : WRITELN('RESULTS OUT OF RANGE');
      3 : WRITELN('ERROR TYPE 3');
    4,5 : WRITELN('UNDEFINED ERROR')
   END (*CASE*)
```

9. (a) TRUE    (b) TRUE    (c) FALSE    (d) FALSE    (e) FALSE
   (f) TRUE    (g) TRUE    (h) FALSE    (i) TRUE    (j) TRUE

10. (a) WRITELN(AREA)
   (b) can't be done—exponent is wrong
   (c) WRITELN(AREA:12:7)
   (d) WRITELN(AREA:7:2)

11. (1) FALSE    (2) TRUE    (3) FALSE    (4) FALSE    (5) TRUE

12. ```
FUNCTION FAC(N : INTEGER) : INTEGER;
   BEGIN
      IF N = 1
         THEN FAC := 1
         ELSE FAC := N * FAC(N-1)
   END;
```

CHAPTER 9

1. (a) ```
TYPE SCHOOL = (LINCOLN, JEFFERSON, ADAMS,
                 WASHINGTON);
```
   (b) ```
TYPE TEAM = (FIRST, SECOND, THIRD, SS,
              LF, RF, CF, CATCHER, PITCHER);
```
   (c) `TYPE FAMILY = (TOM, SALLY, JOE, RUTH);`

2. (a) `TYPE NUMERALS = '0'..'9';`
   (b) `TYPE RANGE = -4..24;`
   (c) `TYPE SUBTEAM = FIRST..SS;`

3. (a) `VAR ARY1 : ARRAY[1..24] OF REAL;`
   (b) `VAR ARY2 : ARRAY['A'..'Z'] OF INTEGER;`
   (c) `VAR ARY3 : ARRAY[-5..4] OF CHAR;`

4. (a) ```
FOR I := 1 TO 24 DO
     ARY1[I] := 0.0
```
   (b) ```
FOR CH := 'A' TO 'Z' DO
     ARY2[CH] := 0
```
   (c) `READ(ARY3[-5], ARY3[-4])`

5. ```
Assume: VAR I, J : 1..10;
             TEMP : THING;

I := 1;
J := 10;
WHILE I < J DO
```
```

```
      BEGIN
         TEMP := LIST[I];
         LIST[I] := LIST[J];
         LIST[J] := TEMP;
         I := I + 1;
         J := J - 1
      END
```

6. Assume: `VAR I : 1..83;`
           `SUM : INTEGER;`

```
   SUM := 0;
   FOR I := 1 TO 83 DO
      IF INSERVICE[I]
         THEN SUM := SUM + 1
```

7. TRUE   8. TRUE   9. FALSE   10. FALSE   11. FALSE

CHAPTER 10

1.
```
FUNCTION INDEX(VAR LIST : ARYTYPE;
                  VALU, LENGTH : INTEGER) : INTEGER;
VAR I : INTEGER;
    FOUND : BOOLEAN;
BEGIN
   I := 1;
   FOUND := FALSE;
   WHILE (I <= LENGTH) AND NOT FOUND DO
      IF VALU = LIST[I]
         THEN FOUND := TRUE
         ELSE I := I + 1;
   IF FOUND
      THEN INDEX := I
      ELSE INDEX := 0
END;
```

2. Assumes integer data
```
PROCEDURE MERGE(VAR ONE, TWO : TEXT; VAR COMB :
                  ARYTYPE; VAR LENGTH : INTEGER);
VAR VALONE, VALTWO : INTEGER;
BEGIN (*MERGE*)
   LENGTH := 0;
   READ(ONE, VALONE);
   READ(TWO, VALTWO);
   WHILE NOT EOF(ONE) AND NOT EOF(TWO) DO
      BEGIN
         LENGTH := LENGTH + 1;
         IF VALONE > VALTWO
            THEN
               BEGIN
```

```
                        COMB[LENGTH] := VALTWO;
                        READ(TWO, VALTWO)
                END
            ELSE IF VALONE = VALTWO
                    THEN
                        BEGIN
                            COMB[LENGTH] := VALONE;
                            READ(ONE, VALONE);
                            READ(TWO, VALTWO)
                        END
                    ELSE
                        BEGIN
                            COMB[LENGTH] := VALONE;
                            READ(ONE, VALONE)
                        END
        END;
    WHILE NOT EOF(ONE) DO
        BEGIN
            LENGTH := LENGTH + 1;
            COMB[LENGTH] := VALONE;
            READ(ONE, VALONE)
        END;
    WHILE NOT EOF(TWO) DO
        BEGIN
            LENGTH := LENGTH + 1;
            COMB[LENGTH] := VALTWO;
            READ(TWO, VALTWO)
        END
    END; (*MERGE*)
```

3. (a) `TYPE CODES = 'A'..'D';`
   `VAR SALES : ARRAY[CODES] OF REAL;`
   (b) `CONST NUMEMPLOYEES = 100;`
   `VAR ID : ARRAY[1..NUMEMPLOYEES] OF INTEGER;`
   `    DEP : ARRAY[1..NUMEMPLOYEES] OF INTEGER;`
   `    RATE : ARRAY[1..NUMEMPLOYEES] OF REAL;`
   `    TRANSID : INTEGER;`
   `    HOURS : REAL;`

4. (a) Get a transaction CODE and AMT.
   Increment SALES[CODE] by AMT.
   (b) This is a parallel arrays problem. One of the files must be read into a set of arrays. The second file must be read one set of values at a time and the ID searched for in the ID array.

5. Only the print procedure needs to be changed. It must read in the characters which are to be printed.

```
PROCEDURE PRINT(FREQ : LIST);
BEGIN (*PRINT*)
    WHILE NOT EOF DO
        BEGIN
```

```
          READ(CH);
          WRITELN(CH, ' OCCURRED ', FREQ[CH]:3, ' TIMES');
          IF EOLN THEN READLN          (*skip over <eoln> character*)
       END
   END; (*PRINT*)
```

CHAPTER 11

1. TRUE

2. (a) FALSE   (b) FALSE   (c) TRUE

3.
```
FOR A := 0 TO 60 DO
     FOR B := 1 TO 36 DO
          TABLE[A,B] := 0
```

4.
```
PROCEDURE INIT(VAR ARY : LIST; CH : CHAR;
                  N : INTEGER);
VAR I : INTEGER;
BEGIN
   FOR I := 1 TO N DO
       BEGIN
          ARY[I,I] := CH;
          ARY[N-I+1,I] := CH
       END
END;
```

5.
```
PROCEDURE MAXVAL(ARY : TABLE; VAR MAX : INTEGER;
                  N, M : INTEGER);
VAR I, J : INTEGER;
BEGIN
   MAX := -MAXINT;
   FOR I := 1 TO M DO
       FOR J := 1 TO N DO
           IF ARY[I,J] > MAX
               THEN MAX := ARY[I,J]
END;
```

CHAPTER 12

1.
```
TYPE BOOK = RECORD
               TITLE : ARRAY[1..100] OF CHAR;
               NUMAUTHORS : INTEGER;
               AUTHORS : ARRAY[1..100] OF CHAR;
               PUBL : ARRAY[1..40] OF CHAR;
               PUBDATE : INTEGER
            END; (*RECORD*)
```

2. (a) TYPE STUDENTREC = RECORD

```
                              NAME : ARRAY[1..20] OF CHAR;
                              SOCSECNUM:ARRAY[1..11]OF CHAR;
                              CLASS : (FRESHMAN,SOPHOMORE,
                                         JUNIOR,SENIOR);
                              GDPT : REAL;
                              SEX : (M, F)
                          END;   (*RECORD*)
   (b) VAR STUDENT : STUDENTREC;
          .
          .
       BEGIN
          .
          .
       WRITELN(' NAME        SOCSEC#         CLASS        GDPT',
               '      SEX');
       FOR I := 1 TO 20 DO
           WRITE(STUDENT.NAME[I]);
       WRITE(' ');
       FOR I := 1 TO 11 DO
           WRITE(STUDENT.SOCSECNUM[I]);
       WRITE(' ');
       CASE STUDENT.CLASS OF
           FRESHMAN : WRITE(' FRESHMAN');
           SOPHOMORE : WRITE(' SOPHOMORE');
           JUNIOR : WRITE(' JUNIOR');
           SENIOR : WRITE(' SENIOR')
       END;   (*CASE*)
       WRITE(STUDENT.GDPT:5:2);
       CASE STUDENT.SEX OF
           M : WRITE(' MALE');
           F : WRITE(' FEMALE')
       END;   (*CASE*)
       WRITELN

   (c) VAR ROLL : ARRAY[1..3000] OF STUDENTREC;

3. PROCEDURE INIT(VAR TOME : BOOK);
   CONST BLANK = ' ';
   VAR I : INTEGER;
   BEGIN
     FOR I := 1 TO 100 DO
         TOME.TITLE[I] := BLANK;
     TOME.NUMAUTHORS:= 0;
     TOME.AUTHORS := TOME.TITLE;
     FOR I := 1 TO 40 DO
         TOME.PUBL[I] := BLANK;
     TOME.PUBDATE:= 0
   END;

4. TYPE PART = RECORD
                 NUM : INTEGER;
```

```
                  PRICE : REAL
              END;  (*RECORD*)
  VAR PARTS : ARRAY[1..MAXLENGTH]OF PART;
      LENGTH, PTR, I : INTEGER;
      FOUND : BOOLEAN;
      NEWPART : PART;
        .
        .
        .

    LENGTH := 0;
    WHILE NOT EOF DO
      BEGIN
        READLN(NEWPART.NUM, NEWPART.PRICE);
        PTR := 1;
        FOUND := FALSE;
        WHILE NOT FOUND AND (PTR <= LENGTH) DO
          IF NEWPART.NUM < PARTS[PTR].NUM
            THEN FOUND := TRUE
            ELSE PTR := PTR + 1;
        FOR I := LENGTH DOWNTO PTR DO
            PARTS[I+1] := PARTS[I];
        PARTS[PTR] := NEWPART;
        LENGTH := LENGTH + 1
      END
5. TYPE STRING = ARRAY[1..30] OF CHAR;
      COURSEGRADE = RECORD
                      COURSEID : INTEGER;
                      GRADE : CHAR
                    END; (*RECORD*)
      GRADELIST = ARRAY[1..50] OF COURSEGRADE;
      DATE = RECORD
                MO : 1..12;
                YR : 1900..2000
             END; (*RECORD*)
      CLASSTYPE = (FRESH, SOPH, JR, SR, GRAD);
      STUDENT = RECORD
                  NAME : STRING;
                  ID,
                  HRSCREDIT,
                  COURSECNT : INTEGER;
                  GRADES : GRADELIST;
                  ENROLLDATE : DATE;
                  CLASS : CLASSTYPE;
                  GPA : REAL
                END; (*RECORD*)
```

6. (a) FALSE   (b) FALSE   (c) TRUE   (d) FALSE   (e) TRUE
    (f) FALSE   (g) TRUE   (h) TRUE   (i) TRUE

7. (a) AREF := AMAP.CHART
    (b) GUIDE[4] := AMAP

```
(c) GUIDE[10].MAPCODE := ACODE

(d) IF ACODE[1] = GUIDE[2].MAPCODE[1]
        THEN
          BEGIN
            FOR I := 1 TO 25 DO
              WRITE(GUIDE[2].MAPCODE[I]);
            WRITELN;
            IF GUIDE[2].STYLE = FORMAL
                THEN WRITELN('FORMAL')
                ELSE WRITELN('BRIEF')
          END

    or

    WITH GUIDE[2] DO
      IF ACODE[1] = MAPCODE[1]
          THEN
            BEGIN
              FOR I := 1 TO 25 DO
                  WRITE(MAPCODE[I]);
              WRITELN;
              IF STYLE = FORMAL
                  THEN WRITELN('FORMAL')
                  ELSE WRITELN('BRIEF')
            END

(e) WITH AMAP.CHART DO
      BEGIN
        FOR I := 1 TO 2000 DO
          BEGIN
            J := 1;
            MATCH := TRUE;
            WHILE MATCH AND (J <= 25) DO
              IF AREF.TOKEN[I,J] = TOKEN[I,J]
                THEN J := J + 1
                ELSE MATCH := FALSE;
            IF NOT MATCH
                THEN WRITELN('TOKEN ', I)
          END;
        FOR I := 1 TO 20 DO
          BEGIN
            J := 1;
            MATCH := TRUE;
            WHILE MATCH AND (J <= 25) DO
              IF AREF.SYMBOL[I,J] = SYMBOL[I,J]
                THEN J := J + 1
                ELSE MATCH := FALSE;
            IF NOT MATCH
                THEN WRITELN('SYMBOL ', I)
          END
      END
```

CHAPTER 13

1.
```
FUNCTION LENGTH(STR : STRING) : INTEGER;
VAR I : INTEGER;
    PAD : BOOLEAN;
BEGIN
  I := 20;
  PAD := TRUE;
  WHILE PAD AND (I>0) DO
    IF STR[I] = ' '
      THEN I := I -1
      ELSE PAD := FALSE;
  LENGTH := I
END;
```

2.
```
PROCEDURE REVERSELINE(VAR DATA : TEXT; VAR LN : LINE);
VAR I, J : INTEGER;
    TEMP : ARRAY[1..80]OF CHAR;
BEGIN
  I := 1;
  WHILE NOT EOLN(DATA) DO                       (*get line*)
    BEGIN
      READ(DATA, TEMP[I]);
      I := I + 1
    END;
  FOR J := 1 TO I-1 DO                          (*reverse line*)
      LN[J] := TEMP[I-J];
  FOR J := I TO 80 DO                           (*pad with blanks*)
      LN[J] := ' '
END;
```

3. The following procedure includes error checking.
```
PROCEDURE GETSYMBOL(VAR DATAFILE : TEXT; VAR SYM :
                    SYMBOL; VAR ERROR : BOOLEAN);
VAR CH : CHAR;
    I : INTEGER;
BEGIN
  ERROR := FALSE;
  IF NOT EOF(DATAFILE)
    THEN READ(DATAFILE, CH);
  WHILE NOT EOF(DATAFILE) AND (CH <> '*') DO    (*find '*'*)
    READ(DATAFILE, CH);
  IF EOF(DATAFILE)
    THEN ERROR := TRUE                          (*no symbol found*)
    ELSE
      BEGIN
        I := 1;
        WHILE NOT EOF(DATAFILE) AND (I<=5) DO
          BEGIN
            READ(DATAFILE, CH);
            SYM[I] := CH;
            I := I + 1
```

```
                        END;
                IF EOF(DATAFILE)
                    THEN ERROR := TRUE          (*premature EOF*)
                    ELSE
                        BEGIN
                            READ(DATAFILE, CH);
                            IF CH <> '*'         (*check terminator*)
                                THEN ERROR := TRUE
                        END
            END
END;
```

(*This procedure would be much shorter without error checking*)

4. The following does not include error checking.

```
   Assume:  VAR LIST : ARRAY[1..20]OF WORD;
                TOKEN : WORD;
                DATAFILE : TEXT;
                FOUND : BOOLEAN;
                LENGTH, PTR, I : INTEGER;
                CH : CHAR;
        .
        .
        .
   RESET(DATAFILE);
   LENGTH := 0;
   WHILE LENGTH < 20 DO
     BEGIN
       FOR I := 1 TO 20 DO                        (*get a word*)
         BEGIN
           READ(DATAFILE, CH);
           TOKEN[I] := CH
         END;
       READLN(DATAFILE);                          (*go to next line*)
       PTR := 1;
       FOUND := FALSE;
       WHILE NOT FOUND AND (PTR <= LENGTH) DO
         IF TOKEN < LIST[PTR]
             THEN FOUND := TRUE
             ELSE PTR := PTR + 1;
       FOR I := LENGTH DOWNTO PTR DO
           LIST[I+1] := LIST[I];                  (*shift words*)
       LIST[PTR] := TOKEN;                        (*insert word*)
       LENGTH := LENGTH + 1
     END;
   REWRITE(DATAFILE);
   FOR I := 1 TO 20 DO                            (*put sorted words in file*)
       WRITELN(DATAFILE, LIST[I]);
        .
        .
        .
```

5.
```
FUNCTION CHECK(STR1, STR2 : WORD) : BOOLEAN;
BEGIN
   CHECK := STR1 = STR2
END;
```

6.
```
WRITELN(PERSON.NME);
WRITELN(PERSON.ADDR);
WRITELN('CLASS - ', PERSON.CLASS:1);
IF PERSON.SEX = M
   THEN WRITELN('MALE')
   ELSE WRITELN('FEMALE')
```

7. (a) T   (b) T   (c) F   (d) T   (e) F   (f) F   (g) F   (h) T
   (i) F   (j) T

8.
```
GET(DATA);
WHILE NOT EOF(DATA) DO
   BEGIN
      FOR I := 1 TO 10 DO
         SUM := SUM + DATA↑[I];
      AVERAGE := SUM / 10;
      WRITELN('AVERAGE - ', AVERAGE:10:3);
      GET(DATA);
   END
```

9. (a) I IN [1..24]
   (b) CH IN ['A', 'J', 'K']
   (c) X IN [1, 51..100]

10. (a) MONTHSET = SET OF MONTHS;
    (b) SUMMERMONTHS := [JUNE, JULY, AUGUST]
    (c) WINTERMONTHS := [DECEMBER, JANUARY, FEBRUARY]
    (d) SCHOOLMONTHS := [SEPTEMBER..DECEMBER, JANUARY..MAY]
    (e) JMONTHS := [JANUARY, JUNE, JULY]
    (f) [JUNE, JULY, AUGUST, DECEMBER, JANUARY, FEBRUARY]
        [JUNE, JULY]
        []
        [SEPTEMBER..DECEMBER, FEBRUARY..MAY]
        [DECEMBER, JANUARY, FEBRUARY]
    (g) TRUE
        TRUE
        FALSE
        TRUE

CHAPTER 14

1.

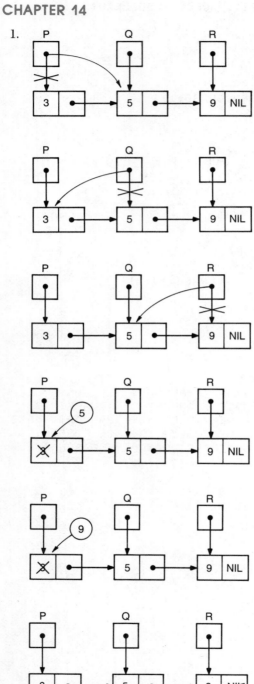

2. (a) P↑.NEXT := P↑.NEXT↑.NEXT
    (b) R↑.NEXT := S
    (c) LIST := P↑.NEXT
    (d) P↑.NEXT↑.NEXT := LIST

3. (a)   1   1
    (b)   2   0

4. False

5.   0   0

6. (a) NEW(P);
        P↑.EMPNO := 0;   (* lowest legit. empno = 1 *)
        P↑.NEXT := NIL;
        EMPLOYEES := P;

    (b) VAR I : INTEGER;
            CH : CHAR;

            .
            .
            .

        NEW(P);
        WITH P↑ DO
          BEGIN
            FOR I := 1 TO 25 DO
              BEGIN
                READ(CH);
                NAME[I] := CH
              END;
            READ(DEPTNO);
            READ(EMPNO);
            READLN(SALARY);
          END

    (c) PROCEDURE INSERT(EMPLOYEES, EMP : PTR);
        VAR P, BACK : PTR;
            PLACEFOUND : BOOLEAN;
        BEGIN (* INSERT *)
          PLACEFOUND := FALSE;
          BACK := NIL;   (* initialize pointer *)
          P := EMPLOYEES;
          WHILE (P <> NIL) AND NOT PLACEFOUND DO
                                        (* find place to insert *)
              IF EMP↑.EMPNO > P↑.EMPNO
                 THEN
                   BEGIN
                     BACK := P;
                     P := P↑.NEXT;
                   END
                 ELSE PLACEFOUND := TRUE;
          EMP↑.NEXT := P;
          BACK↑.NEXT := EMP
        END; (* INSERT *)

Note that there is a header node so we never need to insert at the beginning of the list.

7. (a)
```
FUNCTION EVEN (P : ↑NODE) : BOOLEAN;
BEGIN
   IF P↑.INFO MOD 2 = 0
      THEN EVEN := TRUE
      ELSE EVEN := FALSE
END;
```

Must be a type identifier.

(b)
```
PROCEDURE SUCCESSOR (P : PTR);
BEGIN
   WHILE P↑.NEXT <> NIL DO
      BEGIN
         WRITELN(P↑.INFO, ' IS FOLLOWED BY ',
            P↑.NEXT↑.INFO);
         P := P↑.NEXT
      END
END;
```

The original loop condition would make this an illegal reference when P ↑ .NEXT = NIL.

Programming Assignments

Chapter 2

1. Input and run the following program. Lowercase information within parentheses is to be filled in by you. This information is called *program documentation*.

```
PROGRAM ONE(INPUT, OUTPUT);
(*   PROGRAMMING ASSIGNMENT ONE                    *)
(*   (your name)                                    *)
(*   (date copied and run)                          *)
(*   (description of the problem)                   *)

CONST   DEBT  = 300.0;   (* ORIGINAL VALUED OWED *)
        PAYMT = 22.4;    (* PAYMENT *)
        INTR  = 0.02;    (* INTEREST RATE *)
VAR   CHARG,             (* INTEREST TIMES DEBT *)
      REDUC,             (* AMOUNT DEBT IS REDUCED *)
      REMAIN : REAL;     (* REMAINING BALANCE *)
BEGIN
   CHARG  := INTR * DEBT;
   REDUC  := PAYMT - CHARG;
   REMAIN := DEBT - REDUC;
   WRITELN('PAYMENT ', PAYMT, ' CHARGE ',
           CHARG, ' BALANCE OWED ', REMAIN)
END.
```

The assignments represented here have been collected over a period of years. As they have been used, revised, and used again, the original authors have been forgotten. We therefore wish to acknowledge collectively the people who have taught the courses where the assignments were used: Angus Pearson, Dick Edmiston, Mike Smith, Larry Mahaffey, Woody Bledsoe, Joyce Brennan, Sarah Barron, Tom Rowan, and Bill Bulko.

Note: Several of these assignments make use of random numbers. Most Pascal compilers have random number generators. Since they vary in name and input, we leave the description to the instructor or specific system documentation.

2. Copy and run the following program. Fill in the comments by using the pattern shown in Assignment 1 above. Such information is entered for the clarification of someone reading the program.

```
PROGRAM TWO(INPUT, OUTPUT);
CONST TCOST = 600;
        POUNDS = 10;
        OUNCES = 11;
VAR TOTOZ,
    UCOST : REAL;
BEGIN
  TOTOZ := 16 * POUNDS;
  TOTOZ := TOTOZ + OUNCES;
  UCOST := TCOST / TOTOZ;
  WRITELN('COST PER UNIT ', UCOST)
END.
```

(Note how hard it was to tell what the program was doing without the comments already in the code.)

Chapter 3

1. In Assignment 1 for Chapter 2, the values for DEBT, PAYMT, and INTR were set as constants. For this assignment, rewrite that program so that DEBT, PAYMT, and INTR are read in. You will need to make the following changes:
   1. Change your comments.
   2. Add INTR, DEBT, and PAYMT to the VAR section (after removing them from the CONST section).
   3. Read values into INTR, DEBT, and PAYMT.

2. Write a program to calculate the cost of glasswork and metal stripping for rectangular windows. All windows, no matter what size, use the same quality of glass and aluminum strips, therefore the unit prices are *constants* for all windows:

   glass : 50 cents per square inch (unit area)
   aluminum : 75 cents per inch (unit length)

   The length and width of a window should be read as input data. You may select *any one* out of the following three sets (all measured in inches), as your input data:

$$60, 30$$
$$55, 24$$
$$25, 18$$

Output: (all properly labeled)
   1. Echo print the input data.
   2. The total cost, the sum of the costs of glasswork and metal strips may be expressed as cents.

Note: Area = length × width
   Perimeter = 2 × (length + width)
   100 cents make a dollar

3. The metric system is upon us! Even the daily temperature on the news is given in centigrade. You know the formula for conversion is

$$C = \frac{5}{9} * (F - 32)$$

but it takes too long to calculate. Your friend says that a good approximation when converting Fahrenheit to centigrade is to take half of the Fahrenheit temperature and subtract 15. How good an approximation is it?

    Write a Pascal program that reads in a temperature given in Fahrenheit, computes the centigrade equivalent by the actual formula, computes the approximation, and computes the percent difference between the two. The ouput should be properly labeled of course.

Input: Temperature in Fahrenheit

Output: 1. Temperature in Fahrenheit
        2. Correct temperature in centigrade
        3. Approximated version of temperature in centigrade
        4. Percent difference between approximation and actual temperature

4. Write a program to compute and print the area and the perimeter of the following:

a. a triangle (sides 3, 4, and 5 inches)
b. a rectangle (sides 7 and 9 inches)
c. a circle (6 inches in diameter)

5. Read in three integers representing the blastoff time of a rocket expressed in hours, minutes, and seconds on a 24-hour clock. Then read another integer giving the rocket's flight time in seconds. Use these data values to calculate the time of day at which the rocket will return to earth, and print out this time in a readable format. You may assume that the rocket returns on the same day.

Input: Four integer numbers

Output: The expected time of return

Data: 3   47   32   45678

Remarks: 1. Always echo print the input data.
           2. Always label your output properly.

Chapter 4

1. You want to find the minimum number of rolls of coins (quarters, dimes, nickels, pennies) in a given amount of money. You also want to calculate the minimum number of coins in any amount left over. Use only integer arithmetic in solving this problem.

Input: A data line or card containing a single number that represents the total amount of money.

    Use the following number: 66.69

Output: 1. Echo print and label the input.
        2. Print a line for each coin, giving the number of rolls of that coin. If there are none, print an appropriate message (label each line).

3. Print the amount left over in cents and then the minimum number of coins to make up that amount; label.

Note: The amount in dollars for a roll of each coin is

quarters	$10.00
dimes	5.00
nickels	2.00
pennies	.50

2. Read in two numbers, D and R. D is the balance due for a customer's charge account. R is the amount received from the customer. Compare these two numbers. If they are equal, print the message 'NOTHING OWED'. If the amount received is greater than the amount due, the customer is given credit toward his account. Print out his credit balance. If the amount received is less than the amount owed, the new balance is computed by adding a 1.5 percent service charge to the unpaid amount. Print that amount.

3. Your great-grandmother wants you to paint the floor of her gazebo without wasting any paint. She knows from experience that it takes one quart of paint to cover 37 square feet of surface area. If the gazebo floor is 10 feet in diameter, how much paint should she buy? (Remember a gazebo is round and AREA = πR^2.) Your answer should be in quarts.

4. The Local Pizza Parlor advertises their giant pizza (15 inches in diameter) for $4.76 and their large pizza (10 inches in diameter) for $2.20. Susy and Sarah have decided that two 10-inch pizzas would be a better buy. Are they right?

5. The date for any Easter Sunday can be computed as follows: Let X be the year for which it is desired to compute Easter Sunday.

Let A be the remainder of the division of X by 19.
Let B be the remainder of the division of X by 4.
Let C be the remainder of the division of X by 7.
Let D be the remainder of the division of (19A + 24) by 30.
Let E be the remainder of the divison of (2B + 4C + 6D + 5) by 7.

The date for Easter Sunday is March (22 + D + E). (Note that this can give a date in April.)

Output: Print out the date for Easter Sunday for 1985.

Chapter 5

1. The date for any Easter Sunday can be computed as follows: Let X be the year for which it is desired to compute Easter Sunday.

Let A be the remainder of the division of X by 19.
Let B be the remainder of the division of X by 4.
Let C be the remainder of the division of X by 7.
Let D be the remainder of the division of (19A + 24) by 30.
Let E be the remainder of the division of (2B + 4C + 6D + 5) by 7.

The date for Easter Sunday is March (22 + D + E). (Note that this can give a date in April.) Write a Pascal program that prints out a table showing the dates of Easter Sunday from 1965 to 1980.

Output: A properly labeled table with two columns, one the year and the other the date of Easter Sunday for that year

2. Write a program to assign *letter grades* (A, B, C, D, F) to students and calculate *how many* students got A, B, etc.

    Input: 1. First line or card contains an INTEGER number giving the *total number* of students in the class.

        2. Following are as many lines or cards (one for each student) as the total number of students. Each line or card contains the following data:
   a. social security number (an INTEGER)
   b. *numerical grade* from 0 to 100 (also an INTEGER)

    Output: In tabular form,
   Social Sec. #   Numerical grade   Lettergrade
   for each student, per line of output.

    Following this table there should be five lines of output, one for each letter grade, telling *how many* students got that grade. The letter grade corresponds to the following ranges of numerical grades:

    A—above and including 90,
   B—from 80 to 89 (inclusive)
   C—from 70 to 79 (inclusive)
   D—from 60 to 69 (inclusive)
   F—below 60

3. You are a programmer for a polling service. They have just completed a survey of your area. Each respondent was asked which candidate he or she preferred in the 1980 presidential election. The responses were coded into integer numbers as follows:
   1—Jimmy
   2—Ronny
   3—Teddy
   4—Georgie

Your job is to determine the percentage each candidate got in the poll.

    Input: One number per data line or card. The first line or card in the data is the number of people in the survey.

Output:

```
TOTAL NUMBER IN SURVEY          9

NAME                 NUMBER          PERCENT

JIMMY                  3               33
TEDDY                  3               33
GEORGIE                3               33
RONNIE                 0                0
```

To calculate percentage use the following formula:

$$\text{percent} = (\text{no. favoring a candidate} * 100) / \text{total number in survey}$$

4. You do the accounting for a local soft drink distributorship that sells Coke (ID Num-

ber 1), Sprite (ID Number 2), Diet Coke (ID Number 3), and Diet Sprite (ID Number 4) by the case. Write a program to

a. read in the case inventory for each brand;
b. process all weekly sales and purchase records for each brand;
c. print out the final inventory.

Input: 1. First line or card—eight values representing the initial inventory (ID number followed by number of cases)
2. Remainder of data—an ID number and number of cases (A positive integer represents amount bought, a negative integer represents amount sold.) Use EOF to determine when you are through.

Output: Labeled output for each soft drink—the name, ID number, the number of transactions, and the final inventory for the transaction period

5. Write a program that determines the quantity in pounds and ounces of boxes of laundry soap. Each box will be described by two numbers in the form

total price (cents)	unit price (cents/ounce)
162	2

This box of soap contains 5 lb 1 oz of detergent.

Input: 1. First line or card—the number of boxes or records to follow (N)
2. Next N lines or cards—total price, unit price as described above.

Output: A labeled table giving total pounds, ounces, unit price, and actual price

6. In 1626 Peter Minuit purchased Manhattan Island from the Indians for $24 worth of beads and trinkets. If his money had been invested at 6% interest and the interest had been compounded annually, what would the investment be worth in 1985?

7. You borrow $1000 from a banker to buy a stereo. You pay 12% interest on this three-year loan, compounded semi-annually. What is the total amount you will pay for your stereo when the loan becomes due at the end of three years?

8. Most orb-weaver spiders build their webs at night. Their webs, which are used to capture prey, consist of both "spokes" and a spiral that radiates outward from the center or hub of the web. To be effective, web silk must remain sticky and must be repaired when torn by insects, wind, or other animals.

Assume that an orb-weaver spider must rebuild her web on three successive evenings because of some disturbance factor. For simulating this task the following assumptions may be made:

1. Only one web is built per evening.
2. The web is complete except for the spiral when the orb-weaver begins.
3. She begins the spiral at the hub.
4. Continual disturbances during the building of the web (modeled by calling the random generator) impede her building of the spiral.
5. Seven successful rounds are needed to complete the spiral of the web.
6. Each round is 2 cm greater than the size of the previous round.
7. The first round closest to the center is 2 cm in circumference.
8. Each call to the random generator is equivalent to 1 cm if successful (i. e., one "spin") and a round is completed when exactly 2 cm is reached for the firs round, 4 cm for the second round, etc.

9. You may assume that numbers generated less than 0.5 or greater than 0.5 are equal in probability and that numbers less than 0.5 are equivalent to unsuccessful "spins" and numbers greater than 0.5 are equivalent to successful "spins". The number 0.5 may be treated as part of either case.

Input: None

Output: For each of the three evenings:

    1. Print in a readable format the number of "spins" (each equivalent to 1 cm) necessary for the spider to complete each spiral round up to and including the seventh round.

    2. Print the total number of "spins" necessary to complete all 7 rounds of the spiral.

    For all evenings:

    1. Print the average number of "spins" for each successful round.

    2. If on any of the three evenings the spider does not complete the spiral in a total of 110 tries, abort the building of the web and print 'SHE'LL GO HUNGRY TONIGHT'.

Chapter 6

1. Write a program that reads in a sequence of grades (ranging from 0 to 100) and calculates the following information:

    a. the number of grades
    b. the average grade
    c. the minimum grade
    d. the maximum grade
    e. the number of failing grades (below 60)
    f. the number of passing grades

    Input: A sequence of integer numbers (Use EOF to determine when you have finished reading the numbers.)

    Output: 1. Echo print the numbers.
                  2. The six values described above properly labeled.

2. Knowing you are a computer whiz, a friend has asked you to write a program that calculates the mileage information for the car he drove on a recent vacation. At each stop for gas he recorded the odometer reading and the amount of gas purchased. Assume that he filled the tank each time. In addition assume that gas was purchased immediately prior to leaving for the trip and immediately upon return, taking odometer readings at each point. Design a program to read the total number of stops made (including the first and last), the odometer readings, and gas purchases. Then compute

    a. the gas mileage achieved between every pair of stops on the trip;
    b. the gas mileage achieved through the entire trip;
    c. the best gas mileage on a single tank.

3. The registrar's office would like a program that will process student's semester grades and a grade report for each student. This semester report will include the grade point average for each student.

$$\text{Grade point average} = \Sigma \, C(i)*W(i)/ \, \Sigma \, C(i)$$

where C(i) is credits for the course and W(i) is the weight for the grade (4 for A, 3 for B, 2 for C, 1 for D and 0 for F). If the sum of credits for a student is zero, print zero for the grade point average. All of the records for any one student are together in the input stream.

Input: Each student record indicates the number of courses taken, the course number, credits, and grade, and is written in the following form:

1. First line or card—student ID and number of courses taken
2. Next lines or cards (one for each course taken)—course number, credit hours, and grade (4, 3, 2, 1, 0)

There will be a set of lines or cards like these for each student.

Output: For each student print a report as follows (double space between students):

1. First line—student ID
2. Second lines (one for each course taken)—course number, credit, and grade
3. Last line—total credits taken, total credits received, semester point average; label appropriately

4. A very popular department on campus has problems with growing enrollment in its classes. The department decides that during registration it will go up to room limit on all of its classes, although, because of special permission and errors prior to registration week, some classes already have exceeded room size.

   The department would like to have a list for each day of the registration period, showing enrollment figures for each class. You have been asked to write a program that will print such a list.

Input: 1. First line of data—the number of classes on the list
   2. Other data lines—unique five-digit number, room size, current enrollment

Output: Echo print each line of input, with the following additional information on the same line (whichever applies):

1. If the class is full, a statement to that effect.
2. If the room limit has already been exceeded, a statement to that effect and the number of spaces exceeded.
3. If space is left in the class, a statement to that effect and the number of spaces left.

5. A local savings and loan association plans to use a computer to prepare statements for their new "save-spend" accounts. For each customer, a set of data entries is prepared, containing his or her account number and balance forwarded from the previous month. This is followed by transaction entries, which contain the customer's ID and the amount of the transaction. Account withdrawals will have a negative amount of transaction. The number of transactions is arbitrary. A new customer's leading entry is detected by a change in ID.

Output: For each customer print a report as follows:

1. First line—customer ID
2. Second line—heading line: item, deposits, withdrawals, balance
3. One line for initial balance and each transaction—deposit or withdrawal under appropriate heading; keep a running balance

4. Next line—Service charge (10¢ per withdrawal) and balance
5. Last line—Interest paid (1% on any final balance over $1000.00) and total (label each row correctly, e.g., service charge, interest)

6. A poor soul, considerably intoxicated, stands in the middle of a 10-ft-long bridge that spans a river. He staggers along, either toward the left bank or the right bank, but fortunately cannot fall off the bridge. Assuming that each step taken is exactly 1 ft long, how many steps will be taken before the drunkard reaches either bank of the river? It must be assumed that it is just as likely that a step will be toward the left bank as toward the right. You must do three things.

1. Find how many steps are taken in getting off the bridge.
2. Tell which bank is reached.
3. Let the drunkard go out for five nights and arrive at the same point (the center) of the bridge. Find, on the average, how many steps it takes to get off the bridge.

You will need to have a random number generator to solve this problem. (Check with your instructor for the name of the random function in your system.) You may assume that it is just as likely to generate a number less than .5 as the same or greater. The following is an example of the use of this function:

$$X := RANF(0.0)$$

X can be used to determine the direction of his next step. If the number of steps exceeds 100, print 'HE'LL HAVE TO SLEEP IT OFF'.

Chapter 7 ▬▬▬▬

1. The Chargall Company needs a billing system that takes a customer's current balance, computes the interest and adds it to the current balance, adds the current purchases, and determines the minimum payment due. Your job is to program this for them. The one restriction is that the form of the input data was determined before they hired you and cannot be changed. There are two types: the current balance and purchases. The current interest rate varies from month to month but the payment is always 1/10 of the new balance.

Purchases Format:

1–9	10	11 ⟶
social security number	,	amount of sale with decimal punched (may be credit); i.e., a negative amount

Current Balance Format:

1–9	10	11 ⟶
social security number	,	current balance with decimal punched

Before you receive it, the data has been sorted by social security number, with the current balance the last data item.

Example: 456491217, 12.36 ⎫
456491217, −5.00 ⎭ sales (or credits)
456491217, 242.0 current balance
921007121, 25.00 ⎫
921007121, 31.50 ⎭ sales
921007121, 300.36 current balance

Input: 1. A line or card containing the interest rate to be charged on INPUT
2. The data as described above on file DATA with an end-of-file indicating the end of the run

Output: The output should be a table showing the interest rate at the top and a line of output for each customer showing the social security number and the corresponding new balance and the monthly payment due.

2. You just bought a small computer to help out in your computer classes. It would be nice to make some money with it as well, so you and a friend decide to print and sell a weekly list of prices of common products sold at the three largest grocery chains in town. Your program will print a list of the stores and the items surveyed, and will also print the minimum cost on each particular item and the ID of the store having that minimum price.

Input: 1. First entry—number of stores surveyed
2. Next entries (one line for each store surveyed)—name of store (20 characters), store ID
3. Last entries (a new line for each item)—name of item (20 characters), store ID, price, store ID, price, store ID, price

Output: 1. A heading to the list that includes some appropriate title and the list of store names and their corresponding IDs
2. For each item in the list, the name of the item, the minimum cost, and the ID of the store with the minimum price
3. A final line that prints total savings (accumulation of the savings on each item); label appropriately

3. Summer school is over and it's time for your tour of Europe. However, you are a little concerned about handling all those currencies and wish to be able to convert quickly in your head before you go. The last time you looked the rate of exchange was as follows:

7.2 French francs = 1 dollar
.66 British pound = 1 dollar
2.4 German marks = 1 dollar
1439 Italian lira = 1 dollar

Since this is not very easy to do in your head, you decide to use the following approximations:

7 French francs = 1 dollar
.5 British pound = 1 dollar
2 German marks = 1 dollar
1000 Italian lira = 1 dollar

Write a program that reads in a value in francs, pounds, marks, and lira and computes the actual dollar amount for each using the exchange table, then computes the approximation for each and the difference between the two.

Output: A line for each country that includes the following:

    1. Amount of foreign currency read in

    2. Correct amount in dollars

    3. Approximate amount in dollars

    4. Difference between the two

The output should be properly labeled.

Chapter 8

1. A positive integer p is said to be a *prime number* if p > 1 and the only positive divisors of p are 1 and p.

    Example: 2, 3, 5, 7, 11 are the first five prime numbers.

    (Note that 1 is not a prime number.)

    If two positive integers p and p + 2 are such that both of them are prime numbers, then we say that each of them is a *twin prime* of the other.

    Note that for any positive integer p,

    1. If p is not a prime number then it has no twin prime.

    2. If p is a prime number, then it may have 0, 1, or 2 twin primes.

    Example: 1, 2, 4, 6, 8, 9, . . . have no twin primes; 3, 7 each has one twin prime (5); 5 has two twin primes (3 and 7); etc.

    Given a sequence of positive integers, for each determine whether it is a prime number, and if so, find its twin primes.

2. A local bank has instituted a new credit system and would like to have account numbers that are self-checking in order to have some protection against fraud and clerical errors. They have devised a system as follows: The account numbers will be nine digits long and the ninth digit (rightmost) can be calculated by either summing, subtracting, or multiplying all of the preceding digits and finding the rightmost digit of the result.

    Your job is to write a program that can be used to check the validity of the account numbers that have been sent to the bank as part of its daily transactions.

    Input: 1. Single-digit operation code

            2. Nine-digit account number

        (There will be an arbitrary number of these entries.)

    In the operation code, 1 is addition, 2 is subtraction, and 3 is multiplication. You will also need to check for the correctness of the operation code.

    Output: 1. Echo print the input.

             2. Under each echo-printed line, state whether the account number is valid or invalid or whether the operation code is incorrect.

    Example: If the input were the following:

    1 123456786

    1 represents addition, so

    $$1 + 2 + 3 + 4 + 5 + 6 + 7 + 8 = 36$$

    6 is the rightmost digit of 36, therefore the account is valid.

3. Redo Assignment 3 for Chapter 7 with the following change. Instead of reading in values in francs, pounds, marks, and lira each time, your data is in the form of a code indicating which currency followed by the amount of that currency. The code is as follows:

'F' French francs
'B' British pound
'G' German mark
'I' Italian lira

Use a CASE statement to determine which currency you are converting.

4. Recode the WHILE loops in the assignments for Chapter 5 as REPEAT loops.

5. You are the head programmer at the El Cheepo Manufacturing Company. For years the accounting department has rounded the number of hours worked by each employee to the nearest hour. Now management is considering truncating hours instead of rounding.

   You have been asked to write a program that calculates the payroll both ways and compares the total cost to the company.

Input: UPDATE: 1. Employee ID numbers
                   2. Hours worked

            MASTER: 1. Employee ID number
                     2. Hourly wage
                     3. Number of dependents

Output: 1. A report showing gross pay, tax withheld, net pay based on rounding, and net pay based on truncation
             2. A summary statement showing how much money would be saved using truncation

Processing: Withholding: 15% (gross pay − 10 * number of dependents)

Chapter 9

1. A company wants to know the percentage of its sales from each sales person. Each sales person has a data line or card giving an identification number and the dollar value of his or her sales.

   Input: A record for each sales person

   Output: The total sales, the sales person's ID, sales, and percentage of total sales.

2. The local baseball team is computerizing its records. You are to write a program that computes batting averages. There are 20 players on the team, identified by the numbers 1 through 20. Their batting record is coded on a file as follows. Each line contains four numbers; the player's identification number and the number of hits, walks, and outs he made in a particular game.

   Example: 3   2   1   1

   The above example means player number 3 was at bat 4 times, made 2 hits, 1 walk, and 1 out during one game. For each player there are several records on the file. To compute each player's batting average, add his total number of hits and divide by the total number of times at bat. Note that a walk does not count as either a hit or a time at bat when calculating batting average.

You are to print player ID, batting averages, and number of walks for each player in descending order by batting average, labeled appropriately. (Remember to echo print input.)

3. You have been asked to do a simple analysis of the exam scores for a large freshman class. Write and test a computer program that performs the following:

   1. Reads the test grades
   2. Calculates the smallest and largest scores and the mode (the most frequent score)
   3. Prints a single-page summary showing the smallest score, the largest score, the mode, and a list of grades with the frequency of appearance of each grade

   Input: 1. First data line—the number of exams to be analyzed (not to exceed 100) and an alphanumeric title for the report
              2. Remaining data lines—a nine-digit student ID number followed by a number grade, 0–100

   Output: 1. Echo print the input data.
              2. Print the title beginning on a new sheet of output paper.
              3. Print the minimum, maximum, and mode, all properly labeled.
              4. Print the unique grades and the frequency of occurrence of each.

4. One of the local banks is gearing up for a big advertising campaign and would like to see how long their customers are waiting for service at their drive-in windows. They have asked several employees to keep accurate records for the 24-hour drive-in service. The collected information will be read from a file and will consist of the time of day in hours, minutes, and seconds that the customer arrived, the time the customer was actually served, and the ID number of the teller.

   Write a program that executes the following steps:

   1. Read in the wait data.
   2. Compute the wait time in seconds.
   3. Calculate the mean, standard deviation, and range.
   4. Print a single-page summary showing the values calculated in 3.

   Input: 1. The first data line or card contains a title.
              2. The remaining lines or cards each contain a teller ID, a start time, and an arrival time. The times are broken up into hours, minutes, and seconds according to a 24-hour clock.

   Processing: 1. Calculate the mean and the standard deviation.
                   2. Locate the shortest wait time and the longest wait time.
                   3. The program should work for any number of records up to 100.

   Output: 1. Echo print the input data.
              2. Print the title beginning on a new page.
              3. Print the following values, all properly labeled.
                  a. number of records
                  b. mean
                  c. standard deviation
                  d. the range (minimum and maximum wait)

5. The final exam in your psychology class is to be 30 multiple choice questions. Your instructor says that if you write the program to grade the finals you won't have to take it. You, of course, accept.

Input: Line or card 1: the key to the exam. The correct answers are the first 30 characters followed by an integer number that says how many students took the exam (call it N).

   The next N lines or cards contain student answers in the first 30 character positions followed by the student's name in the next 10 character positions.

Output: For each student, print his or her name, followed by the number of correct answers. If the number correct is 60% or better, print 'PASS' otherwise print 'FAIL'.

Chapter 10

1. The local bank in Assignment 4, Chapter 9, was so successful with its advertising campaign that the parent bank decided to run a contest and collect data from banks all over the state. However, they decided to add several things. Frustration levels will be assigned to wait times as follows:

WAIT < (MEAN − S.D.)	=> 'AMAZED'
(MEAN − S.D.) < WAIT < MEAN	=> 'PLEASED'
MEAN < WAIT < (MEAN + S.D.)	=> 'CALM'
(MEAN + S.D.) < WAIT < (MEAN + 2 * S.D.)	=> 'IRRITATED'
(MEAN + 2 * S.D.) < WAIT	=> 'BERSERK'

where MEAN is the mean waiting time, S.D. is the standard deviation, and WAIT is the wait time.

   We are going to calculate frustration levels for each recorded wait.

Input: Same as Assignment 4, Chapter 9, except that the first two digits of the teller ID will actually correspond to a bank ID; should be treated as one number

Output: Same as Assignment 4, Chapter 9, plus

   1. A bar graph (histogram) showing frustration level distribution
   2. A table sorted by combination ID showing
      a. ID number
      b. wait time
      c. frustration level

The table sorted by ID will allow us to examine the performance of particular banks and tellers and see if any of them are particularly better or worse than the others.

2. The company you are working for has just taken over a smaller company. The accounting department would like to have a combined list of employee social security numbers and department codes for the two groups. They want the list in ascending order by social security number. Your job is to write a program that will print such a list. The 50-entry file is on DATA1; the file of unknown length is on DATA2.

Input: 1. DATA1 Fifty lines or cards (in ascending order by social security number): Social security number (integer), Department code (6 characters)   (1 pair per line)

2. DATA2 An unspecified number of lines or cards (in ascending order by social security number): Social security number (integer), Department code (6 characters) (this is the current file of the larger firm)   (1 pair per line)

Output: An ordered list of social security numbers and department codes (1 pair per line)

Note: You are not required to sort this information. The two lists that are given are already sorted. You are required to merge the two.

3. Your history professor has so many students in her class that she has trouble knowing how well the class did on exams. She found out that you are a computer whiz and has asked you to write a program to do some simple statistical analyses on exam scores, in return for which she will not flunk you even though you flashed on the first quiz. You, of course, cheerfully agree.

Write and test a computer program that performs the following steps:

1. Reads the test grades from data cards
2. Calculates the class mean, standard deviation, and percentage of the test scores falling in ranges <10, 10–19, 20–29, 30–39, . . . , 80–89, and ≥ 90
3. Prints a single-page summary showing the mean and standard deviation, and a histogram of test score distribution. This page will be formatted so that it can be torn off as a complete one-page report.

Input: The data lines or cards are as follows:
1. The first line or card contains the number of exams to be analyzed and an alphanumeric title for the report.
2. The remaining lines or cards have 10 test scores on each line or card until the last, and 1 to 10 scores on the last. The scores are all integers.

Processing: 1. Calculate the mean, XAVG, and the standard deviation, STD.

2. Find the percentage of scores that fall in each of the ten intervals <10, 10–19, 20–29, . . . , ≥90.
3. Your program must work for any size class up to 100 (0 < N < 100).

Output: 1. Print the input data as they are read.
2. Print an analysis report, beginning on a new page. Your report will consist of the title that was read from data, the number of scores, mean, and standard deviation (labeled), and a histogram showing the percentage distribution of scores.

4. A small postal system ships packages within your state. To be accepted, a parcel is subject to the following constraints:

1. Weight limit of 50 lb
2. Parcels are not to exceed 3 ft in length, width, or depth and may not have a combined length and girth exceeding 6 ft. (The girth of a package is the circumference of the package around its two smallest sides; mathematically the formula is

$$\text{GIRTH} = 2 * (S1 + S2 + S3 - \text{LARGEST})$$

where LARGEST is the largest of the three parcel dimensions, S1, S2, and S3)

Your program should process a transaction file containing one entry for each box mailed during the week. Each entry contains a transaction number, followed by the weight of the box, followed by its dimensions (in no particular order). The program should print the transaction number, weight, and postal charge for all accepted packages, and the transaction number and weight for all rejected packages. At the end of the report, you must print the number of packages processed and the number rejected.

Input: 1. *Parcel Post table*—weight and cost (show 25 values). This table should be stored in two one-dimensional arrays. The postal cost of each parcel can then be determined by searching the WEIGHT array and using the corresponding element in the COST array. If a package weight falls between two weight categories in the table, your program should use the cost for the higher weight.

2. *Transaction file*—transaction number, weight, and three dimensions for an arbitrary number of transactions. Assume that all weights are whole numbers and that all dimensions are given to the nearest inch.

Output: 1. First line—appropriate headings
2. Next N records—transaction number, whether accepted or rejected, weight, and cost
3. Last line—number of packages processed, number of packages rejected

5. You work for a local business that has two stores in your town. Both stores maintain inventories of the products sold. Weekly, a listing of the total inventory for both stores is printed by your department and sent to the general manager. Your program must take a list supplied by each store and print a unique list of the total inventory.

Input: Each store list contains the product ID, the number of items currently in the store, and the cost per item (real number)

Note: The ID numbers on each list are sorted in ascending order. ID numbers do not necessarily appear on both lists.

Output: A labeled report containing the following information:
1. Item ID, total items, cost/item, and value of total items
2. A final line that gives the total value of the combined inventory

6. The students for a particular high school class have their names and their school numbers recorded in a file. For example,

DALE   14   (*Note:* No one in the school is allowed to
BROWN   23   have a name longer than 10 characters)

The file is arranged alphabetically. Another file contains the names of newly entered students for the same class; these names are also alphabetically arranged. Your program should read the two files and print all the names alphabetically along with each student's school number. The smaller file (new students) will have no more than 50 entries.

Note: Your program should read the smaller file first and store its names in an array. Then the alphabetized list should be printed at the same time the larger file is read. (Why is it better to read the smaller file first? What is the advantage of printing the list while the second file is being read, rather than waiting till both files are read?)

Chapter 11

1. Photos taken in space by the Voyager spacecraft are sent back to earth as a stream of numbers. Your job is to take a matrix of numbers and print it as a picture.

   If the numbers received represent levels of brightness, then one approach to generating a picture is to print a dark character (like a $) when the brightness level is low and print a light character (like a blank or a period) when the level is high.

   Unfortunately, errors in transmission sometimes occur. Your program will attempt to find and correct these errors and then print a corrected picture on a new page.

   Assume a value is in error if it differs by more than 1 from each of its four neighboring values. Correct the bad value by giving it the average of its neighboring values, rounding it to the nearest integer.

   Example:

5	The 2 would be regarded as an error and would
4 2 5	be given a corrected value of 5.
5	

   Note: Values on the corners or boundaries of the matrix will have to be processed differently from values on the interior.

   Finally, print on a new page a negative image of the corrected picture.

2. The following diagram represents an island surrounded by water (shaded area). Two bridges lead out of the island. A mouse is placed on the black square. Write a program to make the mouse take a walk through the island. The mouse is allowed to travel one square at a time either horizontally or vertically. A random number between 1 and 4 should be used to decide which direction the mouse is to take. The mouse drowns when hitting the water and escapes by crossing a bridge. What are the mouse's chances? You may generate a random number up to 100 times. If the mouse does not find his way by the 100th try he will die of starvation. Restart the mouse in a new array and go back and repeat the whole process. Count the number of times he escapes, drowns, or starves.

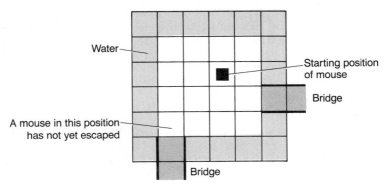

Input: 1. First record—the size of the array, includes border of water and bridges (will not be larger than 20 × 20)
2. Next N records—the rows of the two-dimensional array
The positions containing negative numbers represent the water.
The positions in the edge containing a 0 represent the bridges. The position containing a 1 represents the starting position of the mouse. All others contain zeroes.

Output: For each trip by the mouse you should print the following (double space between trips):
1. A line stating whether the mouse escaped, drowned, or starved
2. A line showing the mouse's starting position and the position of the two bridges
3. A map showing the frequency of the visits of the mouse to each position

3. In competitive diving, each diver makes three dives of varying degrees of difficulty. Nine judges score the dive from 0 to 10 in steps of 0.5. The total score is obtained by discarding the lowest and highest of the judges' scores, adding the remaining scores, and then multiplying the scores by the degree of difficulty. The divers take turns, and when the competition is finished, they are ranked according to score. Write a program to do the above, using the following input and output specifications.

Input: 1. Number of divers
2. Diver's name (10 characters), difficulty (REAL), and judges' ratings (REAL)

There will be a record like the above for each diver. All of the records for DIVE 1 will be grouped together, then all for DIVE 2, then all for DIVE 3.

Output: 1. Echo print in tabular form with appropriate headings, e.g., NAME, DIFFICULTY, judges' number (1–9)
2. A table that contains the following information sorted by final total, in descending order (highest diver first):

NAME	DIVE 1	DIVE 2	DIVE 3	TOTAL

Name is the diver's name; DIVE 1, 2, and 3 are the total points they received for a single dive as described above, and TOTAL is their overall total.

4. You work for the Jet Propulsion Laboratory. They want you to write a program that will take an array containing the digitized representation of a picture of the night sky and locate the stars on it. Each element of the array represents the amount of light hitting that portion of the image when the picture was taken. Intensities range from 0 to 20.

Example input:

0	3	4	0	0	0	6	8
5	13	6	0	0	0	2	3
2	6	2	7	3	0	10	0
0	0	4	15	4	1	6	0
0	0	7	12	6	9	10	4
5	0	6	10	6	4	8	0

A star is probably located in the area covered by the array element i, j if the following is the case:

$$(A(i, j) + \text{sum of the 4 surrounding intensities})/5 > 6.0$$

Ignore possible stars along the edges of the array.

The desired output is a star map containing asterisks where you have found a star and blanks elsewhere, e.g.,

```
 _ _ _ _ _ _ _ _ _ _ _ _ _ _ _ _ _ _ _ _
:
:      *
:
:
:            *
:            *      *   *
:
:
```

Input: 1. A title
2. An array of intensities

Output: A star map. Print two blanks for the "no star" case. The presence of a star will be indicated by a blank followed by an asterisk. The chart should have a border and be labeled with the title.

Chapter 12

1. Write a program to simulate playing the game of Bingo. Each player uses a Bingo card like the one below. Tokens numbered 1 to 75 are drawn at random and announced. If the number appears on a player's card, it is covered by a marker. Play continues until a player or players have a winning combination of markers. The winning combinations are

1. Horizontal row of 5
2. Vertical row of 5
3. Either main diagonal of 5

B	I	N	G	O
0	20	33	47	63
3	0	40	51	68
11	21	0	50	70
1	16	37	0	71
7	29	31	55	0

Note that the central position is a free position on all Bingo cards. The first column contains numbers between 1 and 15, the second column numbers between 16 and 30, etc.

Read three Bingo cards. Generate a number in the range 1–75 using a random number generator. The ranges for appropriate columns are as follows:

B	1–15
I	16–30
N	31–45
G	46–60
O	61–75

The letter and number should be printed. However, no number should be printed more than once. Play continues until there is a winner or winners. Output should include the players' original cards, the letters and numbers generated, and players' cards at the end of the game with positions covered by markers displayed as zeroes, and the winning players' number (1, 2, or 3).

2. The local police department keeps a file of city residents who have marked their belongings with a unique seven-character code (digits and letters). Write a program to match items recovered by the department with codes in the file. First the program reads the file that contains the code, name, and phone number of residents. For example,

         A123456   JOHN SMITH   4527836

means that John Smith, having phone number 4527836, has the unique code of A123456.

Then a file of items recovered will be read. This file contains a code and item description. If the code of a found item matches the code of a person in the first file, print the code, person's name, phone number, and the item description. If not found, print the code number, 'NO MATCH', and item description. Process each found item as it is read, using a linear search.

3. Write a program that maintains a service for lost and found pets. First the program reads a file giving found pets and the finders' names and phone numbers. For example,

         SIAM CAT   MISS MABEL DAVIS   7143261

means Miss Mabel Davis, having phone number 7143261, found a siamese cat. A similiar file for losers of pets is to be processed. If a lost pet matches a found pet, then the program should print the name of the pet as well as the finder, the loser, and their telephone numbers. If the pet not found, print 'NOT FOUND' under the finder column. Process each loser record as it is read, using a linear search.

4. Your cousin—the noisy one—has been sitting in the corner for hours, quietly absorbed with a new game. Being a little bored (and curious), you ask if you can play. The game consists of a black box with numbers on all sides as shown on the left at the top of the next page.

There are five obstructions called BAFFLES, which you cannot see, placed in the box. The object of the game is to find the baffles. You select a number between 0 and 39, which activates a laser beam originating at that location. You are then told where the beam leaves the box. If the beam did not encounter a baffle, it will exit directly opposite where it entered. If the beam encounters a baffle, it will be deflected at right angles, either right or left, depending on the direction of the baffle. You can locate the baffles by shooting beams into the box, using the deflections of the beams as hints to the placement and direction of the baffles.

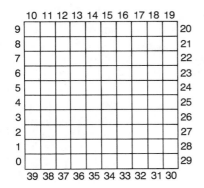

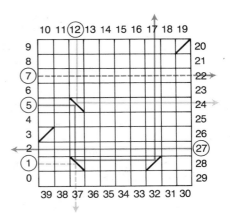

A beam shot from 7 would come out at 22. A beam shot from 1 would be deflected once and exit at 37. A beam shot from 27 would exit at 2 without being deflected. A beam shot from 5 would come out at 17 after three deflections. A beam shot from 12 would be deflected once, exiting at 24.

The game is scored by giving one point for each laser shot and two points for each guess. A lower score, obviously, is more desirable.

When your cousin demands his game back, you decide to write a computer program to simulate the game. (*Note:* Your program is not supposed to *SOLVE* the baffles problem; it is supposed to present the game to be played.) This clearly ought to be an interactive program, where the baffles are set by a random number generator and a player either fires a laser beam or makes a guess as to the position of a baffle. However, you decided to write the program and test it first. You can add the prompts for interactive play later.

Input/Output:

1. In our interactive game, the baffles will be set by a random number generator. For testing this program, however, we will read in the coordinates from an input file. The information for each baffle will be one line of input in the format

X   Y   DIR

where X   is an integer between 0 and 9
       Y   is an integer between 10 and 19
      DIR is either an R or an L

X, Y, and DIR are separated by at least one blank, maybe more.

Example:

5   12   L   sets

9   19   R   sets

Error checking: You are not assured that each line of input will be unique (just as the random number generator may coincidentally come up with the same coordinates for two baffles). You can only place a baffle in a "free" position, i.e., one that has not been previously set. You need to set a total of 5 UNIQUE baffles.

When you have set five unique baffles, skip all input until you encounter a ∗.

2. Input for playing the game follows the ∗. Each command to the game will be on a separate line in the input file. Echo print each command before the specified output. The format for the command input will be the following:

col. 1	col. 2–80	meaning
P		Print the box, showing the locations and directions of all the baffles that have already been found.
L	integer (0–39)	Laser shot. Shoot the laser, with the beam entering the box at the designated location. Output should be: LASER SHOT #____ EXITED THE BOX AT ____.
G	X Y DIR (same format as part 1)	Guess the location of one baffle. X, Y, and DIR refer to the coordinates and direction of the baffle. Output: THIS IS GUESS NUMBER ____. If guess correct, print CONGRATULATIONS, YOU HAVE NOW FOUND ____ BAFFLES. If guess correct, but baffle was found on a previous guess, print YOU HAVE ALREADY FOUND THIS BAFFLE. If guess incorrect, print SORRY, BETTER LUCK NEXT TIME.
S		Score. Output: NUMBER OF SHOTS: ____ NUMBER OF GUESSES: ____ CURRENT SCORE: ____

Continue processing until all five baffles are found. Output message of congratulations and calculated score. Print the box showing the location and direction of all the baffles.

Error checking: In addition to the specific error checking mentioned above, you must check *all input*. If an error is found in any line, that line is not used, and an appropriate warning should be printed. (Use your imagination.) You may assume that the number of items on a line and their respective types *are* correct.

Example:

```
L     40
          *** LASER SHOT OUT OF BOUNDS -- TRY AGAIN ***
B      5     12     R
          *** ILLEGAL COMMAND -- TRY AGAIN ***
```

Sample game

Input file:

```
5      12        L
9  19               R
2  17 J
3               10        R
9      19     L
14     3     R
1       12   L
         1   17       R
   3  13   R
  9            11   L
*
L8
L12
G 5 12 L
P
L 30
G    30 20 R
G   9  19               R
R       17
L 17
G         5 12              L
S
:
:
G      1 10 R
L  1
G      1 12             L
```

Output:

```
*** SET BAFFLES ***
   5      12    L      BAFFLE 1 SET
   9      19    R      BAFFLE 2 SET
   2      17    J      *** error message ***
   3      10    R      BAFFLE 3 SET
   9      19    L      *** error message ***
  14       3   R       *** error message ***
   1      12    L      BAFFLE 4 SET
   1      17    R      BAFFLE 5 SET
```

Ignore rest of input until * is encountered.

```
*** PLAY GAME ***

L    3
     LASER SHOT #1 EXITED THE BOX AT 21.

L    12
     LASER SHOT #2 EXITED THE BOX AT 24.

G    5    12    L
     THIS IS GUESS #1.
     CONGRATULATIONS, YOU HAVE NOW FOUND 1 BAFFLE(S).

P
```

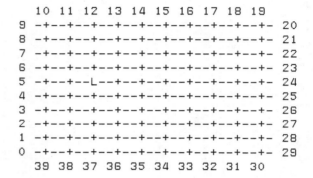

```
L    30
     LASER SHOT #3 EXITED THE BOX AT 20.

G    30    20    R
     *** OPERANDS OUT OF BOUNDS -- TRY AGAIN ***

G    9    19    R
     THIS IS GUESS #2.
     CONGRATULATIONS, YOU HAVE NOW FOUND 2 BAFFLE(S).

K    17
     *** ILLEGAL COMMAND -- TRY AGAIN ***

L    17
     LASER SHOT #4 EXITED THE BOX AT 5.

G    5    12    L
     THIS IS GUESS #3.
     YOU HAVE ALREADY FOUND THIS BAFFLE.

S
     NUMBER OF SHOTS:    4
     NUMBER OF GUESSES:    3
     CURRENT SCORE:    10
```

```
        .
        .
        .
G    1    10    R
     THIS IS GUESS #15.
     SORRY, BETTER LUCK NEXT TIME.

L    1
     LASER SHOT #26 EXITED THE BOX AT 37.

G    1    12    L
     THIS IS GUESS #16.
     CONGRATULATIONS, YOU HAVE NOW FOUND 5 BAFFLE(S).

************** YOU FOUND ALL THE BAFFLES ****************

        NUMBER OF SHOTS:    26
        NUMBER OF GUESSES:    16
        CURRENT SCORE:    58

                10 11 12 13 14 15 16 17 18 19
            9  -+--+--+--+--+--+--+--+--+--R-  20
            8  -+--+--+--+--+--+--+--+--+--+-  21
            7  -+--+--+--+--+--+--+--+--+--+-  22
            6  -+--+--+--+--+--+--+--+--+--+-  23
            5  -+--+--L--+--+--+--+--+--+--+-  24
            4  -+--+--+--+--+--+--+--+--+--+-  25
            3  -R--+--+--+--+--+--+--+--+--+-  26
            2  -+--+--+--+--+--+--+--+--+--+-  27
            1  -+--+--L--+--+--+--+--R--+--+-  28
            0  -+--+--+--+--+--+--+--+--+--+-  29
                39 38 37 36 35 34 33 32 31 30
```

Your output may differ in minor details from this example. (Different error messages, slight format differences, etc.)

Chapter 13

1. The Emerging Manufacturing Company has just installed its first computer and hired you as a junior programmer. Your first program is to read employee pay data and produce two reports: (1) an error and control report and (2) a report on pay amounts. The second report must contain a line for each employee and a line of totals at the end of the report.

Input:

TRANSACTION: 1. Set of five job site number/name pairs
2. One card or line for each employee containing
   a. ID number
   b. Job site number
   c. Number of hours worked
   These data have been presorted by ID number

MASTER FILE: 1. ID number
2. Name
3. Pay rate per hour
4. Number of dependents
5. Type of employee (union/management) (1 is management, 0 is union)
6. Job site
7. Sex (M or F)

This file is also ordered by ID number.

Note: (1) Union members get time and a half for hours over 40; professionals get nothing for hours over 40. (2) The tax formula for tax computation is as follows: If number of dependents is 1, tax rate is 15%; otherwise the tax rate is

$$\left[1 - \left(\frac{\text{No. of dep.}}{\text{No. of dep.} + 6}\right)\right] \times 15\%$$

Output: 1. Error and control report
a. List the input lines or cards for which there is no corresponding master record, or where the job site numbers do not agree. Continue processing with the next line or card of data.
b. Give the total number of employee records that were processed correctly during this run.
2. Payroll report (labeled for management).
a. A line for each employee containing the name, ID number, job site name, gross pay, and net pay
b. A total line showing the total amount of gross pay and total amount of net pay

2. The Emerging Manufacturing Company has decided to use its new computer for parts inventory control as well as payroll. You are to write a program that is to be run each night. It takes the stock tickets from the day's transactions, makes a list of the parts that need ordering, and prints an updated report that must be given to the five job site managers each morning. Note that you are not being asked to update the file.

Input:

TRANSACTION: 1. Set of five job site number/name pairs
2. One card or line for each stock transaction containing
a. Part ID number
b. Job site number
c. Number of parts bought or sold (a negative number indicates that it has been sold)

This data has been presorted by site number within part number.

MASTER FILE: 1. Part ID number
2. Part name (no embedded blanks)
3. Quantity on hand
4. Order point
5. Job site

This file is also ordered by job site number within part ID number. If a part is not in the master file and the transaction is a sale, print an error message. If the transaction is a purchase, list it in the proper place in the out report.

Note: There is a separate entry in the master file for parts at each job site.

Output: 1. Error and control report that contains error messages and a list of the parts that need to be ordered; i.e., quantity on hand is less than order point

2. A report must be generated that contains, for *all* the parts in the master file,
   a. The part number
   b. The part name
   c. The job site name
   d. The number on hand

Remember, this report is for management. Be sure it is written so managers can read it.

3. You have taken a job with the IRS, hoping to learn how to save on your income tax. They want you to write a toy tax computing program in order to gain an idea of your programming abilities. The program will read in the names of members of families and each person's income and compute the tax that the family owes. You may assume that consecutive people in input with the same last name are in the same family. The number of deductions that a family can count is equal to the number of people listed in that family in the input data. Tax is computed as follows:

$$\text{adjusted-income} = \text{income} - (5000 * \text{number-of-deductions})$$
$$\text{tax-rate} = \text{adjusted-income}/100000, \text{ if income} < 60{,}000, \text{ otherwise}$$
$$\text{tax-rate} = .50$$
$$\text{tax} = \text{tax-rate} * \text{adjusted-income}$$

There will be no refunds, so you must check for people whose tax would be negative and set it to zero.

Input entries will look as follows:

last name,   first name.   total income

Example:

JONES,	RALPH.	19765.43
JONES,	MARY.	8532.00
JONES,	FRANCIS.	
ATWELL,	HUMPHRY.	35678.12
MURPHY,	ROBERT.	13432.20
MURPHY,	ELLEN.	
MURPHY,	PADDY.	
MURPHY,	EILEEN.	
MURPHY,	CONAN.	
MURPHY,	NORA.	

Input: The data as described above with an end-of-file indicating the end of the run

Output: A table containing all of the families, one family per line, with each line containing the last name of the family, their total income, and their computed tax

4. Your assignment is to write a program for a computer dating service. Clients will give you their names, phone numbers, and a list of interests. It will be your job to maintain lists of men and women using the service and to match up the compatible couples.

Data structures: The problem requires you to maintain two lists, men and women. The lists must include the following information: NAME (20 characters), PHONE-NUMBER (8 characters); NUMBER OF INTERESTS (maximum number is 10), INTERESTS (10 characters each; must be in alphabetical order), and a variable that gives the position of the client's current match (will be 0 if not matched). When a new client is added to the list, he or she is added to the bottom of the appropriate list. (You do not keep the names of the clients in alphabetical order.)

Input: 1. Number of current clients
  2. Sex (7 characters), name (20 characters), phone number (8 characters), number of interests, list of interests (10 characters for each one; must be sorted; interests are separated by commas with a period after the final interest.) (*Note:* There will be a record like this for each of the current clients)

The rest of the file will include data lines that look like one of the following (all of the lines will start with a 10-character word as outlined below):

NEWCLIENT☐ sex (7 characters), name (20 characters), # of interests, interests (10 characters for each one; see above for description)

If the key word NEWCLIENT occurs, you should add the client to the appropriate list by storing the appropriate information. Match him or her with a member of the opposite sex. (A match occurs when three of the interests are the same. Use the fact that interests are sorted to make the match process easier.) Make sure you then designate both persons as matched as described above. Print the name of the new client, his or her match, and both phone numbers. If no match is found, print an appropriate message.

OLDCLIENT☐ name (20 characters)

Unmatch this name with his (or her) current match by setting the MATCH variables for this name and his (or her) match to 0.

PRINTMATCH

Print list of all matched pairs.

PRINTNOT☐☐

Print the names and phone numbers of clients who are not currently matched.

STOPPROG☐☐

This will be the last line in the file.

Output: Print information as described above with appropriate titles.

Note: You are to use an INSERTION sort to sort interests.

5. Although many people think of computers as large number-crunching devices, much of computing deals with alphanumeric processing. For example, the compiler reads your program as alphanumeric data. To let you get a taste of this type of processing, the input data for this problem will be a Pascal program.

The assignment is to read a Pascal program and find all of the assignment statements. From each of these you will extract the variable being assigned a value (the one before the operator assignment and all of the variables in the expression on the right-hand side. You may assume that no variable contains an embedded blank and that each statement is on a line by itself.

Input: A Pascal program. (Why not this one?)

Output: Print out each assignment statement and next to it the variables that you have extracted. The output should be labeled.

Example output:

ASSIGNMENT STATEMENTS	LEFT	RIGHT		
X := B	X	B		
X := 5.6	X			
TEST:=(X+5.4)*2+Y/A	TEST	X	Y	A
X:=REC+NUM*(AGE-10)	X	REC	NUM	AGE

Chapter 14

1. You are to write a set of utility routines to manipulate a group of three stacks. The specifications for these routines are given in terms of preconditions and postconditions. The preconditions to each routine tell you what the routine may assume to be true on entry to the routine. The postconditions state what the routine guarantees to be true on exit from the routine. The notation is as follows:

> S is the specified stack
> S' is the stack before the last operation on it
> first(S) is the most recent element put in S
> length(S) is the number of elements in S
> // means concatenated with

Stack operations

```
PROCEDURE PUSH(VAR S : STACKTYPE; X : ETYPE;
               VAR OVERFLOW : BOOLEAN);
```
   preconditions: TRUE
   postconditions: (S = <X> // S' and OVERFLOW = not FULLS(S'))
       or (S = S' and OVERFLOW = FULLS(S))

```
PROCEDURE POP(VAR S : STACKTYPE; VAR X : ETYPE;
              VAR UNDERFLOW : BOOLEAN);
```
   preconditions: TRUE
   postconditions: (S' = <X> // S and UNDERFLOW = not EMPTYS(S'))
       or (S = S' and UNDERFLOW = EMPTYS (S))

```
PROCEDURE CLEARS(VAR S : STACKTYPE);
```
   postconditions: S = <>

```
PROCEDURE LOOK(S : STACKTYPE; VAR UNDERFLOW : BOOLEAN;
               VAR TOP : ETYPE);
```
preconditions: TRUE
postconditions: $(S = S'$ and TOP = first(S) and UNDERFLOW =
    not EMPTYS(S))
    or $(S = S'$ and UNDERFLOW = EMPTYS(S) and TOP
    is undefined)

```
FUNCTION EMPTYS(S : STACKTYPE) : BOOLEAN;
```
postconditions: EMPTYS = $(S = <>)$

```
FUNCTION FULLS(S : STACKTYPE) : BOOLEAN;
```
postconditions: FULLS = (length(S) = MAXSTACK);

Testing: The input data consists of a series of commands to test your routines. There are an arbitrary number of blanks between commands. Be sure to echo print each command before you execute it.

    Stacks will be designated by the integers 1 through 3. Elements will be strings of 1 through 20 characters, including embedded blanks, delimited by a period. (The period is *not* part of the element.)

The commands are:

PUSH   stacknumber element.
    Execute procedure PUSH, using element as the value to be put on the designated stack. If an error condition occurs, print an appropriate message.

POP   stacknumber
    Execute procedure POP, using the designated stack, and print the value returned. If an error condition occurs, print an appropriate message.

LOOK   stacknumber
    Execute procedure LOOK, using the designated stack, and print the value returned. If an error occurs, print an appropriate error message.

CLEARS   stacknumber
    Execute procedure CLEARS, using the designated stack,

EMPTYS   stacknumber
    Execute function EMPTYS, using the designated stack, and print the result.

FULLS   stacknumber
    Execute function FULLS, using the designated stack, and print the result.

PRINT   stacknumber
    Print the elements in the designated stack. The stack must be returned to its original state. (*Hint:* Use a temporary stack.)

DUMP
    Print the elements in *all* the stacks.

STOP
    Stop executing.

Note that all the preconditions are TRUE. This means that all the testing for full and/or empty is being done in the utility routines themselves. If the testing were done in the CALLING routine, this would be stated in the preconditions. Which routines would this change? What would the preconditions look like?

2. Given a starting point in a maze, you are to determine if there is a way out of it.

The maze is represented by a 10 × 10 array of 1's and 0's. There is one exit from the maze. The door to the exit contains a *. You may move vertically or horizontally in any direction that contains a 0; you may not move to a cell with a 1. If you move into the cell with the *, you have exited. If you are in a cell with 1's on three sides, you must go back the way you came and try another path. You may not move diagonally.

Input: A 10 × 10 array of characters (1, 0, *). Each data line consists of one row of the maze.

Each succeeding line consists of pairs of values, representing starting points in the maze (i.e., row and column numbers).

Process these entry points until EOF.

Output: For each entry into the maze, print the maze with an E in the entry square, followed by the message 'I AM FREE' if a way out exists from that point or 'HELP, I AM TRAPPED' if a way out does not exist from that point.

Processing: You begin at the entry point and continue moving until you find the way out or you have no more moves to try. Remember, you can move into any cell with a 0, but cells with a 1 block you.

Data structures: There are two distinct sets of data structures for this assignment: the stack utility routines written in Assignment 1 and the data structures used to represent the maze.

Error handling: You may assume that your entry positions are indeed within the maze. You may also assume that the starting position contains a 0.

Index